Baedeker's

IRELAND

Cover picture: Jaunting-car in Muckross Park

126 colour photographs
10 town plans, 13 ground plans, 4 special plans
8 drawings
9 special maps, 1 fold-out map

Text contributions:
Dr Peter Harbison (History)
Dipl.-Ing. Wilhelm Jensen (places in Republic of Ireland)
Brian Reynolds (Economy)
Dr Margit Wagner (General, Climate, Geography, Government and Society, Religion, Education and Culture, Art, Literature, Music)

Editorial work and additional material:
Baedeker Stuttgart (Gisela Bockamp, Peter M. Nahm)
Editorial work, English language edition: Alec Court

Cartography:
Franz Kaiser, Sindelfingen;
Mairs Geographischer Verlag, Ostfildern-Kemnat bei Stuttgart (fold-out map)

Design and layout:
Creativ GmbH;
Ulrich Kolb, Stuttgart

General direction:
Dr Peter Baumgarten, Baedeker Stuttgart

English translation:
James Hogarth

© Baedeker Stuttgart
Original German edition

© The Automobile Association 50225
United Kingdom and Ireland

© Jarrold and Sons Ltd
English language edition worldwide

US and Canadian Edition
Prentice Hall Press

Licensed user:
Mairs Geographischer Verlag GmbH & Co.,
Ostifildern-Kemnat bei Stuttgart

Reproductions:
Gölz Repro-Service GmbH, Ludwigsburg

The name *Baedeker* is a registered trademark

Source of illustrations:

Bilderdienst Süddeutscher Verlag (4), Bord Fáilte (Irish Tourist Board) (27), Commissioners of Public Works (1), Hintze (2), Historia-Photo (2), Kahr (1), Lutz (3), Nahm (1), Neumeister (73), Northern Ireland Tourist Board (5), Green Studio Ltd (2), Thiele (1), Wüchner (3), Xeniel (1)

914. 15

2 235073 NF

Printed in Great Britain by Jarrold and Sons Ltd, Norwich.

0 86145 612 2 UK
0-13-058140-2 US and Canada
3-87504-118-6 Germany

How to Use this Guide

The principal towns and areas of tourist interest are described in alphabetical order. The names of other places referred to under these general headings can be found in the index.

Following the tradition established by Karl Baedeker in 1844, sights of particular interest and hotels and restaurants of particular quality are distinguished by either one or two asterisks.

In the list of hotels, etc., r.=rooms. Only a selection of hotels and restaurants can be given: no reflection is implied, therefore, on establishments not included.

The symbol (i) at the beginning of an entry or on a town plan indicates the local tourist office or other organisation from which further information can be obtained. The post-horn symbol on a town plan indicates a post office.

This guidebook forms part of a completely new series of the world-famous Baedeker Guides.

The English editions are now published for the first time in this country. Each volume is the result of long and careful preparation and, true to the traditions of Baedeker, is designed in every respect to meet the needs and expectations of the modern traveller.

The name of Baedeker has long been identified in the field of guidebooks with reliable, comprehensive and up-to-date information, prepared by expert writers who work from detailed, first-hand knowledge of the country concerned. Following a tradition that goes back over 150 years to the date when Karl Baedeker published the first of his handbooks for travellers, these guides have been planned to give the tourist all the essential information about the country and its inhabitants: where to go, how to get there and what to see. Baedeker's account of a country was always based on his personal observation and experience during his travels in that country. This tradition of writing a guidebook in the field rather than at an office desk has been maintained by Baedeker ever since.

Lavishly illustrated with superb colour photographs and numerous specially drawn maps and street plans of the major towns, the new Baedeker Guides concentrate on making available to the modern traveller all the information he needs in a format that is both attractive and easy to follow. For every place that appears in the gazetteer, the principal features of architectural, artistic and historic interest are described, as are the main areas of scenic beauty-spots in the locality. Selected hotels and restaurants are also included. Features of exceptional merit are indicated by either one or two asterisks.

A special section at the end of each book contains practical information, details of leisure activities and useful addresses. The separate road map will prove an invaluable aid to planning your route and your travel within the country.

Introduction to Ireland

Ireland from A to Z   45–206

Achill Island/Oiléan Acaill · Adare/Ath Dara · Aran Islands/Oileain Arann · Ardara/Arda Rath · Ardmore/Ard Mor · Arklow/Inbhear Mor · Armagh · Athlone/ Ath Luain · Athy/Baile Átha h-I · Ballina/ Beal an Aithe · Ballinasloe/Beal Átha an Sluagh · Ballinrobe/Baile an Rodhba · Ballybunion/Baile an Bhuinneanaigh · Bantry/Beanntraighe · Belfast · Belmullet/Béal an Mhuirthead · Birr/ Biorra · Blarney/An Bhlarna · Bloody Foreland/Cnoc Fola · Boyle/Mainistir na Buille · Boyne Valley · Bray/Bri Cualann · Bundoran/Bun Dobhrain · Burren/ Boirinn · Cahir/Cathair Dhuin Iascaigh · Carlow/Ceatharlach · Carrick-on-Shannon/Cara Droma Ruisg · Carrick-on-Suir/Carraig na Suire · Cashel/Caiseal Mumhan · Castlebar/Caislean an Barraigh · Cavan/An Cabhan · Cliffs of Moher/ Aillte an Mhothair · Clonakilty/Clanna Chaoilte · Clonmacnoise/Cluain Mic Nois · Clonmel/Cluain Meala · Cong/Cunga Feichin · Connemara · Cork/Corcaigh · Dingle Peninsula · Donegal/Dún nu nGall · Drogheda/Droichead Átha · Drumcliffe/ Droim Chliabh · Dublin/Baile Átha Cliath/ Dubhlinn · Dundalk/Dun Dealgan · Dungarvan/Dun Garbhain · Dun Laoghaire · Ennis/Inis · Enniscorthy/Inis Coirthe · Enniskerry/Ath na Scairbhe · Fanad Peninsula · Fermoy/Mainistir Fhear Muighe · Galway/Gaillimh · Glencolumbkille/Gleann Cholaim Cille · Glendalough/Gleann da Locha ·
Glengarriff/Gleann Garb · Gort/Gort Iase Guaire · Grand Canal · Horn Head/Corran Binne · Inischrone/Inis Eascrach Abhan · Inishowen Peninsula/Inis Eoghain · Kells/Ceanannus Mor · Kenmare/An Neidin · Kildare/Cill Dara · Kilkee/Cill Chaoidhe · Kilkenny/Cill Chainnigh · Killaloe/Cill Dalua · Killarney/Cill Airne · Killybegs/Na Cealla Beaga · Kinsale/ Ceann Saile · Letterkenny/Leitir Ceanainn · Limerick/Luimneach · Lismore/Lios Mor Mochuda · Londonderry/Derry/Doire · Longford/Longphort · Lough Corrib · Lough Erne · Lough Neagh · Loughrea/ Baile Locha Riach · Louisburgh/Cluain Cearban · Macgillicuddy's Reeks/ Na Cruacha Dubha · Macroom/ Maghcromtha · Monaghan/Muineachain · Monasterboice/Mainistir Buithe · Mullingar/Muileann Cearr · Nas/Nas na Ri · Navan/An Uaimh · New Ross/Ros Mhic Treoin · Portlaoise/Port Laoise · Ring of Kerry · Roscommon/Ros Comain · Roscrea/Ros Cre · Rosguill Peninsula · The Rosses/Na Rosa · Royal Canal · River Shannon · Skellig Islands/ Skellig Rocks · Skibbereen/Sciobairin · Sligo/Sligeach · Tara/Teamhair na Riogh · Thurles/Durlus Eile · Tipperary/Tiobrad Arann · Tralee/Traigh Li · Trim/Baile Atha Truim · Tuam/Tuaim · Tullamore/Tulach Mhor · Waterford/Port Lairge · Westport/ Cathair na Mart · Wexford/Loch Garman · Wicklow/Cill Mhantain · Wicklow Mountains · Youghal/Eochail

Introduction to Ireland

Republic of Ireland
Northern Ireland

Cross of the Scriptures, Clonmacnoise

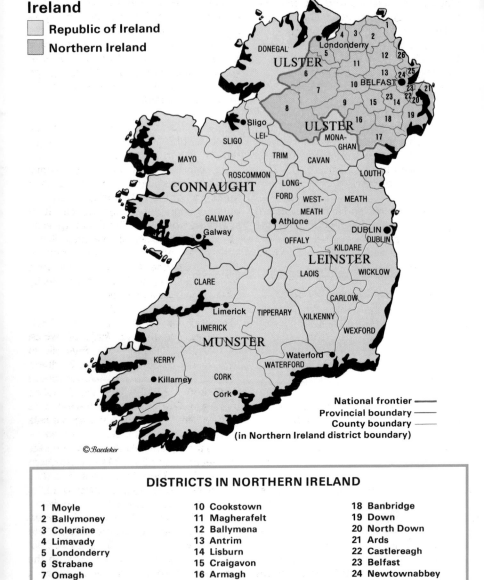

Ireland

- Republic of Ireland
- Northern Ireland

National frontier ▬▬▬
Provincial boundary ▬▬▬
County boundary ▬▬▬
(in Northern Ireland district boundary)

© Baedeker

DISTRICTS IN NORTHERN IRELAND

1 Moyle	10 Cookstown	18 Banbridge
2 Ballymoney	11 Magherafelt	19 Down
3 Coleraine	12 Ballymena	20 North Down
4 Limavady	13 Antrim	21 Ards
5 Londonderry	14 Lisburn	22 Castlereagh
6 Strabane	15 Craigavon	23 Belfast
7 Omagh	16 Armagh	24 Newtownabbey
8 Fermanagh	17 Newry	25 Carrickfergus
9 Dungannon	and Mourne	26 Larne

Political and Administrative Divisions

Ireland is divided into four historic *provinces* – Leinster (Laighean), Munster (Cúige Mumhan), Ulster, and Connaught (Connacht). With the establishment of the Irish Free State in 1921 most of Ulster remained in Northern Ireland, part of the United Kingdom of Great Britain and Northern Ireland. The name Ulster is often applied to the province of Northern Ireland.

The provinces were divided into *counties*, twenty-six in the Republic of Ireland and six in Northern Ireland. (In referring to an Irish county the word "County" is put before the geographical name: e.g. County Down, or Co. Down for short.) Under a reorganisation of local government in 1973 the counties of Northern Ireland were replaced by twenty-six *districts*.

In the **Republic of Ireland**, the province of *Leinster* has twelve counties; *Munster*, the largest of the four provinces, has six; *Connaught* has five; and *Ulster* has three, Monaghan and Cavan in the interior and Donegal – known as "Ireland in Little" – in the north-west.

Northern Ireland takes in the old counties of Londonderry, Antrim, Tyrone, Fermanagh, Down, and Armagh. These names are no longer in official use, having been replaced by the names of the new administrative districts.

Ireland, the green island in north-western Europe, remained for centuries in the shadow of the larger neighbouring island of Great Britain and was almost forgotten by the rest of Europe. Only a very few travellers – such as Prince Pückler-Muskau in the early 19th c. – spoke of the beauty of the Irish countryside, its stone witnesses to a glorious past, the country houses in their beautiful parks and the friendliness and hospitality of the people, however poor they might be, as well as their ready wit.

It is only in more recent times, with the establishment of the sovereign Republic of Ireland and the country's growing prosperity, that the island has begun to attract increasing numbers of holiday-makers and tourists – individualists travelling on their own, looking for something out of the usual, perhaps fishing or playing golf, who like peace and quiet and who appreciate the friendly reception they receive. The first word in the old language of Ireland that the visitor gets to know is "Fáilte", which means "Welcome".

(The old Celtic language of Ireland is known as *Irish* or *Gaelic* or, more rarely, as *Erse*. Since there are variations in the spelling of place-names and personal names, in both their Irish and English versions, the forms adopted in this guide are those used in the publications of the Irish Tourist Board.)

Ireland (in Irish *Eire*) lies between latitude 51°30′ and 55°30′ N and between longitude 5°30′ and 10°30′ W. Along with the main island of Great Britain and various smaller islands and groups of islands it forms part of the British Isles – a term of purely geographical significance. It is separated from Great Britain, to the east, by the North Channel, the Irish Sea – which can often be rough – and St George's Channel; the west coast is open to the Atlantic, with numerous rocky offshore islands and islets.

The total area of the island is 32,600 sq. miles (84,403 sq. km), of which 27,100 (70,283) are in the Republic of Ireland and 5500 (14,120) in Northern Ireland. The population of Ireland is about 5,100,000 – 3,500,000 in the Republic and 1,600,000 in Northern Ireland. This gives a density of 156 to the square mile (60 per sq. km) for the island as a whole – 130 to the square mile (50 per sq. km) for the Republic and 290 (114) for Northern Ireland. The Republic of Ireland is thus one of the most thinly populated countries in Europe. But since the total population of Ireland between the 1840s, the period of the Great Famine, and the middle of the 20th c. fell from 8,000,000 to 4,000,000, the passing of the 3,00,000 mark in the last few decades must be taken as a positive development.

Geography

The interior of the island is a landscape of extensive limestone plains with expanses of moorland, innumerable loughs (lakes) large and small, and here and there low ranges of hills; the Shannon system of rivers and lakes covers something like a fifth of Ireland. Near the coasts the pattern is different, with ranges of hills of some size and varying geological structure. The ranges in the south of Ireland are built of folded red sandstone, separated by river valleys, which are usually well wooded.

The highest peak, at 3417 ft (1041 m), is Carrantuohill (Macgillicuddy's Reeks).

In Connemara, Mayo and Donegal the predominant rock is granite, sometimes overlaid with quartzite. Characteristic of these areas are the isolated bare conical hills which rise abruptly out of the plain. A basaltic plateau covers most of north-eastern Ireland. In the Wicklow Mountains granite again predominates. An area of particular interest both to geologists and to botanists is the karstic landscape of the Burren, near the west coast in Co. Clare.

Ireland went through at least two Ice Ages, which have left their traces in polished and striated rock surfaces and dark hill loughs, in the course of many valleys and in numerous morainic deposits of debris. The drumlins – elongated whale-backed mounds of boulder clay – which occur in swarms across a wide swathe of northern Ireland, broadly between Sligo and Belfast, are deposits of this kind.

Round Ireland's much-indented 2000 mile (3170 km) coastline, with its many wide bays and narrow inlets, there are numbers of beautiful beaches, offering ample scope for long walks or rides in the pure and bracing sea air, even when the weather is not inviting for bathing.

Of the forests which gradually covered the country after the Ice Ages only a few remnants survive. The original tree cover consisted of oak, holly, beech, birch and hazel. In these forests lived elk of a species now extinct, whose huge antlers have been found in bogs; they can be seen on the walls of some Irish castles like Bunratty and Adare Manor.

Today only a small proportion of the country consists of forest, and the Government has made efforts to remedy this by extensive afforestation schemes. Most of the plantings have been Sitka spruce, which has not in fact done particularly well in Ireland. Deciduous trees do, however, flourish, and fine single specimens with wide-spreading, regular branches can frequently be seen.

Tropical and subtropical species originally planted in the parks and gardens of country houses have spread beyond these, particularly in the warm south-west, and in the mild Irish climate many familiar flowering plants flourish luxuriantly and develop vigorous new forms, such as the foxglove and a bluebell with an unusually long stem and a deep blue colour.

In bog country and in thin stony soils the vegetation consists predominantly of mosses, lichens and heather, with broom adding patches of brilliant yellow to this rather monotonous landscape during its flowering season.

Irish farming country is mainly pasture, creating a landscape the greenness of which – in every conceivable shade, varying according to the weather, the

Lough Gartan

cloud cover, the amount of rain, the direction of the wind and the constitution of the soil – has earned Ireland the name of the Emerald Isle and proved a major attraction for visitors. Arable land is found only on the east coast and in certain inland regions, particularly in Co. Tipperary.

Ireland is relatively poor in native fauna, though it has a great variety of birds. Hawthorn hedges provide nesting places for songbirds. In moorland areas the cry of the curlew and the snipe can be heard, and the song of the soaring lark. Oyster-catchers leave their haunts on the coast and move far inland wherever they find sufficient water. Gulls and guillemots nest on crags off the Atlantic coast, and puffins with their gaudy beaks can occasionally be seen. Cormorants patrol the coasts, and gannets, flapping their great wings, plunge down from a great height to seize their prey. Such seabirds as the stormy petrel and fulmar are more rarely seen.

The water of Irish loughs (a term applied both to inland lakes and to major arms of the sea), rivers and streams is frequently brown and peaty, but it is always un-polluted and supports an abundant fish population. Salmon and trout are the most sought-after species; pike and rainbow trout are relatively recent introductions.

Round the coasts of Ireland various species of seal can be encountered.

Climate

Ireland lies in a region of mild south-westerly winds, subject to the influence of the warm water brought by the Gulf Stream. Since no point on the island is more than 70 miles (112 km) from the sea, the whole country has a relatively temperate climate, with mild winters and cool summers. Rain and wind are regular features of Irish weather, but snow is rare except in the hills, and never lies long.

Seasonal fluctuations in **temperature** are small. While the temperature in the coldest months (January and February) ranges between 39 °F (4 °C) in the north-east and 45 °F (7 °C) in the south-west, the thermometer rises to 57–61 °F (14–16 °C) in the warmest months (July and August) and very seldom goes above 77 °F (25 °C). The sunniest months are usually May and June, and in general the south-east of the island gets most sun.

Rainfall is high in the west of Ireland, with an annual average of 118 in (2997 mm), while on the sheltered east coast, around Dublin, it is only 30 in (762 mm). The west of the island lies under the direct influence of Atlantic winds. The moisture-laden air masses are forced upwards by the coastal hills, and the cooling of the air at the higher levels brings down the rain in heavy downpours. Showers of this kind can frequently be seen coming, as they appear on the horizon and move past or draw rapidly closer. When a strong wind whips against the wall of rain it is blown horizontally rather than falling from above. In these conditions good rainwear is of more use than an umbrella.
The moisture content of the air is generally high, with the highest levels in the west.
The weather of Ireland is very changeable. After a rainy day the sky will clear towards evening, with fine light effects and frequently also rainbows.

Government and Society

The island of Ireland is divided into two parts with different systems of govern-ment and social patterns.

Northern Ireland

Northern Ireland, created a self-governing State within the United King-dom by the Government of Ireland Act 1920, was brought under direct rule by the United Kingdom Government in 1972, when the Northern Ireland Parlia-ment was suspended as a result of political difficulties within the province. Subsequent attempts to re-establish some form of self-government having failed, Northern Ireland remains under direct rule as part of the United Kingdom.

Republic of Ireland

The **Republic of Ireland** (Poblacht na hÉireann), established in 1949, succeeded the Irish Free State which came into being as an independent State in 1922. Under a constitution adopted in 1937 it is a parliamentary democracy governed by a House of Representatives (*Dáil Éireann*) and Senate (*Seanad Éireann*), with executive power in the hands of the Prime Minister (*Taoiseach*) and his Ministers. The Head of State is an elected President (*Uachtarán na hÉireann*), whose official residence is in Phoenix Park.

The flag of the Republic is a tricolour, green-white-orange. The national emblem is the harp, together with the three-leaved shamrock, a symbol recalling St Patrick and his interpretation of the Trinity.

The National Anthem is the "Soldier's Song" (written in 1907 by Peadar Kearney, music by Patrick Heeney and Peadar Kearney), a marching song harking back to the fight for independence.

The law of the Republic is based broadly on the principles of British law. The old Irish Brehon law (Law of the Judges), based on traditional Celtic conceptions, was abolished by the British authorities in the 17th c.

The army of the Republic is a volunteer force – there is no compulsory military service in Ireland – which has shown its mettle in United Nations peace-keeping forces in many parts of the world. The Army School of Equitation has demonstrated on the international level the high qualities of Irish competition horses.

Officially the Republic is bilingual. All official documents must be presented in both Irish and English, since the Irish national language (see p. 17) has equal status with English. Representatives speaking in the Dáil usually begin their speeches with a few words in Irish. Road signs, etc., are bilingual. Throughout the country as a whole, however, the language generally spoken is English: Irish predominates as the mother tongue of the inhabitants only in a few areas in the west and south. These islands of Irish, known collectively as the **Gaeltacht**, are the responsibility of a special Government Minister, and the people of the Gaeltacht enjoy certain tax benefits. Whether these and other measures, and the efforts of those concerned to promote the use of Irish, will be successful in preserving the old language remains to be seen.

Gaeltacht
Irish-language areas in Ireland

Londonderry
NORTHERN
BELFAST
IRELAND
Sligo
REPUBLIC
Athlone
Galway OF
DUBLIN
IRELAND
Limerick
Waterford
Killarney
Cork
© Baedeker

The Irish Character

The Irish are great talkers, delighting in argument, and gifted with the liveliest imagination. Even in a difficult situation an Irishman will rarely fall into despondency but – if necessary with the help of alcohol – will seek refuge in a world of dreams. In dealing with strangers the Irish are friendly, receptive and ever ready to help.

The Irish pub, which plays a considerable part in social life, is still primarily a man's place. As in Britain, the pubs are subject to licensing laws controlling their opening hours.

The Tinkers

The tinkers of Ireland are an underprivileged group on the fringe of society who, like the gipsies – to whom, however, they are not related – travel about the country and speak a secret jargon of their own. It is now known that the tinkers are of Irish origin and not, as was once thought, incomers to Ireland.

The Anglo-Irish

The Anglo-Irish are the descendants of members of gentry families and ex-officers who from the mid 17th c. onwards were given possession of expropriated Irish estates. Unlike earlier English settlers, who had learned to speak Irish and adopted the way of life of the native population, these English landlords remained a separate community. They continued to speak English, preserved their Protestant faith and isolated themselves behind high walls from their Irish and Catholic neighbours. Some used their estates only as a source of income, spent little time in Ireland and had stewards to collect the rents for the poor cottages occupied by their tenants. Later, however, the Anglo-Irish ruling class also made their contribution to the country's cultural life. They built themselves country houses and laid out large parks planted with exotic plants which flourished in the mild climate of Ireland.

The Anglo-Irish were responsible for the great period of building activity in Dublin in the 18th c. which yielded such a harvest of fine architecture; in Trinity College they had a university of their own; and they produced many leading Irish figures, politicians and philosophers as well as writers and poets.

During the 18th c., too, the Anglo-Irish established a variety of cultural institutions. The *Royal Irish Academy* collected early manuscripts (including the famous Psalter of Columcille) and produced a many-volumed Irish dictionary. The *Royal Dublin Society*, now best known for its Horse Show, originally also had cultural interests, and its collections formed the nucleus of the National Library and the National Museum.

In the course of time the Anglo-Irish became accustomed to an easy life on their country estates. After the establishment of an independent Irish State covering the greater part of the island they lost their predominant place in the country's life. Many of the old country houses were destroyed by the Irish.

The American Irish

During the 19th c. some 2,000,000 Irish people emigrated to the United States, dissatisfied with political conditions in Ireland or driven by the Great Famine of the 1840s to seek a new life elsewhere. Irish immigrants in New York established a revolutionary movement whose members were known as *Fenians*. From this developed the *Irish Republican Brotherhood*, which worked for the separation of Ireland from Britain by violence. One of its members, Eamon de Valera (born in New York in 1882), was among the leaders of the Easter Rising of 1916; condemned to death, the sentence later commuted, he was released under an amnesty in 1917. He was rearrested in 1918, but in 1919 escaped from Lincoln Gaol and fled to America but returned to Ireland in 1920 and thereafter became Prime Minister and later President of the Republic of Ireland.

The Irish who emigrated to the United States, mostly of rural origin, settled in the large cities of the north, where they soon dominated the market for unskilled labour (e.g. in canal and railway construction). At the same time they developed into a political force to be reckoned with. Between 1870 and 1920 every American city with a substantial Irish population had Irishmen in leading positions, and frequently an Irish mayor, while the police and the fire brigade were always predominantly Irish. In spite of the considerable influence which the Irish thus exercised it was not until 1960 that the first American of Irish descent became President of the United States, in the person of the Democrat John F. Kennedy (1917–63), who was also the first Roman Catholic to become President.

The American dramatist Eugene O'Neill (1888–1953), who had his first play produced in 1916 and received the Nobel Prize for Literature in 1936, was also of Irish descent.

Religion

Celtic Christianity

During the 5th c. the Celtic population of Ireland adopted the Christian faith as it was taught by St Patrick. There were no martyrs. Frequently the old Irish kinship groups went over *en masse* to the monastic life: the head of the clan became abbot and his family, retainers and servants followed him. Nunneries were established for the women. As a result there was a great flowering of religious houses and the number of monks grew rapidly; and just as the kinship group had previously lived in a ring-fort, so they now sought safety within the enclosing walls of the monastic precinct. The Penitentials and Monastic Rules that have come down to us bear witness to the hard conditions of life in the early monasteries.

St Patrick is believed to have received part of his training on the Iles de Lérins, off the Mediterranean coast near Cannes, and it seems likely that while there he met representatives of some of the Eastern churches. This may be how the idea of the *religio arctior*, the strictest ascetic life, came to Ireland, where it was enthusiastically received. Since the faithful were deprived of the opportunity of "red martyrdom", at the cost of their own blood, many of them sought the "*green martyrdom*" of voluntary exile to remote places. While the hermits of the Near East withdrew to the desert, their Irish counterparts retired to a solitary life on very small inaccessible islands off the Atlantic coast.

A typical example of a monastic settlement of the 8th c. is provided by the tiny churches and beehive cells to be seen on the upper terraces of the treeless little islet of *Skellig Michael* (p. 27).

In addition to one or more churches and the cells for the monks a monastery would have a refectory and a guest-house, scriptoria and craftsmen's workshops. Students from England and the Continent and men and women fleeing before the upheavals of the Great Migrations sought refuge in the Irish religious houses, some of which grew to become real monastic cities. Latin as well as Irish was spoken in the monasteries, and not only religious works but the writings of Virgil, Cicero and Ovid were read. There are records, too, of monks who knew Greek.

At the same time there was a movement in the opposite direction. Side by side with the "green martyrdom" there developed the "*white martyrdom*", the *peregrinatio pro Christo*, the pilgrimage for Christ's sake. In frail boats made of animal hides on a timber framework Irish monks ventured out into the "pathless sea" and made their way as itinerant preachers by way of England and France into other European countries. With them they took not only their austere faith but also a humanist education, carrying in leather pouches their precious manuscripts, including copies of the Scriptures which perhaps were already illuminated. The traces of their journeys and their settlements can still be followed today. In regions devastated by war and the passage of armies they established new religious and cultural centres. Later, from the 9th c. onwards, when the process of conversion to Christianity was complete, Irish monks still found their way to Europe as scholars and as advisers to various European rulers. Thus Ireland was able to repay to the Continent, many times over, what it had earlier received from the Continent.

Among the saints of the Early Celtic Church there are some who will constantly be encountered by visitors to Ireland.

St Patrick, who came to Ireland in 432, tells us in his "Confessio" that in him "the spirit glowed". He travelled through the country with a large retinue and treated the High King as an equal, baptising his daughters and lighting the Paschal fire near Tara. Round his life, the exact dates of which are not known, numerous legends have grown up. He is the national saint of the Irish.

St Enda was one of the first to withdraw, in the year 490, to a remote and solitary place in order to devote himself to a life of study and renunciation on the model of the desert hermits. Soon so many disciples followed him to his retreat on Inishmore, one of the Aran Islands, that a large monastic settlement grew up the fame of which spread to the Continent.

Many of the monks who gathered round St Enda themselves founded monasteries and gained a reputation for sanctity, including St Ciarán, who in 548 established the monastic settlement of Clonmacnoise on the Shannon. The learning of the Clonmacnoise monks soon earned it the style of the "University of the West".

Equal to Clonmacnoise in size and importance was Glendalough in the Wicklow Mountains, to which St Kevin, followed by numerous disciples, withdrew to lead a hermit's life.

The leading female saint was St Brigid, who founded a large double monastery for monks and nuns in Kildare in 490. In the "fire house" there burned a perpetual fire − perhaps the continuation of some pre-Christian cult − which was extinguished only at the Reformation. A "St Brigid's cross" woven of straw or reeds, regarded as a protective symbol, is still found in Irish houses, and also on cars and tractors.

St Brendan, who founded a monastery at Clonfert and gathered round him a host of monks, became the model for all those who left home for Christ's sake and ventured on to the open sea, sailing they knew not whither. The "Voyage of St Brendan the Abbot", the account of which survives in numerous medieval copies, is said to have lasted nine years.

St Columba (521 or 543–597) is known in Irish as Columcille and in Latin as Columbanus (the Elder, to distinguish him from the other Columbanus). Columba, who was born at Gartan and, like St Kevin, came from a royal house, went into exile to atone for his guilt. He had secretly made a copy of a psalter belonging to St Finian, who guarded his books jealously and demanded that Columba should give him the copy. When the two could not agree Finian brought the matter before the High King, who gave his judgement that the copy belonged to Finian, on the ground that a copy should go with the original book as a calf goes with a cow. Columba and his supporters refused to accept this verdict, and thereupon fought a battle with the High King on the slopes of Benbulen, north of Sligo. Columba was victorious but left 3000 of his men dead on the field, and by way of penance left home and went into exile. In 563 he landed with 12 companions on the Scottish island of Hy (now Iona), where he founded a monastery. From there he carried on missionary work, mainly among the Picts and Angles. For all the strictness of his faith he is said to have been a kindly man and a lover of nature, particularly of animals.

St Columbanus (the Younger), born in Ireland in 540, was of a less amiable temperament than Columba. About 590, when a disciple of St Comgall in the celebrated Monastery of Bangor and already of advanced years, he resolved to go on pilgrimage. With 12 companions he travelled to the Continent and gained great influence at the Burgundian Court, founding monasteries at Annegray and Luxeuil. He is described as powerful in the faith but uncompromising and irascible.

After a dispute with the Burgundian King he and his companions made their way up the Rhine Valley to Lake Constance and crossed the Alps into northern Italy. His last monastic foundation was at Bobbio in Lombardy, where he died in 615. His monastic rule was an influential contribution to Western monasticism. The disciples whom he gathered round him were thus given a definite pattern for monastic life.

Other Irish saints who propagated their faith on the Continent were *St Gallus*, one of Columba's companions, who founded the Monastery of St Gall in Switzerland; *St Kilian*, Apostle of the Franks, who suffered martyrdom at Würzburg; and *St Virgil*, now Patron Saint of Salzburg.

In later times, when the Vikings were already harrying Ireland, many learned Irish monks found employment at European Courts, and "Scotus" (="Irishman") became a term of honour. Clemens Scotus succeeded Alcuin as head of Charlemagne's famous Palace School, at which Dicuil, described as a grammarian, geographer and astronomer, also taught. Sedulius Scotus, a scholar of outstanding quality, moved from Metz to Cologne. Johannes Eriugena ("Irish-born"), one of the leading spirits of his day, is recorded as having been at the Court of Charles the Bald about 845.

The influence of Iro-Scottish missionaries reached far into eastern Europe, as is shown by the existence of "Scottish houses" (in German Schottenklöster) at Regensburg, Vienna and Kiev. Thus the Early Irish Church was able to transmit to other countries far afield the treasures of its faith and its learning.

Religion in Ireland Today

The Republic of Ireland is overwhelmingly Roman Catholic. The Roman Catholic faith is professed by 94 per cent of the population, while between 4 and 5 per cent are Protestant, the largest Protestant denomination being the Church of Ireland (Episcopalian). In Northern Ireland the Protestants have a majority over the Roman Catholics, some 23 per cent of the population being Presbyterians and 19 per cent belonging to the Church of Ireland, compared with 28 per cent who profess Catholicism. The strains resulting from this religious division are reflected in the history of Ireland in recent years.

More than in any other country in Europe, the tradition of the faith has been maintained unbroken among the Roman Catholic population of Ireland, in spite of the oppression to which they were exposed in past centuries. When Catholic worship was forbidden Mass continued to be celebrated in secret in the open air, at "Mass rocks" in remote places. Those who

wanted to become priests had to seek training and ordination abroad, mainly in France and Spain. When the building of churches was again permitted they had at first to be unobtrusively sited in side streets.

The influence of the Roman Catholic Church makes itself felt in all areas of life in the Republic. On Sundays the numerous services are attended by crowded congregations. Children are commonly baptised with the names of early Irish saints. Marriages are celebrated in church in the presence of the whole family; registry-office weddings are rare. Divorce is prohibited under Irish law. Until recently contraception was also forbidden by law, but at the beginning of 1985, against the wishes of the Church, the Irish Parliament passed a measure authorising the restricted issue of contraceptives.

In large Irish Catholic families it is common for one son or daughter to go into the Church. Priests are part of everyday life in the Republic. Irish priests and nuns are found in many countries, particularly in the Third World, as teachers, nurses and social workers. In the field of private charitable work within Ireland itself the Irish put the inhabitants of wealthier countries to shame.

There are, of course, more negative aspects, including the strict censorship of plays and books – a reflection of the influence exerted by the Church until quite recent times over the whole range of culture in the Republic – which led writers like James Joyce and Sean O'Casey to leave the country, though O'Casey was already living in London before he personally became a victim of it.

Some of the **pilgrimages** which are still popular among Catholics in Ireland indicate that the ascetic aspirations of the Early Celtic Church have persisted into our own day.

On the last Sunday in July every year tens of thousands of people climb Ireland's holy mountain, *Croagh Patrick*, in memory of the 40 days of penance which St Patrick imposed on himself on the summit of the hill in the year 441. The ascent of this bare cone of quartzite with its steep slopes and sharp-edged scree is exceedingly strenuous. The pilgrimage is not performed in a well-ordered procession: people go singly or in groups (school classes, sports clubs, military units); many are non-Catholics or foreigners. Some pilgrims go barefoot. Until some years ago the hill was climbed on the night of Saturday to Sunday, but when, with increasing numbers of pilgrims, the number of mishaps also increased, the Church authorities moved the pilgrimage to the following day.

Station Island in Lough Derg, near the frontier with Northern Ireland, is also associated with St Patrick. In pre-Christian Ireland a cave on the island was thought to be the entrance to the Underworld; and in medieval times the place became famous throughout Europe as St Patrick's Purgatory when a travelling knight claimed to have seen the fires of Purgatory in the cave. The pilgrims who make what has been called "the hardest pilgrimage in Christendom" are now almost exclusively Irish. They spend three days on the island performing the numerous penances prescribed, mainly vigils and fasting. During the pilgrimage season (June to August) visitors are not allowed on the island and photography is forbidden.

Knock (Co. Mayo), the scene of a 19th c. apparition of the Virgin, also attracts large numbers of pilgrims, including sick people seeking a cure. Few foreigners found their way to Knock until the mid 1980s, when the Connaught regional airport was opened there.

In addition to the major pilgrimages there are many local pilgrimages on a particular saint's day ("pattern day"). Thus on *Inisheer*, the smallest of the Aran Islands, the Church of St Cavan, which is in danger of disappearing under drifting sand, is swept clear so that Mass can be celebrated on 14 July.

"Lourdes grottoes" are often set up at crossroads or in natural rock formations. Occasionally visitors will encounter a well surrounded by a wall, round which rosaries or coins or sometimes everyday objects have been deposited; and bushes or posts near the well are hung with rags of clothing. Such **holy wells** are credited with the power of healing particular ailments.

Just as monks were the first to record the ancient popular legends and thus helped to perpetuate them, so the Celtic Church tolerated, and thus preserved, beliefs that attributed some form of life to nature. Hence the various forms of spirit which survive in Irish tradition, such as the fairies (*sidhe*) who dwell on tree-clad hills, and the "little people" or leprechauns who live under hawthorn bushes. To destroy a hawthorn bush, it is believed in the west of Ireland, brings ill luck. There, too, lives a black beast known as the *pooka* which scares lonely travellers and the *banshee*, whose wailing cry foretells the death of a member of one of the old-established families.

The Irish Language

The **Irish** or *Erse* language, also called by the philologically incorrect name of *Gaelic*, belongs to the Celtic group of languages and, within that group, to the Insular Celtic languages. Gaelic in the wider sense includes Scottish as well as Irish Gaelic. Another Insular Celtic language is Breton, which was taken into north-western France by immigrants from the British Isles.

References to the Irish language in this guide are to be taken as meaning the Old Celtic language, not the regional variant of English spoken in Ireland.

Originally Celtic was spoken all over the British Isles. The Germanic peoples who

began to settle in Britain in the 5th c. brought their Germanic languages with them, and the Anglo-Saxon and later English which developed out of these tongues displaced the old language so effectively that it survived only in remote areas without contact with the outside world – and Ireland in those days was such an area. In later centuries, during the period of English rule and the United Kingdom of Great Britain and Ireland – that is, until the establishment of an independent Irish State – the speaking of the Irish language was not only a means of communication but also a declaration of national identity. The latter part of the 18th c. saw an enthusiastic and almost romantic interest in Old Celtic, which prepared the ground for the appearance of such a celebrated literary fraud as Macpherson's "Ossian". Like many languages, spoken by minorities, which have never attained the status of a national or even an official language (e.g. Breton, Provençal, Basque and Catalan), Irish enjoyed a regular renaissance in the late 19th c. – a recollection by the Irish people of their own language, culture and history which involved not only a stock-taking of their inheritance but also a purposeful concern with the old language as a living spoken tongue.

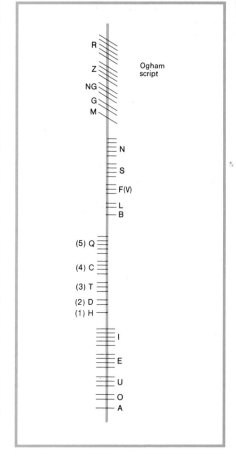

Ogham script

From the 4th to the 7th c. the language was written in the **ogham** script. Although based on the sounds of the Latin alphabet, ogham is quite different from that alphabet in origin and characteristics. The 25 letters of the ogham alphabet take the form of points or horizontal or oblique lines, in groups of from one to five, set on a long vertical line (which often runs down the edge of a stone slab). Later the Latin alphabet was adopted.

Although the Irish language may seem strange and different to one accustomed to the Germanic and Romance languages of Europe – with no parallels to familiar structures, no immediately obvious relationships in the vocabulary – it nevertheless belongs to the great Indo-European family of languages which spans so much of the globe. Having developed independently of other European languages from an early stage, it has evolved grammatical patterns which have no direct equivalent in those languages. There is the additional difficulty, for those seeking to understand or to learn Irish, that it has no "received standard", merely a series of local variants which have equal validity and status.

In spite of the conscious efforts which have been made over the past 200 years to promote the speaking of Irish, the areas within which it is spoken – collectively known as the **Gaeltacht** (see map on p. 12) – have become steadily smaller. Comparison of the situation in 1961 with the evidence for 1851 shows that in the course of just over a hundred years the Irish language area has shrunk by almost 80 per cent – though admittedly this statistic tells us nothing about the actual number of speakers of Irish. Recent estimates suggest that the number is about 55,000. Practically everyone in Ireland speaks English, which is in general official use.

Education and Culture

From time immemorial the Irish have held the spoken and the written word, and indeed all knowledge, in honour, and those who teach are held in high regard. This respect was accorded even to the "hedge-schoolmasters" who travelled the country during the period of the penal laws and taught the country children for a penny a week in the shelter of a hedge. It is said that they carried their ink-well on a chain round their necks and stuffed a Virgil as well as a Gaelic reading-book into their pockets.

When the Irish were again allowed to have schools education was mostly in the hands of the teaching Orders and the secular clergy. The Christian Brothers played a particularly important part in educating the children of the poorer classes.

Republic of Ireland

In the Republic of Ireland education is compulsory from the age of six to sixteen. There is a State system of *national schools* with a uniform curriculum, in which some of the staff are ecclesiastics. As a rule children go to these schools in their fourth or fifth year. Later they go on to *secondary schools*, which are not State-run but are grant-aided and inspected by the Department of Education. The Leaving Certificate at the end of the school course is issued by the Department. In recent years numbers of comprehensive schools have been established. The school day is from nine o'clock to about three o'clock. The yellow school buses which take children to school are a familiar sight in country areas.

For the further education of pupils aiming at a practical trade there are *vocational schools* (which also have further education classes for adults) and a number of *technical colleges*. There is also a technologically oriented college in Limerick, the *National Institute for Higher Education*, opened in 1972. A similar college with the same name was opened in Dublin in 1980.

There are two universities in the Republic, Trinity College in Dublin and the National University of Ireland. *Trinity College*, the oldest university in Ireland, was established by Elizabeth I, exclusively for the education of the sons of the Protestant Anglo-Irish. Irish students were admitted for the first time in 1793, and Roman Catholics were excluded from fellowships and scholarships until 1873. Nevertheless Trinity College has played an important part in the intellectual and political life of Ireland. Among its students have been writers including Oliver Goldsmith and Jonathan Swift, Oscar Wilde and J. M. Synge, the philosopher and statesman Edmund Burke, and also men such as Theobald Wolfe Tone and Robert Emmet who died for the cause of Irish independence. It now has over 5000 matriculated students.

The *National University of Ireland*, which can trace its origins to a college founded in 1845 of which Cardinal Newman was the first Rector, was established as such in 1908. It now consists of three colleges in Dublin, Galway and Cork. Associated with it is St Patrick's College at *Maynooth*, a seminary for priests which also admits lay students; it has a department of Celtic studies. The National University has over 8000 matriculated students in Dublin, 4000 in Cork and 3500 in Galway.

While Trinity College is housed in fine classical buildings in the heart of Dublin, the three colleges of the National University are situated in suburban surroundings. Galway in particular has a fine campus on the banks of the Corrib, with handsome modern buildings. Originally all teaching in the Galway college, including teaching in science, was in Irish, but English is now also used. The college still sees itself, however, as the intellectual and cultural centre for the Irish-speaking areas in the west of Ireland, and seeks to bring fresh impulses to this long-neglected region.

Efforts are also being made in the rest of the Republic to preserve the old national language from extinction. Irish is a compulsory subject at all schools, and in 28 secondary schools the teaching is wholly or partly in Irish. Classes of city children are taken during the summer holidays to places in the Gaeltacht, where they stay with Irish-speaking families. Adults who want to improve their Irish can go to one of the *Irish Colleges* in the Gaeltacht; and their regular courses are also attended by foreigners, usually of Irish origin.

Northern Ireland

Education is compulsory until the age of 16. Central responsibility for the public education system other than university rests with the Department of Education. Local administration is in the hands of five Education and Library Boards established in 1973, with finance provided by the Department, which also inspects the schools. Most schools ("controlled schools") are provided by the boards and wholly financed from public funds, but there are also many privately run voluntary schools which are grant-aided by the boards.

Primary schools, of which there are just over 1000, take children up to the age of 11 or 12, after which they go on to one of a number of types of secondary school. The grammar schools, of which there are 78 (21 controlled and 57 voluntary), provide a seven-year course leading to the General Certificate of Education (ordinary level) at the end of the fifth year and the GCE (advanced level) at the end of the seventh; the "intermediate" schools, of which there are 183 (all controlled schools), provide different types of courses leading to certificates of lesser academic standard; and there are also small numbers of two types of non-selective secondary schools, junior high schools and comprehensive schools. Finally there are 26 institutes of further education.

Northern Ireland, like the Republic, has two universities. *Queen's University*, Belfast, was originally founded in 1845 as the non-denominational Queen's University of Ireland, with colleges in Belfast, Cork and Galway, but in 1908, following difficulties with the Roman Catholic hierarchy, it gained independent status as Queen's University, Belfast. It now has some 6700 students. The *University of Ulster* was formed in 1984 from the merging of the New University of Ulster (itself a quite recent foundation) and the Ulster Polytechnic, with campuses at Coleraine, Jordanstown, Londonderry and Belfast; it has the equivalent of 9000 full-time students.

Economy

After the establishment of the Irish Free State in 1921 most of the country's capital remained in the hands of wealthy Anglo-Irish and the native Irish had little share in the profits. When Eamon de Valera's Fianna Fáil Party came to power in 1932, however, it followed a policy of economic self-sufficiency and fostered the growth of productive industry by protective tariffs. When the new Irish Government refused to pay the "land annuities" – the interest on capital originally advanced to enable Irish farmers to buy their land – as the 1921 Treaty required, an economic war developed between Britain and the Free State. The British Government imposed a 40 per cent duty on Irish goods, which led to a drastic decline in Irish exports. A compromise was reached under which the quota for the export of Irish cattle to Britain was increased on the understanding that the Free State would purchase all its requirements of coal from Britain. The economic war finally came to an end in 1938 when Britain withdrew from its naval bases in southern Ireland.

In the years before the Second World War the Irish Government promoted the country's economic development by a variety of means, including the establishment of partly State-controlled institutions such as the Agricultural Credit Corporation and the Electricity Supply Board. The Republic's withdrawal from the Commonwealth in 1949 gave it greater economic independence.

Although Ireland is relatively poor in minerals, the working of metal ores has been increased in recent years – principally lead, zinc and silver (at Tynnagh, Co. Galway, Navan, Co. Meath, and elsewhere), but also copper, mercury and

Irish cattle

Milk transport

pyrites. Deposits of natural gas have been found at Kinsale.

Foodstuffs, beer, tobacco and textiles are traditional Irish **industries**, but since the late 1950s the Government has promoted the development of new industries and the establishment of foreign firms in Ireland. During the last 20 years numbers of British, United States, West German and Dutch firms have come to Ireland, manufacturing machinery, electrical and electronic apparatus, pharmaceuticals and chemicals as well as textiles and foodstuffs. These export-oriented industries have created many new jobs in Ireland.

Some 70 per cent of the country's total area is devoted to **agriculture**, the great bulk of it as pasture. In Central Ireland cattle are reared for beef, while in the south dairying predominates. After cattle, the most important types of livestock are sheep, pigs and poultry. On good grazing land racehorses are bred for export.

The predominant agricultural crop is barley, which is used in the brewing of beer as well as for fodder. The production of potatoes, sugar-beet, wheat and oats is also of economic importance.

Catches of fish have increased in recent years but are still insufficient to meet the needs of the population.

A third of the Republic's **energy** needs is met by hydroelectric and peat-fired power-stations, rather more than 60 per cent by imported fuels (coal, oil). The largest of the hydroelectric stations on the country's numerous rivers is the one on the Shannon.

Much of the Irish central plain and extensive areas on the north-west, west and south coasts are covered with moorland and bog; and peat has been from time immemorial, and still is, the domestic fuel of Ireland. Since the beginning of industrialisation it has been increasingly worked by mechanical methods for use as industrial fuel, and in 1946 the Government established Bord na Móna, an organisation concerned with all aspects of peat working, processing and use. There are now several peat-fired power-stations; peat briquettes, factory-made from milled peat, provide domestic and industrial fuel; and peat is increasingly being used by gardeners to improve their soil. There is a peat research institute at Droichead Nua, Newbridge, Co. Kildare.

Cutting peat

Peat-fired power station

Britain is the principal customer for Irish **exports**, though the British share of total exports has fallen from two-thirds in the 1960s to under half today. Over the same period exports to the other EEC countries have risen to some 30 per cent of the total. The principal exports are cattle, meat, machinery, textiles and chemicals. In 1983 the value of exports was less than the cost of imports.

Tourism. – With remains of the past, its castles and country houses, its beautiful scenery and hospitable people, Ireland holds powerful attractions for holiday-makers and tourists. The most popular parts of the country are Dublin and the west of the country, where the landscape is still largely unspoiled and the people live their simple traditional life. In 1985 more than 1,900,000 visitors came to the Republic, and income from tourism makes an important contribution to the national economy. In Northern Ireland, in addition to such natural beauties as the Glens of Antrim and the Giant's Causeway, boating holidays on Lough Erne are a particular attraction.

History

Stone Age (c. 7000–2000 B.C.). – The first settlers reach Ireland and bring the land into cultivation. They construct large megalithic tombs.

About 7000 B.C. From this period date the earliest certainly identifiable traces of human activity in Ireland. The first settlers are believed to have come from Scotland, first establishing themselves in what is now Antrim, in the north-east, and moving on from there into the interior of the island. They live by hunting and fishing.

About 4000 B.C. After a second wave of incomers the clearance of forest and scrub land begins, and the population turns to farming and herding.

About 3000 B.C. The first megalithic tombs are constructed.

Bronze Age (c. 2000–500 B.C.). – Implements and weapons begin to be made of metal.

About 700 B.C. Metal axes, daggers and swords are produced, and – towards the end of the Bronze Age – large pots, shields and horns.

Iron Age (c. 500 B.C.–A.D. 400). – The Gaels, a Celtic people, come to Ireland. Numbers of forts are built. Rule by kings. The new iron weapons are superior to the old bronze swords.

From 500 B.C. Various peoples, including the Gaels, move into Ireland from the Continent and subjugate the native inhabitants, the Druid-ruled Tuatha Dé Danann (People of the Goddess Danu). In the prevailing insecurity, with constant warlike raids and cattle-stealing, the people of the island seek safety in strong forts.
A division of Ireland into four provinces develops. Society is split into three classes – priests (druí), warriors and peasants. The king (rí) owes allegiance to an over-king (ruirí), who in turn is subject to a king of over-kings (rí-ruirech) or high king.
Below the king are the nobles of the warrior caste (flaithi), who are patrons of the aes dána, men of art and learning, including poets, doctors and jurists. The family unit is the derb-fine, a four-generation family which possesses land and rights of succession.

Early Christian period (c. 400–1170). – Many of the Irish are converted to Christianity and numerous monasteries are founded. Viking raids on the island are repelled.

About 432 St Patrick, captured by Irish pirates and brought to Ireland as a slave, escapes but later returns to Ireland and converts its people to the Christian faith.

5th–9th c. After Patrick's death numerous monasteries are founded, which during the 6th c. grow in size and influence. Many monks leave home and spread the Christian faith in Scotland (Columba, d. 597) and England and on the Continent (Columbanus, d. 615)

About 800 Viking raids. The Vikings establish settlements on the east coast of Ireland which later develop into towns (Dublin, Wexford, Waterford, etc.). They teach the Irish the art of shipbuilding.

About 1014 In the Battle of Clontarf, near Dublin, the Vikings and their allies are defeated by the Irish under their High King, Brian Boru, who is killed in the battle. This defeat puts an end to the Viking conquest of Ireland.

Norman period (1170–1534). – The descendants of the Normans who had come to Britain with William the Conqueror in 1066 attack Ireland from bases in Wales and seize much land.
King Henry II of England (1154–89) grants fiefs in Ireland to Norman barons and receives the homage of the Irish clan chiefs. The Normans, leaving the Irish only certain areas in western and northern Ireland, occupy the extensive territory which becomes known as the Pale and build mighty castles to defend it. They found numerous monasteries for the new monastic orders (Cistercians, Dominicans, etc.), to which they appoint English abbots. Inland, towns come into being as market-places and centres of authority.

1261 The Battle of Calann, near Kenmare, is one of the first signs of successful Irish resistance to the Normans.

1348–50 Norman power is weakened by the Black Death which ravages the country.

15th c. Decline of Norman rule. A new Irish national feeling emerges – fostered, paradoxically, by one of the great Norman families, the Geraldines. They and the Butlers, another Anglo-Norman family, dominate Irish political life in the second half of the century.

English (and later British) rule (1534–1782). – Ireland is still more closely bound to Britain, and the condition of the Irish people grows steadily worse.

1534 Execution of "Silken Thomas", a Geraldine.

About 1535 Henry VIII (1509–47) breaks with the Pope; Dissolution of the Monasteries.

1541 Henry VIII assumes the title of King of Ireland.

Second half of 16th c. Elizabeth I (1558–1603) continues the political and religious oppression of the predominantly Catholic Irish.

1598 After many years of resistance Hugh O'Neill defeats the English in the Battle of the Yellow Ford.

1601–03 In the Battle of Kinsale the Irish are defeated.

1606 The traditional Irish system of Brehon law is abolished by the British authorities.

1607 "Flight of the Earls": the three leading figures in Ulster – O'Neill, O'Donnell and Maguire – flee to the Continent.

1608 The central and western areas of Ulster, the last bastion of Irish resistance, are settled by Scottish and English Protestants, who are given land confiscated from the native Irish: an event which many see as the root of present-day troubles.

1649 Oliver Cromwell ruthlessly represses an Irish rebellion (1641 onwards) against the Protestants. The Roman Catholic King James II (1685–88), whose attempts to re-establish Catholicism in Britain have met with fierce resistance, seeks to restore his position by a campaign in Ireland.

1690 Battle of the Boyne, in which James is decisively defeated by the Protestant William of Orange (King, as William III, from 1689).

18th c. – There follows a time of severe political and religious repression in Ireland. Penal laws discriminating against Roman Catholics are introduced. Many Irish people emigrate to the United States. The poverty of the native population is in stark contrast to the prosperity of the Anglo-Irish, who possess fine houses and great estates.

Relative independence (1782–1800). – A brief period during which Ireland has a Parliament with a measure of independence.

1782   After several rebellions against the repression of Catholicism Britain recognises an Irish Parliament with a greater degree of independence, in which the leading figure is *Henry Grattan*. The Parliament does something to improve the plight of the poor. Its membership, however, is entirely Protestant.

During the 1790s   The *United Irishmen* led by the Anglo-Irish lawyer *Theobald Wolfe Tone*, influenced by the French Revolution, call for the establishment of a republic in Ireland.

1798   A rising supported by France is defeated.

1800   Britain proposes a union of the British and Irish Parliaments. Influenced by the offer of financial compensation, offices and pensions, the Irish Parliament dissolves itself; it meets for the last time on 2 August.

Religious freedom and Irish nationalism (1800–1922). – More than a century of efforts to secure equal rights for Catholics and national independence for Ireland end with the establishment of the Irish Free State.

1800   The *Act of Union* provides for the establishment of a single Parliament of the United Kingdom of Great Britain and Ireland, meeting at Westminster. Ireland is represented in both the House of Commons and the House of Lords.

1801 (1 January)   The Act of Union comes into force. Wealthy landowners leave Ireland, depriving the country of much of its economic strength.

1829   *Daniel O'Connell*, leader of the Irish Catholic middle classes, elected to Parliament in 1828, secures the admission of Catholics to Parliament and public office (Catholic Emancipation). His objective is to break up the parliamentary union of Britain and Ireland.

1845–49   A devastating famine, brought about by the failure of the potato crop (the staple food of the poor in Ireland), results in the death of more than a million people (out of Ireland's 8,000,000) and the emigration to Britain and the United States of at least another million.

1848   An attempted rising by the *Young Ireland* Party, a movement predominantly of the Protestant middle classes which seeks the establishment of an Irish State on the basis of religious tolerance, collapses because of the general lack of political interest resulting from exhaustion after the famine.

1858   In the United States Irish immigrants found the *Irish Republican Brotherhood*, a secret society aimed at achieving Irish independence by the use of force.

1879   The *Land League* is founded by *Michael Davitt* with the object of securing fair rents and fixity of tenure for Irish tenants.
Charles Stuart Parnell, elected to Parliament in 1875, advocates *Home Rule* – independence for Ireland within the British Empire.

1885   Parnell is the recognised leader of the Irish people, but his attempt to secure the re-establishment of an independent Irish Parliament is frustrated by the House of Lords after his Bill had been passed by the House of Commons.
Most Protestants in the northern counties of Ireland are against Home Rule, since they believe that they do better out of the Union.

1893   Foundation of the *Gaelic League*, with the objective of reviving the Gaelic language and Gaelic literature.

1905   Foundation of *Sinn Féin* (We Ourselves), a group fighting for Irish political and economic independence and advocating passive resistance to British rule.

1912   With the conflict between Britain, Ulster and the nationalist part of Ireland reaching its climax in the years immediately before the First World War, the House of Commons passes a Home Rule Bill (the enactment of which the House of Lords has power to delay until 1914).
In anticipation of the possibility that the Bill will become law, the Ulster opponents of Home Rule form the Ulster Volunteer Force to oppose its introduction by force if necessary.

1913   In Dublin the Irish Volunteers are formed to support the demand for Home Rule.

1914   Outbreak of the First World War.
A new Home Rule Bill is passed leaving it open to the northern counties of Ireland to opt for the continuance of the Union, but the outbreak of war prevents it from coming into operation.

1916 (24 April)   *Easter Rising*: while the British army is fighting in France the Irish Volunteers and an Irish citizen army, with the support of the Fenians, proclaim a republic in Dublin. It is repressed by British forces and a number of its leaders are executed.

1918   In a British general election Sinn Féin gain a majority over the Home Rule party.

1919   In Dublin the Irish Members of the British Parliament establish their own Parliament, the *Dáil Éireann*, declare Irish independence and set up a Provisional Government headed by *Eamon de Valera* (1882–1975).

1919–21   The British attempt to block Irish independence leads to *civil war*, in which the leading part on the Irish side is played by the *Irish Republican Army* (IRA).

1920   Parliament passes the Government of Ireland Act, which provides for two self-governing areas in Ireland, one in the six northern counties with their Protestant majority, the other in the rest of the country.

1921 (6 December)   The British Government and the moderate leaders of the independence movement (Arthur Griffith. Michael Collins) sign a treaty establishing an Irish Free State (*Saorstát Éireann*) within the British Empire.
The six northern counties remain part of the United Kingdom.

1922 (7 January)   The Dáil Éireann ratifies the treaty.

IRISH FREE STATE AND REPUBLIC OF IRELAND

1922   *Arthur Griffith* (b. 1871) becomes first Prime Minister of the Irish Free State, but dies in August. He is succeeded by *William Thomas Cosgrave* (1880–1965), who holds office until 1932.

1922–23   Armed resistance to the Government by opponents of the treaty. The Government wins the day, but at the cost of many lives.

1923 Supporters of the treaty form the *Cumann na nGaedheal*, which later unites with a number of smaller groups to form the *Fine Gael* (Family of the Irish) Party.

1926 Opponents of the treaty, led by Eamon de Valera, form the *Fianna Fáil* (Comrades of Destiny) Party.

1932 After Fianna Fáil's election victory over Fine Gael Eamon de Valera becomes Prime Minister, a post which he holds until 1948 (with two later periods of office).

1937 (29 December) A new constitution comes into force declaring Ireland to be a "sovereign, independent, democratic state" under the name of *Eire*. The constitution provides for the election of a President.

1939–45 Ireland remains neutral during the Second World War.

1948 In a general election Fianna Fáil is defeated, and the Fine Gael leader *John Aloysius Costello* (1891–1976) heads a coalition government.

1949 Ireland becomes a republic, the Republic of Ireland (*Poblacht na hÉireann*), and leaves the British Commonwealth.

1955 Ireland becomes a member of the United Nations.

1963 President J. F. Kennedy of the United States visits Ireland and is given an enthusiastic reception.

1973 (1 January) Ireland joins the European Community.

1979 In Ireland, with its high rate of population increase, just under 10 per cent of all workers are unemployed.
During his visit to Ireland Pope John Paul II calls for an end to violence.

1980 The British Prime Minister (Mrs Thatcher) and the Irish Prime Minister (Charles Haughey), who is an advocate of the union of the Republic of Ireland with Northern Ireland, meet in Dublin to discuss the hunger strike by IRA prisoners in Belfast (which had begun on 27 October).

1982 (14 December) *Garret FitzGerald* (b. 1926) becomes Prime Minister, heading a coalition government of Fine Gael and the Labour Party with the declared objective of putting the economy back on its feet.

1984 United States President Ronald Reagan visits Ballyporeen, the parish from which his ancestors are said to have come (their name then being Regan).
EEC Heads of Government hold a summit meeting in Dublin.

1985 The Irish Parliament decides by a small majority in favour of permitting the restricted use of contraceptives: the first time in the history of the Republic that a government has successfully resisted the influence of the Roman Catholic Church.
On 16 November the British and Irish Prime Ministers (Mrs Thatcher, Garret FitzGerald) sign the *Hillsborough Agreement*, arrived at after long secret negotiations, which provides for the establishment of a secretariat in Belfast and for regular meetings between Irish and British ministers and officials to discuss questions concerning Northern Ireland, with the particular objective of stepping up the fight against terrorism.

1986 The Irish Minister of Justice signs the Council of Europe Convention on the fight against terrorism.

NORTHERN IRELAND

1920–60 The six counties of Northern Ireland (Ulster), with a predominantly Protestant population, form part of the *United Kingdom of Great Britain and Northern Ireland*. Northern Ireland has its own Parliament, at Stormont, and its own government.

1969 Tensions between the Protestant majority and the Roman Catholic minority lead to major outbreaks of violence. The mainly Catholic *Irish Republican Army* (IRA) becomes increasingly active, the Protestant *Ulster Defence Association* (UDA) is formed. The IRA is split into an "Official" wing, which calls for a united socialist Ireland, and a "Provisional" (nationalist) wing which seeks to achieve the incorporation of Northern Ireland in the Republic by acts of terrorism.

1973 Britain and the Republic agree to establish an *All-Ireland Council*.

1976 The Women's Peace Movement, involving both Catholic and Protestant Women, is launched by Mrs Betty Williams and Miss Mairead Corrigan.

1980 (October) IRA prisoners in the Maze Prison, Belfast, go on hunger-strike.

1981 (May) The IRA activist Bobby Sands dies after a 66-day hunger-strike. Other deaths of hunger-strikers follow.

1981 (October) End of the hunger-strike. The Maze prisoners fail to gain their chief objective, to be recognised as political prisoners.

1983 (May) The Irish Prime Minister, Garret Fitz-Gerald, sets up a *New Ireland Forum*, with representatives of the main political parties in the Republic and the Social Democratic and Labour Party (SDLP) of Northern Ireland, to seek a solution of the Irish problem.

1984 (May) The New Ireland Forum puts forward a report with proposals designed to bring about a future united Ireland; but the realisation of any such plans is evidently dependent on the agreement of the Protestant majority in Ulster.

1984 (11–12 October) A powerful bomb, for which the IRA "Provisionals" claim responsibility, kills and injures members of the British Conservative Party in the Grand Hotel, Brighton, during the annual party conference.

1985 (February) IRA activists carry out a mortar attack on a police station in Newry, Northern Ireland, killing nine people.

1985 (November) The Protestant Unionists of Northern Ireland, representing a majority of the population, express violent opposition to the Hillsborough Agreement. When the House of Commons, by a majority representing all the main parties, approves the agreement Ian Paisley, leader of the Democratic Unionist Party in Northern Ireland, and other Unionist Members of Parliament resign their seats in protest, deliberately provoking by-elections in which they are re-elected.

1985 (December) Thousands of Belfast shipyard workers demonstrate against the Hillsborough Agreement.

1986 Resistance to the agreement intensifies. In March there is a 24-hour general strike and, during the Easter holiday, violent clashes between Protestants and the police.

Art and Architecture

Ancient monuments and other features of interest in the country are usually indicated by signposts, which in the Republic are green and white. Many of these places are under State protection as National Monuments. They are usually open and unguarded.

Since the Roman legions never came to Ireland the Celtic inhabitants of the island were able to develop their own distinctive culture and art without influences from outside, and as a result Ireland offers visitors the opportunity of discovering the characteristic forms and figures of Early Celtic art in unique beauty and abundance. Monastic sites and high crosses, metalwork and book illumination are the most impressive manifestations of this Early Irish art; but after this great heyday the late medieval period saw an artistic decline, since the country lacked a wealthy middle class with an interest in art. It was not until the 18th c. that the well-to-do Anglo-Irish ruling class began to build their great country houses, usually in neo-classical style, and the elegant Georgian houses to be seen in the towns, particularly in Dublin and Limerick.

While elsewhere in Europe it is possible to date old buildings by reference to changing styles, in Ireland the style of building in earlier centuries showed little change. The country is littered with the ruins of the past, fitting picturesquely into the landscape; and it has often been possible – as at Ballintubber Abbey and Bunratty Castle, for example – to bring an old building back into use by giving it a new roof and inserting new doors and windows in the gaping holes in its walls.

Stone Age

During the **Stone Age** (*c.* 7000–2000 B.C.) megalithic tombs, built of huge slabs of undressed stone, were constructed all over Ireland. The term *dolmen* is generally applied to the earliest megalithic chambered tombs, with a chamber formed by a number of upright stones (orthostats) which support a capstone weighing many tons and sloping down towards the rear of the tomb. A good example of this type is the gigantic dolmen on *Browne's Hill* near Carlow.

In the *passage grave* the chamber is approached by a passage formed of orthostats. The stones are decorated with spirals, zigzags and other forms of ornament, and the whole structure was originally buried in an earth mound. In some of these tombs there are three side chambers opening off the square, giving them a cruciform plan. The passage graves in the *Boyne Valley* are particularly famed.

In the *gallery grave* there is no distinction between the passage and the burial chamber. The *wedge-shaped gallery grave* has a chamber which is broader at one end than the other, enclosed within a U-shaped formation of orthostats. This type of grave is particularly common in Ireland: there is a good example at *Ballyedmunduff*, near Dublin.

There is also the *court cairn*, a burial mound with a semicircular or oval court serving some ritual purpose in front of the tomb chamber. A tomb of this kind can be seen at *Creevykeel*, north of Sligo.

Bronze Age

Characteristic monuments of the **Bronze Age** (*c.* 2000–500 B.C.) are the *stone circles*, probably used for cult ceremonies, which have left such impressive remains in Ireland. A good example is the *Drombeg* stone circle in Co. Cork.

To this period, too, belong the *standing stones*, known in Irish as *gallain*, which also had some ritual significance.

Evidence of Bronze Age wealth is provided by the finds (e.g. in the Wicklow Mountains) of valuable gold ornaments, including *lunulae* (crescent-shaped collars) of gold sheet.

Iron Age

During the **Iron Age** and the beginning of the Christian period (*c.* 500 B.C.–A.D. 400) *ring-forts* surrounded by stone or earth ramparts, known in Irish as *raths*, were built to provide protection for kinship groups or clans from enemy attacks and plundering expeditions. There are said to be more than 30,000 ring-forts in Ireland, many of them preserved only in the form of fragmentary remains.

There were also more strongly defended *hill-forts*, commandingly situated on elevated sites. An imposing example of a hill-fort – in Irish *lis* – is *Dún Aenghus* on Inishmore in the Aran Islands.

The term *promontory fort* (Irish *dún*) is applied to a ring-fort built on a promontory or projecting tongue of land; sometimes the rampart is built across the neck of the promontory. There is a fine promontory fort at *Dunbeg* on the Dingle Peninsula.

Another type of defensive structure was the *carnnog*, an artificial island in a lough constructed with the aid of piles. Occasionally a natural islet might be used for this purpose. As places of particular security some of the crannogs remained in occupation into the late medieval period.

The Irish terms for the various types of fort feature in many place-names – Dungannon, Lismore, Rathdrum, etc.

During the Bronze Age the Celtic population of Ireland learned the technique of enamelwork, producing beautifully ornamented everyday articles as well as jewellery. They are believed to have acquired the art from the Roman provinces.

Towards the end of the Iron Age the **ogham script**, named after Ogmios, the Celtic god of writing, came into use (see Irish Language, p. 18). Ogham inscriptions are usually found on the edges of erect slabs of stone or diagonally across the stone. Most of those which have been preserved – some 250 out of a total of 300 – are in the counties of Kerry, Cork and Waterford. The inscriptions invariably take the form of standard formulae. The Alphabet Stone at *Kilmalkedar* on the Dingle Peninsula has Latin and ogham inscriptions side by side.

Early Christian Period

The **Early Christian period** (*c.* 400–1170) saw a great flowering of art in Ireland, notably richly carved high crosses and illuminated manuscripts.

The many monastic sites established during this period, however, produced no architecture of any significance. It is known from the chronicles of the time that the buildings were of wattle and daub, or occasionally of timber. Where these materials were not available, as on the rocky islet of *Skellig Michael* in the Atlantic, use was perforce made of stone. On Skellig Michael a flight of more than 600 steps was hewn from the rock to give access to a relatively sheltered terrace on which the monks built their beehive cells and oratories and buried their dead. An upright slab of stone inscribed with a cross was the forerunner of the later elaborately decorated high crosses.

The *beehive hut* of this period (Irish *clochán*) is a small round hut of drystone masonry, corbelled to form a "false vault" and closed at the top by a flat slab of stone. This type of structure is also found in the stony and treeless Mediterranean countries, and probably originated there. On Skellig Michael the monks selected and laid their stones with such care and accuracy that the huts have remained watertight to this day.

The early churches were tiny *oratories* used either for individual devotions or for celebrating Mass. The corbelled walls meet at the roof-ridge, giving the building the form of an upturned boat. The interior was dark, lit only by the door or, later, by a narrow window over the altar. The *Gallarus Oratory* on the Dingle Peninsula is a completely preserved example of the type.

The *gravestones* on the monastic sites show a development from simple forms of ornament to small-scale works of art. In the later period all the arms of the cross which forms the central feature are richly decorated. The inscriptions take the form of a standard formula (*"or do . . ."*) asking for a prayer for the dead man. Built into a wall at *Clonmacnoise* is a notable collection of gravestones and fragments of gravestones. The standing stones of the pagan period were now "baptised" by the carving of a cross, often in very crude form. There are also early attempts at decorating such stones, as on the *Reask Stone* in Kerry, where the stylised cross resembles a flower.

Ireland's celebrated **high crosses**, standing up to 15 ft (4·5 m) high, are believed to have developed out of decorated standing stones of this kind. What are believed to be early forms of the high cross can be seen at *Fahan* and *Carndonagh* on the

Cross-slab, a forerunner of the high cross   High cross with figures

the upright. The whole surface of the cross is divided into panels, each filled with geometric designs: the Celts, it has been said, abhorred an empty surface. It is possible, though not certain, that such crosses were originally made of wood covered with sheet bronze, so that the crosses we have today may be merely stone copies of an earlier form. The studs at the junction of the arms, possibly representing the nails used in the construction of earlier wooden crosses, have been cited as evidence for this theory. On the base are figural representations, not easy to interpret, which may depict scenes of monastic life. The Ahenny crosses have been dated to the 8th c. on the basis of the striking similarity between their geometric patterns and the ornament in the "Book of Kells".

Inishowen Peninsula: stones, ascribed to the 7th c., in the form of a rough cross decorated with interlace ornament and crude figures in relief. The crosses at *Ahenny* in Co. Tipperary show a more developed form with a slender shaft set on a base and a circle linking the arms with

From about the 9th c. the ornamental patterns on the high crosses begin to give place to figural ornament. This is the great age of the Bible crosses, set up in monastic settlements as visible signs of

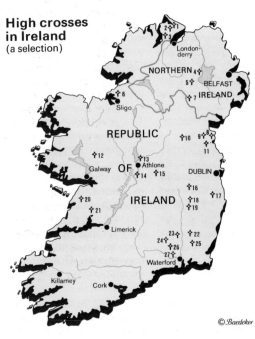

High crosses in Ireland
(a selection)

© Baedeker

1 Clonca	10 Kells	19 Castledermot
2 Carndonagh	11 Duleek	20 Kilfenora
3 Fahan	12 Tuam	21 Dysert O'Dea/Ennis
4 Arboe	13 Bealin	22 Graiguenamanagh
5 Donaghmore	14 Clonmacnoise	23 Kilree
6 Drumcliffe	15 Durrow	24 Killamery
7 Tynan	16 Kilcullen	25 St Mullins
8 Termonfeckin	17 Glendalough	26 Ahenny
9 Monasterboice	18 Moone	27 Kilkieran

piety and means of instruction. The finely carved relief figures, in rectangular panels, depict Old and New Testament scenes. Groups of panels are frequently devoted to miraculous deliveries from difficulty or danger – Daniel in the Lions' Den, the Three Young Men in the Fiery Furnace, the Sacrifice of Isaac, David and Goliath. Figures of Paul and Antony, the desert saints, recall the Eastern prototypes of the Irish hermits, and the fabulous creatures depicted on the sides of many crosses seem to come from the East rather than from western Europe. The central feature, however, is almost always the message of salvation – on the west face Christ crucified, on the east face Christ in glory on Judgment Day. The cross is frequently topped by a small house-like structure in the form of a shrine.

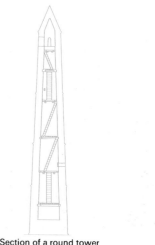

Section of a round tower

The kind of stone used depends on local conditions, but is usually a very fine-grained sandstone. There are quarries of such stone near Kells and Monasterboice in the east of Ireland. One of the finest of such crosses is Muiredach's Cross at *Monasterboice*. The crosses at *Clonmacnoise* were hewn from erratic blocks of sandstone.

The stone used was of very variable quality: the carving on some crosses is still as clear and sharp as on the day it was done, while on others it has been worn smooth and sometimes almost effaced by wind and rain.

Where sandstone was not available and the harder granite had to be used, as at Columba's foundation of *Moone* in south-eastern Ireland, the carving was necessarily simplified almost to the point of abstraction. The figures on the Moone High Cross have an appearance of uniformity, but the faces are not without expression.

From about the 11th c. the representation of Biblical scenes, apart from the Crucifixion, was largely abandoned, and the crosses were again covered with ornament. Sometimes the crosses, with shorter arms and no ring, are carved with individual figures in high relief, such as the limestone crosses of Co. Clare. The *Dysert O'Dea* Cross has a representation of the crucified Christ in a long draped garment and below this the dignified figure of a bishop wearing a mitre and carrying a crosier after the Roman fashion.

While there are a small number of high crosses in Scotland and northern England, the **round tower** found in early monastic settlements is a characteristically Irish development (though there are two examples in Scotland). It is a slender and elegant structure tapering to a height of between 60 ft (18 m) and 100 ft (30 m), with a conical stone roof – the central and most prominent feature of the monastic site. The building of round towers is believed to have begun after the first Viking raids: thus, in addition to serving as a bell-tower, they also provided a place of safety in case of attack. The entrance was several feet above the ground, and within the tower narrow ladders gave access to the upper storeys. The various floors, of which there were usually five, were lit only by narrow windows, all facing in different directions, so that a watch could be kept for the approach of an enemy. In normal peaceful times the monks working in the open were called to services by a hand-bell. A number of these angular metal bells have survived, and examples can be seen in the National Museum in Dublin and the British Museum in London, as well as in churches in remote Scottish glens.

Some 80 Irish round towers are still standing in whole or in part. While the earliest were constructed of undressed stone, without any form of ornament, later examples have elaborately carved stone friezes and decorated doorway arches in Romanesque style. Some round towers, including the one at *Monasterboice*, must still be climbed on ladders. The finest example of a round tower is the one at *Ardmore* in Co. Waterford.

Fine **metalwork** was also produced during the Early Christian period. The excellent examples of metalwork to be seen in the National Museum in Dublin show that the craftsmen of the period could practise and refine techniques inherited from the past, taking as their models articles of earlier periods in bronze, decorated with enamel or vitreous paste, or in beaten gold or silver. Among the examples of their work are such splendid ornamental brooches as the Tara Brooch and, as the monasteries became increasingly wealthy, precious vessels such as the *Ardagh* and *Derrynaflan Chalices* (8th and 9th c.). Later richly decorated cases and containers were produced for objects of particular veneration, including manuscripts and bells, bishops' crosiers and relics of the early saints. In work of this kind the artists made it a point of honour never to repeat themselves.

Irish crosiers have semicircular crooks, but with a straight end, and were kept in a similarly shaped bronze shrine, with a pattern of ornament which frequently ends in an animal's or bird's head. Bell shrines similarly have the same shape as the bell. The *Shrine of St Patrick's Bell* is of bronze, decorated with gold filigree, silver and precious stones.

The covers of a saint's prayer-book were ornamented with bronze mountings. In one example depicting the Crucifixion the angels' garments and wings have spiral and interlace decoration.

The commonest items of this kind to have survived, however, are small house-shaped reliquaries with steeply pitched roofs like those of the Early Irish churches, made of wood with a bronze facing and decoration, which were designed to be carried on a strap round the neck.

Many works of art of this kind were carried off to Norway by Viking raiders and have come to light as grave-goods recovered from tombs, particularly women's tombs. Some are in Norwegian museums; others have been brought back to Ireland.

The *Cross of Cong* (*c.* 1123), brilliantly decorated in gold and blue with animals and fabulous creatures, was the last great achievement of the Irish metalworkers.

The supreme intellectual and artistic contribution of the monks of the Celtic Church lay in the development of an Irish script and in the **illumination of manuscripts**. From the Latin script of their day they evolved a decorative half-uncial script which could be either strong and vigorous or, if the writer's artistic bent so dictated, lively and fanciful. The perfection of this script, written on thick parchment sheets, rivals the work of Islamic and Chinese calligraphers.

The urge to decorate the pages of a manuscript appears at an early stage. In the "Cathach" (Helper in the Fight), St Columba's catechism, for example, the initials break out into a profusion of curls and spirals, while other letters are outlined in dots.

While in the "Cathach" (*c.* 600) only red and blackish-brown ink is used, later illuminated manuscripts glow in many colours. Among the colours used are crimson, bright red, emerald-green, dark blue and yellow. The initials in the chapter-headings of the Gospels are formed by a pattern of interlace ornament ending in human and animal heads, or sometimes by human figures shaped like articulated puppets to form the letters. Later the initials may take up the whole of a page. Above and below the lines appear the animals familiar to the men of that period – cats, mice, cocks and hens, birds,

"Book of Kells": monogram of Christ

fishes. Some of these figures are true to life, but most of them belong to a fantasy world. Words and syllables are linked by curving brackets of grotesque form in the shape of human or animal bodies which can no longer be accommodated within the line and are set above or below it.

The finest achievements of Irish book illumination are the whole-page illustrations, either covered with an all-over pattern of tapestry-like ornament or depicting scriptural scenes. The whole intricate pattern is drawn with such delicacy of line that it requires a magnifying glass to appreciate all the detail. There are evident similarities between these designs and the decorative motifs on metalwork and on high crosses.

On one of the decorated pages of the "Book of Kells", the most magnificent of these illuminated manuscripts, the Virgin and Child are depicted for the first time in the West. The Four Evangelists with their symbols are a favourite theme. Here again the artists have largely broken away from a realistic method of representation and are seeking to give pictorial expression to their own ideas. Thus we find figures with feet turned sideways (as in Egyptian tomb-paintings), a double pair of hands, harlequin-like dress or blue hair.

Numerous examples of Irish manuscript illumination can be seen in Dublin: in the Royal Irish Academy St Columba's "Cathach" (6th c.) and the Stowe Missal (early 9th c.), and in the Old Library of Trinity College the "Book of Durrow" (7th c.), the "Book of Dimma" (8th c., in a silver-plated bronze case or cumdach), the "Book of Armagh" (c. 807), which contains all Four Gospels, and the undisputed masterpiece of Irish book illumination, the "**Book of Kells**".

Recent research indicates that at some time between 790 and 820 four scribes in St Columba's Monastery on the island of Iona, off the Scottish west coast, began work on the "Book of Kells", but after Viking raids on Iona fled to Kells in Ireland, taking with them the partially completed book. In Trinity College, where the book has been preserved since the 17th c., a different page of the manuscript is shown every day.

Most of the holy men of the Celtic Church were active scribes and copyists. When they travelled they carried their manuscripts with them, and their foundations in Britain (e.g. on Lindisfarne) and on the Continent (e.g. at St Gall) also followed the insular style. In consequence a·relatively large number of manuscripts have survived, most of them now in the large European libraries.

Occasionally the Irish scribes noted down personal remarks, or sometimes verses, in the margins of their manuscripts – observations of nature, pious statements, sometimes also thoughts which are by no means pious. In some of these notes they give expression to their fear of the Vikings who brought this great flowering of art to an end.

Romanesque Art

Romanesque art came to Ireland in the 12th c. with the adoption of the Roman form of the Christian faith. Hitherto the Irish had continued to build small churches with steeply pitched stone roofs of the traditional kind; and the new style, too monumental for Irish tastes, was accepted only in part and was so considerably modified as to form a distinctive Irish Romanesque.

The first church in the new style, already a masterpiece, was Cormac's Chapel on the Rock of Cashel, which was consecrated in 1134. Builders from Regensburg in Germany are believed to have worked on this church, and the Schottenkloster (Scots Monastery) in Regensburg is known to have had connections with Ireland. (In the early medieval period the Irish were known as Scoti or Scotti.) For the first time in an Irish church the nave is barrel-vaulted and the chancel groin-vaulted. At the junction of nave and chancel are two square towers. The steeply pitched roof, however, follows earlier Irish models, and the carved fabulous beasts and human heads are typically Irish.

The Celtic head motif is also found in other Irish Romanesque churches, for example at Dysert O'Dea, where the principal doorway has animal masks between bearded human faces, or in Clonfert Cathedral, where the richly decorated west doorway is surmounted by a high triangular pediment with geometrically arranged human heads and ornament. Zigzag mouldings on the doorway and richly sculptured chancel arches are found on other Romanesque churches in Ireland.

After a national synod in 1110 the Irish Church was gradually assimilated to the Roman Church. Diocesan government was introduced, and the power and influence of the old monasteries declined sharply.

At the same time Bishop Malachi of Armagh brought in the Cistercians, the first of the great new religious Orders to come to Ireland. *Mellifont Abbey*, where a Burgundian architect built the fine monastic church, was the mother house of some two dozen other foundations. These new abbeys had a whole complex of buildings in addition to the church – cells for the monks, a refectory, a cloister, domestic offices, etc. The church was often called a cathedral, even though it was not a cathedral in the strict sense of a bishop's church. The monks from the older monasteries now flocked to these new foundations, bringing about the final demise of the Celtic Church.

When the Anglo-Normans conquered Ireland they built castles to provide security in a hostile country. An early form of castle was the *motte and bailey*, with a timber tower built on a circular or oval mound (the motte) and an outer court (the bailey) defended by wooden palisades.

A more substantial fortification was the stone-built keep, with thick walls and a few windows. This might either stand by itself or be enclosed within an outer ward surrounded by curtain-walls. Many ruins of these almost indestructible strongholds have survived to the present day.

In course of time still more powerful fortresses were built, on the pattern of English castles, with corner towers and massive battlemented walls.

Gothic Art

During the Norman period, from the 13th c. onwards, the **Gothic** style came to Ireland. Buildings in Gothic style were erected only by the Norman incomers, with the help of native craftsmen, and by the new religious Orders – first the Cistercians and Augustinians, later the Dominicans and Franciscans.

The churches and cathedrals which were now built, in disturbed times and with limited means, were sturdy structures with little decoration and were smaller than their counterparts on the Continent. The monasteries were built in accordance with the rules and requirements of the various Orders, but these, too, were on a smaller scale than elsewhere. Ruins such as those of *Rosserilly*, Co. Galway, with tower and cloister, refectory and reader's desk, bakery and fish-tank, are like a miniature edition of a Franciscan friary.

Ireland's contribution to the art of this period consists of gravestones of traditional Irish type and a few works of sculpture. Most of the artists are practically unknown. There seem to have been a number of gifted sculptors named O'Tunney in the Kilkenny area, the most notable of them being *Rory O'Tunney*, whose work is to be seen in the cloister of Jerpoint Abbey, on tombs at Jerpoint and at Kilcooley Abbey, near Urlingford, and in Kilkenny Cathedral. On these tombs the figure of the dead man, in full armour, lies on a stone sarcophagus under a sculptured canopy, which sometimes has Late Gothic tracery, with figures of angels, Apostles, saints and holy men round the sides; in 15th-17th c. tombs the dead man and his wife may be lying side by side. The figures are notable for the meticulous treatment of the hair and the garments and for the curiously impenetrable expression of the faces.

Also typically Irish are the *sheila-na-gigs* – small carvings of obscene female figures which may be fertility symbols or intended to ward off evil spirits – which can be found in unobtrusive positions on churches.

From the End of the Middle Ages to the Present Day

Thereafter, given the poverty of the native Irish population, art and architecture stagnated for several centuries. It was not until the **18th c.** that the Anglo-Irish ruling classes, having risen to prosperity and wealth, began to build country mansions and town houses appropriate to their status. Following the models provided by Palladio in Italy and Inigo Jones in England, they built mostly in the classical style. A typical example is

Castletown House, near Dublin, built by Alessandro Galilei and Sir Edward Lovett Pearce in 1722–32 for William Conolly, Speaker of the Irish Parliament, with plasterwork by the Francini brothers.

This flowering of architecture was followed, on a much more modest scale, by the other arts. Since the owners of the new country houses preferred an outdoor life, they were more interested in the layout of their parks and gardens than in the interior decoration of their houses. Exotic trees, immaculate lawns and terraces (as at *Powerscourt* in the Wicklow Mountains) meant more to them than pictures, furniture or carpets.

Nevertheless there were some notable achievements in the minor arts, such as the elegant silver of the period. Some of the more eccentric wishes of the landowners were given expression in the "follies" they built on their estates – Greek or Egyptian temples, obelisks or artificial ruins.

From the middle of the 17th c. a period of great building activity began in Dublin, and within a bare hundred years what had been an unimportant and not particularly salubrious little town was transformed into the second city of the British Empire. Four new bridges were built over the Liffey, its banks were lined with quays, and the old town centre was surrounded by wide modern streets and squares laid out in gardens. The Royal Hospital for old and disabled soldiers, designed by Sir William Robinson, was built in 1670–87.

This building activity reached its peak in the 18th c. Dublin Castle and Trinity College were rebuilt. The short-lived Irish Parliament was housed in a new building (now the Bank of Ireland) designed by Edward Lovett Pearce. As in the rest of Europe, architects of different nationalities were at work in Dublin. Richard Castle or Cassels (1690–1751), a German, built Tyrone House and Leinster House, which is now the Parliament building. James Gandon (1743–1823), an Englishman of Huguenot origin, built the Custom House and the Four Courts, whose elegant silhouette and domes are reflected in the waters of the Liffey, and began the King's Inns on Constitution Hill. Francis Johnston (1761–1829), who built both in the fashionable classical and in the neo-Gothic style, was responsible for the

Chapel in Dublin Castle and the General Post Office which featured so prominently in the fighting of 1916, also the Grecian St George's Church, often considered his best work.

In addition to such large public buildings this period also saw the building of the handsome mansions of the aristocracy and the prosperous business classes, with imposing façades behind railed front gardens. This was the heyday of the **Georgian style**. The brick fronts of these Georgian houses with their tall windows are beautifully proportioned; their only form of ornament, in endless variation, lies in their painted doors with brilliantly polished knockers, flanked by columns and surmounted by an architrave and a semicircular fanlight with a light or the house number. The interior of these houses is often decorated with fine plasterwork by the Francini brothers. Similar houses and terraces can be found in other towns including Limerick and Cork. Dublin's terraces of Georgian houses remained almost intact until well into this century. Since then they have fallen victims, individually or in whole streets, to the housebreaker, to give place to new development. It is only in recent years and at the cost of great efforts that it has been possible to save and to restore properly some of the city's finest streets and squares.

During the 19th c., with Catholic Emancipation, many new churches were built, and the art of **stained glass** enjoyed a great flowering. The first workshops soon developed into schools of stained-glass artists; new techniques were tried out and links were established with the Continent. Pioneers in this development, which was considerably influenced by the Art Nouveau movement, were Michael Healy, Harry Clarke, Sarah Purser and Evie Hone.

20th Century

It is interesting to see how Irish architects and artists of the present day have taken up the forms and themes of the early period of Irish art. In church-building architects such as Liam McCormick have designed round churches of notable quality, reflecting the plan of Ireland's prehistoric stone forts. Such new churches, and churches reconstructed on the remains of older buildings, have tabernacles, Stations of the Cross, fonts and doors of modern design by such artists as Imogen Stuart, a native of Munich.

Smaller objects of bronze (by Edward Delaney, Oisín Kelly and others), again showing the influence of models of the Early Celtic period, have also evolved their own characteristically Irish style. An affinity can perhaps be detected here with the brush drawings of Louis Le Broquy, who illustrated Thomas Kinsella's modern version of the "Cattle Raid of Cooley".

Literature

In the Early Celtic period poets occupied a leading position in Irish society. Seers as well as poets, they acquired their skills in special schools, usually under the direction of Druids, where, lying in the dark, they learned their texts and verses by heart.

During this period (600–1200) there came into being the great cycles of Irish/Celtic *heroic sagas*, which took the form of prose epics and were set against a pagan background.

In the early years of the Christian period the sagas were written down by monks; but alongside this written record an oral tradition was maintained by the *shanachies*, men skilled in the art of telling tales.

A number of different cycles can be distinguished.

In the tales of the *mythological cycle* mortals still hold intercourse with divinities, who have a double aspect, now mild, now terrifying. There is no firm boundary between life and death; and the final goal for man is Tir na n'Og, the Land of the Ever Young, somewhere westward in the Atlantic.

The *Red Branch cycle* of tales is concerned with the Ulaid, a people who gave their name to Ulster. Their royal stronghold was Eamhain macha (Navan Fort, in Northern Ireland), their great hero CuChulainn. The subjects of the tales are cattle raids and their consequences, described in graphic, colourful and sometimes grotesque scenes. In the best known of these sagas, the "Táin Bó Cúailnge" ("Cattle Raid of Cooley"), Queen Maeve, dissatisfied with her husband's possessions, plays the role of the evil opponent of the hero, CuChulainn. The tragic love-story of Deirdre of the Sorrows is in this cycle – often likened to Tristan and Isolde – inspired plays by Yeats and Synge.

The third cycle, which is to be dated after the year 1000, centres on the exploits of *Finn MacCool* and his war band, the Fianna, which seens to anticipate some of the ideals of the later knightly culture. The theme of tragic love – the story of Diarmaid and Grainne, who, too, can be compared with Tristan and Isolde – also appears in these tales.

The *Folklore Commission* began to record the tales of the shanachies in 1935, and they were later issued on records and tapes.

The middle period (1200–1650) was the Age of the Bards – Celtic poets who composed and sang songs in praise of their lord or their king. The prose literature of this period was mainly devoted to the *Fenian cycle*, the fourth of the great cycles: fairy-tale-like tales of adventure, often incorporating ballads.

The characteristic feature of the late period (1650–1850) was the oppression of the Irish by the English conquerors, which had a detrimental influence on the development of Irish language and literature. The predominant element in literature was now folk poetry, cherished by country people and craft workers. Many of

Jonathan Swift   George Bernard Shaw   William Butler Yeats

the poems gave expression to sorrow and the love of nature. Since this poetry flourished particularly in the southern Irish province of Munster it is also known as *Munster poetry*.

From the 17th c. onwards the names of individual Irish authors – writing in English – begin to feature in the history of literature.

The first of these was *Jonathan Swift* (1667–1745). His principal work, "Gulliver's Travels" (1726), though often thought of as a children's book, is in fact a bitter satire directed against England. Many of Swift's other works are also directed against wrongs and abuses of his day. He is buried in St Patrick's Cathedral, Dublin, where he was Dean for 30 years.

Typical Irish qualities – wit and humour, delight in telling stories – can be seen in the work of *Laurence Sterne* (1713–68), scion of an old Irish family, who spent his life as a country clergyman in England. His principal work is the humorous novel "The Life and Opinions of Tristram Shandy", in which the action of the story takes second place to the author's own personality and whimsical fantasy.

Witty comedies were written by the Anglo-Irish playwright *Richard Brinsley Sheridan* (1751–1816), best known for "The School for Scandal" (1777).

Oliver Goldsmith (1728–74), known as the author of a novel, "The Vicar of Wakefield" (1766), poems ("The Deserted Village", 1770) and plays ("She Stoops to Conquer", 1773), describes in his works the country around Athlone, still known as Goldsmith Country. When a poor student at Trinity College, Dublin, Goldsmith wrote ballads for street singers

to earn a few coins and would creep out at night to hear them sung.

Thomas Moore (1779–1852), a talented musician as well as a poet, sought to build a bridge between the world of Celtic traditions and the rather frivolous attitudes of the Anglo-Irish society which he admired by fitting the old sagas to traditional airs in his "Irish Melodies". With these songs, which were soon popular in English drawing-rooms and on the Continent, he won new friends for Ireland and the Irish cause.

The beginning of the modern period was marked at the end of the 19th c. by the establishment of the *Gaelic League* (1893). The object of the League, whose members included Douglas Hyde, first President of the Republic (1938–45), and the writer George Moore (1852–1933), was the revival of Irish language and literature – which came to be called the *Celtic Renaissance*. About the turn of the century Pádraic Pearse (1878–1916), Pádraic O Conaire (1882–1928), Peadar O Laoire (1839–1929) and others began to produce literary work in the Irish language, and in 1899 Lady (Augusta) Gregory founded the Irish National Theatre in Dublin (known from 1904 as the *Abbey Theatre*), in which plays in both English and Irish were performed.

Some of the writers of the modern period, including William Butler Yeats, John Millington Synge and Sean O'Casey, concerned themselves with Irish traditions and the problems of Ireland; others, like Oscar Wilde and George Bernard Shaw, turned more towards Britain; but even those Irish writers who spent most of their life away from Ireland, such as James Joyce, reflect in their work the mentality and language of their native country.

Sean O'Casey

James Joyce

Brendan Behan

Oscar Wilde (1856–1900), born in Dublin, went as a young man to London, where his novel "The Picture of Dorian Gray" was published in 1890 and became a great popular success. Thereafter Wilde turned to play-writing and wrote in rapid succession a series of sparkling comedies, among them "Lady Windermere's Fan" (1892). The dialogue of his plays reflects the wit and quick give-and-take of Irish conversation. His masterpiece was "The Importance of Being Earnest" (1895), a comment on the society of his time.

George Bernard Shaw (1856–1950), an Anglo-Irish dramatist ("Pygmalion", 1912; "Saint Joan", 1923; etc., etc.) who achieved world fame and won the Nobel Prize for Literature in 1925, was noted for his finely polished language and his sceptical wit. The only one of his works that shows any feeling for his native Ireland is "John Bull's Other Island" (1904).

The Anglo-Irish poet *William Butler Yeats* (1865–1939) was a co-founder of the Irish National Theatre and played a major part in initiating the Celtic Renaissance. He had an interest in the occult and created his own personal mythology, in which he incorporated the old Celtic sagas. His works – poems, plays, essays – have a mystical and often symbolic character. His later works, imbued with philosophical ideas, are among the finest English poems of the 20th c. He celebrated the Easter Rising of 1916 in a poem containing the famous line "A terrible beauty is born". He also wrote one-act plays, influenced by the Japanese Noh theatre, which were performed at the Abbey Theatre; in one of these the victorious heroine is a woman with a beggar's staff who personifies Ireland. He was awarded the Nobel Prize for Literature in 1923.

As a Senator of the Irish Free State Yeats was instrumental in securing that the animals which appear in the "Book of Kells" (a hare, a dog, a fish, a bird) should feature on Irish coins.

The Irish playwright *John Millington Synge* (1871–1909) was encouraged by W. B. Yeats to spend some time on the Aran Islands in order to study the way of life and the language of the islanders, and he published a description of the islands and their people in 1907 ("The Aran Islands"). His plays are concerned with the life of Irish peasants and fishermen ("The Tinker's Wedding", 1907). Synge brought the Anglo-Irish dialect on to the stage for the first time. His successful comedy "The Playboy of the Western World" (1907) perfectly reproduces the vigorous and yet delicate language of the islanders. In 1904 Synge became Director of the Abbey Theatre.

The dramatist *Sean O'Casey* (1880–1964), who began by earning his living as a labourer on the railways, joined the Irish national movement at an early age. The Irish struggle for independence is the background both to his six-volume autobiography and to his early plays, such as "The Shadow of a Gunman" (1923), most of which reflect the life of the poor and wretched. In his dramas O'Casey combines comedy and humour with tragic irony. The Abbey Theatre turned down "The Silver Tassie", a new play he offered them in 1928 but staged it some years later. The rejection is often cited as the reason he left Ireland for ever, but he had been living in London for a year when it happened.

Of one of Ireland's greatest writers, *James Joyce* (1882–1941), it could be said that in his intricate play with words and ideas he brought to literature the masterly skills of the old Celtic book illuminators. Just as the Celtic artists "abhorred a vacuum", so Joyce sought in "Ulysses" (1922) to depict the whole of one particular day in the life of Leopold Bloom, the 16th of June 1904, following out every convolution and ramification of events, ideas and feelings. Before "Ulysses" Joyce had published "Dubliners" (1914), a collection of short stories, and "Portrait of the Artist as a Young Man" (1916), a largely autobiographical work in which he portrays the tensions between a young artist and his surroundings.

In his last work, "Finnegans Wake" (1939), Joyce seeks, as in "Ulysses", to give linguistic expression to the unconscious or subconscious mind. Since he employs words from more than 20 different languages and refers to a variety of esoteric myths and religions, "Finnegans Wake" must rank as one of the most difficult works in all literature.

Samuel Beckett, born near Dublin in 1906, worked for some time in Paris as James Joyce's secretary, and in 1936 made his home there. Some of his works are written in English, some in French, and then translated by himself into the other language. Among his many works –

poems, plays, novels, essays – it is principally his plays ("Waiting for Godot", 1952), in which the action is reduced to the minimum, that have brought him fame. In 1969 Beckett was awarded the Nobel Prize for Literature.

Brendan Behan (1923–64) became involved as an adolescent in the activities of the Irish Republican Army and spent several years in British penal establishments. His experiences during this period are described in his autobiographical novel "Borstal Boy" (1958) and his posthumous "Confessions of an Irish Rebel" (1965). The heroes of his plays, with their fierce social criticism, are the outsiders of society ("The Hostage", 1958; "The Quare Fellow", 1959).

The Irish are particularly noted as writers of short stories, which are concerned with the precise depiction of a particular situation or state or mind, their expressive force resulting from the tension between linguistic precision and the humour of the situation, between pessimism and cheerfulness. The subjects are mostly taken from Irish everyday life. Among particular masters of the genre are Liam O'Flaherty (1897–1984), Sean O'Faoláin (b. 1900) and Frank O'Connor (1903–66).

Music

The heyday of Irish music was in the medieval period, the favourite instrument being the harp. In the banqueting hall of the High King, at lesser Courts and in the houses of the magnates of the day the "three tunes, of laughing, of weeping and of sleep" were played.

We know the names of only a few of the most celebrated harpists (many of whom were blind) and of the tunes ascribed to them. Later we hear of itinerant troubadours, who specialised in folk music. More than 200 compositions by *Turlough O'Carolan* (1670–1738), a blind poet and harpist, have been preserved.

During the centuries of English rule the poverty of the people ruled out any serious musical interests, and most of the Anglo-Irish landlords, preferring an outdoor life, had little time for the arts. Dublin during its 18th c. heyday was the exception, and in 1742 Handel's "Messiah" had its first performance in the city, conducted by the composer.

Nevertheless the musical talents of the Irish managed to find expression. The instruments used in performing light music or dance music were of the simplest – fiddles, played with great virtuosity; tin whistles, with which they produced unexpectedly strong and harmonious sounds; and goatskin drums (*bodhran*). The Irish pipes (*uilleann*) were a softer-toned variant of the Scottish bagpipes, held under the arm and operated by movements of the elbow. These traditional instruments have been supplemented in more recent times by the concertina, the guitar and the banjo.

Folk groups all over the country use these various instruments in a rich repertoire of Irish but also Scottish, English and American tunes and songs, establishing an international reputation not only in concert halls but also in the popular "folk clubs".

In the late 18th c. much effort was devoted to collecting the traditional Irish songs, and several volumes of old folk tunes were published. Using these folk-songs and the traditional melodies, Sean O'Riada (1931–71) composed important works which opened up new avenues and pointed the way for younger colleagues after his early death.

Scenery and Sights

Province of Leinster
(Laighean: Republic of Ireland)

Leinster, in the east of Ireland, has flat sandy coasts, along which are numerous port towns of varying size, some of them with ferry services to and from Britain and the Continent. The largest of these ports is **Dublin**, capital of the Republic, which lies at the head of a large crescent-shaped bay between the *Howth Peninsula* to the north and the hills around *Dalkey* to the south. From the bay ships can sail up the River Liffey into the centre of the city.

In Dublin itself the inner area bounded by the city's two canals is of most interest to the visitor, with its museums and cathedrals, its shopping streets and park-like squares, and above all the fine public buildings and terraces of Georgian houses which recall the city's 18th c. heyday. The doors of these houses, approached by short flights of steps, often flanked by white columns, brightly painted, with brass plates and knockers, fanlights and lamps, are a particular feature of Dublin.

South of Dublin are the lonely and beautiful **Wicklow Mountains**, with bare conical granite peaks which gleam in the sun. In a narrow wooded valley in the hills is the once-celebrated monastic city of **Glendalough.**

The area north of Dublin, with the **Boyne Valley**, is particularly rich in antiquities, from prehistoric burial sites by way of Early Celtic high crosses and the ruins of later monasteries to the imposing remains of medieval castles. The road from Dublin to Belfast runs close to the coast, passing through the towns of **Drogheda** and *Dundalk*, with the railway following a roughly parallel line.

The interior of the province is an undulating region of pastureland, with fields bounded by hawthorn hedges, which when the hawthorn is in blossom mark out long strips of lighter colour against the varying shades of green of the fields. This pastureland, on limestone soil, is horse country, with famous stud farms and an old and celebrated racecourse, the **Curragh**, which are open to visitors.

To the west, almost without transition, is a level expanse of moorland. Here the most modern machinery is used to work the vast resources of peat, and the cooling towers of peat-fuelled power-stations are prominent landmarks.

The boundary between Leinster and the province of Connaught is formed for some distance by Ireland's longest river, the **Shannon**, on the banks of which is **Clonmacnoise**, the second of the great monastic cities of the Early Christian period.

Farther south is the medieval city of **Kilkenny**, seat of the powerful Butler family, Earls of Ormond, with many historic old buildings, but also a thriving modern town. The work of the *Kilkenny Design Centre* has had a powerful influence on the design of Irish industrial products; and credit is also due to the Centre for the good-quality souvenirs which visitors can buy at many places in Ireland.

In the extreme south-east of the province is the old-world town of **Wexford**, an example of the settlements established near the sea by Ireland's foreign conquerors. Wexford, originally a Viking foundation, later passed into the hands of the Normans. The surrounding countryside with its trim square fields and orchards still has an un-Irish air.

The migrant birds who fly over Ireland in great numbers in spring and autumn or spend the winter there – particularly wild geese and wild ducks – find a safe and suitable habitat in the **Saltee Islands** and the *Wexford Wildlife Reserve*.

Province of Munster
(Cúige Mumhan: Republic of Ireland)

In the province of Munster ranges of hills running from east to west enclose beautiful river valleys and separate landscapes of very different types.

Dominating the fertile surrounding plain is the steep-sided crag of the **Rock of Cashel**, for centuries a great spiritual and political centre.

The people of the southern counties of Munster, particularly the inhabitants of **Cork** and **Waterford**, have a reputation for nimble-mindedness and determination. The southern and western coasts of the province, with the projecting *Beara*, *Iveragh* and *Dingle* peninsulas, are wide open to the influence of the Gulf Stream, and around **Glengarriff**, for example, it is common to see palms growing in people's front gardens. The roads are bordered by high fuchsia hedges, and subtropical plants flourish on the crumbling walls of old castles.

In the **Killarney** lake district a dense mantle of ivy covers the trunks of huge trees, forests of rhododendrons reach up the hillsides to a considerable height and the strawberry tree (arbutus) has established itself and flourishes.

On the south coast of Munster there are many little holiday resorts, with cheerful rows of brightly painted houses, often situated on river estuaries or on bays reaching far inland, which have remained little known and have preserved their peace and quiet. The beautiful west coast, however, has been extensively developed for the holiday and tourist trade, and the roads along the Atlantic carry a heavy traffic. From the scenic road known as the **Ring of Kerry**, on clear days, the bizarre rock cones of the **Skellig Islands** can be seen far out to sea.

Kerry is rich in antiquities, from **Staigue Fort** to the standing stones and beehive huts of the **Dingle Peninsula**.

To the west of **Limerick** is the estuary of the **Shannon**, with its flat shores and its expanses of salt water blown into waves by the Atlantic winds.

A car ferry between *Tarbert* and *Killimer* saves motorists who want to follow the coast some considerable detours. The Shannon marks the boundary of Kerry: to the north of the river is Co. Clare. From the county town of **Ennis** roads reach out in all directions to the main beauty-spots and features of interest in the area.

In the karstic terrain of the **Burren** rare plants of Arctic and Alpine or Mediterranean origin make their home in sheltered crevices in the rock. This is the haunt of large butterflies whose beauty of form and colour is even surpassed by some of the wild orchids which grow here. The numerous ring-walls and hill-forts show that Clare had a considerable population in the first century of our era.

The **Cliffs of Moher** on the Atlantic coast, rising sheer from the sea to a height of over 600 ft (180 m), are one of the most spectacular sights in Ireland, particularly if the sea is stormy.

Province of Connaught
(Connacht: Republic of Ireland)

The province of Connaught was always scorned by the conquerors of Ireland, who preferred to seize more fertile land elsewhere on the island and drive its former owners into this extreme westerly region. In the words attributed to Cromwell: "To Hell or to Connaught."

Lying off the city of **Galway** and its beautiful bay are the **Aran Islands**, whose appeal to visitors lies not only in the great prehistoric fort of **Dún Aenghus** on *Inishmore* but in the old way of life, in the hard conditions of these remote islands, which has been preserved on the smaller islands of *Inishman* and *Inisheer*.

The coastal regions of Connaught are bare and stony, with great expanses of unpopulated high moorland. These lonely territories with their limitless horizons, their clouds sweeping high overhead and their brilliant colouring after rain have now become a favoured tourist area, the haunt of painters and photographers. Carefully stacked piles of peat alternate along the roadside with water-filled peat cuttings and bog pools, lying like mirrors between rock and moorland. The most useful domestic animals here are donkeys, which carry their loads in wicker saddle-baskets. The low whitewashed cottages, some of them still thatched, are surrounded by hedges of rhododendrons. The road signs often show only the Irish form of place-names in the old script.

In **Connemara**, with its bare conical hills, the *Twelve Bens*, all these features, these various forms and colours, are brought together within a relatively small area. The finest view, farther north, is to be had from Ireland's holy mountain, **Croagh Patrick**, on the coast of Co. Mayo; it extends over scattered groups of islands to the cliffs and beaches of **Achill Island**.

At the north end of the province the counties of **Sligo** and **Leitrim** provide an unexpected contrast with their green and gently beautiful landscapes. Their most striking feature is the great table mountain of **Benbulben**, with which numerous legends are associated.

The strings of lakes in the interior, with their apparently endless maze of waterways, offer quite a different landscape pattern. They are popular with anglers, whose boats can be seen dotted about amid dense green islets of vegetation.

Province of Ulster
(Republic of Ireland)

Donegal, the most northerly county in the Republic of Ireland, is accessible from the rest of the Republic, without crossing into Northern Ireland, on only one road. The long journey, however, is well worth the trouble. Even in these northern parts the influence of the Gulf Stream can still be felt. On steep rock faces, washed by salt spray, cushions of thrift contrive to flourish. In the evening the rocks which form a backdrop to crescent-shaped beaches of white sand take on a rosy tinge, earning Ireland's north-west corner its name of **Bloody Foreland**. From the coast quiet little roads run east over treeless grassland, moors and lonely passes. Isolated hills rear up abruptly from the lower ground, visible from a long way off. **Mount Errigal** with its smooth quartzite flanks looks as if it were covered with snow.

In the extreme north, on the **Inishowen Peninsula**, there are weathered stone crosses of the Early Christian period; the one of *Carndonagh* is famous as a forerunner of the later high crosses. From the great hill-fort known as the **Grianán of Aileach** the view extends in good weather over *Lough Swilly* and *Lough Foyle* to the open sea and eastward into Northern Ireland.

In the village of **Gartan**, above Lough Gartan, a cross and a stone slab remind the visitor that one of the greatest of the Early Christian saints, St Columba or Columcille, was born here in the year 521. There are also cross-slabs recalling associations with St Columba in **Glencolumkille**. This valley, which had been almost abandoned by its inhabitants, was given new life through the efforts of the local priest and now has small home industries, holiday homes and an open-air folk museum. Here, as elsewhere in the county, high-quality hand-woven Donegal tweeds are produced. From nearby *Bunglass Point* there is a magnificent view of the cliffs of **Slieve League** falling sheer down to the sea.

Province of Ulster
(Northern Ireland)

The industrial city and port of **Belfast**, the political, economic and cultural centre of Northern Ireland – and in recent years the scene of much sectarian violence – lies at the mouth of the River Lagan, which here flows into *Belfast Lough*.

Picturesquely situated above the north side of Belfast Lough is the Norman stronghold of **Carrickfergus**. On the south side is the popular seaside resort of *Bangor*.

Londonderry (Derry), Northern Ireland's second largest city, situated at the north-west corner of the province, is still surrounded by a complete circuit of 17th c. walls.

Northern Ireland offers visitors a wealth of beautiful scenery – the great expanse of Lough Neagh to the west of Belfast; the intricately patterned *Lough Erne* in the south-west of the province; the **Mourne Mountains** in the south-east; the **Glens of Antrim** north of Belfast; and – perhaps the most spectacular sight of all – the bizarre rock formations of the **Giant's Causeway** on the north coast of the province.

The city of **Armagh**, where St Patrick founded a monastery in the year 445, is now the religious centre of Ireland, the seat of both a Catholic and a Protestant archbishop.

Suggested Itineraries

In the following suggested itineraries places which have a separate entry in the A to Z section of this Guide are in **bold** type.

The itineraries are designed to take in the major cities, beauty-spots and features of interest (high crosses, round towers, etc.) in the countryside. Many of the places described in the Guide, however, can be reached only on side roads off the main routes. The map at the end of the book will help in detailed planning.

All the places mentioned in the Guide, whether the subject of a separate entry or not, are included in the Index on p. 233.

Dublin to Drogheda and Belfast (about 95 miles)

From Dublin the N1 runs north to *Swords*, an ancient little town with a ruined castle and a round tower. Continuing at some distance from the sea, it reaches the coast at *Balbriggan* (water-sports) and then runs north-west to **Drogheda** on the River Boyne.

A detour can be made to the **Boyne Valley** with the famous *Newgrange*, *Knowth* and *Dowth* passage graves, by turning left into the N51 immediately after crossing the Boyne.

From Drogheda the N1 runs to Dunleer. About half-way there, to the left of the road, is the old monastic site of **Monasterboice**, with fine high crosses.

From Dunleer the N1 continues, crossing a number of rivers flowing into Dundalk Bay, to the port of **Dundalk**, only a mile or two short of the Northern Ireland border. Over the border the A1 heads north for Belfast. From *Newry* the A28 runs north-west to **Armagh**, from which the A3 leads north-east to Lisburn, on the main road to **Belfast**.

Dublin to Arklow and Wexford (about 90 miles)

The coast road south from **Dublin** comes in a few miles to **Dun Laoghaire**, from which there are ferry services to Holyhead (Anglesey). There the N11 turns away from the coast, running along the pro-montory of Dalkey, on the south side of Dublin Bay. A side road on the left leads to **Bray**, one of Ireland's leading seaside resorts. The N11 then runs along the east side of the **Wicklow Mountains**, past country of great scenic beauty and tracts of forest, to Ashford and Rathnew.

From Rathnew the R750 follows the coast to **Wicklow**, continuing to *Wicklow Head* (lighthouses).

From Rathnew it is possible either to continue on the N11 or to take the coast road (Brittas Bay, Mizen Head) to the seaside resort of **Arklow**, where the Avoca River flows into the sea. A detour can be made from here to the *Vale of Avoca*, to the north-west.

From Arklow the N11 continues to Gorey and **Enniscorthy**, an attractive town on the River Slaney. The N11 then goes on to **Wexford**, where the Slaney reaches the sea. (Wexford can also be reached from Gorey on the R741 and R742, which keeps fairly close to the coast.)

From Wexford various roads continue south to the seaside resort of *Rosslare* and the ferry port *Rosslare Harbour*.

Dublin to Waterford and Cork (about 160 miles)

From **Dublin** the N7 runs south-west to **Naas**, once the seat of the kings of Leinster. South of the town is *Punchestown Racecourse*.

From Naas the N9 goes south, crossing the River Liffey at Kilcullen. Beyond this the road passes **Moone**, with a famous high cross, and *Castledermot* (round tower). It then descends into the Barrow Valley to **Carlow**, an industrial town with a ruined castle, to the east of which is *Browne's Hill dolmen*, Ireland's largest megalithic chambered tomb.

From Carlow the N9 continues south along the right bank of the River Barrow. At Leighlinbridge it crosses the river, and then runs south-west (from Whitehall as the N10) to **Kilkenny** on the River Nore, one of the most attractive towns in Ireland. From there the N10 (with possible detours to *Kilree*, which has a round tower and a high cross, and the Augustinian Priory of *Kells*) and the N9 (beyond

Knocktopher) continue to **Waterford** on the River Suir, celebrated for the production of Waterford glass.

From Waterford visits can be made to the coastal resorts of *Dunmore East* (R683, R684) and *Tramore* (R675).

The main route continues from Waterford, at some distance from the coast, to **Dungarvan**, **Youghal** (detour, a short distance before the town, on the R673 to **Ardmore**, with a round tower) and **Cork**, the principal city in the south of Ireland and a major port.

Dublin to Limerick and Killarney (about 125 miles)

From Dublin the N7 runs south-west to **Naas** and **Kildare**, Ireland's great horse-breeding centre. East of the town is the *Curragh Racecourse*, on which there are race-meetings from spring to autumn. Crossing the River Barrow and the **Grand Canal**, the N7 continues to **Portlaoise**, an important traffic junction in the centre of Ireland. The route then continues, with the *Slieve Bloom Mountains* on the right, to **Roscrea**, and from there via Nenagh to the attractive town of **Limerick**, on the Shannon.

From Limerick the N24 runs south-east to **Tipperary**, from which the N74 continues east to **Cashel**, at the foot of the famous *Rock of Cashel*.

The main route continues from Limerick on the N20 and N21 (beyond Patrickswell) via **Adare** and *Newcastle West* to Abbeyfeale, from where the route continues south on the N21 (to Castleisland), the N23 (to Farranfore) and the N22 to **Killarney**, in the centre of the beautiful Killarney lake district, one of the most popular holiday areas in south-western Ireland.

Killarney is a good base from which to drive round the Iveragh Peninsula on a beautiful scenic road, the **Ring of Kerry**, which runs close to the coast for most of the way, with superb views.

Dublin to Athlone and Galway (about 135 miles)

From **Dublin** the N4 goes west, skirting the **Royal Canal** for part of the way, to *Maynooth* and Kinnegad. From there the route continues on the N6, via Kilbeggan and Moate, to **Athlone**, at the point where the River **Shannon** flows out of Lough Ree.

South of the town, on the east bank of the river, are the remains of the monastic settlement of **Clonmacnoise** (high crosses), which can be reached from Athlone either by boat or on the Shannonbridge road.

From Athlone the main route continues on the N6 to **Ballinasloe** and **Loughrea** (from which there is a possible detour to the *Turoe Stone*), and then via Craughwell and Oranmore to **Galway**, on Galway Bay.

Galway, the largest town in the west of Ireland, is a good starting-point for trips to **Lough Corrib** and around **Connemara**, a region on the Atlantic coast where Irish is still spoken. From Galway, too, there is a ferry service to the **Aran Islands** (and also an air service).

Dublin to Carrick-on-Shannon and Londonderry (about 205 miles)

From Dublin the N3 runs north-west via Dunshaughlin to Navan.

Roughly half-way between Dunshaughlin and Navan, at the village of **Tara**, a road goes off on the left to the *Hill of Tara*, once the stronghold of the high kings of Ireland.

Navan is an important road junction; just north of the town, at *Donaghmore*, stands a round tower. From Navan the N51 and N52 (from Delvin) lead south-west to **Mullingar**, from where the N4 runs north-west to **Longford** and **Carrick-on-Shannon**, the starting-point for cabin-cruiser trips on the Shannon. From here the route continues via **Boyle** to **Sligo**, on Sligo Bay, to the east of which is beautiful *Lough Gill*. From Sligo the N15 goes north and north-east to **Donegal** and then over the Barnesmore Gap and through hilly and wooded country to *Balleybofey*.

From Ballybofey a detour can be made to the north-west coast of Ireland. The N56 runs north into the N13, from which the

N56 can be followed along the coast, by way of various promontories and peninsulas – **Horn Head**, the **Rosguill Peninsula**, the **Fanad Peninsula** – and then on the N13 to the **Inishowen Peninsula**, with the *Grianán of Aileach*, a mighty stone fort.

The main route continues east on the N15 to *Lifford*, where, at Strabane Bridge, there is a border crossing into Northern Ireland. From here the A5 runs north, parallel to the River Foyle but at some distance from it, to **Londonderry** (Derry), a port on *Lough Foyle*, the old centre of which is surrounded by its 17th c. town walls. Londonderry is a good base for coastal trips – for example to the *Giant's Causeway* or the *Glens of Antrim*.

Sligo to Enniskillen and Belfast
(about 105 miles)

From **Sligo** the N16 leads east and after crossing the border into Northern Ireland

continues as the A4 to *Enniskillen*. From Enniskillen a short detour can be made to **Lough Erne**. The route then continues via Dungannon and past the great expanse of **Lough Neagh** to the Northern Ireland capital, **Belfast**.

Londonderry to Belfast
(about 60 miles)

From **Londonderry** the route runs inland on the A6 and B74 and then (from Feeny) on the B40 through the *Sperrin Mountains*, a hilly and wooded region of beautiful and varied scenery with the tourist centre of *Gortin*, and then via Draperstown to Magherafelt.

From Magherafelt the route (A31, A6, M22) continues to the north of **Lough Neagh** to *Antrim*, near which is a well-preserved round tower. The M2 motorway then goes on to **Belfast**, near which is the interesting *Ulster Folk and Transport Museum*. From Belfast there are attractive trips along the coast north and south of the city.

Ireland
A to Z

Within each entry in this part of the Guide the various buildings and other features of interest are described in a sequence that can conveniently be followed by a visitor, either on foot or by car.

The surroundings of the various towns – with some exceptions where this arrangement did not seem appropriate – are described in a clockwise direction, starting from the north.

A note on Irish terminology may be useful. It should be remembered that in Ireland the name "cathedral" is frequently given to a church which is not a cathedral in the strict sense of an episcopal church; that the term "mountain" may be applied to hills which are by no means of Alpine proportions; that the old term "demesne" is still commonly used for an estate or property; and that a "gap" is a pass. Some of the special terms applied to particular types of prehistoric remains are explained in the introductory section of this Guide (see Art and architecture, p. 26).

It is also worth bearing in mind that references to the Blackwater River are not always to the same river. Ireland has large expanses of peatbog, which give the water of the local streams a dark tinge: not surprisingly, therefore, there are three rivers on the island all called Blackwater. The first, to the west of Armagh, forms the frontier between Northern Ireland and the Republic, then turns north-east and flows into Lough Neagh; the second, a left-bank tributary of the Boyne, flows through Lough Ramor, north-west of Kells, and joins the Boyne at Navan; the third, the longest of the three, rises a little way north-east of Killarney and thereafter flows in an easterly direction past Fermoy and Lismore, takes a right-angled turn to the south and reaches the sea in Youghal Bay.

On the banks of the Shannon

Achill Island/ Oiléan Acaill

Map reference: B/C1/2.
Republic of Ireland.
Province: Connacht. – County: Mayo.
Population: 3100.
ⓘ **Tourist Information Office,**
   Achill Sound;
   tel. (098) 4 32 49.
   Open July and August.

HOTEL. – *Achill Sound*, B*, 36 r.

With an area of 55 sq. miles (142 sq. km), Achill Island (Oiléan Acaill) is Ireland's largest offshore island. It lies off the west coast of the main island, separated from it by the narrow Achill Sound, which is spanned by a swing bridge. This hilly L-shaped island is almost entirely covered by heath and bog, with cultivated land only in valleys and near the coast. The hills on the north and west coasts rise to 2200 ft (671 m), dropping down to the sea in magnificent cliffs.

Near the bridge is **Achill Sound**, the island's market town. It offers facilities for bathing and deep-sea angling; motor boats and sailing craft can be hired.

Near the south end of the island, on the shores of Achill Sound, are the ruins of *Carrickkildavnet Castle* (15th c.: National Monument), with part of a vaulted stone roof and remains of an old slipway for boats. The castle belonged to the legendary Grace O'Malley, who ruled extensive territories in this area in the 16th c. (see Louisburgh).

SURROUNDINGS. – 7 miles (11 km) north-west of Achill Sound, on the north coast, is *Dugort*, which has a good sandy beach. In the surrounding area there are many remains of cairns and chamber tombs.

It is worth climbing *Slievemore* (2169 ft (661 m)), a cone of quartzite and mica, for the sake of its extensive views to the north and south. Below the hill, accessible only from the sea and in good weather, are the Seal Caves; the best way to see them is to take a boat, with an experienced boatman, from Dugort (2 miles (3 km)).

4 miles (6 km) south-west of Dugort lies *Keel* (Achill Head Hotel, B, 24 r.; Amethyst Restaurant), an attractive holiday resort with a sheltered sandy beach 2 miles (3 km) long extending south-east to the foot of the Minaun Cliffs, which fall sheer 800 ft (240 m) to the sea at one point. Keel is the centre of the island's fish-processing industry.
There is fishing for brown trout in Keel Lough.

3 miles (5 km) west of Keel is *Dooagh*, the prettiest place on the island, with white houses and white roofs.

There is a particularly picturesque stretch of coastal scenery on the road to *Keem* (5 miles (8 km)), which has a beautiful sandy beach (several parking places).

The beach at Keem (Achill Island)

Adare Manor

From Keem there is a rewarding climb up *Croaghaun* (2068 ft (630 m)), to the west. On the seaward side it ends in a 4 mile (6 km) long line of cliffs. From here there is a magnificent view over the Atlantic.
It is unsafe to go too near the edge of the cliffs, which are much undercut by the sea.

5 miles (8 km) west of Achill Sound lies the pretty little resort of *Dooega*, a convenient point from which to climb Minaun Mountain (1530 ft (466 m)) and Minaun Cliffs.

Adare/Ath Dara

Map reference: D3.
Republic of Ireland.
Province: Munster. – County: Limerick.
Population: 800.

ⓘ **Tourist Information Office,**
Church View,
Adare;
tel. (061) 8 62 55.
Open June to August.

HOTEL. – *Dunraven Arms*, HA, 24 r.

RESTAURANTS. – *Dunraven Arms Hotel*; *Ferriers Restaurant*

Adare (Ath Dara, "Ford of the Oak Tree") lies on the wooded west bank of the River Maigue, some 9 miles (16 km) south-west of Limerick on the busy road which leads to Killarney. With its thatched roofs and old grey-walled church, it has something of the air of an English village.

From the 14-arched stone bridge there is a very attractive view of the beautifully planted banks of the river and the old buildings in the background.

SIGHTS. – **Adare Manor** (Mon.–Sat. 10.30 a.m.–4 p.m., Sun. 2–4.30 p.m.; admission charge) is a neo-Gothic mansion (1832) set in a park. The principal rooms, including the hall and picture-gallery, are open to the public; from the house there are fine views of the gardens and terraces. The tea-room is open only from June to August. In the park, on the banks of the river, are the extensive ruins of *Desmond Castle* (13th c.), a romantic sight with its semicircular towers and lush growth of vegetation.

Also in the park are the ruins of a *Franciscan friary* founded in 1464, with later additions. The nave, choir and south transept of the church survive; fine fonts, niches and stalls in choir. Beautiful cloister with an old yew tree in the centre; conventual buildings.

Near the bridge over the River Maigue are the restored remains of a 14th c. Augustinian abbey, used since the 19th c. as a Protestant church and school.

The Roman Catholic parish church originally belonged to a Trinitarian abbey built in the 13th c. It reached its present size and form, however, only in the 19th c.

SURROUNDINGS. – 5 miles (8 km) south-east of the town on the N20 is *Croom*, with a 12th c. castle restored in the 19th c. In the 18th c. it was the meeting-place of the "Maigue poets". West of Croom are the ruins of a 15th c. church (National Monument) and a massive round tower (12th c.), the top part of which is missing.

2½ miles (4 km) east of Croom we come to the remains of *Monasteranenagh Abbey* (National Monument), a Cistercian house dating mainly from the 12th c., with good carving.

7 miles (11 km) south-west of Adare on the N21, on the River Deel, lies the little market town of *Rathkeale*, round which are a number of ruined castles. One of them, Castle Matric (1440; open June–Sept., Sat., Sun., Mon. and Thu. 2–4.30 p.m.; admission charge) has been restored; period furniture and *objets d'art*.

Early in the 18th c. many German refugees from the Palatinate were resettled in the district around Adare and Rathkeale, which then became known as the *Palatine*. They preserved much of their way of life until late in the 19th c., and German family names can still be met with in the area.

5 miles (8 km) west of Adare stands *Cappagh Castle* (15th c.), a strongly fortified keep 70 ft (21 m) high, with 16th c. turrets at the eastern corners.

Aran Islands/ Oileain Arann

Map reference: C2.
Republic of Ireland.
Province: Connacht. – County: Galway.
Population: about 2000.
ⓘ **Tourist Information Office,**
Kilronan;
tel. (099) 6 12 63.
Open March to October.

GUEST-HOUSE. – *Johnston Hermon's Kilmurvey House*, B, 8 r.

ACCESS. – By air or by sea. Aer Arann flies daily to all three islands from Carnmore, 4 miles (6 km) north-east of Galway. There are daily boat services (CIE line) from Galway to the main harbour of Kilronan on Inishmore and also to the two smaller islands.

The Aran Islands (Oileain Arann) lie in the Atlantic between 25 and 30 miles south-west of Galway. There are three islands: Inishmore (area 12 sq. miles (30·54 sq. km)), Inishmaan (3½ sq. miles (9 sq. km)) and Inisheer (2¼ sq. miles (5·6 sq. km)).

Thanks to the remoteness of the islands their inhabitants have preserved much of the old Irish culture which elsewhere has been lost, and the language of the islands is still predominantly Irish. The hard traditional life of the Aran fisherfolk is depicted in the works of J. M. Synge and other writers and in Robert Flaherty's film "Man of Aran".

The islands, of karstic limestone, are rugged and infertile. At the cost of un-remitting toil the inhabitants have built up successive layers of sand and seaweed into small and irregularly shaped fields, which they call "gardens", sheltered by drystone walls.

Visitors and freight are conveyed to the two smaller islands in currachs – light boats made of laths and tarred canvas, which are also sailed far out into the open sea to fish and catch lobsters.

Until a few years ago the islanders still wove their own clothing and wore hand-made shoes of hide without heels, known as "pampooties". Still to be seen are the

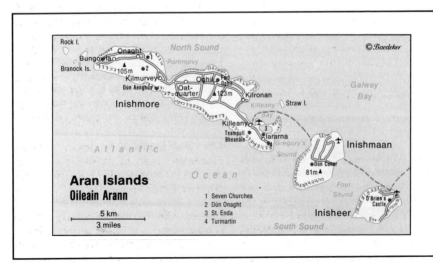

Aran Islands Oileain Arann

5 km
3 miles

1 Seven Churches
2 Dún Onaght
3 St. Enda
4 Turmartin

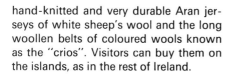
Currachs ready to put to sea

Fields enclosed by drystone walls

hand-knitted and very durable Aran jerseys of white sheep's wool and the long woollen belts of coloured wools known as the "crios". Visitors can buy them on the islands, as in the rest of Ireland.

There are the remains of so many old buildings on the islands that only the most important sites (all scheduled as National Monuments) can be mentioned. Since the dating of the early structures is subject to great uncertainty, no dates are given here.

Inishmore

On the edge of the cliffs fringing the south-west coast of Inishmore is the great stone fort of **Dún Aenghus**, a mighty semicircle of three roughly concentric enclosures on the brink of sheer cliffs dropping 300 ft (90 m) to the sea. The inner court, 150 ft (45 m) in diameter, is surrounded by a stepped drystone wall, 20 ft (6 m) high and 18 ft (5·4 m) thick at the base, containing various passages and chambers. The middle rampart is surrounded by a defence consisting of thousands of sharp-pointed stones set close together (*chevaux-de-frise*), in the manner of a modern tank barrier. From the edge of the cliff there is a breath-taking glimpse of the surf far below, with magnificent views over the sea.

Farther east is *Oghil Fort* (National Monument), a stone fort with two concentric ring-walls and steps leading up to the ramparts.

North of Dún Aenghus, at the hamlet of *Kilmurvey*, are the 9th c. Church of St Brecan and Temple MacDuagh, an early church with a choir.

On a ridge north-west of Kilmurvey stands the stone fort of *Dún Onaght*, which is almost exactly circular in form.

Kilronan, at the south-east end of Inishmore, is the chief place on the island. 2 miles (3 km) south, around *Killeany*, are the remains of numerous religious buildings. Of particular interest is *Tighlagh Eany*, an early church with later features which is all that remains of the monastic settlement of St Enda (Eany); there is a very fine cross shaft with interlace ornament and a relief figure of a horseman.

Also in this area is *St Benan's Church* (Teampall Bheanáin), one of the smallest churches in the world, measuring only $10\frac{3}{4}$ ft by 7 ft (3·20 by 2·10 m).

Visitors who have time to explore the smaller islands will find many remains of old buildings scattered about in a landscape of stony soil and drystone walls.

Inishmaan

On a steep-sided hill on Inishmaan rises the oval fort of *Dún Conor* (National Monument), with a number of hut sites (restored) in the interior; it affords fine views. There is also a fine dolmen. The old way of life of the Aran islanders is particularly well preserved on Inishmaan (clothing).

Inisheer

Among the remains on Inisheer are the medieval tower of *O'Brien's Castle*, prominently situated on a rocky hill; *St Gobnet's Church* (Cill Gobnet), a small oratory with the characteristic features of Early Irish architecture; and the *Church of St Cavan*. Every year on 14th June this little church is cleared of the sand which continually drifts over it so that an early service can be held; the Saint's tomb is also swept clear of sand for the occasion.

Ardara/Arda Rath

Map reference. B3.
Republic of Ireland.
Province: Ulster. – County: Donegal.
Population: 650

(i) **Tourist Information Office,**
  Campbell's,
  Ardara;
  tel. 34.
  Open June to August.

HOTEL. – *Nesbitt Arms*, B, 27 r.

RESTAURANTS. – *Nesbitt Arms Hotel; Ferrier's*.

Ardara (Arda Rath, "Earth Hills") is prettily situated on the little River Owentocher, near the eastern shore of Loughros More Bay, an arm of the sea which reaches far into the land. It is noted for the manufacture of homespun tweeds. Hand knitting, hosiery and hand embroidery are also produced here.

SURROUNDINGS. – 7 miles (11 km) north-east of Ardara, on the River Owenea, lies *Glenties*, situated in a wooded region, with good fishing in its loughs and rivers. There is a Government fish-hatchery in the little town.

Glenties has several times won the contest for Ireland's tidiest town.

North-east of Glenties, rising above the long narrow Lough Finn, is *Aghla Mountain* (1933 ft (589 m): fine viewpoint). The River Finn, which flows out of the lough, is followed for several miles by the road, which runs along the hillside high above it, with magnificent views.

2 miles (3 km) south-west of Ardara an unclassified road branches off on the right and winds its way up through a rugged landscape of bare hills, with tight bends and gradients of up to 25 per cent, to the *Glengesh Pass* and on to *Glencolumbkille* (see entry).

To the west of Ardara extends a long narrow peninsula ending in *Loughros Point*, with superb views.

From the north side of Loughros Beg Bay, at low tide, it is possible to enter the *Maghera Caves*. Near by is the *Essaranks Waterfall*. From here there are footpaths continuing along the coast, through beautiful scenery, or through the Slievetooey Mountains (1500 ft (450–460 m)) to Glencolumbkille.

North of Ardara the R261 branches west off the N56. A prominent feature on this road is a huge dolmen at *Kilclooney*. Beyond this are the twin holiday villages of *Narin* and *Portnoo*, beautifully situated in the shelter of hills on the south side of Gweebara Bay. Narin has a fine sandy beach 1½ miles (2·5 km) long and an 18-hole golf-course. At low tide it is possible to walk (or, more usually, paddle) to the little islet of *Inishkeel*, with the ruins of an old chapel on the shore.

Farther west, on Dunmore Head, are two old ring-forts from which there are fine views.

On an island in *Lough Doon*, 1½ miles (2·5 km) south of Portnoo, stands a massive and well-preserved circular stone fort (reached by boat, at a small charge; signpost).

The quiet little resort of *Rosbeg*, 3 miles (5 km) south of Portnoo, has a good sandy beach and fishing for brown trout in the local loughs.

Ardmore/Ard Mor

Map reference: E4.
Republic of Ireland.
Province: Munster. – County: Waterford.
Population: 300.

HOTEL. – *Cliff House*, B, 16 r.

GUEST-HOUSE. – *Melrose*, B, 6 r.

Ardmore (Ard Mor, "Great Hill") is an attractive little resort half-way along the south coast of Ireland, 2½ miles (4 km) off the N25 to the east. It offers a good beach and fine cliffs; the village itself mingles old buildings and modern villas.

SIGHTS. – The well-preserved *round tower (12th c.: National Monument) of Ardmore is one of the latest of Ireland's round towers. It rises to a height of 97 ft (29·6 m), in four tapering storeys, with its round-arched doorway high above the ground. In the interior are projecting stones carved into grotesque heads.

Dolmen, Kilclooney

Adjoining the tower is the ruined *St Declan's Church or "Cathedral" (13th c.: National Monument). It bears the name of a bishop who founded a monastery here in Early Christian times and is honoured by a pilgrimage here on 24 July every year. The blind arcading on the west gable contains very fine Romanesque reliefs, unfortunately much weathered. In the upper row the figure of the Archangel Michael weighing souls can be distinguished; below this are Adam and Eve, the Judgment of Solomon and the Adoration of the Kings.

In the choir of the church are two ogham stones.

St Declan's Church: relief in the blind arcading

Built on to the "Cathedral" is St Declan's House, which is believed to contain his tomb. This is an important station on the annual pilgrimage.

½ mile (800 m) east of the main group of buildings are the ruins of *Dysert Church*, once a church of some size. Near by is St Declan's Well (restored 1798), a holy well in which pilgrims bathed.

At the south end of the beach can be seen an erratic boulder known as *St Declan's Stone*. It is said that anyone who crawls under the stone – which cannot be done by those in a state of sin – will be cured of rheumatism.

SURROUNDINGS. – There are many pleasant walks along the cliffs – to the sea-caves in Ardmore Head and Ram Head, east and south of the village, to Whiting Bay (west of Ardmore) and to the beautiful Bay of Monatray (sandy beach).

Arklow/ Inbhear Mor

Map reference: D5.
Republic of Ireland.
Province: Leinster. – County: Wicklow.
Population: 8650.
ⓘ **Community Tourist Information Office,**
Grand Parade,
Arklow;
tel. (0402) 3 24 84.
Open June to September.

HOTELS. – *Arklow Bay*, B*, 20 r.; *Royal*, B, 20 r.; *Hoyne's*, B, 15 r.

RESTAURANTS. – *Arklow Bay Hotel*; *Royal Hotel*; *Marine*, Main Street; *Viking Café*, Main Street.

Arklow (Inbhear Mor, "Broad Estuary") lies on the N11, the main road south from Dublin. Here the River Avoca, from which the Vale of Avoca takes its name, flows into the Irish Sea.

HISTORY. – Arklow has had an eventful history. There is a tradition that St Patrick landed here. In later centuries there was much fighting for possession of the town, which changed hands several times. The last battle fought here, during the 1798 Rising, is commemorated by a memorial in front of the Roman Catholic church.

Arklow is a seaside resort with good bathing beaches, but it is also a busy little town noted for its boatyards and its potteries (conducted visits). There is an interesting Museum of the Sea.

Along the South Strand past the golf-course is *Arklow Rock* (fine views), on which is Our Lady's Well, still much venerated.

SURROUNDINGS. – From Arklow the R747 runs north-west along the River Avoca. To the right of the road stands *Shelton Abbey*, now a State forestry school, set in a park with magnificent rhododendrons and other beautiful shrubs.

Beyond this is *Woodenbridge* (side road into the Vale of Avoca: see below), where two other streams flow into the Avoca. The village has a golf-course (9 holes) and a trout-hatchery (which visitors can inspect).

From here the R747 continues west along the River Aughrim, via Aughrim and Tinahely, to *Shillelagh* (9-hole golf-course). From the woods in this area came the stout cudgels, "shillelaghs", with which the Irish were accustomed to settle their differences at a time when they were not allowed to bear arms. There is trout fishing in the local streams.

In the hills west of Shillelagh the ruined *Aghowle Church* (12th c.: National Monument) has an interesting doorway, a plain granite cross and old gravestones.

From Woodenbridge the R752 leads north into the lovely *Vale of Avoca*, a favourite beauty-spot celebrated by Thomas Moore. The road runs through Avoca village, a good trout-fishing centre. In spring the valley, fringed by green hills, is gay with the white blossom of the wild cherry trees. In pre-Christian times copper, lead, zinc and sulphur were worked here. The area now contains a variety of industry.

3 miles (5 km) farther up the valley Croneblane looks down from its crag on the famous *Meeting of the Waters*, where the Avonmore and Avonbeg flow into the Avoca. There is a good view of the junction from the Lion's Bridge.

2 miles (3 km) beyond this is the *Avondale Forest Park*, with a mansion of 1797 (beautiful interior), birthplace in 1846 of patriot Charles S. Parnell, now occupied by the State forestry school. Near by is a nature trail (open all year).

The Vale of Avoca ends at Rathdrum.

Armagh

Map reference: B5.
Northern Ireland.
District: Armagh. – Population: 13,000.
ⓘ **Armagh District Council,**
The Palace,
Friary Road,
Armagh;
tel. (0861) 52 40 52.

HOTELS. – *Drumsill*, Moy Road, B*, 14 r.; *Charlemont Arms*, English Street, B, 10 r.

RESTAURANTS. – *Dobbin's*, 30 Scotch Street; *Drumsill House*, Moy Road; *Milestone*, 30 Upper English Street.

Armagh (Ard Macha, "Macha's Hill") lies in Northern Ireland, south-

west of Lough Neagh. Situated at the junction of a number of main roads, it is the chief town of its district, and as the seat of both a Roman Catholic Cardinal and a Protestant Archbishop it takes an important place in the religious life of Ireland. It has textile and meat-processing industries.

HISTORY. – The town takes its name of Macha's Hill from the legendary Queen Macha, who in the 3rd c. built a stronghold, now known as Navan Fort, on a hill 2 miles (3 km) to the west. Remains of its ring-wall can still be seen on the hill.

Armagh gained importance in Early Christian times, when St Patrick founded a monastery and a church about 445. The settlement developed into a centre of missionary activity, and the "Book of Armagh" was written in the monastery. In the course of the centuries the town was several times burned down and rebuilt.

SIGHTS. – In the centre of the town lies the wide avenue known as The Mall, flanked by many Georgian houses. In this street can be found the *County Museum*, with material on archaeology and local history. Facing the north-west end of the museum is the *Court House* (by Francis Johnston, 1805–09).

From the Court House College Hill runs north-east, passing on the right the Royal School (1608), founded by James I, to the Armagh Astronomy Centre.

The *Observatory*, established in 1791, is open to the public. The Centre also includes a Planetarium opened in 1968 (presentations in July and August) and a Hall of Astronomy which displays astronomical apparatus and a model of a spacecraft.

Going south-west from The Mall, we pass the 18th c. Market House and come to the Protestant *St Patrick's Cathedral*. It occupies the site of the church founded by St Patrick in the 5th c. The cathedral's present aspect dates from a 19th c. restoration by Lewis Cottingham. Notable features of the interior are a 10th c. crypt, a number of monuments (including that of Sir Thomas Molyneux) and a bust of the 18th c. Archbishop Richard Robinson, who did much to give Armagh its present attractive appearance. On the outside wall can be seen a tablet marking the supposed position of the grave of High King Brian Boru, killed in the Battle of Clontarf (1014), buried here by his own wish.

To the north-west of the town, also commandingly situated on a hill, is the Roman Catholic *St Patrick's Cathedral*, a neo-Gothic building (1840–73) with interior decoration (mosaics) by Italian artists.

To the south of the town are the remains of a *Franciscan friary*.

SURROUNDINGS. – 9 miles (14 km) west of Armagh is the village of *Caledon*. 2 miles (3 km) south-west of this is Caledon House (1779), a part-Georgian, part-Regency mansion set in beautiful gardens.

At *Tynan*, south of Caledon, are a number of high crosses carved with Biblical scenes (12th c.).

Armagh

1	Planetarium	6	County Museum
2	Court House	7	Orange Tree
3	Library	8	Gate
4	Market House	9	Drelincourt School
5	Pavilion	10	Palace Gardens

Athlone/Ath Luain

Map reference: C4.
Republic of Ireland.
Province: Leinster. – County: Westmeath.
Population: 9450.
ⓘ **Tourist Information Office,**
   17 Church Street,
   Athlone;
   tel. (0902) 7 28 66.

HOTELS. – *Royal*, B*, 55 r.; *Prince of Wales*, Church Street, B*, 42 r.; *Shamrock Lodge*, B, 31 r.; *Newpark House*, B, 17 r.

RESTAURANTS. – *Le Château*, Abbey Lane; *Prince of Wales Hotel*, Church Street; *Shamrock Lodge Hotel*.

EVENTS. – *Athlone International Freshwater Gala Angling Festival*; *Shannon Boat Rally* (July).

View of Athlone

Athlone (Ath Luain, "Ford of Lun"), situated almost in the exact geographical centre of Ireland, lies on the Shannon, which flows through Lough Ree, to the north of the town, here forming the boundary between the provinces of Leinster and Connacht.

HISTORY. – The crossing of the Shannon at this point was important from time immemorial. By the end of the first millennium A.D. there was already a wooden bridge over the river here, and in the 13th c. a bridgehead was formed, with a castle and river-bank defences, which in later centuries was repeatedly fought over, destroyed and rebuilt.

The town is a busy rail and road junction and a harbour on the Shannon (see entry) and Lough Ree. In addition it has developed a number of light industries and become the main marketing and distribution centre for the surrounding area. To the east of the town is the powerful Athlone long-wave transmitter.

SIGHTS. – On the west bank of the Shannon, above the town and the bridge, is the 15th c. *King John's Castle* (National Monument), which now houses a local museum. Near the bridge stands the Church of SS Peter and Paul, a fine modern building (1937) with stained glass depicting well-known people, among them the tenor John McCormack (1884–1945), a native of the town.

The station, in Galway Road, is a good example of early railway architecture.

SURROUNDINGS. – From Athlone the N55 runs north-east through the *Poets' Country* of Oliver Goldsmith and John Keegan Casey. Goldsmith went to school in Lissoy, which he describes in his "Deserted Village".

4½ miles (7 km) east, on a by-road near the Athlone transmitter, is *Bealin*. On a hill near the village, in the grounds of Twyford House, can be seen a 9th c. *high cross* (National Monument) carved with hunting scenes, intertwined animal figures and other ornamental patterns.

Athy/Baile Átha h-I

Map reference: D5.
Republic of Ireland.
Province: Leinster. – County: Kildare.
Population: 4300.

HOTEL. – *Leinster Arms*, B, 18 r.

Athy (Baile Átha h-I, "Ford of Ae"), the largest town in Co. Kildare, lies south-west of Dublin on the River Barrow, at a ford which was an important crossing-place and at the junction of two roads, the N78 and R417. A branch of the Grand Canal (see entry) runs into the Barrow here.

SIGHTS. – *White's Castle*, built by the Earl of Kildare in the 16th c. to protect the bridge over the Barrow, is a massive rectangular structure with turrets at the corners. The bridge has the unusual name of Crom-a-boo, from the war-cry of the Desmonds – an Earl of Desmond was English Governor about 1420.

$\frac{1}{2}$ mile (800 m) north on the L18 is *Woodstock Castle* (13th c.), also built to defend the river crossing. It suffered severe damage in 1649.

Downstream from White's Castle stands the *Dominican church* (by John Thompson, 1963–65), on a pentagonal plan, with an ingenious spherically vaulted roof structure. It contains a number of notable works of art, including fine stained glass and Stations of the Cross by George Campbell.

The old *Court and Market House*, a fine Georgian building, is now the fire station.

SURROUNDINGS. – 4$\frac{1}{2}$ miles (7 km) north-east of the town, on the N78, is the *Motte of Ardskull*, a 30 ft (9 m) high circular earthwork of the 12th c.

5 miles (8 km) east of the Motte of Ardskull lies *Ballitore*, once a flourishing Quaker settlement with a celebrated school.

South of Ballitore, at *Moone*, just off the N9, is a slender *high cross* 17$\frac{1}{2}$ ft (5 m) high with magnificent low reliefs, naïvely stylised. On the east side can be seen Daniel with seven lions, Abraham's sacrifice, Adam and Eve, and the Crucifixion; on the west side the Twelve Apostles, the Crucifixion, the Virgin and St John; on the north side the Miracle of the Loaves and Fishes, the Flight into Egypt, the Three Young Men in the Fiery Furnace and various animals; and on the south side a number of figures and animals. The cross stands in the churchyard beside a ruined 13th c. church which contains remains of another cross with figures of animals and centaurs.

Going south from Moone on the N9, we come in 5 miles (8 km) to *Castledermot* (Kilkea Castle Hotel, A, 53 r.), with the ruins of a very ancient monastery (National Monument; Romanesque doorway), a *round tower* (upper part medieval) and two granite high crosses carved with Biblical scenes. The relief of David with his harp on the North Cross is of particular interest as one of the few representations of an Irish harp.

On the south side of the town are the ruins of a Franciscan friary (National Monument), founded in the 14th c. and dissolved in the 16th.

The road from Castledermot back to Athy, running north-west, comes in 3 miles (5 km) to *Kilkea Castle*, which dates from 1180. After undergoing much alteration in the 19th c. it now houses a luxury hotel and a health farm.

Ballina/Béal an Aithe

Map reference: B2.
Republic of Ireland.
Province: Connacht. – County: Mayo.
Population: 6850.
(i) **Tourist Information Office,**
   Ballina;
   tel. (096) 2 24 22.
   Open July and August.

HOTELS. – *Downhill*, A, 54 r.; *Belleek Castle*, B*, 16 r.; *Bartra House*, B, 30 r.

GUEST-HOUSE. – *Mount Falcon Castle*, A, 11 r.

RESTAURANTS. – *Downhill Hotel*; *Swiss Barn*, Foxford Road.

Ballina (Béal an Aithe, "Mouth of the Ford") lies in the north-west of Ireland, in bog country on the banks of the River Moy, at the point where it widens out before entering Killala Bay, on the Atlantic. As the largest town in Co. Mayo Ballina is the marketing centre for an extensive hinterland.

For anglers it is a good base from which to fish the River Moy and two well-stocked loughs, Conn and Cullin.

SIGHTS. – The modern Roman Catholic cathedral has fine stained glass. Near by are the remains of a 15th c. Augustinian friary.

Near the railway station a dolmen (National Monument) marks the grave of four brothers who are said to have murdered their foster-father, a bishop, in the 6th c.

SURROUNDINGS. – The R310 runs south to the narrow strip of land between *Lough Conn*, famed for its pike, and *Lough Cullin*; fine views from the bridge. In both loughs fishing is free. *Pontoon* (Pontoon Bridge Hotel, A, 24 r.) is a favourite fishing resort; boats can be hired.

The R315 follows the south and west sides of Lough Conn, heading north. On the left *Nephin Mor* rises above the plain to a height of 2626 ft (800 m); seen from the north-east at some distance, its handsome and striking silhouette suggests the majesty of a holy mountain.

At the north-west end of Lough Conn, on the N59, is *Crossmolina*, where there is a peat-fired power-station. There are numerous remains of ring-forts and other ancient structures in the area. 6 miles (10 km) south-east, on a peninsula reaching out into the lough, are the ruins of *Errew Abbey* (13th c.: National Monument).

From Crossmolina the R315 continues north to *Ballycastle*, with beautiful coastal scenery on the Atlantic. On Downpatrick Head, 4 miles (6 km) north, natural forces have carved fantastic shapes out of the sandstone cliffs bordering the shore and the isolated stacks in the sea.

For an attractive run from Ballycastle, take the minor road which runs east following the coast via Rathlackan to Carrowmore and turns left there to reach Lackan Bay. The road ends at *Kilcummin*, where the picturesque ruins of a little 7th c. church, with a holy well and old gravestones, stand in lonely isolation by the sea.

From Carrowmore the road goes south past the remains of *Rathfran Friary* (13th c.: National Monument); of the church there remain the nave, choir and a chapel (15th c.).

4 miles (6 km) farther south, at *Killala*, stands a well-preserved *round tower* 84 ft (26 m) high. Adjoining it is a small 17th c. "Cathedral". In 1798 French forces who had landed in Kilcummin Bay to support the rebels held out for some time in Killala against British troops.

A little way beyond Killala a side road branches off on the left and runs south-east to *Moyne Abbey (National Monument), a 15th c. Franciscan house of which considerable remains survive, though in a state of ruin – the nave, choir (with side chapel) and tower of the church, the cloister with its vaulting, the chapter-house, refectory, kitchen and dorters.

2½ miles (4 km) south is *Rosserk Friary* (National Monument), another 15th c. Franciscan house which preserves extensive remains. A richly carved doorway leads into the aisleless church, with two chapels in the south transept. It has beautiful windows, a double font (with a round tower carved on one of the supports) and a square tower. The conventual buildings are two-storeyed.

Ballinasloe/Béal Átha an Sluagh

Map reference: C3.
Republic of Ireland.
Province: Connacht. – County: Galway.
Population: 6400.
ⓘ **Tourist Information Office,**
Ballinasloe;
tel. (0905) 4 21 31.
Open July and August.

HOTELS. – *Hayden's*, Dunlo Street; *East County*, Dunlo Street.

RESTAURANT: *Oriental House*, Society Street.

EVENT. – *Horse Fair* (Oct.).

Ballinasloe (Béal Átha an Sluagh, "Ford-Mouth of the Hosts") lies in the centre of Ireland, south-west of Lough Ree on the N6. In earlier times a place of military importance, it is now a busy market town, famous for its horse, cattle and sheep fairs. The great October Fair is the largest in Ireland. Before the days of motor traction, when cavalry played an important part in warfare, this fair could claim to be Europe's largest horse market. Ballinasloe is the terminal harbour at the western end of the Grand Canal (see entry) – though the last section of the canal is no longer navigable.

Rosserk Friary

Clonfert Cathedral: doorway

SIGHTS. – The town has a number of handsome 18th c. houses.

Above the River Suck stands *Ivy Castle* (19th c.), built on the foundations of an earlier stronghold.

On the south-west side of the town, in a park, is the Late Georgian mansion of *Garbally*, a handsome building in the local limestone; it is now a school.

SURROUNDINGS. – 5 miles (8 km) south of the town on the R355 are the ruins of an Augustinian house, *Clontuskert Abbey* (National Monument). The west doorway of the church (1471) is notable for its carvings – Michael weighing souls, saints, a pelican, a mermaid with a mirror, etc.

From Clontuskert the R355 continues to Laurence-town, beyond which a side road on the left leads to *Clonfert*, 13 miles (21 km) south-east of Ballinasloe, the site of an ancient monastic settlement. The doorway of the *"Cathedral", under its massive west tower, is a supreme masterpiece of Irish Romanesque sculpture. Above six orders of round-headed arches borne on inward-inclined columns richly decorated with stylised patterns rises a high triangular pediment containing a row of five tall blind arches and, above these, a pattern of small triangles alternating with human heads and ornaments. Within the arches and in other vacant spaces are more human heads, alternately bearded and clean-shaven. The east windows in the choir are among the finest examples of Late Romanesque art. The decoration of the later work in the interior – the arches supporting the tower, with figures of angels and a mermaid, the chancel arch and the 15th c. windows – is also of notable quality.

7 miles (11 km) west of Ballinasloe, on the R348, stands **Kilconnell Abbey** (National Monument), a Franciscan friary founded in 1353. The church, with its slender and graceful tower over the crossing, is a fine example of Gothic architecture, with a beautifully carved west doorway. It contains two notable canopy tombs in the north wall. The one to the left of the entrance doorway has figures of saints (probably showing French influence); the other is in the choir. Around the church are conventual buildings with numerous masons' marks.

2½ miles (4 km) south-east of Kilconnell is *Aughrim*, with a local museum which contains material from the Stone Age onwards.

Ballinrobe/Baile an Rodhba

Map reference: C2.
Republic of Ireland.
Province: Connacht. – County: Mayo.
Population: 1450.
ⓘ **Tourist Information Office,**
    Ballinrobe;
    tel. 131.
    Open July and August.

HOTEL. – *Lakeland*, B, 17 r.

RESTAURANT: *Lakeland Hotel.*

Ballinrobe (Baile an Rodhba, "Town of the Robe River") lies in the west of Ireland at the point where the N84 crosses the River Robe. To the west of the town is Lough Mask (good fishing), and beyond this the chain of the Partry Mountains, rising to their highest point in Benwee (2206 ft (672 m)). Ballinrobe is popular both as an angling centre and as a base from which to explore the surrounding area.

SURROUNDINGS. – The road from Ballinrobe to Ballintubber (T40) runs along a narrow strip of land between the much-indented shores of *Lough Mask* and *Lough Carra*, which are linked by an underground stream. On an islet in the green waters of Lough Carra is a cairn marking the grave of the writer George Moore (1852–1933).

9 miles (15 km) north of Ballinrobe, on a by-road to the right of the N84, is *Ballintubber or Ballintober Abbey, an Augustinian house founded in 1216. Since then – in spite of the devastation wrought by Cromwell's troops in 1653 – it has continued in use as a place of worship down to the present day. The church is cruciform in plan. In a chapel on the south side of the choir is an elaborate altar-tomb with a row of finely carved figures on the pediment. The church and cloister were excellently restored in 1963–66.

The abbey lay on the pilgrim road to Ireland's holy mountain, Croagh Patrick (see Louisburgh), which can be glimpsed in the distance through the arches of the cloister.

6 miles (10 km) south of Ballinrobe, on a by-road running towards the east side of Lough Mask, is *Lough Mask House*, surrounded by its park. In the last quarter of the 19th c. this was the residence of Captain Charles Boycott (1832–97), the agent of an English landlord, who treated his Irish tenants so badly that on a certain day in the year 1880 they resolved to have nothing more to do with him; without offering him any violence, they refused to work for him or to sell him their produce. Workers had thereupon to be brought in from the northern counties to gather in the potato harvest, under military protection, so that the crop was quite unprofitable. This form of passive resistance compelled Boycott to retreat to England, having given a new word to the language.

In Lough Mask, separated from the park of Lough Mask House by a narrow strip of water, lies the islet of *Inishmaine*, on which are the ruins of a small Augustinian friary (13th c.: National Monument). The cruciform church has good carving (animals, foliage).

The Atlantic coast at Ballybunion

Bantry House

Ballybunion/Baile an Bhuinneanaigh

Map reference: D2.
Republic of Ireland.
Province: Munster. – County: Kerry.
Population: 1350.
(i) **Tourist Information Office,**
Ballybunion;
tel. (068) 2 72 02.
Open July and August.

HOTELS. – *Ambassador*, B*, 85 r.; *Marine*, Sandhill
Road, B, 21 r.; *Atlantic*, C, 11 r.

GUEST-HOUSES. – *Southern*, B, 12 r.; *Eagle Lodge*,
B, 11 r.

RESTAURANTS. – *Eagle Lodge; Seafood Restaurant,
Marine Hotel*, Sandhill Road.

**Ballybunion (Baile an Bhuinne-
anaigh, "Town of the Sapling"), a
popular family resort, lies on a
coast open to the west where the
Shannon, emerging between two
promontories, at last reaches the
Atlantic in the Mouth of the Shannon. With its sea-caves, rugged
cliffs, coves and beaches, it offers
a variety of attractions for seaside
holidays.**

SIGHTS. – In the cliffs to the north of the
town there are many caves, some accessible only by boat, others which can be
reached on foot at low tide. A 3 mile
(5 km) long footpath runs along the top of
the cliffs between *Doon Cove* and Doon
Point, both of which have remains of
promontory forts, past the old fortress of
Lick Castle.

To the east of Ballybunion, rising out of
the flat surrounding country, is *Knocka-
nore Mountain* (866 ft (264 m)), from
which there are superb views of the
Mouth of the Shannon.

SURROUNDINGS. – From Ballybunion the R551
leads north-east to *Ballylongford*, at the head of a
narrow inlet. On the west side of the inlet is
Carrigafoyle Castle (15th c.: National Monument),
with an 85 ft (26 m) high keep (fine views). To the
east of the little town are the ruins of a beautiful
Franciscan house, *Lisloughtin Abbey* (15th c.:
National Monument). The church has a fine west
window. There are remains of conventual buildings.

5 miles (8 km) beyond Ballylongford on the R551 is
Tarbert, from which there is a car ferry over the
Shannon to Killimer (Co. Clare: see Kilkee).

1¼ miles (2 km) north, on *Tarbert Island*, are a
lighthouse and an old battery. The islet is connected
with the mainland by a causeway.

4 miles (6 km) south-east of Ballybunion we come to
Listowel, a thriving little town which has become
known for its Writers' Week, held annually in June.
The writer John B. Keane (b. 1928) keeps a pub here.

To the south of Ballybunion the River Feale flows
through a fjord-like estuary, *Cashen Bay*, into the
sea. Here there is a well-known salmon-hatchery,
Cashen Fishery, which visitors can inspect.

1¼ miles (2 km) south, on the site of an old monastic settlement (Rattoo), are a 15th c. church and the excellently preserved *Rattoo Round Tower (National Monument), 92 ft (28 m) high.

Bantry/ Beanntraighe

Map reference: E2.
Republic of Ireland.
Province: Munster. – County: Cork.
Population: 2900.
ⓘ Tourist Information Office,
Bantry;
tel. (027) 5 02 29.
Open July and August.

HOTELS. – *Westlodge*, B*, 106 r.; *Bantry Bay*, B, 16 r.

GUEST-HOUSE. – *Vickery's Inn*, B, 15 r.

RESTAURANT. – *Westlodge Hotel.*

Bantry (Beanntraighe, "Descendants of Beann") lies at the extreme south-western tip of Ireland, sheltered by its surrounding hills, at the head of the famous and beautiful bay which bears its name. The influence of the Gulf Stream can be seen in the climate and vegetation of the area, where high fuchsia hedges and palms are frequent features of the landscape. Bantry's harbour is sheltered from the sea by Whiddy Island. The harbour affords anchorage for sea-going vessels and supertankers, which discharge their cargoes on Whiddy Island. There are remains of old fortifications on the island.

HISTORY. – Bantry Bay was twice entered by French fleets in 1689, in support of James II, and in 1796, to bring aid to the Irish rebels. Both expeditions were unsuccessful: in 1796 the ships could not even put in to land on account of fog and violent storms.

SIGHTS. – On the outskirts of the town, set in a beautiful park, is *Bantry House. Both the park and the house are open to the public. The house was altered in 1771 by the first Earl of Bantry, and in 1840 was enlarged by the addition of two side wings into a long and finely proportioned building of 14 bays. It contains a valuable art collection from all over Europe (icons, tapestries, French furniture). The stables are of notable architectural quality.

The park, with Italian-style terraces and statues, is laid out on the slopes of the hill.

From the terraces there are extensive views over Bantry Bay with its islands and inlets.

SURROUNDINGS. – Two roads of particular scenic beauty are the road to *Macroom* (see entry) over Cousane Gap (to the north-east) and the coast road to *Glengarriff* (see entry), with magnificent views of the sea and the hills.

To the north of the town, on the Glengarriff road, are the Donemarc Falls on the River Mealagh. There is good fishing in the river and in Drombrow Lough, above the river, and Lough Bofinna.

3 miles (5 km) north of Bantry, where the R584 branches off for Macroom, is *Ballylickey*, which also offers good fishing in the surrounding area.

South-west from Bantry extends the long and scenically magnificent *Sheep's Head Peninsula*, with good beaches at Kilcrohane and Ahakista on the south coast.

There is a rewarding drive round the peninsula to its westerly tip, the Sheep's Head. The road from Kilcrohane to Gouladoo runs past the foot of Seefin (1116 ft (340 m)), from which there are beautiful views to the north over Bantry Bay and the hills of the Bear Peninsula.

Belfast/Béal Feirste

Map reference: B5/6.
Northern Ireland.
Province: Ulster. – District: Belfast.
Population: 362,000.
ⓘ Belfast City Council,
City Hill,
Belfast;
tel. (0232) 22 02 02.

HOTELS. – *Forum*, Great Victoria Street, A*, 100 r.; *Culloden*, 142 Bangor Road, A*, 76 r.; *Conway*, Dunmurry, A*, 76 r.; *Stormont*, 587 Upper Newtownards Road, A, 67 r.; *Drumkeen*, Upper Galwally, A, 28 r.; *La Mon House*, 41 Gransha Road, B*, 30 r.; *Lansdowne Court*, 657 Antrim Road, B*, 24 r.; *Park Avenue*, Holywood Road, B, 42 r.; *York*, 59–63 Botanic Avenue, C, 18 r.

RESTAURANTS. – *Ambassador*, 462 Antrim Road; *Crown* (old-established and well known), 46 Great Victoria Street; *La Mon House*, 41 Gransha Road; *Maysfield Leisure Centre*, East Bridge Street; *Park Avenue Hotel*, Holywood Road; *Skandia*, 50 Howard Street; *Strand*, 12 Stranmillis Road.

EVENTS. – *Lord Mayor's Show* (parade with decorated floats and bands, May); *Belfast Festival of Queen's* (drama and music at Queen's University, Nov.).

Belfast (Béal Feirste, "Sandy Ford") lies in the north-east of Ireland at the outflow of the River Lagan into Belfast Lough. The "capital" of Northern Ireland since 1920, it is an

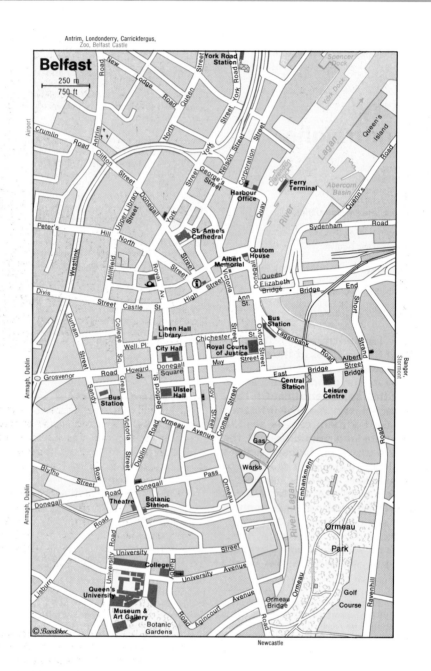

important industrial city and port. On Queen's Island is the Harland and Wolff shipyard, one of the largest of its kind; the "Titanic" was built here in 1912.

HISTORY. – Belfast already possessed a fort in the early Middle Ages, but this was destroyed in 1177. Thereafter a castle was built, the possession of which was often disputed between the native Irish and the English conquerors. In 1613 the town which had grown up around the castle was granted a charter by James I.

The manufacture of linen had long been an important industry in Belfast, and it received additional impetus in the latter part of the 17th c. when Huguenots fleeing from France introduced improved industrial methods. The newcomers also contributed to the development of the town's intellectual life, and this led to a considerable influx of both Irish and British settlers, who built their own churches, giving Belfast its present multiplicity of religious denominations and sects.

The centre of Belfast lies on the west bank of the River Lagan, which is spanned by several bridges within the area of the city.

City Hall, Belfast

Some streets in the city centre are closed to cars, and vehicles must expect to be checked. Pedestrians, whether local people or visitors, must be prepared to produce proof of identity.

Central area

The central feature of Belfast is the **City Hall** in *Donegall Square*, a huge Renaissance palazzo (by Sir Brumwell Thomas, 1898–1906) with four corner towers and a massive dome. In front of it are statues of Queen Victoria and prominent citizens of Belfast, and on the west side, in the *Garden of Remembrance*, stands a war memorial. There is also a sculptured group commemorating the sinking of the "Titanic". On the north side of the square is the *Linen Hall Library* (1788), with an exhibition on the history of linen manufacture. Donegall Place and the adjoining streets, particularly *Royal Avenue*, are the city's main shopping streets, with large department stores.

To the north, by way of Royal Avenue and Church Street, is **St Anne's Cathedral**, the principal church of the (Anglican) Church of Ireland, begun in 1898 (architect Sir Thomas Drew). It has three fine west doorways decorated with sculpture.

The baptismal chapel has a mosaic ceiling made of hundreds of thousands of tiny pieces of glass; it contains the tomb of Lord Duncairn (Sir Edward Carson, d. 1935), leader of the Ulster Unionists.

South-east of the cathedral, near the River Lagan, are the *Custom House* (1854–57) and the **Albert Memorial Clock-Tower**, popularly known as the Big Ben of Belfast, which was built in 1869 to commemorate the Prince Consort.

South Belfast

$\frac{3}{4}$ mile (1207 m) south of Donegall Square, reached by way of Bedford Street, Dublin Road and University Road, stands the red-brick Tudor-style *Queen's University* (1845–94), independent since 1909. It contains a historical museum.

To the south of the university in the *Botanic Gardens*, is the **Ulster Museum** (Mon.–Fri. 10 a.m.–5 p.m., Sat. 1–5 p.m., Sun. 2–5 p.m.), which has much material of the Celtic and Early Christian periods (swords, harps, jewellery, etc.). An important recent acquisition is the collection of gold and silver objects recovered in 1968 from the "Girona", a Spanish galleon sunk off the northern Irish coast in the 16th c.

The *Art Gallery* is particularly strong in European paintings of the 17th and 18th c. and Irish art of different periods; it also has collections of Irish glass and silver. Evidence of the scale of Irish emigration down the centuries, particularly to the United States, is given by the portraits of prominent people of Northern Ireland origin, including ten American Presidents.

North Belfast

To the north of the city are the *Zoological Gardens* and various parks, sports grounds and golf-courses, as well as *Belfast Castle* (1870), once the home of Lord Shaftesbury. Here, too, rises *Cave Hill* (1182 ft (360 m)), a hill of volcanic origin which is supposed to resemble Napoleon's profile. It is worth climbing the hill for the sake of the fine **views* which it affords in good weather of the city, Lough Neagh to the west and the coast to the east, with the Isle of Man in the distance.

Stormont

$3\frac{1}{2}$ miles (5·6 km) outside the city to the east, at **Stormont**, stands the imposing classical-style building erected in 1928–32 to house the Parliament of Northern Ireland. In front of it is a monument to Sir Edward Carson.

3 miles (5 km) to the north, in the grounds of Cultra Manor, is the **Ulster Folk Museum**, an open-air museum of traditional Ulster buildings illustrating domestic life and agriculture (May–Sept., Mon.–Sat. 11 a.m.–4 p.m., Sun. 2–4 p.m.; Oct.–Apr., Mon.–Sat. 11 a.m.–5 p.m., Sun. 2–5 p.m.; admission charge).

SURROUNDINGS OF BELFAST. – **Lough Neagh:** see entry.

On the north and south sides of *Belfast Lough*, the wide inlet into which the River Lagan flows, are a series of popular seaside resorts. The coast immediately north of the lough is particularly beautiful.

Half-way along the north side of the lough, 7 miles (11 km) from Belfast, lies *Carrickfergus* (Coast Road Hotel, B*, 20 r.; Dobbin's Inn, B, 13 r.), which was a considerable port before its displacement by Belfast. It is famed for its splendidly preserved Norman castle, one of the finest in Northern Ireland.

*Carrickfergus Castle (known in medieval times as Kragfargy's Castle) stands on a spur of black basalt which was originally surrounded by water except on

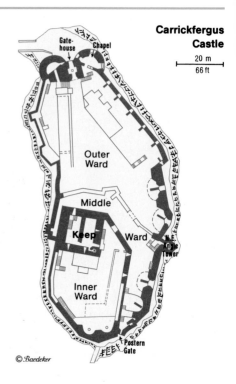

Carrickfergus Castle

20 m
66 ft

Gatehouse · Chapel · Outer Ward · Middle Ward · Keep · Ward · N.E. Angle Tower · Inner Ward · Postern Gate · FEET

© Baedeker

the north side. For some 750 years it was a place of great military importance, strategically situated to control the harbour and Belfast Lough.

Begun by the Norman magnate John de Courcy between 1180 and 1204, it was taken by King John in 1210 after a year-long siege. In 1316 it fell into the hands of the Scots. In the 16th c. it was renovated and more strongly fortified, but thereafter it fell into decay. It was captured by the French in 1760 – the last time it was taken by an enemy. In the 18th c. it was used as a prison. Later, after further strengthening of its defences, it became (until 1928) a military store and arsenal. During the Second World War the keep served as an air-raid shelter.

The castle's most notable features are the massive *Keep* (on the third floor a magnificent Norman Great Hall; from the top, fine views), the two-storey *Gatehouse* (in the east tower a room known as the Chapel on account of its unusual window) and a number of cannon of the 16th–19th c.

From Carrickfergus a particularly beautiful section of the coast road runs by way of the popular seaside resort of *Whitehead* to **Island Magee**, a peninsula 7 miles (11 km) long by 2 miles (3 km) wide. A striking feature on the east side of the peninsula is the *Gobbins*, a stretch of basalt cliffs 250 ft (76 m) high containing a number of caves. There are numerous legends associated with the cliffs and the caves. At the end of the peninsula can be seen a megalithic chambered tomb (dolmen).

A series of quarries and cement works disfigure the coast road to **Larne** (Magheramorne House Hotel, A, 23 r.; Highways Hotel, B, 11 r.), a busy industrial town and seaside resort on Larne Lough. There are notable remains of *Olderfleet Castle* (three-storey keep).

From Larne there are ferry services to Scotland (Stranraer and Cairnryan) and also a ferry to Island Magee (above).

Carrickfergus Castle

A romantic and beautiful stretch of coast road leads from Larne to Cushendun. After passing through the Black Cave Tunnel the road rounds Ballygalley Head with its great basalt crags. Ballygalley is a popular seaside resort, with an old castle which is now a hotel (Ballygalley Castle Hotel, A, 30 r.). From here to Glenarm, a little port at the mouth of the River Glenarm, the road is flanked by white limestone cliffs. The next seaside resort is Carnlough, with a small harbour and a good sandy beach.

Waterfoot, at the near end of the Red Bay, is delightfully situated on the Antrim coast in a kind of amphitheatre of sandstone cliffs at the mouth of *Glenariff, one of the most beautiful of the Glens of Antrim (Glens of Antrim Feis – Irish dancing and music, July). Just beyond Waterfoot are the little resort of Cushendall and the better known Cushendun.

The road along the south side of Belfast Lough and down the coast also has beautiful scenery and a number of attractive little places. Holywood, a suburb of Belfast, has remains of the 12th c. Franciscan Friary of Sanctus Boscus (Holy Wood). From here the road continues via Crawfordsburn to Bangor (O'Hara's Royal Hotel, A, 32 r.; Winston Hotel, B, 46 r.), the most popular of Northern Ireland's seaside resorts, with wide sandy beaches, beautiful promenades and plentiful facilities for sport and entertainment. Features of interest are the Castle and Castle Park, and the Abbey Church, on the site of a monastery founded in 555. – On the way to Bangor, Helen's Tower, near Crawfordsburn, should not be missed.

Beyond Bangor Copeland Island can be seen out to sea. Farther south, at Donaghadee, is the 20 mile (32 km) long Ards Peninsula. From Donaghadee a road runs along the coast of the Irish Sea to Ballywalter (beautiful beach), Ballyhalbert and Cloghy, from which it turns inland to Portaferry, on the southern tip of the peninsula.

There is a ferry service from Portaferry to Strangford (p. 66) on the mainland. From Portaferry it is possible to return along the west side of the peninsula on the A20, following the shores of Strangford Lough. After passing through Ardkeen (ruined castle) and Kircubbin the road comes to Greyabbey, with remains of a Cistercian abbey founded in 1193, one of the best preserved in Ireland. Notable features are the fine Perpendicular windows and the magnificent west doorway.

The road continues, passing Mount Stewart House (beautiful park with many dwarf trees), to Newtownards, a noted linen-making centre and a good base from which to explore the coastal region and the Mourne Mountains to the south. It has a Town Hall of 1770 and a ruined Dominican church (1244). In the High Street stands the Old Cross, which has been several times restored.

From here it is possible to return direct to Belfast (6 miles (10 km)), or alternatively to turn south via the whiskey-distilling town of Comber and continue down the west side of Strangford Lough to Downpatrick (21 miles (34 km)). Garden-lovers will prefer the road which turns away from the lough via the little town of *Saintfield, enabling them to see the beautiful Rowallane Gardens, with many rare flowers and plants.

On the west shore of the lough is the resort of Killyleagh (birthplace of Sir Hans Sloane, founder of the British Museum), with Hilltop Castle overlooking the town. The scenery is very beautiful, with the Mourne Mountains shimmering blue in the distance.

Downpatrick is the county town of Co. Down. Here St Patrick began the conversion of Ireland in 432. 2 miles (3 km) north is Saul, where he landed, built his first church and is said to have died. Downpatrick

Cathedral, the seat of a bishop, was built in 1790 on the remains of an earlier church; there are a number of capitals and a font (17th c.) from the earlier church. The granite stone in the churchyard which is said to mark his tomb dates only from 1900.

From Saul a road goes east along the coast to **Strangford**, an old Viking settlement beautifully situated at the south end of Strangford Lough (p. 65). The strategic importance of this area is indicated by the presence of four Anglo-Norman castles (16th c.) here and in the immediate vicinity. Audley's Castle is open to the public.

No fewer than seven castles protected *Ardglass*, to the south of Strangford; there are remains of one of them, Jordan Castle, with a square keep. Formerly a considerable port, Ardglass is now a small fishing village.

West of *Killough*, on the opposite side of the bay, extends a beautiful bathing beach.

At *St John's Point* begins a magnificent *scenic road*, along probably the most beautiful stretch of coast in Northern Ireland, to Newry (39 miles (63 km)). It encircles the wide bay of Dundrum, large areas of which are exposed at low tide, to New-castle. *Dundrum* is a picturesque fishing village with good sandy bathing beaches and a tower surrounded by a moat, all that is left of the old castle.

Newcastle (Slieve Donard Hotel, Downs Road, A, 118 r.) offers all the amenities of a seaside resort, including a golf-course. It lies at the west end of Dundrum Bay at the foot of *Slieve Donard* (2796 ft (853 m)), the highest of the **Mourne Mountains**. The climb takes some 2 hours, and is rewarded by a magnificent *view* from the top, extending as far as the Scottish coast.

From Newcastle the road begins to climb, with the sea on the left and the ever-changing backdrop of the Mourne Mountains (the home of many rare plants) on the right. It passes through a number of quiet little fishing and farming villages including *Glasdrumman* and *Annalong*, from which a number of peaks between 1700 ft (518 m) and 2450 ft (747 m) – Rocky Mountain, Slieve Bignian, etc. – can be climbed.

Kilkeel is a favourite resort with fishermen, since there are good catches to be had both in the sea and in the River Kilkeel and nearby Carlingford Lough. Around Kilkeel are a number of prehistoric chambered tombs.

Between *Greencastle* in the north and *Greenore* in the south **Carlingford Lough** cuts deep inland, with a road along each side.

The road from Kilkeel to Hilltown, however, runs through the Mourne Mountains, with steep climbs and descents. *Hilltown*, beneath the north-west side of the hills, is a good base for climbs and walks in the hills, richly coloured with the changing hues of their granites and schists.

On the north side of Carlingford Lough, surrounded by woodland (mainly oaks), is **Rostrevor**, a pretty and peaceful little holiday resort (boating, pony-trekking, fishing, walking).

The port and industrial town of **Newry** lies on the River Newry and a canal, with the Mourne Mountains to the south-east and the *Camlough Mountains* to the

west. The tower of St Patrick's Church, Ireland's first Protestant church, dates from 1578. The neighbour-ing *Cathedral* (RC) is neo-Gothic. Near the town are the picturesque village of *Bessbrook* (to the north-west) and Derrymore House, an 18th c. thatched villa in Georgian style.

Belmullet/Béal an Mhuirthead

Map reference: B2.
Republic of Ireland.
Province: Connacht. – County: Mayo.
Population: 1000.
(i) **Tourist Information Office,** Belmullet;
tel. 78.
Open July and August.

HOTEL. – *Western Strands*, C, 10 r.

Belmullet (Béal an Mhuirthead, "Ford on the Sea") lies in the north-west of Ireland on the narrow strip of land which links the Mullet Penin-sula with the mainland. This isolated little place is a good base from which to explore the 15 mile (25 km) pen-insula and the country to the north.

SURROUNDINGS. – The west coast of the *Mullet Peninsula*, exposed to the storms of the Atlantic, is completely denuded of vegetation; the east side, with numerous little coves, almost completely encloses *Blacksod Bay*. On both sides of the peninsula there are beautiful beaches, particularly at its narrowest point, around Elly Bay on the east side.

The peninsula has many remains of ancient structures. On *Doonamo Point*, 5 miles (7 km) from Belmullet, are notable remains of a clifftop fortress with a great rampart, 200 ft (60 m) long and 18 ft (5·5 m) high at some points, stretching across the neck of the headland and enclosing three beehive-shaped huts and the ruins of a ring-fort.

At Fallmore, on the southern tip of the peninsula, are the ruins of St Dairbhile's Church (National Monu-ment).

From *Blacksod Point*, at the end of the peninsula, there is a fine view of *Achill Island* (see entry), with the tall peak of Slievemore. From the west side, where there was formerly a signal tower, there are views of the offshore islets, which were inhabited in early times and preserve many Early Christian remains.

3 miles (5 km) south of Belmullet the R314 branches off the R313 and runs north-east. From *Glenamoy* there is an attractive detour of 10 miles (16 km) northward to *Benwee Point*, which rises in sheer and rugged cliffs to a height of 843 ft (257 m) above the sea (magnificent views). To the north of *Portacloy* are the *Stags of Broadhaven*, a group of seven precipitous rocks rising out of the sea to a height of 328 ft (100 m).

From Glenamoy the R314 goes over the moors to *Belderg*, 1¼ miles (2 km) short of the north coast with its rugged cliff scenery. From the *Hill of Glinsk* (1017 ft (310 m)), 4 miles (6 km) west, there are panoramic views of the whole area. 1¼ miles (2 km) farther west is *Moista Sound*, an inlet totally surrounded by cliffs.

Birr/Biorra

Map reference: C4.
Republic of Ireland.
Province: Leinster. – County: Offaly.
Population: 3700.

ⓘ **Tourist Information Office,**
Emmet Square,
Birr;
tel. (0509) 2 02 06.
Open May to September.

HOTELS. – *County Arms*, B*, 18 r.; *Dooly's*, B. 14 r.

RESTAURANTS. – *County Arms Hotel*; *Dooly's Hotel*.

Birr (Biorra, "Spring Wells"), a thriving little market town, lies in the centre of Ireland at the intersection of two main roads (N52 and N62), on the western edge of Co. Offaly. Immediately west of the little town is the junction of two good fishing rivers, the Little Brosna and the Camcor.

SIGHTS. – The town is well laid out, with four main streets meeting in Emmet Square. It has many handsome houses of the 17th and 18th c., particularly in Oxmantown Mall and St John's Mall. In St John's Mall is a monument to the third Earl of Rosse, a famous astronomer.

Birr Castle (not open to the public) was frequently besieged in earlier centuries; in the 18th and 19th c. it was several times altered and enlarged. About 1840 the third Earl of Rosse, to whose descendant the castle still belongs, designed and constructed a giant telescope – for some 80 years the largest in the world – and set it up in the grounds of the castle. With this telescope he was the first to discover spiral nebulae. The building in which the telescope (now in the Science Museum in London) was housed can still be seen in the park. There is also an Exhibition Gallery with a small display of optical apparatus which is open to the public from June to September (Wed.–Sun. 2.30–5.30 p.m.).

In the beautiful *park (open daily 9 a.m.– 1 p.m. and 2–6 p.m.: admission charge), extending along the River Camcor to the west of Emmet Square, are an arboretum, lakes, clipped hedges over 30 ft (9 m) high and flower gardens, some of them laid out in geometric patterns.

SURROUNDINGS. – 8 miles (13 km) north-west of Birr, on a hill on the west bank of the Shannon, is *Banagher*. The gun positions constructed by English forces in the 17th c. can still be seen. At the bridge are

Birr Castle

mooring facilities for motor cruisers. Anthony Trollope worked as a post office clerk and wrote some of his early novels here.

The local Crannog Pottery is well worth a visit.

5 miles (8 km) north-east of Birr, by the roadside, rise the imposing ruins of *Clonony Castle* (16th c.). The road to the castle runs past *Shannon Harbour*, where the Shannon and the Grand Canal (see entries) join. Old warehouses and a hotel of 1806 bear witness to the former importance of this little port.

To the east of Birr are the Slieve Bloom Mountains. At their foot is the pretty village of *Kinnitty*, from which an excursion into the pretty little *Forelacka Glen* can be made.

On the road which runs south-west from Kinnitty, beyond the Clareen crossroads, a hawthorn known as *St Ciaran's Bush* grows in the middle of the roadway. Ciaran was a 5th c. saint who founded a monastery here.

A mile or two south stands *Leap Castle*, burned down in 1922 but still impressive even in its ruined state.

Blarney/An Bhlarna

Map reference: E3.
Republic of Ireland.
Province: Munster. – County: Cork.
Population: 2000.

HOTELS. – *Blarney*, A, 70 r.; *Christy's Country House*, B, 11 r.; *Blarney Castle*, C, 10 r.

RESTAURANT. – *Blarney Hotel*.

Blarney (An Bhlarna, "The Plain") lies near the south coast of Ireland, 5 miles (8 km) north-west of the county town, Cork.

SIGHTS. – **Blarney Castle** (May–Sept., Mon.–Sat. 9 a.m.–6.30 or 8.30 p.m., Sun. 9.30 a.m.–5.30 p.m. or dusk; Oct.–Apr., 9 a.m.–dusk; admission charge), a massive 5th c. keep with walls 18 ft (5·5 m) thick and a 82 ft (25 m) high tower is the strongest castle in the province of Munster. In one of its walls is the famous Blarney Stone, which is believed to bestow the gift of eloquence on anyone who kisses it. The origin of the tradition is unknown.

The castle has given a new word to the English language. Queen Elizabeth I had instructed her Governor in Ireland to call upon Cormac MacCarthy, then Lord of Blarney, to give up the traditional system by which the clans elected their own chiefs and instead to accept the grant of his lands from the Crown. Cormac Mac-Carthy, while seeming to agree to this proposal, repeatedly put forward plausible excuses for failing to carry it out, until the Queen declared in exasperation: "This is all Blarney: what he says he never means." Hence the use of "blarney" to mean fair words intended to deceive without offending.

On the vaulted upper floor of the castle is a large chimney. Round the top of the building runs a battlemented parapet walk, and here a visitor who wants to kiss the Blarney Stone must lie on his back and, with someone holding him, lean backwards and downwards to kiss the underside of the stone. From the battlements there are magnificent views.

The castle grounds, laid out in the 18th c., contain a grove of trees, grottoes and a pretty dell with a circle of large stones known as Rock Close.

Bloody Foreland/ Cnoc Fola

Map reference: A3.
Republic of Ireland.
Province: Ulster. – County: Donegal.
ⓘ **Tourist Information Office,**
   Falcarragh;
   tel. 1 75.
   Open June to August.

Bloody Foreland (Cnoc Fola) is a broad headland at the north-west corner of Ireland, between Ballyness Bay to the north and Gweedore to the south. It gets its name from the reddish tinge which the rocky coast takes on at sunset. The sea is then bathed in the same hue, and Tory Island, lying a few miles offshore, becomes a glowing dream island in the dusk.

There is a good road encircling the area. This is one of the parts of Ireland where Irish is still the predominant spoken language, and two well-attended summer schools in the language are held here, at Bunbeg and Cloghaneely.

SURROUNDINGS. – To the south-east is the long, narrow *Lough Dunlewy*, with fishing for salmon and trout.

From the north side of the lough *Mount Errigal* (2429 ft (740 m) can be climbed. This gleaming white

Mount Errigal

of 200. There are the remains of various ancient structures, including an unusual round tower (National Monument) of undressed stone, 55 ft (17 m) high. For a boat to Tory Island, apply at the post office in Meenlaragh, near the pier. The boat service is very much dependent on the weather; but a trip to this outpost of Europe, though something of an adventure in rough weather, is a very rewarding one.

Boyle/Mainistir na Buille

Map reference: C3.
Republic of Ireland.
Province: Connacht. – County: Roscommon.
Population: 1750.

ⓘ Tourist Information Office,
Bridge Street,
Boyle;
tel. (079) 6 21 45.
Open June to August.

HOTELS. – *Forest Park*, B*, 12 r.; *Royal*, Bridge Street, B, 16 r.

RESTAURANTS. – *Forest Park Hotel*; *Royal Hotel*.

Boyle (Mainistir na Buille, "Monastery of the Pasture River") lies in north-western Ireland at the foot of the Curlew Hills and on the north bank of the River Boyle, which links Lough Gara and Lough Key. The river is spanned by an old bridge. A market centre, Boyle is one of the chief towns in Co. Roscommon.

cone of quartzite, with two peaks (30 ft (9 m)) apart linked by a ridge known as One Man's Path, also offers scope for rock-climbers. From the top there are magnificent views – northward towards the wild and lonely *Lough Altan*, with Aglamore (1313 ft (400 m)) rising sheer from its waters; eastward towards the glaciated *Derryveagh Mountains*; southward towards the rocky Poisoned Glen, so called because of the spurge that grows there; and westward over the great expanse of Gweedore and the Atlantic coast.

In the Gweedore area are two power-stations, which are still partly fuelled by hand-cut peat. During the early 19th c. Lord George Hill became widely known for the reforms he carried through for the benefit of the poor cottagers of this area.

Between *Bunbeg* (Gweedore Hotel, A. 30 r.; Seaview Hotel, B*, 28 r.), which has an attractive little harbour, and *Derrybeg* (Radharc an Eargail Hotel, B, 25 r.) is *Middletown*, with a 9-hole golf-course.

From Bunbeg a boat can be taken to the islands in *Gweedore Bay* – Innishinny, Gola, etc. – all with beautiful rock and cliff scenery. There are beautiful beaches on the coast of the mainland, such as Magheraclogher Strand.

To the north, in Ballyness Bay, are *Gortahork* (McFadden's Hotel B*, 26 r.) and *Falcarragh*, from which *Muckish Mountain* (2166 ft (660 m)) can be climbed. It is a stiff climb, but the views from the top are magnificent. Gortahork and Falcarragh offer accommodation for those attending the summer school in the Irish language in Bunbeg.

Near Falcarragh, in *Myrath* churchyard, is a large ancient cross hewn from a single block of stone.

Tory Island is the largest island in the area. A religious centre from early times, it began to decline during the reign of Elizabeth I. The island still has a population

Boyle Abbey

SIGHTS. – On the north side of the town stand the ruins of **Boyle Abbey** (National Monument), a Cistercian house founded from Mellifont in 1161. Of the cruciform church, now roofless, there survive in a good state of preservation the nave, choir and transepts (beautiful capitals carved with human figures, animals and foliage); of the conventual buildings the guest-house and kitchen.

SURROUNDINGS. – To the north-east of the town is forest-fringed Lough Key, with numerous little inlets, promontories and islets. Along its south side extends the **Lough Key Forest Park**, with an excellently equipped camping site, restaurant, children's paddling-pool, picnic sites, etc. There are also facilities for boating, cruising, fishing and walking. There is an interesting Bog Park.

On an island in the lough can be seen the ruins of an old abbey, picturesquely mantled in green.

South-east of Boyle, between Elphon and Strokestown, lies a lake district with no fewer than 65 little loughs which offer excellent coarse fishing.

Strokestown itself is a little town laid out on a regular plan about 1800, with workshops in which traditional Irish crafts are practised (exhibition and shop). Adjoining the town, in a large park, is a handsome country house belonging to Lord Hartland.

There are many prehistoric remains in this area. Most of these are to the west of Boyle, between the town and the village of Ballaghaderreen, to the south-west of Lough Gara. Numerous pile dwellings and 31 boats have been excavated, as well as implements and ornaments. (The excavation site is not open to the public.)

Near Boyle, just off the R294 at *Drumanone*, is a large chambered tomb, with a massive capstone measuring 15 by 11 ft (4·5 by 3·3 m).

West of Lough Gara, in Co. Sligo, is *Monasteraden*, with one of the most celebrated of the many holy wells in this area, dedicated to St Attracta. It is surrounded on three sides by walls, on one of which is a relief of the Crucifixion.

Boyne Valley

Map reference: C5.
Republic of Ireland.
Province: Leinster. – County: Meath.
ⓘ **Tourist Information Office,**
Newgrange;
tel. (041) 2 42 74.
Open May to September.

On the east coast of Ireland, near the town of Drogheda, between Belfast and Dublin, the River Boyne describes a wide bend southward, beginning at Slane, and then turns north again. Here there is a large pre-Christian burial ground. The royal tombs, **some 4500 years old, lie south-east of Slane – at Knowth, Newgrange and Dowth. All three are National Monuments.**

Newgrange

****Newgrange** (visitors are shown round by a custodian; daily 10 a.m. to 6 p.m., in summer to 7 p.m.; admission charge) is the largest of the three tombs. It consists of a roughly heart-shaped mound of turf and stones some 295 ft (90 m) in diameter and 36 ft (11 m) high with a retaining kerb of horizontal slabs. The vertical retaining wall is a reconstruction of the original based on the results of archaeological investigation. A few yards outside the kerb there was originally a ring of 38 pillar-stones, of which 12 survive.

The entrance to the tomb, marked by a kerbstone on the south-east side with carved spiral decoration, leads into a narrow passage 66 ft (20 m) long formed of 43 stone uprights between 5 and 8 ft (1·5 and 2·4 m) high and roofed with massive lintels. At the end of the passage is the main tomb chamber, with a 20 ft (6 m) high vaulted roof. The structure is so designed that the sun shines directly into the chamber at the winter solstice. Three side chambers open off the main chamber, giving the tomb a cruciform plan. Many

Newgrange: the entrance

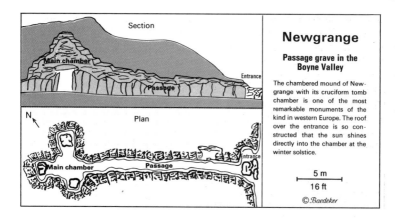

Section

Main chamber

Passage

Entrance

N

Plan

Main chamber   Passage

Entrance

Newgrange

**Passage grave in the
Boyne Valley**

The chambered mound of New-grange with its cruciform tomb chamber is one of the most remarkable monuments of the kind in western Europe. The roof over the entrance is so constructed that the sun shines directly into the chamber at the winter solstice.

5 m
16 ft

© Baedeker

of the stones are carved with spirals, lozenges, wave patterns, snake-like designs or zigzag ornament, which contribute to the powerful effect of the whole. The tomb was constructed with great precision, so that in the course of 4500 years there has been no penetration of rainwater.

Beside the car park is an exhibition centre (open May to September) giving background information on the tomb.

The tombs at *Dowth* and *Knowth* are smaller than Newgrange. Each contains two passage graves under the mound. Dowth can be entered only with difficulty; Knowth has not yet been completely excavated.

In the immediate vicinity of the principal tomb are numerous smaller tombs, standing stones and tumuli.

To the north of Slane rises *Slane Hill* (492 ft (150 m)), where in 433 St Patrick is believed to have proclaimed the victory of Christianity in Ireland by lighting the Paschal fire in defiance of a royal prohibition. On the hill are the ruins of a Franciscan friary (National Monument), with a 16th c. church and conventual buildings laid out round a cloister (rooms with fireplaces, alcoves and aumbry).

To the west of Slane is *Slane Castle*, a fine early 19th c. neo-Gothic mansion. It is one of the Irish country houses where the owners welcome visitors to stay or have a meal. In the grounds are the ruins of a 15th c. Gothic church. Festivals of popular music in the grounds are a recent innovation.

Farther up the valley are *Beauparc House* (1750) and, facing it, the picturesque ruins of *Castle Dexter*.

Roof of the main chamber

Bray/Bri Cualann

Map reference: C5.
Republic of Ireland.
Province: Leinster. – County: Wicklow.
Population: 23,000.
ⓘ**Tourist Information Office,**
Bray;
tel. (01) 86 71 28–29.
Open July and August.

HOTELS. – *Royal*, B, 52 r.; *Crofton Bray Head*, B, 31 r.; *Esplanade*, Seafront, B, 26 r.; *O'Shea's*, B, 20 r.; *Lacy's*, B, 10 r.

GUEST-HOUSES. – *Cois Farraige*, Strand Road, B, 28 r.; *Ulysses*, Esplanade, B, 15 r.

RESTAURANTS. – *Eamon's*, Seafront; *Esplanade Hotel*; *Hunt's*, Main Street; *Old Bray*, Seafront; *Tree of Idleness*, Seafront.

Bray (Bri Cualann, "Hill of Cuala") lies a little way south of Dublin in a beautiful sheltered bay on the Irish Sea, between the Dalkey Promontory to the north and Bray Head to the south. It is one of Ireland's largest and oldest seaside resorts, mainly favoured by Dubliners.

Bray's most popular feature is the *Esplanade*, a spacious promenade which extends along a beach of sand and shingle more than a mile (2 km) long, with a bandstand, putting and other amusements. At the north end is the boating harbour; to the south is *Bray Head*, rising steeply from the sea to a height of nearly 800 ft (240 m). A footpath known as the Great White Way runs from the south end of the Esplanade, passing a small ruined church (13th c.), to the summit of the head (1½ hours there and back). Half-way up, at the Eagle's Nest, is a café (reached in summer by a chair-lift). From the top there are fine views over the sea and inland.

Bray has excellent sports facilities – tennis courts, golf-courses (9 holes and 18 holes), swimming, sailing, motorboating.

SURROUNDINGS. – 2½ miles (4 km) north-west of Bray are the 16th c. Church of *Rathmichael* and the stump of a round tower (National Monument). On the south wall of the church are a number of unusual early gravestones and a cross.

2½ miles (4 km) west of Bray the River Dargle, which flows through the town to reach the sea, forms a densely wooded valley, the rugged and romantic *Glen of the Dargle*, with Lover's Leap, a massive projecting crag. A narrow path runs alongside the river, and a winding road leads into the upper part of the valley.

On the right of the R761, which leads south from Bray, is *Kilruddery*, an Elizabethan-style mansion of 1820 with beautiful gardens (late 17th c.).

Also to the south are the imposing outlines of the *Sugar Loaf Mountains* – the Little Sugar Loaf (1106 ft (337 m)) and Great Sugar Loaf (1628 ft (496 m)), both of which afford fine views.

5 miles (8 km) south of Bray the R761 comes to the resort of *Greystones* (La Touche Hotel, B*, 36 r.), in wooded country, with tennis courts, a golf-course (18 holes) and good bathing in the bay; sailing boats and motor boats can be hired.

The Bray Harriers hunt in the surrounding district.

1½ miles (2·5 km) south-west of Greystones, away from the coast, lies *Delgany*, a pretty little village in a wooded setting, with a golf-course (18 holes). From here an excursion can be made to the *Glen of the Downs* (Glenview Hotel, A, 23 r.), a State forest with a well-laid-out nature trail.

Bundoran/Bun Dobhrain

Map reference: B3.
Republic of Ireland.
Province: Ulster. – County: Donegal.
Population: 1600.

ⓘ **Tourist Information Office,**
Bundoran;
tel. (072) 4 13 50.
Open June to August.

HOTELS. – *Great Northern*, A, 96 r.; *Holyrood*, Main Street, B*, 61 r.; *Maghery House*, B, 26 r.

RESTAURANTS. – *Great Northern Hotel; Holyrood Hotel.*

Bundoran (Bun Dobhrain, "Mouth of the Dobhran") is situated far to the north on the Atlantic coast of Ireland, on the N15 from Donegal to Sligo. This popular seaside resort, with excellent facilities for sport and recreation, lies on the south side of Donegal Bay, with Benbulben to the south of the town.

The beach of fine sand is flanked by a promenade, with cliffs at each end carved into fantastic shapes by the sea. From here there are a number of attractive walks. One of these goes north to the cliffs and caves on Aughrus Head, with the Puffing Hole, a funnel-like cavity through which water is ejected with great force. Beyond this is Tullan Strand, with a cairn, a dolmen and a stone circle.

SURROUNDINGS. – North-east of Bundoran, on the River Erne, which flows out of Lough Erne, is the busy little town of *Ballyshannon*. There are a number of places of interest in the area, including the ruins of *Assaroe Abbey*, a Cistercian house, and St Patrick's Well.

3 miles (5 km) north-west, on the coast, are the ruins of *Kilbarron Castle*, seat of Michael O'Clery, chief of the Four Masters (see Donegal) and one of the writers of the famous "Annals" recording the history of Ireland and its leading families from the legendary origins to the 17th c.

South of Bundoran lies *Lough Melvin* (rough fishing). Near the lough is the village of Kinlough.

Another road leads west to *Bundrowes*, with a 15th c. castle which was much fought over.

Ballyshannon

Kilfenora: carved head on the Cathedral

Burren/Boirinn

Map reference: C/D2/3.
Republic of Ireland.
Province: Munster. – County: Clare.

 Tourist Information Office,
Lisdoonvarna;
tel. (065) 7 40 62.
Open July to September.

The Burren (Boirinn, "Great Rock"), half-way along the Irish west coast, is an extraordinary tract of karstic country on the south side of Galway Bay, a flat tableland of unfolded carboniferous limestone strata rising in stages above the coast. When Cromwell's soldiers came here they are said to have complained that there were "too few trees to hang anyone on, too little water to drown anyone in, and too little earth to bury anyone in."

It is worth taking some times to explore this lunar landscape, with its rounded hills of porous grey rock and its barren terraces, its little streams which seep away in the scarred surface of the land, its underground rivers, caves and swallow-holes, its loughs which are full one day and empty the next, its Alpine flora finding a foothold in any crevice or cranny which can hold humus.

Cavers should be warned that although it is frequently easy to enter the caves, deeper down they can be extremely dangerous for the inexperienced or ill-equipped. If possible a guide should be taken.

AROUND THE BURREN. – There are three possible routes through the Burren – the N67, which runs direct from Ballyvaughan in the north-east to Lisdoonvarna in the south-west; the R480/R476, running eastward across the middle of the area; and the R477, mostly following the coast, which offers a good return route from Lisdoonvarna to Ballyvaughan.

Ballyvaughan is a small fishing village and a good centre from which to explore the surrounding area. 6½ miles (10 km) north-east, in a valley just off the N67, are the ruins of *Corcomroe Abbey (National Monument)*, a Cistercian house founded in 1180. The church is well preserved (choir, nave, south aisle, transepts with chapels). The choir has figural carving, fine masonry, beautiful vaulting and simple but appealing tombs.

The N67 cuts across the Burren from Ballyvaughan in the north-east to Lisdoonvarna (p. 75) in the south-west. A few miles from Ballyvaughan, on the right, is the unusually shaped keep of *Newtown Castle*, circular in form over a pyramidal base.

After a steep climb the road, here known as the "Corkscrew Road", reaches its highest point (720 ft (220 m)). To the west rises *Slieve Elva* (1109 ft (338 m)), round which a number of streams disappear under ground. Here, too, is *Pollnagollum Cave*, Ireland's longest cave, of which some 7½ miles (12 km) have so far been explored (open to visitors). A few miles before Lisdoonvarna, on the left of the road, is *Cahermacnaghten (National Monument)*, a

The barren landscape of the Burren

stone fort with a ring-wall 100 ft (31 m) in diameter and the remains of a castle in which the O'Davoren family ran a celebrated school of Irish jurisprudence until the late 17th c.

1¼ miles (2 km) south of Ballyvaughan the R480 turns left off the Corkscrew Road and runs south. Off this road is the *Ailwee Cave*, with over 300 yd (274 m) of passages, which has been well laid out for visitors (Mar.–Nov. 10 a.m.–6.30 p.m.).

The R480 traverses a lonely area with many remains of ancient structures to *Caherconnell*, with a fine ring-fort. Near by is the *Poulnabrone Dolmen*, the imposing remains of a chambered tomb. 3 miles (5 km) east is *Carran*, in an area rich in remains of the past. 1¼ miles (2 km) north-east is *Temple Cronan* (National Monument), an Early Christian church with grotesque Romanesque heads on the outside walls. 2 miles (3 km) south-east of this, high above a steep-sided valley, stands *Cahercommaun* (National

Poulnabrone Dolmen

Monument), a 9th c. stone ring-fort with three circuits of ramparts. The innermost ring, almost exactly circular, contains three chambers; the two outer rings, linked by radial walls, are semicircular, ending at steep drops. Excavations in the 1930s revealed the presence of buildings of various periods within the area of the fort.

At the junction of the R480 with R476 are the imposing ruins of *Leamaneh Castle* (National Monument), which consists of a tower house of 1480 with a residential wing built on in 1640. 2½ miles (4 km) east, in *Killinaboy*, are the ruins of an interesting church (16th c.?) with a well-preserved "sheila-na-gig" over the south doorway and the stump of a round tower. The R476 runs south-east past beautiful *Lough Inchiquin*, surrounded by wooded hills, and the ruins of Inchiquin Castle (1459) to *Corofin*, in a beautiful setting, with good trout and coarse fishing in the numerous local loughs and the River Fergus.

From Leamaneh Castle the R476 leads west to *Kilfenora*, which was the see of a bishop until the 18th c. The west end of the modest "Cathedral" (12th c.: National Monument) is roofed and still used for worship; the roofless choir contains fine 13th and 14th c. gravestones. There are a number of crosses, including a high cross carved with a Crucifixion and rich ornament standing in a field 109 yd (100 m) west. The finest is the *Doorty Cross*, on the east side of which are figures of three bishops and a two-headed bird.

The very modern *Burren Display Centre* (open from Easter to October: tea-room; admission charge) has informative displays on the history and environment of the Burren, its flora and fauna, etc.

2 miles (3 km) north-east of Kilferona the ring-fort of *Ballykinvarga*, has remains of huts and chevaux-de-frise within a double ring-wall.

4½ miles (7 km) north-west of Kilfenora is *Lisdoonvarna* (Imperial Hotel, B*, 44 r.; Hydro, B, 72 r.; Lynch's Hotel, B, 18 r.), Ireland's best-known spa and a resort very popular with Irish holiday-makers (tennis, pitch and putt course, amusement park). The radioactive springs contain sulphur, magnesium, iron and iodine. The Spa Wells Health Centre is open from June to October.

5 miles (8 km) west of Lisdoonvarna lies the fishing village of *Doolin*, with good bathing and fishing. From Doolin Pier fast motor launches sail several times daily in good weather to Inisheer, the smallest of the *Aran Islands* (see entry).

There is an attractive run to the west of Lisdoonvarna, along the coast of the Burren. The R477 follows a winding course north-westward, passing Ballynalackan Castle, descends to the coast and turns north. To the left are the Aran Islands, to the right the western slopes of the hills (Slieve Elva) with the occasional ruins of a church or a stone fort. From the bare and wind-swept *Black Head*, where the coast road reaches its most northerly point, there are extensive views over Galway Bay. From here the road runs south-east along Ballyvaughan Bay. To the left can be seen *Gleninagh Castle* (16th c.: National Monument), a four-storey tower house with corner turrets. Beyond this the road comes to Ballyvaughan.

Cahir/Cathair Dhuin Iascaigh

Map reference: D4.
Republic of Ireland.
Province: Munster. – County: Tipperary.
Population: 2100.
ⓘ Tourist Information Office,
Castle,
Cahir;
tel. (052) 4 14 53
Open July and August.

HOTELS. – *Kilcoran Lodge*, B, 18 r.; *Keane's Cahir House*, B, 14 r.; *Galtee*, C, 20 r.

RESTAURANT. – *Earl of Glengall*, The Square.

Cahir (Cathair Dhuin Iascaigh, "Fortress of the Dun abounding in Fish") lies in southern Ireland on the River Suir, at the junction of the N8 and N24. To the west of the town the Galtee Mountains rise to a height of 2954 ft (900 m). There is evidence that the small rocky islet in the Suir was occupied by a fort as early as the 3rd c.

SIGHTS. – Until the 16th c. *Cahir Castle* (National Monument) was one of the largest castles in Ireland. After a long and eventful history of destructions and rebuildings the castle was restored in 1970 and now houses a small museum.

The castle consists of a massive three-storey keep and a great hall, with two spacious wards or courts, all enclosed within strong high outer walls, reinforced by round and rectangular towers. The castle is open to the public (conducted tours Tue.–Sun. 10 a.m.–8 p.m.; closed Mon.).

The castle is best seen from the opposite bank of the river, reflected in the water. It is occasionally used as the setting for films.

Cahir Park, along the banks of the Suir, has been well preserved with its plantings and its avenues. In the park is a charming *cottage orné* built by the Regency architect John Nash. The Protestant church (1817–20), also by Nash, is an early experiment in neo-Gothic.

SURROUNDINGS. – 4 miles (6 km) north of Cahir stands an interesting group of medieval structures (National Monuments) – the *Motte of Knockgraffon*, a 12th c. Anglo-Norman stronghold built to protect a

Cahir Castle

ford on the Suir; the ruins of a 13th c. church and tower; and remains of a 16th c. castle. Near by is a churchyard with another ruined church.

5 miles (8 km) south of Cahir is *Ardfinnan*, a picturesquely situated village with a 15-arched bridge over the Suir. On the banks of the river are two towers belonging to a castle which was believed to be impregnable until Cromwell's troops bombarded it with artillery and took it by storm.

The R665 runs south-west from Ardfinnan, passing Castlegrace, a fine ruined castle (13th c.?) just beyond Clogheen, from which the R668 (the "Vee") winds its way south, with many hairpin bends, through the *Knockmealdown Mountains*. There are far-ranging views from the highest hill, Knockmealdown (2658 ft (810 m)).

South-west of Cahir, on a minor road which branches off the N8 on the left 5 miles (8 km) from the town, is *Burncourt Castle* (National Monument), the empty shell of a many-gabled mansion built in 1641–45 and burned down by Cromwell only five years later, in 1650.

North-west of Cahir, between the Galtee Mountains and a wooded ridge of hills running parallel to them on the north, extends the wide *Glen of Aherlow*, once an important pass between the plains of Co. Tipperary and the low-lying territory of Co. Limerick which was the scene of many battles and later became a refuge for dispossessed and outlawed Irishmen. This attractive and fertile glen is good walking country.

Carlow/ Ceatharlach

Map reference: D5.
Republic of Ireland.
Province: Leinster. – County: Carlow.
Population: 12,000.
ⓘ **Tourist Information Office,**
   Carlow;
   tel. (0503) 3 15 54.
   Open July and August.

HOTELS. – *Royal*, Dublin Street, B*, 36 r.; *Carlow Lodge*, B*, 10 r.; *Seven Oaks*, B, 18 r.

RESTAURANTS. – *Reddy's Grillroom*, 67 Tullow Street; *Royal Hotel*.

Carlow (Ceatharlach, "Fourfold Lake"), county town of Co. Carlow, lies south-west of Dublin on the River Barrow, at the intersection of the N9 and N80. It has a variety of industry, including a beet-sugar factory, flour-mills and maltings.

HISTORY. – Strategically situated on the border of the English Pale, Carlow was a stronghold of the Anglo-Normans. In 1361 it was surrounded by a wall, and thereafter was frequently besieged, captured and burned down. The last time it was a scene of battle was in 1798, when 640 Irish rebels were killed. The battle and those who lost their lives are commemorated by a modern high cross in Celtic style which stands in Church Street, where the dead were buried.

SIGHTS. – *Carlow Castle* (National Monument) is reached from Castle Hill

Street through the premises of Corcoran's Mineral Water Factory (apply to the office for permission and the key – not on Sat. or Sun.). Of the main structure of the castle, which was originally square, there remains only the east side with two massive round towers at the corners (13th c.).

At the junction of Athy Road and Dublin Road is the handsome neo-classical *Court House* (1830).

St Patrick's College (1793) was one of the first seminaries for priests to be established in Ireland with the permission of the British authorities.

SURROUNDINGS. – 2 miles (3 km) north-east of Carlow on the Dublin road (N9) is the beautifully wooded Oak Park, with a golf-course (18 holes).

2 miles (3 km) east of the town, in the *Browne's Hill* demesne, is a huge *dolmen (National Monument), 4000 years old, the largest in Ireland. The front end of the capstone, weighing 100 tons (102 tonnes), is borne on three uprights; the rear end has collapsed and rests on the ground.

Continuing east, the R725 comes in 7½ miles (12 km) to the little town of *Tullow*, a centre for fishing the River Slaney and its tributaries.

3 miles (5 km) east of Tullow, in Co. Wicklow, is the ring-fort of *Rathgall* (National Monument), a hilltop stronghold with three concentric ramparts and ditches, probably built in the early centuries A.D. as the seat of the kings of South Leinster. North of the fort can be seen the well-preserved *Haroldstown Dolmen* (National Monument), with a double capstone borne on 10 uprights.

South of Carlow the N9 comes to *Leighlinbridge* with the ruins of the 16th c. Black Castle (National Monument). An earlier castle was built on the site in 1180 to protect the crossing of the River Barrow.

2 miles (3 km) west is the older settlement of *Old Leighlin*, where there was already a monastic establishment in the 7th c. The ruins of a church built in the 13th c. and much altered in the 16th c. still exist. Notable features are the Gothic doorway into the choir, the font, stalls and tombs (16th c.).

From Leighlinbridge the R705 runs south-east to *Muine Bheag* or *Bagenalstown*, an attractive little town which is a good centre for fishermen. In the vicinity are two 13th c. castles, both National Monuments – Ballymoon Castle, an empty shell with walls 8 ft (2·5 m) thick and 20 ft (6 m) high and rectangular towers, and Ballyloughan Castle, the remains of which are notable for the number of fireplaces.

The R705, continuing into the southern tip of Co. Carlow, comes to *Borris*, which has a 9-hole golf-course. Between the town and the river is Borris House.

Borris is the best starting-point for a visit to the *Blackstairs Mountains*, to the east of the town. On the highest peak, Mount Leinster (2576 ft (785 m)), stands a television tower.

At the southern tip of the county, 9 miles (15 km) south of Borris, is *St Mullins*, which has both Early Christian and medieval remains (National Monuments) in the churchyard. They include a church with a spiral staircase, an oratory (St James's Chapel), various other buildings, the stump of a round tower and a granite high cross.

Outside the monastic precincts is a Norman fortress.

A little way west of Carlow is the village of *Clonmore*, with the early 13th c. Clonmore Castle, a building with corner towers typical of its period.

The churchyard, which is cut in two by the road, also contains interesting remains. On the north side of the road is a beautiful and excellently preserved *high cross*, on the south side a fine cross fragment; both are designated National Monuments.

Just over a mile (2 km) farther west, in the churchyard of *Killeshin* village (Co. Laois), is a 12th c. Romanesque *church*, with a doorway which is notable for its carving and its high-pitched pediment.

From the churchyard there is a beautiful view over the plain, with the Wicklow Mountains in the distance.

Carrick-on-Shannon/Cara Droma Ruisg

Map reference: C3.
Republic of Ireland.
Province: Connacht. – County: Leitrim.
Population: 2000.
ⓘ **Tourist Information Office,**
Bridge Street,
Carrick-on-Shannon;
tel. (078) 2 01 70.

HOTELS. – *Bush*, B*, 26 r.; *County*, B*, 17 r.; *Cartown House*, C, 10 r.

RESTAURANTS. – *Bush Hotel*; *County Hotel.*

Carrick-on-Shannon (Cara Droma Ruisg, "Weir of the Marshy Ridge"), county town of Co. Leitrim, lies in northern central Ireland in the upper valley of the Shannon. It is the starting-point for cabin-cruiser trips on the Shannon (Lough Allen) and the River Boyle (Lough Key).

Carrick-on-Shannon has preserved few buildings from earlier centuries. Among them are the Court House (1825) and the Protestant church (1827).

SURROUNDINGS. – The R280 runs north through the prettily situated village of *Leitrim*, from which the county takes its name, to *Drumshanbo*, at the south end of Lough Allen, with the best pike fishing in the country.

From Drumshanbo the R280 follows the west side of *Lough Allen*, passing the mining area of Arigna (Co. Sligo). To the east, beyond the lough, are the *Iron Mountains*, rising to 1893 ft (577 m).

8 miles (13 km) north-east of Carrick-on-Shannon is *Fenagh*, with two old churches (National Monuments) on the site of a former monastery. The one to the south has a fine west doorway and east window (14th/15th c.), the one to the north (15th c.) dressed stones from a pre-Norman building; both have barrel-vaulted west ends.

9 miles (14 km) east of Carrick the R201 comes to *Mohill*, another fishing centre. To the south of the village is Lough Rinn, on the north-east side of which is *Lough Rinn House*, surrounded by a beautiful park.

31 miles (50 km) north of Carrick, in the northern part of Co. Leitrim, is *Manorhamilton*, where the N16 and R280 join at the meeting-point of four fertile valleys, which combine with the step scarps and narrow glens of the limestone hills to form a landscape of great variety and beauty. In the little town can be seen a ruined baronial mansion built by Sir Frederick Hamilton in 1638.

7 miles (11 km) south-west of Manorhamilton is *Dromahair*, which has its place in history. In the 12th c. Dervorgilla, wife of an O'Rourke, eloped from here with the King of Leinster, Dermot MacMurrough. Outlawed by the High King, Dermot appealed for support to Henry II of England, who refused to help but allowed his vassals to do so. This was the first incursion into Ireland by the Anglo-Normans, who landed at Wexford in 1169. The ruins of Breffni Castle, the stronghold of the O'Rourkes, adjoin the Old Hall (1626) on the banks of the River Bonet.

On the opposite bank of the river are the ruins of *Creevelea Abbey* (National Monument), a Franciscan house founded in 1508. The remains comprise a church, with choir and tower, and conventual buildings surrounding a cloister. The columns on the north side of the cloister have a number of fine carvings, including a representation of St Francis with the stigmata preaching to the birds.

3 miles (5 km) north of Dromahair rises a flat-topped hill known as *O'Rourke's Table*, covered with colourful ferns and mosses. From the top there is a fine view of Lough Gill (Co. Sligo) and the Dromahair Plain. Picturesquely situated on the shores of Lough Gill is *Parkes Castle* (17th c.: National Monument), a square three-storey building in a spacious courtyard, the walls of which are reinforced by two round corner towers.

8 miles (13 km) west of Manorhamilton on the N16 lies the little **Glencar Lough*, at the east end of which is a waterfall surrounded by trees.

North-west of Manorhamilton the R280 traverses the Bonet Valley, between high hills, to *Lough Melvin* and the pretty village of *Kinlough*. From here a detour can be made to the sea, joining the coast road (N15) at *Tullaghan*.

On the return trip from Kinlough via Rossinver to Manorhamilton the road skirts the very beautiful south side of Lough Melvin. The lough is well stocked with trout and salmon. From its south end the R282 leads through the hills to Manorhamilton.

Carrick-on-Suir/ Carraig na Suire

Map reference: D4.
Republic of Ireland.
Province: Munster. – Counties: Tipperary and Waterford.
Population: 5600.

(i) **Tourist Information Office,**
41 The Quay,
Waterford;
tel. (051) 7 57 88.

HOTEL. – *Tinvane*, Main Waterford Road, B, 10 r.

Carrick-on-Suir (Carraig na Suire, "Rock of the Suir") lies near the south coast of Ireland on the River Suir. Since the river marks the boundary between Co. Tipperary and Co. Waterford, the town extends into both counties.

HISTORY. – In 1541 Henry VIII of England assumed the title of King of Ireland. Thereafter, particularly during the reign of Elizabeth I, England sought to gain control of Ireland by establishing English landowners in the country. During the 16th and 17th c. these magnates built numbers of fortified Tudor mansions, the finest of which is Ormond Castle in Carrick-on-Suir.

SIGHTS. – **Ormond Castle** (National Monument), once the seat of the Earls of Ormond, consists of a fortified tower of 1450 and a manor house built on to it in 1568. It was built for Queen Elizabeth, but the Queen seems never to have lived in it. It is a typically Elizabethan house: externally a long front with gables and dwarf gables; in the interior a large hall and a gallery extending almost the whole length of the building, decorated with stucco likenesses of the Queen and members of the Ormond family. From the tower there is a magnificent view of the river and the surrounding countryside.

In the centre of the town, near the medieval bridge, stands the old Tholsel (Town Hall), originally a town gate, topped by a clock-tower.

SURROUNDINGS. – North of Carrick-on-Suir, on the boundary between Co. Kilkenny and Co. Tipperary, are two places with notable high crosses, Kilkeeran (5 miles (8 km)) and Ahenny (6 miles (10 km)).

Of the three crosses in the churchyard of *Kilkeeran* the **West Cross* (9th c.) is particularly fine. On the east side of the base are eight horsemen, on the other sides interlace work and geometric patterns. The lower part of the shaft is divided into panels with various patterns, among them intertwined goose-like creatures.

In the churchyard of *Ahenny* are two particularly fine crosses (both National Monuments), with figural decoration only on the bases. The *North Cross has figures of monks carrying crosses, a headless man on a pony, other horsemen and horses, a procession of seven ecclesiastics carrying crosiers and various animals. The base of the South Cross is badly weathered.

The crosses themselves are covered with finely carved geometric designs (spirals, interlace work, rosettes). The patterns are so similar to those in the "Book of Kells" that they are assumed to date from the 8th c.

South-west of Carrick-on-Suir the *Comeragh Mountains* and *Monavullagh Mountains* extend towards the sea. This is good climbing country, particularly around little Lough Coumshingaum, which is surrounded by a horseshoe-shaped line of cliffs rising to the highest peak (2560 ft (780 m)).

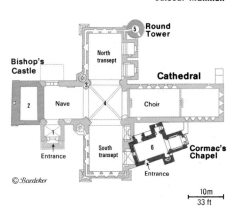

Cashel
Caiseal Mumhan

1 Porch
2 Archbishop's Palace
3 Staircases
4 Central tower
5 Round tower
6 Cormac's Chapel

Cashel/Caiseal Mumhan

Map reference: D4.
Republic of Ireland.
Province: Munster. – County: Tipperary.
Population: 2400.

(i) **Tourist Information Office,**
Town Hall, Main Street,
Cashel;
tel. (062) 6 13 33.

HOTELS. – *Dundrum House*, A, 30 r.; *Cashel Palace*, A, 20 r.; *Rectory House*, Dundrum, B*, 10 r.; *Quirke's Castle*, C, 12 r.

RESTAURANT. – *Cashel Palace Hotel.*

Cashel (Caiseal Mumhan, "Stone Fort of Munster") lies in southern Ireland on the N8. On all the roads which converge on Cashel over the plain the famous Rock of Cashel is a prominent landmark: a steep-sided crag to the north of the little town, crowned by a magnificent group of ruins. These fine monuments of Ireland's past make Cashel one of the country's most-visited sites.

HISTORY. – The rock was fortified by the kings of Munster as early as the 4th c. In 450 St Patrick baptised King Aengus here and made Cashel the see of a bishop, and a number of later kings were also bishops. The celebrated Brian Boru was crowned here, and in 977 made Cashel his principal seat. An O'Brien presented the Rock to the Church, and soon afterwards, in 1127, Bishop Cormac MacCarthy began the construction of Cormac's Chapel. In 1152 the bishopric became an archbishopric. After the Reformation Elizabeth I appointed Protestant archbishops.

The Cathedral, built in the 13th c., was damaged by fire in 1495 and again in 1647. After being restored in 1686 it was abandoned in 1749 and thereafter fell into decay. Finally in 1874 it was taken over by the State and declared a National Monument.

Rock of Cashel

The **Rock of Cashel** (National Monument) rises 200 ft (60 m) above the plain. The entrance to the complex of buildings on the site is reached from the town by way of Ladyswell Street. The walled precinct is entered through the *Hall of the Vicars Choral* (15th c.), which housed laymen or minor canons.

At the entrance stands St Patrick's Cross, on a base richly decorated with geometric designs which may have been the coronation stone of the kings of Munster. It stood in the open air, on the spot where St Patrick baptised King Aengus. Tradition has it that during the ceremony the Saint accidentally struck the King's foot with his crosier; but Aengus made no remark, believing that this was part of the ritual.

In addition to the Hall of the Vicars Choral the complex of buildings includes the Cathedral, built against a round tower, Cormac's Chapel and the Archbishop's Castle.

Cormac's Chapel (1127–32), which is enclosed by the choir and south transept of the cathedral, is the most interesting Romanesque church in Ireland. The architecture and sculpture show the influence of German (probably Regensburg) and English masters, while preserving a distinctively Irish character (expressed, for example, in the steeply pitched stone roof and the corbelling of the barrel vaulting).

Cashel: transept of Cathedral

The transepts are like towers. The wall surfaces, externally and internally, are relieved by blind arcading and a variety of sculptural decoration. The old main doorway (north doorway: now facing the angle between the choir and south transept) is richly articulated and has a fine tympanum depicting a centaur hunting a lion with a bow and arrow. The chapel contains a 12th c. stone sarcophagus finely carved with Scandinavian-type ornament.

The north transept of the Cathedral is built on to a well-preserved **round tower** dating from the same period as Cormac's Chapel. It is 92 ft (28 m) high, with its doorway 12 ft (3·6 m) above ground-level.

The **Cathedral** itself, now roofless, still preserves something of the majesty of a medieval episcopal church. The choir and transepts are longer than the (unfinished) nave. The transepts have preserved their three-bayed gable-ends and their corner turrets. In the angles between the nave and the transepts spiral staircases (127 steps) run up in small round towers to the massive central tower and to roof walks round the nave and transept, linked with one another and with the round tower by various passages and flights of steps within the thickness of the walls – forming

a well-contrived defensive system. In the north transept are a number of fine tombs, one of them with figures of Apostles and saints, including St Thomas Becket.

In the choir is the tomb of Archbishop Myler MacGrath, who died in 1622 at the age of 100. Having gone over to the Protestant Church, he was for several years both a Protestant Archbishop, appointed by Elizabeth I, and a Roman Catholic one, since he had not been dismissed by the Vatican!

At the west end of the Cathedral is the *Archbishop's Palace*, a massive square tower (15th c.) which is more of a fortified castle than a palace. The west wall is thick enough to accommodate a staircase within it. It is well worth climbing to the top for the sake of the magnificent view.

OTHER SIGHTS. – When the castle on the rock was no longer required for protection the Protestant archbishops built a residence, *Cashel Palace*, in the town. This handsome brick building of 1730 is now the Cashel Palace Hotel, furnished in 18th c. style; the entrance is on the north side of Main Street.

Almost exactly opposite stands *Quirke's Castle*, a 15th c. tower house which is now also a hotel.

Turlough Round Tower

Near the base of the Rock the *Dominican Friary* (National Monument) preserves a number of handsome old windows.

The *Cathedral of St John the Baptist* in John Street is a good neo-classical building (1750–83; tower 1812) erected to replace the cathedral on the rock, then falling into disrepair. Set into a wall in the churchyard are a fine series of tomb effigies from the medieval churches of Cashel.

Near by is the *Diocesan Library*, with a collection of rare printed works.

SURROUNDINGS. – West of Cashel we come to *Hore Abbey* (National Monument), a Cistercian house founded in 1266, with the ruins of the church and conventual buildings; the chapter-house is well preserved.

Castlebar/Caislean an Barraigh

Map reference: C2.
Republic of Ireland.
Province: Connacht. – County: Mayo.
Population: 6400.

(i) **Tourist Information Office,**
Castlebar;
tel. (094) 2 12 07.
Open July and August.

HOTELS. – *Welcome Inn*, New Antrim Street, B, 28 r.; *Imperial*, B, 18 r.

RESTAURANTS. – *Breaffy House Hotel*; *Upper Crust*, Bridge Street.

EVENT. – *International Song Contest* (Oct.).

Castlebar (Caislean an Barraigh, "Barry's Castle"), county town of Co. Mayo, lies in the north-west of Ireland, at the junction of the N5 and N60.

HISTORY. – In 1798 a French and Irish force landed at Castlebar and routed a British unit – an engagement known as the "Castlebar Races".

The central feature of this little market town, which also has some light industry, is The Mall, lined with lime trees. There is a small local airport.

SURROUNDINGS. – 3 miles (5 km) north-east on the N5 lies *Turlough*, with a well-preserved *round tower* (National Monument), unusually short and squat, in the churchyard. Adjoining it is a ruined 17th c. church.

Beyond this, on the road to Foxford, *Straid* has a ruined abbey church containing fine *sculpture and tombstones.

From Castlebar the N60 runs south-east over the Plains of Mayo. 3 miles (5 km) beyond Balla a road goes off on the right to the village of *Mayo*, with remains of a once-famous abbey founded in the 7th c. by St Colman.

Sculpture in Straid Abbey

The N60 continues to *Claremorris* (Imperial Hotel, B, 15 r.; Central Hotel, B, 14 r.), from which the N17 leads north-east to *Knock*, a place of pilgrimage which attracts a million visitors every year. The new church (1974) which dominates the village can accommodate 7500 worshippers. The local airport, constructed after a determined campaign by the local priest, has been the subject of some controversy.

The R323 runs east from Knock to *Ballyhaunis* (Central Hotel, B, 15 r.), with remains of an Augustinian priory; the church has been restored.

The loughs south of Castlebar – Lough Mallard, Castlebar Lough and Islanddeady Lough – are a fisherman's paradise.

Cavan/An Cabhan

Map reference: C4.
Republic of Ireland.
Province: Ulster. – County: Cavan.
Population: 3200.
ⓘ **Tourist Information Office,**
Town Hall Street,
Cavan;
tel. (049) 3 19 42.
Open June to September.

HOTELS. – *Kilmore*, B*, 40 r.; *Farnham Arms*, Main Street, C, 15 r.

RESTAURANT: *Gallery*, Main Street.

Cavan (An Cabhan, "Hollow Place"), county town of Co. Cavan, lies in a pleasant district of hills and lakes near the Northern Ireland border, at the junction of the N3, coming from the south-east, with the north–south road, the N54/N55. The town was completely destroyed by British forces in 1690. An old tower marks the site of an abbey founded about 1300, round which the original settlement grew up.

SURROUNDINGS. – 5 miles (8 km) north is *Bally-haise*, with a good 18th c. Market House borne on arches and Ballyhaise Castle (by Richard Cassels, 1731), now occupied by an agricultural college.

From Cavan the R188 runs north-east to the little town of *Cootehill* (White Horse Hotel, B*, 30 r.). North of the town lies *Bellamont Forest*, in which, on the shores of Dromore Lough, is the fine Palladian mansion of Bellamont House (1729: not open to the public).

3 miles (5 km) south-east of Cootehill on the R192 is *Cohaw Giant's Grave* (National Monument), a double-court cairn with five chambers excavated in 1949.

The road continues to *Shercock*, near *Lough Sillan* (camp site), which is renowned for its large pike.

8 miles (13 km) farther south, at the eastern extremity of the province, is *Kingscourt* (Cabra Castle Hotel, B*,

21 r.; Mackin's Hotel, B, 14 r.), where rich deposits of gypsum have led to the development of modern industries. The main street has attractive 17th and 18th c. houses. In St Mary's Parish Church are beautiful stained-glass windows by Evie Hone (1947–48).

The R165 goes west through the hills to the little market town of *Bailieborough* (Bailie Hotel, B*, 21 r.), which has a Court House of 1817 and a Market House of 1818.

9 miles (15 km) south of Bailieborough lies *Virginia*, named after the Virgin Queen, Elizabeth I. Prettily situated on the wooded shores of Lough Ramor, it offers a wide range of sport and recreational facilities (9-hole golf-course, fishing in Lough Ramor, bathing beach, boat hire).

North of Virginia is the site of Cuilcagh House, a mansion belonging to the Sheridan family, in which Swift began to write "Gulliver's Travels".

To the south of *Ballyjamesduff* (Percy French Arms Hotel, B*, 12 r.), on the R194, we come to the village of Mount Nugent, with good fishing in *Lough Sheelin*.

There is also good coarse fishing in *Lough Gowna*, 12 miles (20 km) south of Cavan, reached by way of Gowna, or direct from Lough Sheelin, going west.

North-west of Cavan, past the golf-course, stands *Farnham House*, in a beautiful park.

Farther west is *Lough Oughter*, an intricately patterned maze of inlets and channels through which the River Erne flows. On an island in the lough are the ruins of *Cloughoughter Castle*, a typical example of an Irish circular tower castle of the 13th c.

Near by, at Cornafaen, is a privately run local museum.

To the south of Farnham House in *Kilmore*, a small cathedral town, stands a 19th c. Protestant Cathedral which incorporates a fine Late Romanesque doorway. In the churchyard can be seen a richly decorated tomb of Bishop William Bedell, who made the first translation of the Bible into Irish in the 17th c. Also in the town is a well-preserved motte and bailey.

On the west side of Lough Oughter, reached from Cavan by way of Kilmore, lies *Killeshandra*, surrounded by small loughs, with a church of 1688.

The R201, running west from this lake district, comes in 3 miles (5 km) to *Drumlane*. Here, beautifully situated between two loughs, are a *round tower* and a *church* (National Monuments), both belonging to a former monastery. The church dates from the 13th and 15th c.; the tower, still standing 45 ft (14 m) high, with badly weathered carvings of birds, from the 12th.

The road continues north to *Belturbet*, near the Northern Ireland border, starting-point for cabin-cruiser trips on the River Erne (good fishing). To the north, over the border, is *Lough Erne* (see entry).

The hilly countryside with its many loughs continues west of Belturbet for another 10–12 miles (15–20 km). *Ballyconnell*, a popular coarse-fishing centre, has a 17th c. church.

The R200 climbs steeply up into the *Iron Mountains*, goes over the Bellavally Gap and descends to *Glengevlin*, at the foot of the highest hill in the range, Cuilcagh Mountain. In this area is the *Shannon Pot*, source of the River Shannon. Good climbing country.

Cliffs of Moher ▶

Cliffs of Moher/ Aillte an Mhothair

Map reference: D2.
Republic of Ireland.
Province: Munster. – County: Clare.
ⓘ Tourist Information Office,
Lahinch;
tel. (065) 8 11 71.
Open March to October.

HOTELS. – IN LAHINCH: *Vaughan's Aberdeen Arms*, A, 48 r.; *Atlantic*, B, 24 r.; *Sancta Maria*, B, 20 r.

The Cliffs of Moher (Aillte an Mhothair, "Cliffs of Ruin") rise vertically out of the sea on the west coast of Ireland, just south of Galway Bay.

The sheer *cliffs extend from Hag's Head in the south, where they are 400 ft (120 m) high, to *O'Brien's Tower in the north, where they reach a height of 656 ft (200 m). Between these two points extends a generally flat plateau 5 miles (8 km) long. From the top of the cliffs can be seen narrow strips of vegetation clinging to the cliff face and, far below, isolated pinnacles of rock, with the surf perpetually surging and thundering against the land and, high above, seabirds wheeling and crying. From O'Brien's Tower, built as a tea-house in 1835, there are breath-taking views, extending in clear weather as far as the Aran Islands. The tower is just off the road (R457); in summer it houses an information centre.

SURROUNDINGS. – From the cliffs the road leads east to the fishing village of *Liscannor* (Liscannor Golf Hotel, B*, 24 r.), past the ruins of Kilmacreehy Church (15th c.) and along Liscannor Bay with its beautiful sandy beach to the popular resort of *Lahinch* (hotels: see above), which has something of a southern air with its square white houses and its promenade running along above the surf. It has two 18-hole golf-courses and a variety of sport and recreational facilities (including surfing).

In a wooded valley 2½ miles (4 km) east of Lahinch is the resort of *Ennistymon* (Falls Hotel, B*, 31 r.), where the River Cullinagh cascades down through a rocky gorge. Good brown trout fishing.

7½ miles (12 km) south of Lahinch on the N67 a side road branches off to *Spanish Point*, a rugged promontory on which one of the vessels of the Spanish Armada was wrecked in 1588, with the loss of hundreds of lives. Near the point are a 9-hole golf-course and a good sandy beach.

Clonakilty/Clanna Chaoilte

Map reference: E3.
Republic of Ireland.
Province: Munster. – County: Cork.
Population: 2700.
ⓘ Tourist Information Office,
Clonakilty;
tel. (023) 3 32 26.
Open July and August.

HOTEL. – *Inchydoney*, B, 29 r.

RESTAURANT. – *An Sugan*, Wolfe Tone Street.

Clonakilty (Clanna Chaoilte, "O'Keelty's Sept") lies in Clonakilty Bay on the south coast of Ireland. The head of the bay is almost totally enclosed by the Inchadoney Peninsula. There are good sandy beaches and facilities for water-sports and sea fishing.

Clonakilty was established in 1614 by the first Earl of Cork for occupation by English settlers. It is now a small market town in a fertile agricultural area with an interesting local museum and a beautiful park, Kennedy Gardens.

SURROUNDINGS. – 6 miles (10 km) east on the T71 and R600 lies *Timoleague*, with an abbey founded in 1240 which in its day was an important religious centre. The present ruins (church with south aisle and transepts, tower, remains of conventual buildings) date from later centuries.

From Timoleague it is 2½ miles (4 km) on the R601 to *Courtmacsherry* (Courtmacsherry Hotel, B*, 16 r.), a fishing village on the south side of a narrow inlet.

On the large peninsula south-west of Clonakilty, near Castle Freke, are the ruins of *Benduff Castle* and the remains of a Templar establishment.

At the head of Rosscarbery Bay, picturesquely situated on a hill by the sea, the little town of *Rosscarbery* (Owenahincha Hotel, B, 22 r.), once had a 6th c. monastery famous for its school. There are some remains of this near the ancient cathedral (restored in the 17th and 19th c.).

2 miles (3 km) west of Clonakilty stands *Coppinger's Court* (National Monument), a ruined 17th c. manor-house with picturesque turrets, gables and chimneys.

On a hill just off the road to Glandore (R597) can be found the *Drombeg Stone Circle* (National Monument) of 17 stones, which dates from about the beginning of the Christian era. Near by are the remains of two circular huts.

Glandore is a prettily situated resort with a mild climate and good fishing and bathing.

North-west of Clonakilty, to the right of the R588, is another stone circle, with a single white stone 11 ft (3·3 m) high standing in the centre.

Clonmacnoise/ Cluain Mic Nois

Map reference: C4.
Republic of Ireland.
Province: Leinster. – County: Offaly.
ⓘ Tourist Information Centre,
    Clonmacnoise;
    tel. (0905) 7 41 34.
    Open June to September.

The ancient monastic settlement of Clonmacnoise (Cluain Mic Nois, "Meadow of the Son of Nos") lies in the heart of Ireland, on high ground above the east bank of the Shannon. The walled precinct of the monastery is like a large and lonely churchyard with its numbers of graves scattered about amid the ruins of buildings and high crosses of the Early Christian and medieval periods. The site is a National Monument.

ACCESS. – The pleasantest – if slowest – way to reach Clonmacnoise is by boat from Athlone (see entry). The road from Athlone to Shannonbridge runs just past the site.

HISTORY. – According to tradition the monastery was founded in January 545 by St Ciaran, who died in the same year. It developed into the most celebrated religious centre in Ireland and soon gained the status of a university. The monks working in its scriptoria produced valuable manuscripts including the "Annals of Tighernach" and the "Book of the Dun Cow", and it also had craftsmen producing crosiers, reliquaries and other articles. The precious objects it contained no doubt attracted the raiders who plundered and burned the monastery several times between 834 and 1204 – first the Vikings, then in the 12th c. the Normans, who in 1179 reduced more than a hundred buildings to ashes. The monastery fell into final ruin, however, only after English troops from Athlone had carried off all they could lay their hands on in 1552 and the site had been devastated once again by Cromwell's troops a hundred years later. Since 1955 Clonmacnoise has been under State protection as a National Monument.

The **Monastic Site

The walled enclosure (open May–Sept.: conducted visits) is entered from the car park on the west side. It is a typical Irish monastic site, laid out in a manner very different from monasteries in the rest of Europe, with a number of small churches scattered about the site. Between them there would originally be numerous wattle and daub huts for the members of the community.

In the centre of the main group of buildings stands the *Cathedral*, which incorporates work of the 10th to the 15th c. A notable feature is the medieval figure of St Patrick with two other saints above the north doorway. The sacristy dates from the 16th c.

To the east of the cathedral is the cell-like *Oratory of St Ciaran* (Temple Kieran), a tiny 9th c. church probably containing the tomb of the founder.

At the north end of the precinct are *Temple Connor* (11th c.), now a Protestant church (closed), and *Temple Finian* (12th c.), which has a 56 ft (17 m) high round tower. Another round tower, *O'Rourke's Tower*, 60 ft (18 m) high, stands by itself close to the Shannon; it has an entrance doorway.

Clonmacnoise has three crosses. Outside the cathedral is one of the finest crosses in Ireland, the *Cross of the Scriptures (10th c.: see plan below). On the west face are the Watching of the Tomb, the Arrest, the Betrayal and, above, the Crucifixion. On the east face, below, King Dermot is depicted helping St Ciaran to lay the corner-post of the church; above

Clonmacnoise
Cluain Mic Nois

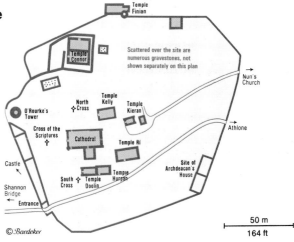

© Baedeker

this are a number of unidentified figures, and above these again the Last Judgment. On the south face are a bishop and David with his harp. On the north face are another bishop, a man with Pan pipes and a falconer. On the base of the cross can be seen a hunting scene with horsemen, chariots and various animals. To the north of this cross is a cross fragment with figures and ornamental patterns. To the south of it a third high cross (9th c.) has a Crucifixion on the west face and panels containing intertwined animals and plants.

To the left of the entrance are some 200 Early Christian gravestones, including some with ogham inscriptions. They are set into the enclosure wall in groups, offering an excellent survey of the different types from the 8th to the 12th c. Many have inscriptions containing the formula "OR DO" ("a prayer for") followed by a name; and many are very beautiful and of high artistic quality.

To the east of the monastic enclosure, reached by a paved way from the Oratory of St Ciaran, lies the ruined *Nun's Church*. The entrance doorway and the choir arch, both richly ornamented, are well preserved; the designs on the capitals of the choir arch are particularly intricate.

Every year on 9 September, the Feast-day of St Ciaran, there is a pilgrimage to Clonmacnoise, when a service is held at a canopied altar in the open air.

Clonmel/Cluain Meala

Map reference: D4.
Republic of Ireland.
Province: Munster. – County: Tipperary.
Population: 12,400.

ⓘ **Tourist Information Office,**
   Clonmel;
   tel. (052) 2 29 60.
   Open July and August.

HOTELS. – *Clonmel Arms*, A, 33 r.; *Minella*, A, 32 r.; *Hearn's*, B, 25 r.

RESTAURANT. – *Clonmel Arms Hotel*

Clonmel (Cluain Meala, "Honey Meadow"), county town of Co. Tipperary, lies near the Irish south coast on the north bank of the River Suir. To the south of the town are the Comeragh Mountains.

Clonmel is a market town, with some industry (principally cider production), the centre of a horse- and dog-breeding area. Laurence Sterne, author of "Tristram Shandy", was born in Clonmel in 1713.

High crosses and gravestones, Clonmacnoise

In 1815 the first regular passenger transport service between two Irish towns was established in Clonmel. An Italian immigrant named Charles Bianconi, a picture-framer by trade, who had risen to prosperity and become Mayor of the town, started a service of horse-drawn cars ("Bianconi cars") between Clonmel and Cahir which later extended over the whole of southern Ireland.

SIGHTS. – *St Mary's Church* (Protestant: National Monument), with an octagonal tower, stands on the site of an earlier 14th c. church; its most recent reconstruction was in 1857. Notable features are the tracery of the east window and a number of 16th and 17th c. monuments. Adjoining the church are remains of the old town walls, with three towers.

Westgate, which closes the west end of O'Connell Street, occupies the site of a medieval town gate. Outside it in Irishtown is St Mary's Roman Catholic Church, with a neo-classical façade and a good plasterwork ceiling.

At the other end of the street is the *Main Guard*, said to have been designed by Christopher Wren, but more probably the work of Sir William Robinson, with the coats of arms of Clonmel and of the Earls of Ormond, whose courts were held here. In Parnell Street stands the *Town Hall*, where the civic insignia are kept. Beyond this are the Court House (1800) and, obliquely opposite this, the *Municipal Library*, which also houses the Clonmel Museum and Art Gallery.

SURROUNDINGS. – 5 miles (8 km) north, on a side road off the R688, *Donaghmore* has a ruined Romanesque *church* (National Monument) with a fine doorway and chancel arch.

4½ miles (7 km) beyond this is the old-world little town of *Fethard*. The Protestant parish church incorporates parts of an earlier 15th c. church, while the Roman Catholic church, at the east end of the town, preserves enough of the substance of an old Augustinian church to give something of the impression of the original. Part of the old town walls still survives.

Slievenamon (2330 ft (710 m)), north-east of Clonmel, and the *Comeragh Mountains* (highest peak Knockamaffrin, 2439 ft (743 m)), south of the town, offer ample scope for climbers and hill-walkers.

Along the banks of the Suir to the east of Clonmel are a number of ruined castles and churches. 2½ miles (4 km) from the town, on the north bank of the river, is Anner House, with the *Falconry*, which has a collection of birds of prey (demonstrations of falconry). Farther east, on the south bank, the beautiful wooded grounds of *Gurteen le Poer* (18th c.) extend up the hill.

Cong/Cunga Feichin

Map reference: C2.
Republic of Ireland.
Province: Connacht. – County: Mayo.
Population: 200.
ⓘ **Tourist Information Office,**
Ballinrobe;
tel. 1 31.
Open July and August.

HOTELS. – *Ashford Castle*, A*, 77 r.; *Ryan's*, B. 17 r.

RESTAURANT. – *Ashford Castle Hotel.*

The village of Cong (Cunga Feichin, "Isthmus of Feichin") lies in the far west of Ireland, on the isthmus between Lough Mask and Lough Corrib (good fishing in both loughs), to the north of Galway Bay and close to the boundary between the counties of Mayo and Galway. The last High King of Ireland, Roderick O'Conor, died in Cong in 1198, after 15 years spent in monastic seclusion.

SIGHTS. – At the entrance to the village are the ruins of **Cong Abbey* (National Monument), an Augustinian house. Only fragments of the church remain, but a finely sculptured doorway and a number of capitals in the cloister are striking examples of Irish Romanesque art.

The processional Cross of Cong, made for King Turlough O'Conor about 1123, is now in the National Museum in Dublin. In the main street of the village is a 14th c. stone market cross, with inscriptions.

Near the abbey, in a park on the shores of Lough Corrib (see entry), stands *Ashford Castle*, an 18th c. house which in the 19th c. belonged to a member of the Guinness family. It is now a hotel.

SURROUNDINGS. – *Lough Mask* and *Lough Corrib* are linked by underground streams flowing beneath the isthmus which divides them. In the limestone rock of this area there are numerous caves, the most interesting of which are *Kelly's Cave* (National Monument), which is thought to have been a Bronze Age burial-place, and the *Pigeon Hole*. Both are easily accessible; the key for Kelly's Cave is kept in Cong.

To the west, beyond the isthmus, extends *Joyce's Country*, a hilly region traversed by green valleys and lonely roads which takes its name from a Welsh family who settled here in the 13th c.

For a rewarding round trip, with a harmonious mingling of hill, valley and river scenery, take the road which runs west from Cong via Clonbur to *Lough*

Ashford Castle (Hotel)

Nafooey, with views of the Partry Mountains, and then, crossing a saddle into the valley of the River Joyce, continue on the L101 round the western tip of Lough Corrib, and so back to Cong.

Connemara

Map reference: C1/2.
Republic of Ireland.
Province: Connacht. – County: Galway.
(i) **Tourist Information Office,**
    Clifden;
    tel. (095) 2 11 63.
    Open June to August.

HOTELS. – IN CLIFDEN: *Abbeyglen House*, A, 40 r.; *Rock Glen Country House*, A, 30 r.; *Clifton Bay*, B*, 40 r.; *Ardagh*, B*, 17 r.; *Celtic*, B, 18 r.

GUEST-HOUSE. – *Atlantic Coast*, B, 19 r.

RESTAURANTS. – IN CLIFDEN: *O'Grady's Seafood*; *Rock Glen Country House Hotel*.

EVENT. – *Connemara Pony Show* (Aug.).

Connemara is the district in western Galway extending between Lough Corrib and the much-indented Atlantic coast of Ireland, to the north of Galway Bay. **Scenery of superb grandeur – ranges of hills and bare isolated peaks, valleys enclosing the black waters of many loughs, a coastline of alternating rocky cliffs and sandy bays: all this makes

Connemara one of Ireland's supreme attractions, appealing to tourists, to sportsmen and to holiday-makers who seek quiet and relaxation.

Irish is still spoken in large areas of Connemara, and road signs are all in Irish script. Here, too, have been preserved the living traditions of singing and story-telling.

The ubiquitous domestic animal is the donkey, which can be seen carrying heavy loads (particularly peat) in baskets slung over his back, or roaming about in freedom. Peat cuttings and neatly stacked piles of cut peat are regular features of the landscape.

Clifden

The chief place in Connemara is **Clifden**, a little market town in the extreme west of the area. It lies at the head of Clifden Bay, one of the numerous narrow inlets which reach inland, heading towards the Twelve Bens which are Connemara's great landmarks. The Connemara Pony Show is a well-known annual event which attracts many visitors in August; it is also the occasion for traditional contests and competitions. Below the town the River Owenglin makes its way down to the sea in picturesque waterfalls.

Clifden, chief town of Connemara

On the hills to the west of the town (fine views) stands *Clifden Castle* (1815), now unoccupied.

An interesting sight in the season is at Weir Bridge, to the south of the town, where large numbers of salmon can be seen struggling against the current.

Farther south are the remains of the first transatlantic wireless transmitting station set up here by Guglielmo Marconi (1874–1937), the Italian pioneer of radio who went to live in England in 1896. Also in this area is a monument to Sir William Alcock and Sir Arthur Whitten Brown, who on 14–15 June 1919 made the first non-stop flight across the Atlantic, taking off from St John's, Newfoundland, and crash-landing here.

Inland from here extends *Lough Fadda*, the haunt of innumerable wildfowl.

TOURS IN CONNEMARA. – The contrasts in the scenery of Connemara – whether in the nature of the landscape or in the play of light and colour – can best be appreciated in a series of separate trips.

From Clifden the N59 runs northward skirting the coast, passing little white cottages scattered about amid stony fields, drystone walls and rocky coves.

At *Streamstown*, a few miles north of Clifden, light-coloured marble is worked; the quarries can be visited. A side road goes off on the left to the fishing village

of *Cleggan* (lobster-catching), from which a boat can be taken to the island of *Inishbofin* (for departure times enquire in Clifden). The island was occupied by monks in the 7th c. On it can be seen ancient promontory forts, stone houses and the remains of a barracks built by Cromwell's forces (1652–57), who made this a kind of concentration camp for priests and monks. But the island is also well worth visiting for the sake of its beautiful sandy beaches and rugged cliffs and the scope it offers for sailing and sea fishing.

The N59 goes via Moyard to *Letterfrack*, a settlement founded by Quakers in the 19th c. The mild climate here allows tall fuchsia hedges to flourish. The loughs and inlets offer good fishing and bathing. Here, too, is the **Connemara National Park** (information pavilion), with waymarked footpaths.

From Letterfrack a side road on the left leads to Tully Cross and *Renvyle* (Renvyle House Hotel, A, 68 r.). At the end of the Renvyle Peninsula, which has beautiful coastal scenery – sandy beaches alternating with cliffs – are the remains of a 14th c. castle and a church, and a dolmen.

The N59 runs east from Letterfrack up the valley of the River Dawros to the Kylemore loughs, nestling amid hills. This area is at its most beautiful when the rhododendrons and fuchsias are in bloom. To the left, above the first lough, stands the palatial *Kylemore Abbey* (19th c.), now a girls' school run by Benedictine nuns, who also operate a pottery and restaurant.

The road passes Kylemore Lough and Lough Fee and winds its way down to *Killary Harbour*, a 10 mile (16 km) long fjord-like inlet the shores of which have a gloomy aspect when in shadow but are charming when the sun shines on them. There was formerly a British naval base here.

Over the water to the north there is a glimpse, between the Mweelrea Mountains and Bengorm (2297 ft

(700 m)), of the Vale of *Delphi, a beautiful rocky valley of classical aspect which owes its name to a young Marquess of Sligo who, returning from the Grand Tour, called his fishing-lodge Delphi.

The road continues along the south side of the fjord to *Leenane*, a good centre for fishermen and climbers. Here, on the River Erriff, which flows down through Co. Mayo into Killary Harbour, is the beautiful *Ashleag Waterfall*.

From Leenane there is a direct route south to Maam Cross (below) on the R336.

The southern coasts of Connemara can be seen by following a coastal route under various road numbers. From Clifden take the N59, which runs east to *Ballynahinch Lough*. Near its southern shore stands Ballynahinch Castle Hotel (A, 20 r.), an 18th c. mansion built by the Martin family, who during the Great Famine of 1845–49 sold much of their property to help the poor. On a wooded islet in the lough can be seen a ruined castle.

Beyond *Recess* is the important intersection known as *Maam Cross*, where the N59 (Clifden–Oughterard–Galway) cuts across the R335/R336 (Louisburgh–Leenane–Screeb–Galway).

From here the route leads south through a maze of little loughs, coming in 6 miles (9 km) to *Screeb*, on a narrow and much-indented arm of the sea which could be taken for another lough were it not for the tide-marks along its shores. The tiny fields in this area are built up from successive layers of seaweed and sand and protected by irregularly shaped drystone walls.

At Screeb the coast road (R340, R342 and R341) branches off to the right, describing wide sweeps round a succession of bays and inlets and reaching Clifden in some 50 miles (80 km), through a landscape which alternates between heath, bog and hills.

From Screeb the R340 follows the shores of Kilkieran Bay to *Carna*, with fishing for sea trout in the bay and for brown trout in the neighbouring loughs. On two islets in *Lough Skannive* are crannogs.

From Carna a boat can be taken to *St MacDara's Island*, named after the 6th c. saint Sionnach MacDara who lived here with other hermits. Here can be seen a church built of large stones (National Monument) and some Early Christian cross-slabs.

The coast road (R340, R342) comes in another 8 miles (13 km) to a minor road on the left which descends to Cashel Bay. *Cashel* (Cashel House Hotel, A, 29 r.; Zetland Hotel, A, 15 r.) is a favourite fishing centre. From here the road runs west and then south to *Roundstone*, a settlement established in the early 19th c. for Scottish fishermen. It is now a holiday resort much favoured by artists and nature-lovers, with beautiful shell beaches.

The coast road (here the R341) continues round Ballyconneely Bay to *Ballyconneely* (Erriseask House Hotel, B, 10 r.), 2½ miles (4 km) south of which, on the sea, is an 18-hole golf-course. It then continues north to Clifden.

The interior of Connemara, with the **Twelve Bens** (east of Clifden) and the *Maamturk Mountains*, is lonely and thinly populated – very different from the coastal areas. Its central feature is the group of 12 peaks which are the great landmark of Connemara; the highest is Benbaun (2356 ft (718 m)), and the others are not much lower. Their steep rock faces are colourful with mosses and lichens, heather and the white quartzite of which they are composed. Access to the hills is over meagre grassland and barren expanses of heath into the side valleys which climb up through the foothills into the mountain world of the Twelve Bens.

At the east end of Lough Kylemore (p. 89) a side road branches off the N59 and runs south in wide curves through the glacial depression between the Twelve Bens to the west and the Maamturk Mountains to the east, along the shores of *Lough Inagh* and *Derryclare Lough*, to rejoin the N59 at *Recess*. The beautiful scenery and the good fishing make this a very popular holiday resort.

To the east of the Maamturk Mountains, running south-east from Leenane, is the valley of the River Joyce, bordering the beautiful region known as Joyce's Country (see Cong).

Cork/Corcaigh

Map reference: E3.
Republic of Ireland.
Province: Munster. – County: Cork.
Population: 136,000.

ⓘ **Tourist Information Office,**
Tourist House, Grand Parade,
Cork;
tel. (021) 27 32 51.
Tourist Information Office,
Cork Airport;
tel. (021) 96 43 47.
Open July and August.

HOTELS. – *Jury's*, Western Road, A , 140 r.; *Metropole*, MacCurtain Street, A, 121 r.; *Imperial*, South Mall, A, 80 r.; *Silver Springs*, Tivoli, A, 72 r.; *Moore's*, Morrison's Island, B , 38 r.; *Arbutus Lodge*, Montenotte, B , 20 r.; *Ashbourne House*, B , 26 r.; *Victoria*, 33–34 Cook Street, B, 30 r.; *Sunset Ridge*, Killeens, B, 28 r.; *Cork Airport*, Kinsale Road, B, 20 r.

RESTAURANTS. – *Arbutus Lodge Hotel*, Montenotte; *Black Castle*, Blackrock; *Café de Paris*, Shopping Centre; *Henning's*, 3A Market Lane; *Hunter's Lodge*, Lower Glanmire Road; *Jury's Hotel*, Western Road; *Lovett's*, Churchyard Lane; *Maple*; *Silver Springs Hotel*, Tivoli; *Turf 'n Surf*, The Square (Passage West).

EVENT. – *International Band Competition* (May).

Cork (Corcaigh, "Marshy Place") is Ireland's largest city after Dublin and Belfast, with an international airport. It lies on the south coast, apparently inland but in fact linked with the sea by way of Cork Harbour and the narrow channel called Passage West. The central area of Cork is in effect an island enclosed between the two arms of the River Lee, the North and South Channels. The

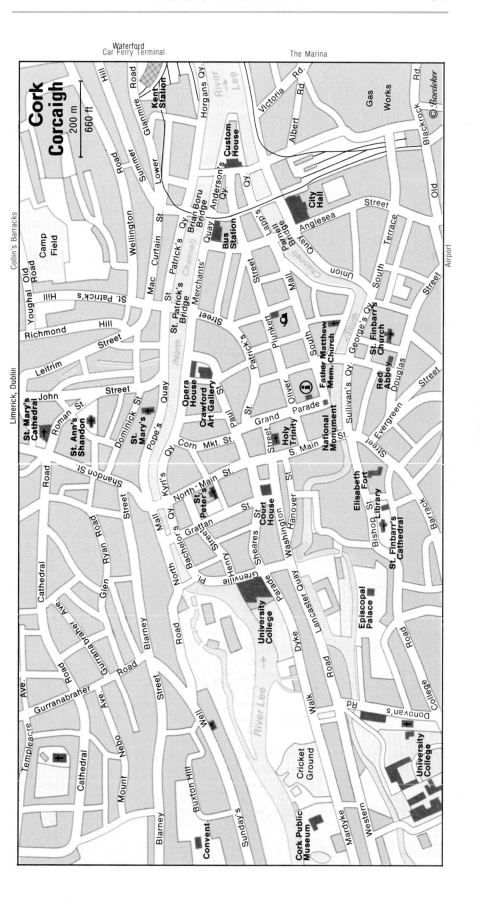

Cork
Corcaigh

200 m
660 ft

river, spanned by several bridges within the city, flows into Lough Mahon as Cork Harbour is also called.

Cork is the intellectual centre of southern Ireland, with many cultural institutions, including the Cork Literary and Scientific Society, founded in 1820. It has a college of the National University of Ireland and two cathedrals, Roman Catholic and Protestant.

Cork is also a considerable port, mainly shipping agricultural produce. Its industries include brewing, foodstuffs, textiles, boots and shoes, and chemicals. There is also a shipyard.

HISTORY. – Cork's history began with the founding of a monastery by St Finbarr (7th c.) on a small alluvial island in the River Lee, where St Finbarr's Cathedral now stands. The monastery and the settlement which grew up around it flourished in spite of several Danish raids, and later were incorporated in the fortified base which the Danes developed here. After the arrival of the English King Henry II in Ireland in 1172 the town was several times captured, recovered and retaken, with the English and the Irish alternating as its masters. In 1284 it was surrounded by a new circuit of walls; in 1378 it was burned down by the Irish; in 1495 it was taken by Perkin Warbeck, the Yorkist Pretender to the English throne; and in 1642 it was captured by Irish insurgents, who were driven out of the city in 1644 and again in 1649. In 1690 the city walls were pulled down.

During the Civil War, in 1920, two mayors of Cork were killed and large areas of the city were damaged by fire.

As a result of this history of war and destruction Cork has preserved hardly any old buildings. It has, however, some fine 18th c. buildings, and the central area between the two arms of the river is given its architectural character by the churches and other buildings of the early 19th c. The house fronts are frequently colour-washed, and the quays along the river, with their limestone walls, are lined with trees.

Cork has a *Tourist Trail* marked out for visitors. A brochure describing it can be obtained from the Tourist Information Office.

Sightseeing in Cork

The following circuit through the central area will allow a visitor to see many of the city's features of interest: From St Patrick's Bridge, spanning the North Channel, Merchants' Quay and its continuation Anderson's Quay run east to the tip of the island, on which is the Custom House. Then along Lapp's Quay, on the South Channel, to Parnell Bridge, from which the city's principal commercial street, South Mall, continues west into the spacious Grand Parade. At the point where this joins the narrower Cornmarket Street turn right into St Patrick's Street, which leads back in a wide curve to St Patrick's Bridge.

Central Area

From Lapp's Quay there is a good view of *City Hall*, which has an assembly hall seating 2000, and its reflection in the sluggishly flowing river. Turning left off South Mall and following the bank of the South Channel, which here describes a sharp bend, we come to the *Father Matthew Memorial Church* (Holy Trinity Church, 1825), a neo-Gothic building designed by G. R. Pain. It commemorates the "Apostle of Temperance", Father Matthew (1790–1861), who preached the unpopular doctrine of abstinence and "made an idea into a crusade".

At Parliament Bridge we come back to South Mall, which has a number of buildings of the first half of the 19th c. To the south of the bridge, enclosed by later buildings in Abbey Street, is the *Red Abbey Tower*, one of the few relics of medieval monastic houses in Cork.

Near the Red Abbey Tower is *St Finbarr's Church*, also known as the South Chapel. Built in 1766, it has late 18th c. furnishings, including a figure of the dead Christ by Hogan.

Farther west, in Bishop Street, can be seen the prominent spires of *St Finbarr's Cathedral* (1865–80), in French Early Gothic style. It is richly decorated and furnished, with fine mosaics in the choir. Its eight bells, cast by Abel Rudhall of Gloucester, are from an earlier church of 1750 on the same site.

At the corner of South Mall and Grand Parade we come to the Cork Lending Library, with the Tourist Information Centre in Tourist House almost opposite it. In Grand Parade are a monument to Irish patriots of 1798–1867 and the Berwick Fountain. To the left, in Washington Street, stands *Holy Trinity Church*, also known as Christ Church (by Coltsman, 1720); it contains some relics of an earlier church, including the mid 16th c. tomb of Mayor Ronan and his wife. Two

View of Cork from St Anne's Church, Shandon

streets farther on, on the north side of Washington Street, is the *Court House* (1832), with a handsome portico.

Northern District

North-west of St Patrick's Bridge stands one of the city's landmarks, ***St Anne's Church, Shandon** (1722). Its handsome tower – which looks rather like a telescope drawn out in three stages and is also popularly known as the "pepperpot" – is of parti-coloured stone, red sandstone on the north and east sides, grey limestone on the other two. It contains eight bells cast by Abel Rudhall in 1750 and has a celebrated carillon; for a small charge visitors can ring the bells themselves. Although the tower is only 120 ft (36 m) high it affords a wide panorama of the city thanks to the church's elevated situation.

Two streets higher up is the neo-classical *St Mary's Cathedral* (1808). The interior was renewed in neo-Gothic style in 1820 after a fire.

To the east, in Old Youghal Road, lie *Collins Barracks*, with a three-light stained-glass window by Evie Hone (1939) in the chapel (seen by appointment).

South of the barracks, near Lower Glanmire Road, stands the Corinthian-style *St Patrick's Church* (by G. R. Pain, 1836), the effect of which is spoiled by an extension of 1894.

From here we go over Brian Boru Bridge to return to the island. To the right can be seen the large bus station, to the left the *Custom House* (1814), now the Harbourmaster's office.

Western and Southern Districts

From the Court House Liberty Street and Sheares Street lead into Mardyke Walk, which runs parallel to the River Lee. To the right, above the north bank of the river, is the *Sunday's Well* district, with houses picturesquely scattered about in the hills. Between Mardyke Walk and the river are sports grounds and the Fitzgerald Park, in which is the *Cork Public Museum* (Mon.–Fri. 11 a.m.–1 p.m. and 2.15–5 or 6 p.m.). The museum offers a comprehensive view of the history of the region from prehistoric times to the present day, and also has collections of silver, glass and the crochet-work and lace for which Cork was formerly celebrated.

Farther south, beyond Western Road and the South Channel, is the *University College* (founded 1845), part of the National University of Ireland, with some 4000 students. Many of the neo-classical buildings are well preserved; particularly fine is the Gaol Gate (1818). The Honan Chapel has beautiful stained glass by Sarah Purser and Harry Clarke. The college possesses interesting collections (e.g. of ogham stones and early prints of Cork) which can be seen by appointment.

On the way back to the city centre we can turn left off Dyke Parade into *Bachelor's Quay*, which has a number of fine Georgian houses along the river-front. Continuing along the quays, we come to Cornmarket Street (on the right).

Across the river to the north is the Dominican *St Mary's Church* (1832–39), on the High Altar of which is a miraculous image of the Virgin (14th c. Flemish work in ivory).

Cornmarket Street, with the Old Market, leads into Grand Parade (p. 92). To the left is *St Patrick's Street*, the city's main shopping street, built over an old arm of the river, extending in a wide arc to St Patrick's Bridge. To the left, in Emmet Place, is the *Crawford Municipal Art Gallery* (sculpture and modern Irish painting; Mon.–Sat. 10 a.m.–5 p.m.). Beyond this we come to the Opera House (1963). At the end of the street, on the corner of Lavitt's Quay, is a statue of Father Matthew, at a busy stop which is known simply as the "Statue".

SURROUNDINGS OF CORK. – 4½ miles (7 km) north-east of the city is *Riverstown House*, with sumptuously decorated rooms (open May–Sept. 10 a.m.–4 p.m.; admission charge).

South-east of Cork, surrounded by arms of the sea, lies Great Island, on the south coast of which is the port of *Cobh* (International Folk-Dance Festival). This relatively modern town, 15 miles (24 km) from Cork, was formerly an important port of call for ocean-going vessels. It is the headquarters of the Cork Yacht Club. There are facilities for all kinds of water-sports. – Above the harbour stands a richly decorated neo-Gothic cathedral.

In the area around *Cork Harbour*, a large, almost land-locked inlet south of Great Island, are fortifications of many different periods. There are also a number of little resorts the mild climate of which attracts many holiday-makers.

At the outer end of Passage West stands *Monkstown Castle* (17th c.: National Monument), now the clubhouse of a 9-hole golf-course.

The R609 and R612 run south to Carrigaline (8 miles (13 km)) and then east to *Crosshaven*, a popular holiday resort with good sandy beaches at the outflow of the River Owenboy into an inlet off Cork Harbour.

View south from the Dingle Peninsula

Dingle Peninsula

Map reference: D1/2.
Republic of Ireland.
Province: Munster. – County: Kerry.
ⓘ **Tourist Information Office,**
Dingle;
tel. (066) 5 11 88.
Open July and August.

HOTELS. – IN DINGLE: *Sceilig*, A, 79 r.; *Hillgrove*, C,
12 r.

GUEST-HOUSE. – *Alpine House*, B, 15 r.

RESTAURANTS. – IN DINGLE: *Doyle's Seafood Bar*,
John Street; *Half Door*, John Street; *Whelan's*, Main
Street.

**The Dingle Peninsula is the most
northerly of the hilly promontories
which reach out from the south-
western corner of Ireland, extending
westward for more than 30 miles
(50 km) from the low-lying country
around Tralee and Killorglin. The
highest point on the peninsula,
Brandon Mountain (3085 ft (940 m)),
rears up at the end of a chain of
hills which at Brandon Head plunge
almost straight into the sea from a
height of 2462 ft (750 m). To the west
of this range is a rolling coastal plain
studded with typical Irish villages
and hamlets. Here there are few
stone walls; corn is grown in small
square fields, and red fuchsia
hedges, pale green ferns and black
moss add their distinctive colour-
ings to the landscape.**

This is a predominantly Irish-speaking
area (Gaeltacht), and old traditions, customs and crafts are still very much alive.

The area is littered with prehistoric and
Early Christian remains, only the most
important of which can be mentioned
here.

SURROUNDINGS. – The road from Tralee runs west
along Tralee Bay to *Camp*. South-east of the village
rises Caherconree (2668 ft (813 m)), which can be
climbed by way of a western spur. At a height of
2000 ft (613 m) is a massive promontory fort, not
reached only by a steep and difficult ascent (not
recommended).

At Camp the R559 bears south-west and winds its
way up through hilly country. In 5 miles (8 km) a side
road branches off on the left and runs south to *Inch*, a
sheltered seaside resort from which a 3 mile (5 km)
long ridge of dunes extends into the sea.

4½ miles (7 km) west, around *Anascaul*, is an area
where wild orchids grow in great variety. The road
then continues on its way to Dingle between the

hills and the sea. 1½ miles (2·5 km) from the little
town it passes *Ballintaggart*, with an old circular burial
ground containing a number of ogham stones
(National Monument), some of them with crosses.

Dingle itself, the chief place on the
peninsula, lies in a sheltered bay with
good beaches, surrounded on three sides
by hills. It is an excellent centre for sea
fishing and boating, and also has a 9-hole
golf-course; but above all it is a good base
from which to visit the many antiquities at
the western end of the peninsula.

West of Dingle, at *Milltown*, is a large standing stone
known as the Milestone, and near this are two others,
the Gates of Glory. Continuing west, the road comes
to Ventry, 2 miles (3 km) north-west of which, on the
Ballyferriter road, are the ruins of *Rahinnane Castle*
(15th c.: National Monument), in a circular enclosure
surrounded by a 30 ft (9 m) deep moat.

From Ventry the road follows the rocky south coast.
On the left, directly above the sea (path to the site
dangerous!), is the fine promontory fort of *Dunbeg*,
with four earthen ramparts and a stone wall. Within
the fort are the remains of a house, square in plan
within its circular outside wall. An underground
passage leads from the interior of the fort to the outer
defences.

Near by, at *Glanfahan*, can be seen a remarkable group
of remains, including 417 beehive huts (built without
the use of mortar), 19 souterrains and 18 standing
stones (all National Monuments). A charge is made
for entry to some of the sites.

The south-western tip of the peninsula is formed by
Slea Head. From the narrow road below Mount Eagle
(1695 ft (517 m)) there are extensive views of the
cliffs and the offshore islands.

Slea Head

The **Blasket Islands** which lie off the end of the peninsula can be reached by boat, weather permitting, from the little fishing harbour of *Dunquin*. The main island, *Great Blasket*, was inhabited until 1953, when the inhabitants – said to have been, in their well-settled way of life, the "happiest people in the world" – were moved to the mainland. In the centre of the island are the ruins of a church (National Monument) of uncertain age. From the island's highest point (937 ft (285 m)) there is a view over Blasket Sound to the rugged coast of Kerry. One of the vessels of the Spanish Armada, the "Santa Maria de la Rosa", ran aground in the sound in 1588.

4 miles (6 km) north-west of Great Blasket lies the little island of *Inishtooskert*, with the ruins of a small church, a well-preserved beehive hut and three crosses (National Monuments).

At Clogher Head, a rocky promontory north of Slea Head, the road turns inland and runs north-east to *Ballyferriter* (Dún an Oir Hotel, B*, 22 r.). At *Reask*, amid the remains of a settlement of hermits, is a notable cross-pillar decorated with tendril patterns.

To the north of Ballyferriter is a broad inlet, *Smerwick Harbour*, on the east side of which, on a rock promontory, stands Dún an Oir, the "Fort of Gold". Here in 1580 600 Spanish and Irish soldiers who gave themselves up to English forces were massacred.

From Ballyferriter a road leads east to **Kilmalkedar**, one of the most important ecclesiastical sites on the peninsula, where a monastery (National Monument) was founded in the 7th c. It preserves a Romanesque church (12th c.) with fine sculpture in the tympanum of the doorway and on the chancel arch. The blind arcading in the interior – like the rest of the church – shows the influence of Cormac's Chapel at Cashel (see entry). In the church is the Alphabet Stone, with ogham and Latin characters side by side. In the churchyard can be seen an old sundial, a large monolithic cross and another ogham stone. 150 yd (140 m) away is St Brendan's House (15th c.), and near this St Brendan's Oratory.

2 miles (3 km) south-west we come to one of the few castles to have been preserved on the peninsula, *Gallarus Castle* (16th c.: National Monument), a four-storey keep with some vaulted rooms. $\frac{3}{4}$ mile (1 km) away is *Gallarus Oratory (National Monument). Shaped like an upturned boat, it has walls over 3 ft (1 m) thick, so carefully constructed, without the use of mortar, that the little chapel (measuring only 15 by 10 ft (4·5 by 3 m)) is still watertight after 1200 years.

On the coast north-west of Kilmalkedar lies the fishing village of *Ballydavid*, where the traditional currachs – light but seaworthy vessels of tarred canvas on a framework of laths – are still made.

At *Ballynavenooragh*, some distance inland at the foot of Brandon Mountain, can be found a large group of beehive huts, several of them double, and two stone ring-forts (all National Monuments). The coast at *Brandon Head*, where Masatiompan (2461 ft (750 m)) falls down to the sea, has a series of mighty cliffs.

On **Brandon Mountain** are the remains of St Brendan's Oratory and a number of stone huts (National Monuments). The climb (best tackled from Cloghane) is well worth the effort, for its own sake and for the magnificent views to be had from the top.

Cloghane lies on the east side of the hills, at the head of Brandon Bay. It can be reached direct from Dingle by a road over the *Connor Pass*, through a grandiose landscape of rugged gorges and steep rock faces. At the foot of the pass the road to the left leads to Cloghane and Brandon; the one straight ahead returns to Camp. To the right of this road is Beenoskee (2713 ft (827 m)), to the left a long promontory reaching out into the sea. The road continues to *Castlegregory*, a quiet little resort between Tralee Bay and Lough Gill. From here it is 4½ miles (7 km) to the tip of the promontory, *Rough Point*, off which is a group of small islands.

Donegal/Dún na nGall

Map reference: B3.
Republic of Ireland.
Province: Ulster. – County: Donegal.
Population: 2000.

ⓘ **Tourist Information Office,**
Donegal;
tel. (073) 2 11 48.
Open June to August.

HOTELS. – *Hyland Central*, A, 59 r.; *Abbey*, The Diamond, B*, 40 r.; *National*, C, 15 r.

RESTAURANT. – *Abbey Hotel*.

Gallarus Oratory

Donegal Castle

Donegal (Dún na nGall, "Fortress of the Foreigners"), county town of Co. Donegal, lies in Donegal Bay, near the north end of the Irish west coast, at the point where the River Eske flows into the bay and the N15 runs into the N56. Originally a Celtic settlement, the town owes its present form to the regular plan, centred on the market square appropriately called the Diamond, laid out by the British authorities in the early 17th c.

SIGHTS. – *Donegal Castle* (National Monument) is an imposing ruin situated on the rocky bank of the River Eske. The chief seat of the O'Donnells, princes of Tir Chonaill, it fell into English hands in 1607. The large square keep (1505) was then altered by the insertion of windows, and a splendid fireplace carved with coats of arms was constructed on the main floor. In 1610 a fortified manor-house was built on to the tower.

Picturesquely situated at the mouth of the River Eske are the remains of *Donegal Abbey*, a 15th c. Franciscan house (National Monument). Here the Four Masters, Michael O'Clery and his three assistants, compiled their celebrated "Annals" between 1630 and 1636. They are commemorated by an obelisk in the Diamond.

SURROUNDINGS. – 5 miles (8 km) north-east of the town is *Lough Eske*, which offers good fishing. From the north end of the lough, which is circled by a road, a detour can be made to a waterfall in a valley 2 miles (3 km) north. The valley climbs up into the *Blue Stack Mountains* and a beautiful little lough enclosed by high rock walls, *Lough Belshade*.

3 miles (5 km) south of Donegal on the N15 a road on the left (R232) leads to Pettigo, from which the R233 runs north through a barren landscape to *Lough Derg*. In the lough lies **Station Island**, known in the Middle Ages as St Patrick's Purgatory, to which there is an important pilgrimage every year. The churches and pilgrim hospices on the island can be seen from the shores of the lough. During the pilgrimage season (June–August) only pilgrims are allowed on the island.

In pagan times a cave on Station Island was believed to be the entrance to the Underworld. It gained its name of St Patrick's Purgatory when a travelling medieval knight claimed to have seen the fires of Purgatory in the cave.

The pilgrims who make what has been called the "hardest pilgrimage in Christendom" are now almost exclusively Irish. They spend three days on the island, performing the numerous penances prescribed, mainly vigils and fasting.

12 miles (18 km) south of Donegal, on the Atlantic, is *Rossnowlagh* (Sand House Hotel, A, 40 r.), a holiday resort with a beautiful sandy beach. The modern Franciscan friary houses the *Donegal Historical Society Museum* (daily 9 a.m.–6.30 p.m.), with Stone Age and Bronze Age material, including a finely wrought sword found during building work in the neighbouring town of Ballyshannon.

$4\frac{1}{2}$ miles (7 km) west of Donegal on the N56 is *Mountcharles*, on a steep-sided hill, with a beautiful view and good fishing in the Eany Water.

Drogheda/ Droichead Átha

Map reference: C5.
Republic of Ireland.
Province: Leinster. – County: Louth.
Population: 23,000.

(i) **Tourist Information Office,**
Drogheda;
tel. (041) 3 70 70.
Open July and August.

HOTELS. – *Boyne Valley*, Stameen, A, 20 r.; *Glenside*, Smithstown, B*, 15 r.; *Rossnaree*, B, 20 r.; *White Horse*, B, 18 r.

RESTAURANTS. – *Monasterboice Inn*; *Sennhof* (Boyne Valley Hotel); *Buttery* (Rossnaree Hotel).

Drogheda (Droichead Átha, "Bridge of the Ford") lies on the north-eastern Irish coast on the River Boyne, at the point where it is crossed by the N1 shortly before its outflow into the Irish Sea. With its port and and its various industries – cement works, steelworks, footwear – it is a considerable industrial centre.

HISTORY. – In 911 the Danes captured the little town, which occupied the site of an earlier settlement at a ford, and developed it into a well-defended stronghold. Later the Anglo-Normans built a bridge and fortified the settlements on both sides of the river. In the 14th and 15th c. Drogheda was one of the four principal towns of Ireland, with the right of coining and, from 1465, a university. Thereafter until the 17th c. Parliament met in Drogheda several times. In 1649 the town was taken by Cromwell's forces, and in 1690, after the Battle of the Boyne, it surrendered to William of Orange's troops.

SIGHTS. – The town had originally 10 gates, of which only one, **St Lawrence's Gate** (National Monument) in St Lawrence's Street, survives. It has two massive round towers with a loopholed connecting wall, a vaulted arch on the upper level and a barrel vault on street-level, all crenellated, enclosing the low entrance passage.

At the other end of St Lawrence's Street, on the left, is the old *Tholsel* (Town Hall), a domed building which is now occupied by a bank. To the right, at the corner of St Peter's Street and William Street, stands the handsome *St Peter's Church* (by Francis Johnston, 1748; Church of Ireland), which has fine Rococo plasterwork in the interior.

On the right-hand side of West Street, the continuation of St Lawrence's Street,

the neo-Gothic St Peter's Church (RC) was built in memory of St Oliver Plunkett, Archbishop of Armagh, who was executed at Tyburn in London in 1681. His embalmed head is in a reliquary in the church.

On the south side of the river, beyond the bridge at the end of Shop Street, *Millmount Fort* (National Monument) was built over a passage grave like Newgrange in the Boyne Valley (see entry); it was used as a Viking thing mote; fortified in the 12th c., it continued in use as a fort until 1800.

Lower downstream the river is spanned by the Boyne Viaduct, a fine example of railway engineering, built in 1932, virtually inside its 1851–55 predecessor.

SURROUNDINGS. – 4 miles (6 km) north-east of Drogheda, at *Baltray*, is a championship golf-course. There is also good bathing on a sandy beach 3 miles (5 km) long.

2 miles (3 km) farther north *Termonfeckin* boasts a three-storey tower house (15th c.: National Monument) which has a fine spiral staircase and an unusual vaulted roof, constructed in exactly the same fashion as the vault of Newgrange, 4000 years older. Beside St Feckin's Church is a richly decorated high cross (10th c.: National Monument): on the east side a Crucifixion, on the west side Christ in Glory, on the other sides geometric designs and interlace.

Just over a mile (2 km) beyond this we come to *Clogherhead*. On the north side of the promontory which ends in Clogher Head lies the little harbour of Port Oriel, with beautiful sandy beaches.

In *Dunleer*, 5 miles (8 km) north-west of Clogherhead, is the *Rathgory Transport Museum* (Sat. and Sun. 2–6 p.m.; admission charge), with a fine collection of veteran and vintage vehicles.

To the east of Drogheda, at Mornington on the Boyne Estuary, stands a lighthouse of the Elizabethen period known as the *Maiden Tower* (a reference to the Virgin Queen).

South-east of Drogheda, in Co. Meath, are the seaside resorts of *Bettystown* (Neptune Hotel, B, 32 r.; 18-hole golf-course) and *Laytown*. Both have beaches 6 miles (10 km) long.

Farther south, on the N1, *Gormanston*, a mansion of 1786, is now occupied by Franciscans. In the park, on the east side of the house, are an extensive system of walks and a "tea-house" of clipped yew hedges.

Inland from here, between the R108 and R152, can be seen the important prehistoric site of **Fourknocks** (1800–1500 B.C.: National Monument), consisting of a large passage grave and two smaller burial mounds. The large grave has a number of scribed stones, including one which depicts a face, drawn in a few simple strokes – the clearest representation of a human face in prehistoric Ireland.

5 miles (8 km) south-west of Drogheda, on the River Nanny (good fishing), lies *Duleek*, with the ruins of a

Mellifont Abbey

priory church and a high cross (National Monuments). The church contains a number of fine monuments and tomb carved with figures of saints, a Crucifixion, angels and coats of arms. The rather squat cross has a Crucifixion, various figures, ornaments and the symbols of the Evangelists. The *Dowdall Cross* (1601: National Monument) by the roadside shows continental influence; it has figures of saints and a coat of arms. – Bridge of 1587.

3 miles (5 km) south of Duleek stands *Athcarne Castle*, a fortified Elizabethan mansion of 1587.

2½ miles (4 km) north-west of Drogheda on the R168 (signposted to Collon), at Tullyallen, a side road on the left leads to Mellifont. Here, on the River Mattoch, are the ruins of *Mellifont Abbey (National Monument), once an important Cistercian house founded in 1142 and built with the help of French monks. By 1271 it had become the mother house of 24 other monasteries. After the Dissolution of the Monasteries (1539) it was converted into a fortified manor-house. Only a few remains of the original building have been preserved – a castle-like gatehouse with a massive tower, the fine crypt of the church, part of the two-storey lavabo in the cloister (arches reconstructed) and the finely vaulted chapterhouse (14th c.) in which a variety of architectural fragments are now kept. Part of the floor of the chapter-house has been laid with attractively patterned glazed tiles from the church. Stumps of walls and marks on the ground indicate that the abbey was laid out on the Clairvaux model.

Drumcliffe/Droim Chliabh

Map reference: B3.
Republic of Ireland.
Province: Connacht. – County: Sligo.
ⓘ **Tourist Information Office,**
Aras Reddan, Temple Street,
Sligo;
tel. (071) 6 12 01.

The village of Drumcliffe (Droim Chliabh, "Back of the Baskets") lies in the deep bay of the same name in north-west Ireland, just to the north of Sligo. St Columba founded a monastery here in 574, the last Abbot of which died in 1503.

SIGHTS. – The grandfather of W. B. Yeats was for many years the parish priest here, and the great Irish poet is buried in the churchyard. His gravestone bears the inscription which he himself composed:

> Cast a cold eye
> On life, on death:
> Horseman, pass by!

On the path leading to the church is a *high cross* (National Monument) of about 1000. On the east side are Adam and Eve, Daniel in the Lions' Den and

Benbulben

Christ in Glory, on the west side the Presentation in the Temple, two figures and the Crucifixion; the cross is also decorated with fabulous beasts and interlace ornament.

SURROUNDINGS. – To the north of the village *Benbulben (1697 ft (517 m)), a flat-topped hill with steeply scarped sides furrowed by gullies, rises abruptly out of the plain. This extraordinary table mountain features prominently in Irish legend. Here Queen Maeve and the Ulster hero CuChulainn fought for possession of a herd of great cattle, and here Diarmaid bled to death after his struggle with the great mountain boar of Benbulben. The slopes of the hill were also the scene of a historical event, the "Battle of the Books" in 561, which was followed by St Columba's departure from Ireland.

The hill, which forms part of the Dartry Mountains, is of interest to geologists and botanists. From the top there are extensive views over the plain and the Atlantic.

4 miles (6 km) west of Drumcliffe, in a park, is *Lissadell House* (open May–Sept., Mon.–Sat. 2.30–5.15 p.m.; admission charge), built in 1834 for the grandfather of Countess Constance Markievicz and her sister Eva Gore-Booth. Countess Markievicz (*née* Gore-Booth) became involved in politics in Dublin and took part in the 1916 Rising. Eva Gore-Booth was a writer. Yeats, who wrote a poem about Constance, stayed in the house on several occasions.

South-west of Lissadell a small peninsula reaches out into Drumcliffe Bay. On it, at the fishing village of Raghly, are the *Pigeon Holes* – two holes in the rock into which the sea is driven with enormous force through underground channels.

Also in this area are the picturesque ruins of Ardtermon Castle (17th c.).

5 miles (8 km) north of Drumcliffe on the N15 is Grange, from which a side road runs west to Streedagh. There a boat can be hired to go to the island of **Inishmurray** (which can also be reached from Mullaghmore, below).

The island, 4½ miles (7 km) west of Streedagh, was still inhabited in the earlier part of this century. On it is an excellently preserved monastic establishment (National Monument) founded by St Molaise in the early 6th c. and abandoned 300 years later after being raided and plundered. The monastic buildings were used by the later inhabitants and were thus preserved. The remains give an excellent impression of what such a settlement was like. A ring-wall between 10 and 15 ft (3 and 4 m) high and of the same thickness at the base, with five entrances, surrounds an oval precinct measuring 60 by 45 yd (53 by 41 m) divided into four enclosures of differing sizes. Within the precinct are the Men's Church, the little Oratory of Teach Molaise, the Church of the Fire, a beehive hut and altar-like masonry structures. On one of these are the famous Curse Stones, round speckled stones which are believed to be effective in putting a curse on an enemy. All round the island are various memorial stones and station chapels, which were visited by pilgrims in a prescribed sequence. From St Patrick's Memorial, at the eastern tip of the island, there is a fine view of the mainland.

5 miles (8 km) north of Grange, near the village of Cliffoney, is the *Creevykeel Court Cairn (National Monument), one of the finest in Ireland. A wedge-shaped stone wall encloses an open court, beyond which are a double-chambered gallery, two other chambers and remains of still another. The site is thought to be about 4500 years old.

From Cliffoney a minor road leads on to the *Mullaghmore Peninsula* (Beach Hotel, B, 20 r.), with a sheltered sandy beach, a boating harbour and good sea fishing. The hotel arranges trips to the island of Inishmurray (above).

Dublin/Baile Átha Cliath/Dubhlinn

Map reference: C5.
Republic of Ireland.
Province: Leinster. – County: Dublin.
Population: 978,000 (including suburbs).

ⓘ **Tourist Information Office,**
14 Upper O'Connell Street and
51 Dawson Street,
Dublin;
tel. (01) 74 77 33.
Dublin Airport;
tel. (01) 37 63 87–88 and 37 55 33.

HOTELS. – *Burlington*, Upper Leeson Street, A*, 472 r.; *Jury's*, Pembroke Road, A*, 310 r.; *Berkeley Court*, Lansdowne Road, A*, 262 r.; *Shelbourne*, 27 St Stephen's Green, A*, 166 r.; *Westbury*, Clarendon Street, A*, 134 r.; *Montrose*, Stillorgan Road, A, 190 r.; *Dublin International*, A, 187 r.; *Gresham*, O'Connell Street, A, 179 r.; *Royal Dublin*, O'Connell Street, A, 110 r.; *Skylon*, Upper Drumcondra Road, A, 88 r.; *Bloom's*, Anglesea Street, A, 86 r.; *Tara Tower*, Merrion Road, A, 84 r.; *Green Isle*, Naas Road, A, 74 r.; *Ashling*, Parkgate Street, A, 56 r.; *Marine*, Sutton, A, 27 r.; *Sachs*, Morehampton Road, A, 20 r.; *Clarence*, 6–8 Wellington Quay, B*, 70 r.; *Wynn's*, Lower Abbey Street, B*, 64 r.; *North Star*, Amiens Street, B*, 36 r.; *Ormond*, Upper Ormond Quay, B, 70 r.; *Powers*, Kildare Street, B, 30 r.; *Lansdowne*, Pembroke Road, B, 28 r.; *Hollybrook*, Howth Road, B, 26 r.; *Waldorf*, 11 Eden Quay, B, 24 r.

GUEST-HOUSES. – *Mount Herbert*, 7 Herbert Road, A, 88 r.; *Egan's*, 7–9 Iona Park, A, 23 r.; *Aerial*, 52 Lansdowne Road, A, 15 r.; *Iona House*, 5 Iona Park, A, 14 r.; *Kilronan House*, 70 Adelaide Road, A, 11 r.

RESTAURANTS. – *Amory Grand*, 39 Arran Quay; *Bailey*, 2–4 Duke Street; *Berkeley Room* (Berkeley Court Hotel), Lansdowne Road; *Blazes Boylan Grill Room* (Bloom's Hotel), Anglesea Street; *Celtic Mews*, 109A Lower Baggot Street; *Coq Hardi*, 35 Pembroke Road; *Granary Buffet*, 34–37 East Essex Street; *Grey Door*, 23 Upper Pembroke Street; *Jonathan's*, Irish Life Mall; *Kish* (Jury's Hotel), Pembroke Road; *Lock's*, 1 Windsor Terrace; *Lord Edward Seafood Restaurant*, 23 Christchurch Place; *Mitchell's Cellars*, 21 Kildare Street; *Murph's*, 99 Lower Baggot Street; *Murph's*, 21 Bachelors Walk; *Old Dublin*, 91 Francis Street; *Snaffles*, 47 Lower Leeson Street; *Solomon Grundy's*, 21 Suffolk Street; *Stag's Head*, 2 Dame Court; *Tandoori Rooms*, 27 Lower Leeson Street; *Unicorn*, 12B Merrion Court.

PUBS. – See Practical Information, Pubs.

EVENTS. – *Grand Opera Season* (Apr.); *Spring Show and Industrial Fair* (May); *Feis Ceoil* (folk-music, May); *Festival of Music in Great Irish Houses* (June); *International Folk Festival* (July); *Antiques Fair*; *Dublin Horse Show* (Aug.); *All Ireland Hurling and Gaelic Football Finals* (Sept.); *City Marathon* (Oct.); *Grand Opera Society Winter Season* (Dec.).

TRANSPORT. – Dublin International Airport is 5 miles north of the city on the N1; the town terminal is in the Bus Station (Busarus), Store Street.

There are two main railway stations, Heuston Station at Heuston Bridge (Kingsbridge) with services to Cork, Limerick, Galway, Waterford and Westport and Connolly Station in Amiens Street with services to Belfast, Sligo and Wexford. There is a direct bus service between the two stations.

The terminal for the car ferry service between Dublin and Liverpool is reached by East Wall and Alexandra Road. Sailings to Holyhead in summer.

Most city and suburban bus services pass through the city centre, long-distance services start from the Bus Station (Busarus) in Store Street.

POST OFFICE. – The General Post Office is in O'Connell Street, at the corner of Henry Street. Poste restante mail can be collected between 8 a.m. and 8 p.m.

Dublin (Baile Átha Cliath, "Town of the Hurdle Ford", or Dubhlinn, "Dark Pool") lies in the wide sweep of Dublin Bay, between the rocky promontory of Howth in the north and the headland of Dalkey to the south. The River Liffey, which flows into the harbour, divides the city into a northern and a southern half, with the city centre shared between the two. The river is spanned by a number of bridges, the most important of which is the O'Connell Bridge. Upstream the Father Matthew Bridge marks the position of the ancient ford over the Liffey.

Dublin is the capital of the Republic of Ireland, and in spite of the vicissitudes of Irish history, which have inevitably had their effect on the city, it has preserved all the air of a capital in its atmosphere and the way of life of its citizens.

The architectural character of Dublin is set not only by the numerous public buildings of the 18th and early 19th c., whose neo-classical façades and domes bear witness to the skills of architects such as Sir Edward Lovett Pearce, Richard Cassels, Thomas Cooley, James Gandon and Francis Johnston, but also by the numerous private houses of the same period, in a plain but elegant style which gives architectural unity to street after street. Many of these houses have already disappeared and others are threatened with destruction. The city is in an age of change – the result of the still-recent achievement of independence and also of new and closer links with other countries, combined with a modest but growing prosperity. Old buildings which have fallen into a state of disrepair are being pulled down and replaced by new but not usually better ones. Nevertheless there is

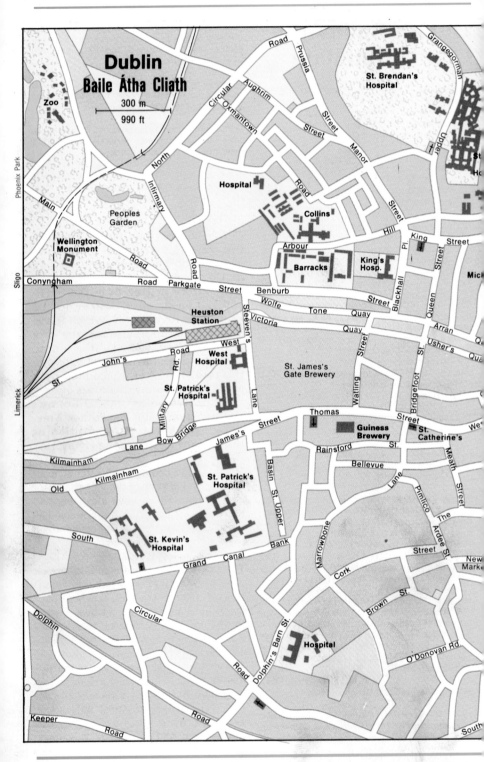

Dublin
Baile Átha Cliath
300 m
990 ft

also a recognition of the values which many of these older buildings represent, and efforts are being made to save them and adapt them to serve new purposes.

HISTORY. – The oldest Irish name of the city and the one still generally used, Baile Átha Cliath, refers to the ancient ford which crossed the Liffey here. The place is mentioned by the classical geographer Ptolemy in A.D. 140 under the name of Eblana. St Patrick is believed to have visited Dublin in 448 and converted many of the inhabitants. Subsequently a Christian community grew up around the ford; then in 840 a first party of Danes occupied the town and established a fortified base for their raiding and trading activities. Their power was broken by Brian Boru's victory at Clontarf in 1014, but it was not until 1170 that the

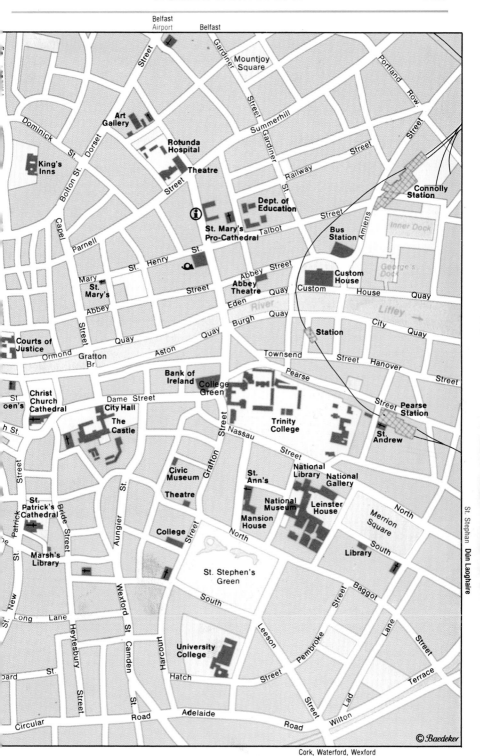

Belfast
Airport Belfast

Mountjoy Square

Art Gallery

Rotunda Hospital

Theatre

King's Inns

Dominick St.

Dorset

Bolton St.

Capel

St.

Parnell

Mary St. Henry

St. Mary's Abbey

Courts of Justice

Ormond Gratton Br.

Christ Church Cathedral

St. oen's

h St.

City Hall

Dame Street

The Castle

Civic Museum

Theatre

St. Patrick's Cathedral

Bride Street

Marsh's Library

New

Long Lane

Heytesbury Street

bard St.

Circular

Gardiner Street

Summerhill

Gardiner Street

Railway St.

Talbot

St. Mary's Pro-Cathedral

Dept. of Education

Street

Abbey Street

Abbey Theatre Quay

Eden Quay

Burgh Quay

River Liffey

Aston Quay

Townsend Street

Pearse

Bank of Ireland College Green

Gratton

Nassau Street

Street

Trinity College

National Library National Gallery

St. Ann's

National Museum Leinster House

Mansion House

College St.

North

St. Stephen's Green

South

University College

Hatch Street

Adelaide Road

Aungier St.

Wexford St.

Camden St.

Harcourt St.

Road

Portland Row

Street

Connolly Station

Inner Dock

Bus Station

Amiens

Custom House

Custom House Quay

City Quay

George's Dock

Station

Hanover Street

Street

Street Pearse Station

St. Andrew

Merrion Square

North

South

Library

Baggot Street

Leeson Street

Pembroke Street

Lad Lane

North

Terrace

Wilton Road

© Baedeker

St. Stephan **Dún Laoghaire**

Cork, Waterford, Wexford

Danes were driven out by the Anglo-Normans. Two years later Henry II came to Dublin to receive the homage of the Irish chieftains. The town now became the capital of the area under English control, the Pale, which was defended by the castles of Anglo-Norman knights. During the conflicts of the 15th and 16th c. the Dubliners usually supported the opponents of the English king. In the 17th c., however, they sided with the Royalists against Cromwell – who captured the

town in 1649 – and later with James II against William of Orange.

In 1697 public street lighting was introduced.

In the 18th c. Dublin prospered, and the population rose from 65,000 to 200,000. A Wide Street Commission and a Paving Board were established to promote the development and improvement of the city, and there was a great boom in building both by public authorities and by Dublin's prosperous citizens.

At the beginning of the 19th c. a brief period of independence was brought to an end by the political union with Great Britain. There followed a time of repression and resistance: in 1844 the Lord Mayor of Dublin, Daniel O'Connell, was imprisoned for "incitement to discontent", and a few years later the leaders of the Land League movement, among them Charles Stuart Parnell, were thrown into Kilmainham Gaol. Political assassinations were carried out by a secret society, and separatist agitation grew.

In 1916 the Easter Rising took place in Dublin, and the General Post Office and other public buildings were occupied by the rebels. In 1919, on the initiative of the Sinn Féin (We Ourselves) movement, an independent parliament met in the Mansion House, presided over by Eamon de Valera. On 25 May 1921, during the Civil War, the Custom House was set on fire. In spite of the ratification of the treaty of January 1922, which established the Irish Free State, domestic conflict continued in Dublin until 1927. It was not until 1931 that most of the public buildings were restored.

During the Second World War Ireland remained neutral. In 1941, however, some German bombs were dropped in error on Dublin, killing 37 people.

Sightseeing in Dublin

A number of *Tourist Trails* are signposted in the city centre; a brochure about them can be obtained from Tourist Information Offices.

Street names are shown in both English and Irish. In many of the older streets the houses are still numbered in a continuous sequence, up one side and down the other.

Although apart from the two cathedrals few Dublin buildings are older than the 18th c., the city's handsome Georgian streets and squares, its public buildings, museums and libraries offer so much interest that they are best seen in a series of separate tours. A good starting-point is *O'Connell Bridge*, which spans the Liffey (here 45 yd (42 m) wide) in the centre of the city. Built in 1792–94, it was widened in 1880. The river, flanked by quays on both sides in its passage through the city, is crossed by a total of 10 road bridges.

Central Area – South-East

At the south end of the O'Connell Bridge the street forks. D'Olier Street, to the left, leads south-east into Pearse Street. Westmoreland Street, straight ahead, runs in a gentle curve to College Green, with the main entrance to *Trinity College, in spacious park-like grounds which are open to the public. In front of the 300 ft (90 m) long Palladian façades are statues of Oliver Goldsmith and Edmund Burke

Trinity College

Trinity College Dublin

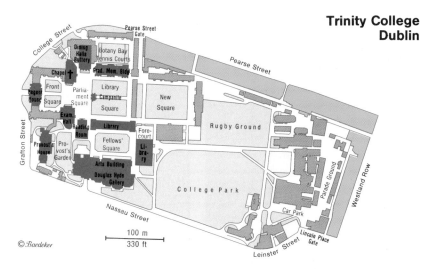

(by Henry Foley, 1863 and 1865). The university, founded by Elizabeth I in 1591, was confined to Protestants until 1793, and Roman Catholics were excluded from fellowships and scholarships until 1873. In 1903 women were admitted to degrees for the first time. Alumni of Trinity College have included Samuel Beckett, Edmund Burke, Robert Emmet, Oliver Goldsmith, Jonathan Swift, J. M. Synge and Oscar Wilde. It has now over 5000 students.

After the noisy traffic of College Green the entrance courtyard of Trinity College is a haven of peace. On the left stands the Chapel (since 1973 open to all denominations which have a university chaplain), on the right the Examination Hall (1779–91; originally a theatre), both designed by Sir William Chambers. Beyond the Chapel is the Dining Hall (by Richard Cassels, 1743), which is hung with portraits of notable members of the university. In the second courtyard is a piece of sculpture by Henry Moore.

Beyond this lies Library Square, on the right-hand side of which is the *Old Library (1712–32; open Mon.–Fri. 9.30 a.m.–4.45 p.m., Sat. 9.30 a.m.–12.45 p.m.; admission charge). Since 1801 the library has been a copyright library, i.e. it is entitled to receive a copy of every book published in Ireland and Great Britain. It now has some 5000 manuscripts and 2,000,000 printed books.

Among its principal treasures are the important manuscripts kept in the Manuscript Room, incunabula and other early printed books. From the ground floor a handsome staircase by Richard Cassels

leads up to the Long Room, 200 ft (60 m) long with a timber barrel-vaulted roof. Here precious illuminated manuscripts are displayed, including the ***"Book of Kells" (8th c.), the ***"Book of Durrow" (7th c.), the "Book of Dimma" (8th c.) and the "Book of Armagh" (9th c., with an 11th c. leather binding). The "Book of Kells", a manuscript of the four Gospels, has 340 sumptuously decorated pages, one of which is on show each day; the beginnings of the Gospels and of individual chapters have particularly elaborate decoration. Also on display in the Long Room is an Irish harp, one of the earliest of its kind. Attached to the library is a bookshop, where a wide range of facsimiles are on sale.

South-east of the Old Library is the New Library (by Paul Koralek, 1967).

To the rear of the New Library, with its façade on Nassau Street, stands the Arts Building, with the Douglas Hyde Gallery (contemporary Irish art, etc.).

On the east side of Library Square are Trinity College's oldest buildings, the Rubrics (1690), in red brick.

Another notable building is Richard Cassels's Printing House (1732) in New Square.

Around College Park with its sports pitches are other university buildings.

To the east of Trinity College, in Westland Row, is the handsome neo-classical St Andrew's Church (1832–37). Immediately adjoining it is Pearse Station

Crucifixion (7th c.)

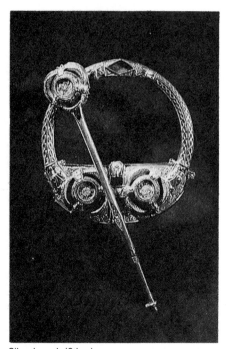

Silver brooch (8th c.)

(services to Wexford). From here Pearse Street leads past the main building of Dublin City Library and over the Grand Canal (with its docks to the left) to *Shelbourne Park*, with a greyhound-racing track.

Facing the main entrance to Trinity College is the large building now occupied by the **Bank of Ireland**, originally designed (by Sir Edward Lovett, 1729) to house the Irish Parliament but in 1820, after the Act of Union, sold to the Bank of Ireland. The curving façade with its different orders and sculpture groups – resulting from alterations carried out at different times – ranks as one of Dublin's finest. The noble banking hall, converted from the Old Commons' Chamber, can be seen during banking hours. Visitors are sometimes admitted in small groups to the former Lords' Chamber, which has a coffered ceiling and a fine chandelier.

From the Bank of Ireland Grafton Street runs south. In 164 yd (160 m) Nassau Street branches off on the left, running alongside the grounds of Trinity College and into Leinster Street and Clare Street. Off Nassau Street, on the right, is Kildare Street, which leads to a complex of important buildings – the National Library, Leinster House and the National Museum.

The *National Library* (1890), to the left of the entrance gateway, has collections of early printed books (notably 17th c. Irish literature), old maps and topographical works, and a newspaper archive.

To the right of the gateway is the ****National Museum** (open Mon.–Thu. 10 a.m.–5 or 9 p.m., Fri. 10 a.m.–5 p.m., Sat. 10 a.m.–1 p.m.), which has a rich collection of Irish antiquities from pre-historic times to the end of the medieval period.

At present, when new rooms are being opened and old ones renovated, exhibits are liable to be moved around and some rooms may be closed.

The entrance rotunda (used for special exhibitions) leads into the Great Hall. Among the most notable items to be seen here are gold jewellery, mainly of the Bronze Age; 11th and 12th c. crosiers; the *Ardagh Chalice* (early 8th c.), silver with gilt ornament, enamel and glass decoration, gold filigree handles; among the processional crosses, the *Cross of Cong* (1123), of oak with silver and gilt-bronze animal ornament; among a number of shrines, the *Shrine of St Patrick's Bell* (12th c.), decorated with silver gilt, gold filigree and ornamental stones; and various reliquaries, including the *Breac*

Cross of Cong (12th c.)

Bell shrine (10th–15th c.)

Maodhóg Reliquary (11th c.), with an exact depiction of the dress of the period.

In the gallery of the Great Hall are antiquities covering a period of more than 7000 years (c. 6000 B.C.–A.D. 1000). Particular treasures to be seen here are the *Tara Brooch* (700–750), of gilt silver, inlaid with silver, copper and enamel, and the *Moylough Belt Shrine* (8th c.), a reliquary of silvered bronze with enamel ornament designed to be attached to a belt.

There are also a number of ogham stones. A collection of sheila-na-gigs (female figures in obscene postures) can be seen on application.

On the upper floor are metal objects, glass, textiles and ceramics. Of particular interest are the cases displaying Irish silver.

To the rear of the Library and Museum, set back from the street, stands **Leinster House**, the Republic's Parliament, the seat of the Dáil Éireann (House of Representatives) and Seanad Éireann (Senate). This sober and dignified building (by Richard Cassels, 1745) was originally the town house of the Dukes of Leinster. Visitors are admitted when Parliament is not sitting (entrance in Kildare Street).

Behind Leinster House, to the left, is the ****National Gallery** (Mon.–Sat. 10 a.m.–6 p.m., Thu. to 9 p.m., Sun. 2–5 p.m.), with the entrance in Merrion Square, to the south-east. Originally opened in 1864, the gallery has since been extended, most recently in 1968.

In addition to representative works by Irish painters the collection, displayed on the ground and upper floors, includes works by American, British, Dutch, Flemish, French, German, Italian and Spanish artists. Among them are:
Irish: George Barrett, James Barry, Francis Darnby, Nathaniel Hore the Elder and Younger, Robert Hunter, James Latham, James Arthur O'Connor, Walter Osborne, Thomas Roberts, Patrick Tuohy, Jack Butler Yeats (W. B. Yeats's brother), John Butler Yeats (the poet's father).
American: J. S. Sargent, Gilbert Stuart, Benjamin West, J. M. Whistler.
British: John Constable, Thomas Gainsborough, William Hogarth, Thomas Lawrence, Henry Raeburn, Joshua Reynolds, William Turner.
Dutch: Peter Claesz, Jan van Goyen, Pieter de Hooch, Jan Steen, Rembrandt, Salomon and Jacob van Ruisdael, Emanuel de Witte.
Flemish: Gerard David, Anthony Van Dyck, Jacob Jordaens, Rubens, Jan Van Scorel, David Teniers the Younger.

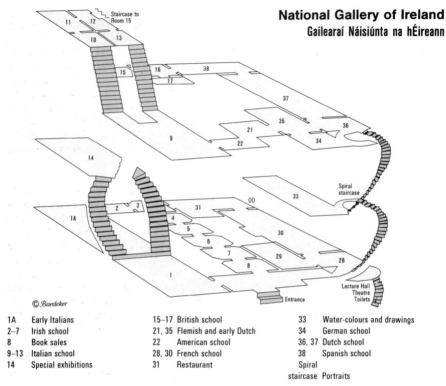

National Gallery of Ireland
Gailearaí Náisiúnta na hÉireann

© *Baedeker*

1A	Early Italians	15–17	British school	33	Water-colours and drawings
2–7	Irish school	21, 35	Flemish and early Dutch	34	German school
8	Book sales	22	American school	36, 37	Dutch school
9–13	Italian school	28, 30	French school	38	Spanish school
14	Special exhibitions	31	Restaurant	Spiral	
				staircase	Portraits

French: Camille Corot, Edgar Degas, Eugène Delacroix, Claude Lorrain, Jean-François Millet, Claude Monet, Alfred Sisley.
German: Lucas Cranach the Elder, Wolfgang Huber.
Italian: Fra Angelico, Giovanni Bellini, Michelangelo, Tintoretto, Titian, Veronese.
Spanish: Goya, El Greco, Murillo, Zurbarán.

The gallery has large numbers of portraits. The older portraits of prominent figures in Irish history, formerly hung in the front rooms, are now in Malahide Castle, 9 miles (14 km) north of Dublin. The more recent ones, including portraits of Brendan Behan, Roger Casement, Eamon de Valera, James Joyce, Sean O'Casey, George Bernard Shaw, J. M. Synge, Oscar Wilde, Charles Stuart Parnell and W. B. Yeats, are in Room 14 (reached from Room 1A).

There are also a fine collection of miniatures (Room 29), a series of portrait miniatures on the upper ground floor and an important collection of water-colours, also on the upper ground floor (Room 32), which can be seen only by appointment. The gallery also possesses 31 water-colours by Turner which, under the terms of the donor's bequest, can be displayed only during the month of January to avoid over-exposure to light; they can, however, be seen by appointment during the rest of the year.

16th c. to the present day, including works by Auguste Rodin and Aristide Maillol.

On the ground floor of the gallery are a book counter and a restaurant, and in the basement a library and lecture hall.

To the south-west of the National Gallery lies Leinster Lawn, with a monument commemorating the founders of the Irish Free State (including Arthur Griffith, the first Prime Minister). This opens into elegant *Merrion Square*, which is surrounded on three sides by handsome Georgian houses. Among residents in the square have been Oscar Wilde's parents, Daniel O'Connell and W. B. Yeats. On the west side of the square is the Rutland Fountain (1791).

From the south-east corner of the square Fitzwilliam Street runs south to *Fitzwilliam Square* (c. 1825), Dublin's best-preserved Georgian square. Fitzwilliam Street is also Georgian, with the additional attraction of a view of the Wicklow Mountains on the horizon.

Another thoroughfare of architectural interest is *Upper Mount Street*, which also leaves the south-east corner of Merrion Square. Passing St Stephen's Church (1824), it continues to the old Huband Bridge (1791) over the *Grand Canal* (see entry).

Turning right from the National Gallery and continuing along Upper Merrion Street, we come to the *Natural History Museum* (Thu.–Sat. 10 a.m.–5 p.m., Sun. 2–5 p.m.), which has a large collection displaying the fauna of Ireland (including skeletons of prehistoric animals). It also contains the Blashka Collection (glass models of marine creatures). Opposite the museum, at No. 24, is the house in which the Duke of Wellington was born.

Farther south along Upper Merrion Street, beyond Merrion Row, we come to *Ely Place*, a cul-de-sac of elegant Georgian houses of about 1770. The finest is Ely House (No. 8), with a handsome staircase and good stucco ceilings; it is now the headquarters of the Knights of Columbanus.

Opposite Ely House Hume Street leads to the east side of *St Stephen's Green*, a 20 acre (9 ha) park with flower-beds, ponds and a variety of monuments, including a fountain ("The Three Fates") by Joseph Wackerle, a gift from the German people in thanksgiving for Irish help in relieving distress after the Second World War, and a memorial stone to W. B. Yeats by Henry Moore. The park is a popular resort of Dubliners, particularly during the midday break (deck-chairs can be hired); there are lunchtime concerts of Irish music in July and August.

On the south side of the square are the *Department of External Affairs* (Iveagh House, No. 80), with a large garden; Clanwilliam House (No. 85, by Richard Cassels) and Newman House (No. 86, by Robert West), both now part of University College, and the Roman Catholic University Church (1854), in neo-Byzantine style.

Immediately south of these buildings stands *University College*. The Republic of Ireland has two universities, Trinity College and the National University of Ireland, to which University College in Dublin and colleges in Cork and Galway belong. Particular attention is given at this university to the Irish language. Following the considerable expansion of University College the original buildings in Earlsfort Terrace now house only the faculties of medicine and architecture; the rest of the university occupies a new site at *Belfield*, 3 miles (5 km) south-east on the N1, on a spacious campus developed since the mid 1960s, with some interesting modern buildings. The old Aula Maxima at Earlsfort Terrace is now the National Concert Hall.

In Dawson Street, to the north of St Stephen's Green, are the *Mansion House* (1705), seat of the Lord Mayor since 1715, with the Round Room (by John Semple, 1821), and the *Royal Irish Academy*, with a library (open Mon. 9.30 a.m.–5.30 or 8 p.m., Tue.–Fri. 9.30 a.m.–5.30 p.m.; closed in second half of August) which contains a priceless collection of manuscripts of the 6th to the 17th c., including the "Cathach", a psalter possibly written by St Columcille. Visitors normally see only facsimiles; the originals can be seen by special arrangement.

Also in Dawson Street is *St Ann's Church* (by Isaac Wills, 1720), with a mid 19th c. neo-Romanesque façade and good woodwork in the interior.

On the west side of St Stephen's Green stands the Royal College of Surgeons (1806). From the north-west corner of the square *Grafton Street*, Dublin's principal shopping and commercial street, runs north, back to Trinity College.

Before returning to Trinity College, however, a detour can be made from the north-west corner of St Stephen's Green along South King Street, which runs west to South William Street, with the *Civic Museum* (originally headquarters of the Society of Artists, built 1765–71; Tue.–Sat. 10 a.m.–6 p.m., Sun. 11 a.m.–2 p.m.; exhibition of old plans, models, etc., of Dublin in the Octagonal Room).

Farther along the street we come to *Powerscourt House*, an imposing mansion (1771–74) built by Robert Mack for Viscount Powerscourt, now converted to commercial purposes (Powerscourt Town House Centre). The beautiful stucco work in the staircase hall, main hall and reception rooms can be seen on application.

The extension of South William Street leads back by way of College Green to Trinity College.

Central Area – South-West

From O'Connell Bridge we go right, along the Liffey quays with the painted doorways of their Georgian houses, to Grattan Bridge and turn left into Parliament Street, which leads to City Hall and Dublin Castle. Alternatively we can go past the Bank of Ireland and along College Green, Dublin's old main street, in the centre of which is a handsome fountain with a statue of Thomas Davis (by Edward Delaney, 1966); then along Dame Street to the City Hall.

The **City Hall** (by Thomas Cooley, 1769–79), an imposing domed building, was originally the Royal Exchange. In the entrance hall are statues of local notabilities. In the Muniment Room are the city archives, including royal charters, the earliest of which (1172) grants the territory of Dublin to the city of Bristol.

Beyond the City Hall stands **Dublin Castle**, the main entrance of which is on Cork Hill. The hill now occupied by the Upper Yard was probably the site of a Celtic and later a Danish fort. In 1204 King John began the construction of a castle (completed 1226) of which little survives, much altered, in the present building. From the reign of Elizabeth I to the establishment of the Irish Free State in

1921 the Castle was the seat of the Viceroy and the headquarters of British administration.

To the right of the main entrance is the Genealogical Office, where people of Irish descent can seek to trace their ancestry. The *State Apartments* (Mon.–Fri. 10 a.m.–12.15 p.m. and 2–5 p.m., Sat. and Sun. 2–5 p.m.; admission charge) are shown to visitors in a conducted tour lasting about half an hour (entrance in Upper Yard, opposite the main entrance to the Castle). Notable features are the colourful Donegal and Killybegs carpets, the chandeliers of Waterford glass and the pavement of green Connemara marble in the entrance hall. (If you want to see the State Apartments it is advisable to check in advance that they will be open, since the Castle is frequently closed at short notice.) The conducted tour takes in the following rooms; St Patrick's Hall, with a painted ceiling (1778) and the banners of the Knights of St Patrick; the blue Wedgwood Room, with paintings by Angelica Kauffmann (?); the Picture Gallery, with portraits of Viceroys; the Throne Room, richly decorated in gold (1740), with an 18th c. throne; the long State Drawing Room with its original furniture; and the Apollo Room or Music Room, with a ceiling of 1746.

At the east end of the Upper Yard a passage leads into the Lower Yard. On the right of this is the Record Tower, one of the four old corner towers, well preserved with its 16 ft (5 m) thick walls, which

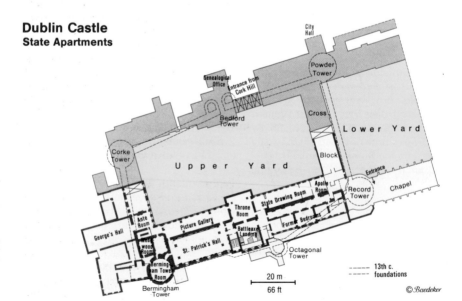

Dublin Castle
State Apartments

Throne Room, Dublin Castle

gives some impression of what the medieval castle was like. The neo-Romanesque Chapel (1807–14) is notable for its unusual external decoration of over a hundred limestone heads of famous Irishmen.

From the Castle a narrow street, Castle Street, runs west. At Nos 7–8 is the entrance to little *St Werburgh's Church* (1759), with a beautiful interior which can be seen by appointment (tel. 72 06 73).

Castle Street leads into Christchurch Place, in which is one of Dublin's two principal churches, **Christ Church Cathedral** (open May–Sept., Mon.–Fri. 9.30 a.m.–5 p.m., Sat. to 12.45 p.m.;

Christ Church Cathedral

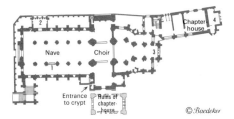

1 Tomb of Strongbow
2 Baptistery
3 Lady Chapel
4 Library

20 m
66 ft

Oct.–Apr., Tue.–Fri. 9.30 a.m.–12.45 p.m. and 2–5 p.m., Sat. to 12.45 p.m.), the cathedral of the Anglican dioceses of Dublin and Glendalough. In its present form it is the result of a major reconstruction in 1871–78; of the original 13th c. church there remain the crypt, which extends under the whole length of the nave, a doorway in the south transept and perhaps parts of the transepts. Enough remains, however, including some sculpture, to give some impression of the magnificence of the old church. The crypt contains numerous architectural fragments of different periods and 17th c. statues of Charles II and James II. In the nave is a fine recumbent tomb effigy of a knight, identified as Strongbow, and beside this a small half-length figure wrongly described as ''Strongbow's Son''.

Other monuments in the choir include the tomb of a 13th c. bishop.

Christ Church Cathedral continued to play a leading part through all the vicissitudes of Irish history over the centuries, although in the 13th c. another church, only $\frac{1}{4}$ mile (400 m) away to the south, was raised to the status of cathedral and has retained that status, in spite of all subsequent changes, down to the present day. This is **St Patrick's

St. Patrick's Cathedral

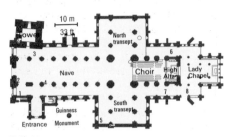

© Baedeker

1 Baptistery
2 Boyle Monument
3 Monument of Turlough O'Carolan
4 Tombs of Swift and Hester
   Johnson ("Stella")
5 Monument of Lady Doneraile
6 Effigy of Archbishop Fulk de
   Saundfort
7 Brasses of Dean Sutton, Dean
   Fyche, etc.
8 Effigy of Archbishop Tregury

Cathedral, the largest church in Ireland (305 ft (93m) long), which is also an Anglican cathedral (Mon–Fri. 9 a.m.–6 p.m., Sat. to 4 p.m.).

At the time of its foundation in the 11th c. the church stood on a marshy site outside the town walls. Like Christ Church Cathedral, it has suffered from over-restoration (1864–69). The massive tower at the north-west corner dates from the end of the 14th c., the steeple from 1739.

The church is entered from the south side. The high interior in severe Early English style is of impressive effect. It contains numerous monuments and tombs. At the second pier, to the right of the entrance, are the tombs of Jonathan Swift (1667–1745) and his "Stella" (Hester Johnson, 1681–1728). To the left of the nearby door is a bust of Swift, with an epitaph which he himself composed: "He lies where furious indignation can no longer rend his heart." Swift was Dean of St Patrick's for 35 years.

Other notable monuments are the following: to the right of the baptismal chapel (old font) the Boyle Monument (1631) commemorating the Earl of Cork, with a number of coloured figures, including a child who is believed to be Richard Boyle, later the celebrated physicist; on the north wall, opposite the entrance, the monument of Turlough O'Carolan (1670–1738), last of the Irish bards; on the north wall of the choir a marble effigy of Archbishop Fulk de Saundfort (d.

1271); on the south wall of the Lady Chapel an effigy of Archbishop Tregury (d. 1471); on the south wall of the choir four brasses, the finest of which are those of Dean Sutton (d. 1528) and Dean Fyche (d. 1539); and, at the south-west corner of the south transept, the typically 18th c. monument of Lady Doneraile.

The choir was from 1783 to 1869 the Chapel of the Order of the Knights of St Patrick, whose banners, swords and helmets can be seen above the stalls.

Near St Patrick's in the courtyard of Molyneaux House, a *bird market* is held every Sunday, 10.30 a.m. to 12.30 p.m.

To the right of St Patrick's a narrow street runs in a curve to *Marsh's Library (Mon. 2–4 p.m., Wed.–Fri, 10.30 a.m.–12.30 p.m. and 2–4 p.m., Sat. 10.30 a.m.–12.30 p.m.), the city's oldest public library, founded by Archbishop Marsh and built in 1701 by Sir William Robinson. The façades were renewed in 1863–69, but the attractive interior has been preserved practically unchanged, including the "cages" in which readers of rare books were obliged to work under the eye of the custodian.

Returning along Patrick Street and St Nicholas Street to Christ Church Cathedral and turning left into High Street, we see on the right the two *St Audoen's Churches*. The Protestant one is a National Monument and is Dublin's only surviving medieval church. Of the original structure there remain the nave (13th c.), in which services are still held, the choir and south aisle (both roofless) and two chapels. In the porch are the Portlester Monument (1496) and a number of gravestones.

High Street continues by way of Cornmarket into Thomas Street, passing on the right the towering Augustinian church by Pugin and on the left the massive façade of *St Catherine's Church* (by John Smyth, 1769). Robert Emmet, who had led a rising against the British, was hanged in front of the church in 1803.

Some 550 yd (500 m) farther west is the 60 acre (24·3 ha) site of *St James's Gate Brewery*, better known as **Guinness's**, where 60 per cent of the beer drunk in Ireland is brewed. Guinness's stout, like all the principal Irish beers, is top-fermented;

it is dark in colour, with a high hop content and, therefore, bitter. Nothing but barley, hops, yeast and water is used in its manufacture.

The St James's Gate Brewery was founded by Arthur Guinness in 1759, and prospered in spite of subsidised competition from imported English beers. In the early 19th c. Napoleon's Continental System brought economic problems, as did the catastrophic famine of the 1840s; but in spite of this Guinness's grew to become Ireland's largest brewery, and by about 1870 the largest in the world. Exports also continued to grow. The first Guinness brewery outside Ireland was established in London in 1936, and there are now breweries as far afield as Nigeria, Ghana, Jamaica and Malaysia. The Dublin brewery exports 40 per cent of its total production.

From an early stage the Guinness brewing dynasty showed themselves munificent public benefactors, mainly for the benefit of the city of Dublin. Thus they helped to finance the reconstruction of St Patrick's Cathedral, built housing estates, supported welfare agencies and took an interest in the economic well-being of their work-force. They can also be credited with the sponsoring of "The Guinness Book of Records".

In the brewery's Visitors' Centre (reached from the main entrance in James's Street; Mon.–Fri. 10 a.m.–3 p.m., closed on bank holidays) visitors are shown a film on the story of the firm and the brewing of beer and then invited to sample the product.

A little way south of the brewery was a harbour at the end of a branch, now filled in, of the Grand Canal (see entry), St James's Harbour. The Grand Canal, constructed in the second half of the 18th c., was used, in conjunction with the Shannon, for the conveyance of passengers and freight including the brewery product, between Dublin and the west of Ireland. After the construction of a railway line to the western part of the country in the mid 19th c. the canal and the harbour lost much of their importance.

Central Area – North

Going downstream from O'Connell Bridge on Eden Quay, we come, passing under the unsightly railway bridge (1889), to the *Custom House, a magnificent building designed by James Gandon (1743–1823), an English architect of Huguenot descent who was responsible for many buildings in Dublin. After the building had been completely burned out in 1921, during the Civil War, the exterior was restored on the basis of the original plans. The long façade with the Doric portico and the 125 ft (38 m) high domed tower which surmounts it is best seen from the opposite side of the river. Most of the fine statues and sculpture are by the Dubliner Edward Smyth.

The north front, although less magnificent than the main façade, is also of notable quality. Opposite it, to the right, is the new Bus Station (Busarus).

From the Custom House the Custom House Quay and North Wall Quay lead to the *Harbour*. North Wall Quay crosses the Royal Canal at the point where it branches off the Liffey to run north-west. Turning left off North Wall Quay, we come to Alexandra Road and the Car Ferry Terminal, where the car ferries from Liverpool arrive. From here can be seen, to the left, the *Bull Wall*, a breakwater built to prevent the silting up of the harbour. To the right is the South Bull (p. 118), the pier on the south side of the harbour.

To the west of the Custom House, dominating the skyline of the city, is the 16-storey *Liberty Hall*, headquarters of the Irish Transport and General Workers Union. Near by is the new *Abbey Theatre* (by Michael Scott, 1966); the main theatre has 638 seats, the small Peacock Theatre 157 seats. It occupies the site of the original Abbey Theatre, the first directors of which were W. B. Yeats and Lady Gregory. Plays in Irish as well as English are presented here.

Going north along Marlborough Street, we pass on the right *Tyrone House* (by Richard Cassels, 1741), with a handsome staircase and good stucco work by Francini. It is now occupied by the Department of Education.

Facing it, stands *St Mary's Pro-Cathedral*, Dublin's principal Roman Catholic church, built in 1816–25 on the model of the Temple of Theseus in Athens. The High Altar was the work of Peter Turnerelli. Masses are also said here in Italian and Spanish.

Parallel to Marlborough Street, one street farther west, is **O'Connell Street**, Dublin's main north–south artery. Originally a good residential street, it lost many of its fine old buildings during the fighting of 1916–22 and is now a shopping and commercial street, with cinemas and restaurants. Along the middle of the street are a series of statues of Irish patriots, including Daniel O'Connell and Charles Stuart Parnell, as well as the "Apostle of Temperance", Father Matthew. On the west side of the street stands the imposing *General Post Office* (by Francis Johnston, 1815–17), which in 1916 became the headquarters of the rebels under the leadership of Patrick Pearse and James Connolly. The Irish patriots are commemorated by a monument in the main hall ("Death of CuChulainn").

In Henry Street, round the corner, is the philatelic counter. Farther north, at 14 Upper O'Connell Street, is the *Tourist Information Office*.

From Upper O'Connell Street, turning right into Parnell Street and then left along Gardiner Street, we come into *Mountjoy Square* (1792–1818), an example of a once-fashionable and elegant square which has come down in the world and is now gradually being rehabilitated. From the north-west corner of the square Gardiner's Place leads into Great Denmark Street, on the right-hand side of which is *Belvedere House* (by Michael Stapleton, 1785), a dignified building with a fine interior. Since 1841 it has been a Jesuit school, James Joyce being its most celebrated pupil.

Great Denmark Street leads via Gardiner's Row into Parnell Square North, on the right-hand side of which is *Charlemont House* (1762), by the English architect Sir William Chambers, with a porch added in 1930. It is now occupied by the ***Municipal Gallery of Modern Art**, founded in 1908 (Tue.–Sat. 9.30 a.m.–6 p.m., Sun. 11 a.m.–5 p.m.), with pictures by Pierre Bonnard, Camille Corot, Edgar Degas, Juan Gris, Edouard Manet, Claude Monet, Pablo Picasso, Camille Pissarro, Auguste Renoir, William J. Leech and Jack B. Yeats.

The Gallery overlooks *Parnell Square*, where there are three fine 18th c. buildings – the Gate Theatre (founded in 1928 in part of the old Assembly Rooms), the Rotunda (now rebuilt as the Ambassador Cinema) and Richard Cassels's *Rotunda Hospital*. The main building, linked with the wings by colonnades, is topped by a domed tower. A beautiful staircase leads up to the Chapel, which has a fine stucco ceiling with numerous figures in strong relief.

In Parnell Square lies the *Garden of Remembrance*, laid out in 1966, with a sculpture by Oisín Kelly ("Lir's Children", 1970). The garden is dedicated to all who gave their lives for Ireland's freedom.

To the west of Parnell Square, in Granby Row, can be found the *National Wax Museum* (Mon.–Sat. 10 a.m.–5.30 p.m., Sun. 1–5.30 p.m.), with wax figures of Irish politicians (Charles Stuart Parnell, Douglas Hyde, Eamon de Valera), actors and writers (James Joyce), and prominent international personalities (Ronald Reagan, Pope John Paul II).

Going south from the end of Granby Row down Upper Dorset Street (the main road north to the airport, the N1) and Bolton Street, we come to Henrietta Street, a cul-de-sac on the right, at the far end of which, on a high base, are the ***King's Inns** (by James Gandon and Caron Baker, 1795; the two wings on the west front are later additions), the headquarters of the ruling body of the Irish legal profession, with a fine Dining Hall (sculpture by Edward Smyth) and a large library.

Continuing down Bolton Street and Capel Street, we come to Mary Street (on the left), in which is *St Mary's Church* (1702), Dublin's oldest unaltered Protestant church, with rich carving on the organ-loft and galleries. The churchyard was presented to the city by the Church authorities in 1966 as a Wolfe Tone memorial garden. Near by is Wolfe Tone Street, named after the leader of the United Irishmen.

Capel Street descends to the Liffey at Gratton Bridge. $\frac{1}{4}$ mile (400 m) upstream, on Inns Quay, is a masterpiece by James Gandon, the ***Four Courts**, seat of the Irish High Court and Supreme Court. Built between 1786 and 1802, it incorporated plans by Thomas Cooley, who died before

◀ **View of the Liffey**

The Four Courts, on the banks of the Liffey

building began. After being badly damaged by gunfire during the Civil War in 1922 it was restored in 1931 with minor alterations. The 456 ft (139 m) long river-front with its Corinthian portico is dominated by a great domed rotunda which is a prominent Dublin landmark. The central hall beneath the dome gave access to the four courts from which the building takes its name – the Exchequer, Common Pleas, King's Bench and Chancery Courts.

West of the Four Courts in Church Street is *St Michan's Church* (1095; much restored), in the crypt of which can be seen a number of mummified bodies (open Mon.–Fri. 10 a.m.–12.45 p.m. and 2–4.45 p.m., Sat. 10 a.m.–12.45 p.m.; admission charge).

½ mile (805 m) farther west, in Blackhall Place, we come to *King's Hospital*, also known as the Bluecoat School. The School was founded in 1669, but the present handsome building (by Thomas Ivory) dates only from the last quarter of the 18th c.; the dome was added in 1894. The interior has fine stucco work and carving. This is the headquarters of the Incorporated Law Society.

Immediately west of the school are the large *Collins Barracks* (18th c.).

Outer Districts – North

From Collins Barracks Parkgate Street leads west to *Phoenix Park. This large public park (1752 acres (767 ha)) owes its name not to the phoenix on a column set up in 1747 by the Viceroy, Lord Chesterfield, who established the park, but to the Irish name of a nearby spring, Fionn Uisg ("Clear Water"). To the right of Main Road, which runs in a straight line through the park, are the People's Garden, the *Zoological Gardens* (Mon.–Sat. 9.30 a.m.–6 p.m., Sun. 11 a.m.–6 p.m.; admission charge), noted for its successful breeding of lions, a polo ground, the residence of the President of the Irish Republic and previously of the Viceroy (by Nathaniel Clements, 1751–54), and the Apostolic Nunciature. To the left of the road are the huge obelisk of the Wellington Monument (200 ft (60 m) high), an eye-catching landmark for visitors coming from the city, followed by various sports grounds, the residence of the United States Ambassador and, at the far end, the Ordnance Survey Office. At the north end of the park is the *Phoenix Park Racecourse*, on the south side St Mary's Hospital, with a chapel designed by Cooley (1771).

Leaving the park by either of the two northern exits, Cabra Gate or Ashtown Gate, and turning right along Navan Road and Cabra Road, then left along Phibsborough Road, we come to *Glasnevin* or *Prospect Cemetery*, an extensive burial ground with the graves of Daniel O'Connell, Charles Stuart Parnell, Roger Casement and many other Irish patriots. North-east of the cemetery, bounded by the River Tolka, are the 50 acre (20 ha) *Botanic Gardens*, with a fine wrought-iron Palm House (by Richard Turner, 1842–50).

Going east along the streets beside the River Tolka, we come to *Fairview Park*, laid out on land reclaimed from the sea adjoining the harbour. North of this, past the junction of Griffith Avenue and Malahide Road, stands the *Marino Casino* (by William Chambers, 1765–71: National Monument), a country villa built for the first Earl of Charlemont, with eight sumptuously appointed rooms set round a handsome staircase. In the basement are extensive domestic offices, below a terrace flanked by four lions. The casino is open to the public (10 a.m.– 7 p.m., each day in summer; 10 a.m.– 4 p.m. Saturday and Sunday in winter). Guides are available.

From Fairview Park Clontarf Road borders the north side of the bay in the direction of Howth. To the right can be seen the flat *North Bull Island*, with two golf-courses (Royal Dublin and St Anne's). Beyond this is a rocky promontory of quartzite and schist, along the slopes of which extends the attractive residential town and holiday resort of *Howth* (Sutton Castle Hotel, A, 20 r.; Howth Lodge Hotel, B*, 14 r.; Deer Park Hotel and Golf-courses, B, 35 r.; St Lawrence Hotel, B, 31 r.). The older part of the town is on the north-east side of the peninsula. Here there is a large fishing and boating harbour, from which a boat can be taken to *Ireland's Eye*, a rocky islet rather more than a mile (1·6 km) offshore, with a little church and a Martello tower (a watch-tower dating from Napoleonic times).

Above Howth harbour are the ruins of *St Mary's Church* (14th–15 c.: National Monument), with two aisles of different length. In the south aisle is the handsome tomb of the Lawrence family (*c.* 1470). West of the church is *Howth Castle*, a battlemented stronghold of irregular plan, much restored. In the beautiful park (open throughout the year) is an 18th c. French-style garden with 30 ft (9 m) high beech hedges and a profusion of rhododendrons. Near by are a fine chambered tomb and a ruined 16th c. tower house.

The highest point on the peninsula (best reached from the Summit district at its east end) is *Ben Howth* (568 ft (173 m)), on

Howth Castle

which can be seen a burial mound; from the top there are panoramic views.

There is an attractive *cliff walk* along the east and south sides of the Howth Peninsula, passing the Baily Lighthouse (1814), a short distance off the path at the south-eastern tip of the peninsula, and St Fintan's Chapel (9th c.). The view over the expanse of Dublin Bay to Dún Laoghaire (see entry) is magnificent.

Outer Districts – South

The quays along the south side of the Liffey are interrupted by the Grand Canal (see entry) and the River Dodder, which join the Liffey together. In order to reach the South Bull (pier), therefore, it is necessary to go along Pearse Street and its continuation Ringsend Road to Ringsend Park. The route (about 3 miles (5 km)) runs along a peninsula through a typical harbour quarter to the old Pigeon House Fort (1748), now the Electricity Works. Beyond this, at the end of the pier, is *Poolbeg Lighthouse* (1762). Cromwell landed at Ringsend in 1646 with an army of 12,000 men on his expedition to subdue the Irish.

$\frac{3}{4}$ mile (1 km) south of Ringsend, on both sides of the Dodder, is the residential district of *Ballsbridge*, with handsome early 19th c. houses, parks and sports grounds.

At the junction of Shelbourne Road and Pembroke Road are the United States Embassy, a circular building of 1964, and a number of new hotels.

Beyond the bridge (1791) over the Dodder, on the right of Merrion Road, are the *Royal Dublin Society Showgrounds*. This extensive area with its carefully tended turf, low white fences and handsome buildings is the setting of the Dublin Horse Show which is held in August every year, a huge show, with more than 2000 horses and a full programme of races, displays, trials, presentations of prizes and auctions, which attracts visitors and purchasers from far and wide. It is also a great social event, with dances in the large hotels. The Spring Fair, held at the beginning of May, is devoted to livestock and agricultural implements and machinery; with it is associated an industrial display.

The Royal Dublin Society is now mainly concerned with scientific agriculture and stock-breeding, but also has a cultural programme of concerts and lectures on subjects of more general interest. It has a library of over 150,000 volumes.

500 yd (457 m) farther south Shrewsbury Road branches off Merrion Road on the right. Here, at No. 20, is the *Chester Beatty Library and Gallery of Oriental Art* (Tue.–Fri. 10 a.m.–5 p.m., Sun. 2–5 p.m.; conducted visits Wed. and Sat. 2.30 p.m.), founded by an American who settled in Dublin in 1953. Among the principal treasures in this valuable collection are, in the Garden Library, French Books of Hours of the 14th and 15th c. and a prayer-book which belonged to Philip II of Spain; and, in the New Gallery, works of Far Eastern art, including Chinese cups of rhinoceros horn (11th c.), Japanese coloured woodcuts, Islamic prints, Sanskrit manuscripts (12th–13th c.), Indian miniatures, Babylonian clay tablets (2500–2300 B.C.) and numerous texts in all the languages of the Near East. The displays in the New Gallery are changed from time to time, since lack of space prevents it from showing the whole riches of its collection.

Merrion Road then runs south-east to *Merrion Strand* and along the shores of Dublin Bay to Dún Laoghaire (see entry).

Beyond the River Dodder, in the *Donnybrook* district, is the national radio and television station, with a tall transmission tower. This was the site of the famous Donnybrook Fair, established by King John in 1204 and suppressed in 1855 after it had become notorious for disorder.

A mile (1·5 km) farther south, at 20 Palmerston Park, we come to the *Museum of Childhood*, with a collection of dolls from 1730 to 1940, rocking-horses, toys, etc. (July and August, daily 2–5.30 p.m.; September and November to June, Sun. 2–5.30 p.m.; closed in October; admission charge).

To the south-west is the *Rathfarnham* district. Between two golf-courses stands Rathfarnham Castle (1587), now modernised, with good ceiling-paintings by Angelica Kauffmann in the hall.

North-west of Rathfarnham lies the *Drimnagh* district. Between Naas Road (N7) and Long Mile Road is Drimnagh Castle (15th c.), with a well-preserved moat and outer ward; the castle itself is incorporated in a later building occupied by the Christian Brothers. Formerly outside the town, the castle was built to deter cattle-raiders.

Returning towards the city on Naas Road, we cross the Grand Canal and come into the Kilmainham district. Between Emmet Road and Inchicore Road is *Kilmainham Gaol* (1792), in which numerous Irish patriots were imprisoned and many were executed. In the entrance archway is a carving of intertwined snakes and chains which gives a sinister foretaste of the atmosphere within. Since 1960 the prison has been restored and now houses a historical museum commemorating the patriots who were confined here (open Sun. 3–5 p.m., in June and July Wed. 10 a.m.–noon and 2.30–4 p.m.; conducted visits; admission charge).

Going towards the city along Kilmainham Lane and turning left into Military Road, we come to an entrance of the *Royal Hospital (by Sir William Robinson, 1680–87), founded by Charles II for "maimed and infirm officers and soldiers". It is a handsome classical building in French/Dutch style, with a tower added in 1701. The chapel ceiling is a copy of the original, which collapsed in 1902. The hospital, after thorough restoration, is now a congress and cultural centre; a number of rooms are occupied by the National Museum (p. 106).

550 yd (500 m) farther on, in Bow Lane, stands *St Patrick's Hospital* (by George Semple, 1746–57), also known as Swift's Hospital, having been endowed by Swift in his will; it is now a psychiatric unit.

In Swift's own bitter words:

He gave the little wealth he had
To build a house for fools and mad;
And show'd, by one satiric touch,
No nation wanted it so much.

Adjoining St Patrick's Hospital, in Steevens Lane, is *Steevens's Hospital* (by Thomas Burgh, 1720–33), Ireland's oldest public hospital. It has a fine library, the Edward Worth Library.

SURROUNDINGS OF DUBLIN – NORTH. – The N1, going north from Dublin, runs through *Santry*. St Pappin's Church (1709) has a 14th c. font, a reredos of 1709 and a fine pulpit. In the churchyard is the 17th c. tomb of Richard Barry and his wife.

Farther north, to the left of the road, we come to *Dublin International Airport* or Collinstown Airport (1937–43), with a church and a small Aviation Museum (at present closed).

2 miles (3 km) farther on is *Swords*, with the ruins of Swords Castle (13th–15th c.: National Monument). The castle, pentagonal in plan, was the seat of the archbishops of Dublin. It preserves a chapel, the gatehouse and towers. Adjoining the village church are a 74 ft (22·5 m) high *round tower* (entrance and roof modern) and the tower (14th c.) of a former monastic church.

2 miles (3 km) beyond this the R127 branches off the N1 on the right to *Donabate*. The parish church has a gallery with rich stucco decoration. To the east is Portrane House (home of Swift's Stella), now occupied by a mental hospital; the round tower is modern. There are beautiful beaches on the coast here.

A little farther north the R127 diverges off the N1 on the right for *Lusk*, which has a *round tower* (National Monument), all that remains of a 9th c. monastery suppressed by the Anglo-Normans. The square tower belongs to a later structure. The church (1847) contains a number of good medieval tombs.

On the coast to the east of Lusk is the village of *Rush*, a bulb-growing centre. From here a boat can be taken to *Lambay Island*, a rocky islet of porphyry (highest point 427 ft (130 m)) which is now a bird sanctuary; it can be visited only with the permission of the owner, Lord Revelstoke.

From Lusk the R127 passes the ruined church (15th c.: National Monument) and castle of *Baldongan* to *Skerries* (good sandy beach, 9-hole golf-course). Just offshore are three little islets – *St Patrick's Island*, with a ruined church; *Colt Island*; and *Shenick's Island* (which can be reached on foot at low tide), with a lighthouse.

The R127 continues along the coast to *Balbriggan* on the River Delvin, a quiet seaside resort with beautiful beaches and a 9-hole golf-course. Its stocking factories, established in the 18th c., still play an important part in the local economy.

SURROUNDINGS OF DUBLIN – NORTH-EAST. – North of Dublin the coastline runs some 3 miles (5 km) east of the N1. There is no road all the way along the coast, however, because of the two river mouths which form inlets cutting deep inland. From the city's north-eastern suburbs or from Howth the R106 leads to the little resort of *Portmarnock*, with its beautiful 2 mile (3 km) long Velvet Beach and well-known championship golf-course.

1¼ miles (2 km) west of Portmarnock we come to *St Doolagh's Church (13th c.), with its original stone roof, a chapel and a battlemented tower (15th c.). Cells in the tower, over the chapel and in the crypt suggest that this may have been a community of hermits. In a field 110 yd (100 m) north-east is St Doolagh's Well, in a stone-roofed octagonal well-house.

From Portmarnock the R106 follows the coast to *Malahide* (Grand Hotel, B*, 48 r.; Johnny's Restaurant, 9 James Terrace; Malahide Castle Restaurant), a popular little seaside resort with a good sandy beach and a 9-hole golf-course. South-west of the town stands *Malahide Castle, which from the 13th c. to 1975 was owned and occupied by the Talbot family and now belongs to the city of Dublin. Much rebuilt and altered in the course of its history, it shows a variety of architectural styles – medieval, Georgian and modern. The Great Hall with its oak roof is the only one in Ireland to have preserved its medieval aspect and to have continued (until 1975) to serve its original purpose. The castle now houses the *National Portrait Gallery* (Mon.–Fri. 10 a.m.–12.45 p.m. and 2–5 p.m.; Apr.–Oct. Sat. 11 a.m.–6 p.m., Sun. 2–6 p.m.; Nov.– Mar. Sat. and Sun. 2–5 p.m.; admission charge), a branch of the National Gallery in Dublin. The pictures in this collection are of interest either for the artist (William Hogarth, Joshua Reynolds, etc.) or the sitter (Anne Boleyn, Robert Dudley, James Gandon, Jonathan Swift, Daniel O'Connell, etc.). In a ruined chapel near the castle can be seen the grave of Maud Plunkett (15th c.), "maid, wife and widow in one day".

SURROUNDINGS OF DUBLIN – SOUTH. – See Dún Laoghaire

SURROUNDINGS OF DUBLIN – WEST. – 2½ miles (4 km) south-west of the city on the N81 is *Tallaght*. Beside the church is a tower with loopholes, the only remnant of a fortified abbey. Within 2½ miles (4 km) of the town, now dwarfed by a huge housing estate, are a number of 18th c. mansions. To the south, at the foot of the Wicklow Mountains, lies an area with numerous burial mounds, chambered tombs and standing stones. *Glenasmole*, the upper valley of the River Dodder, with two reservoirs, is of great scenic beauty.

2½ miles (4 km) north-west of Tallaght on the R113 is *Clondalkin*, a monastic settlement founded by St Mochua in the 7th c. of which nothing remains but an 84 ft (25·5 m) high *round tower* (National Monument), with its original roof and an external staircase (18th c.), and, in the churchyard, two granite crosses and a font (all National Monuments).

The N4 follows the course of the Liffey through the suburb of *Chapelizod* (West Country Hotel, B, 67 r.) to *Lucan* (Lucan Spa Hotel, B, 67 r.; Henry's Restaurant, 4 The Mall), once a much-frequented spa. To the west is Lucan House (1776), with beautiful interiors by James Wyatt, Michael Stapleton and Angelica Kauffmann.

On the N2, on the outskirts of Dublin, *Finglas* has a ruined medieval church and a 12th c. high cross in the churchyard. On a hill 2 miles (3 km), west stands Dunsink Observatory, from 1782 to 1921 the observatory of Trinity College, Dublin (p. 104).

3 miles (5 km) north of Finglas, to the right of the N1, we come to *Dunsoghly Castle (15th c.: National Monument), which, unusually among Irish castles, still preserves its original roof beams. It is a square tower with rectangular corner turrets; far-ranging views from the parapet walks. The roof structure provided the model for the reconstruction of Bunratty Castle (see Ennis). To the south of the castle are the remains of a small chapel (1573).

Dundalk/Dún Dealgan

Map reference: B5.
Republic of Ireland.
Province: Leinster. – County: Louth.
Population: 26,000.

(i) **Tourist Information Office,**
   Dundalk;
   tel. (042) 3 54 84.
   Open July and August.

HOTELS. – *Imperial*, A, 50 r.; *Ballymascanlon*, A, 36 r.; *Derryhale*, Carrick Road, B*, 23 r.; *Fairways*, B, 40 r.; *Lorne*, C, 18 r.

RESTAURANTS. – *Angela's*, Rockmarshall; *Carrick-dale*, Newry Road.

Dundalk (Dún Dealgan, "Delga's Fort") lies on the Irish east coast near the frontier with Northern Ireland, in Dundalk Bay, which forms a sheltered harbour. It is at the meeting-place of three main roads – the N1, N52 and N53. With a variety of industry (engineering, printing, tobacco, two breweries, footwear), the town has a busy and prosperous air.

HISTORY. – In the 10th c. the Irish inhabitants of the area were attacked by Viking raiders, and a naval battle was fought in the bay. The town was fortified in 1185. In 1253, and again in 1315, it was burned down. Thereafter for 300 years it was a cornerstone in the defence of the Pale (the territory in the east of Ireland under English control) and was subjected to repeated attacks. In 1690 it was taken by William of Orange, and in 1724 its fortifications were pulled down.

SIGHTS. – In the centre of the town, in Crowe Street (near the bus station), are two handsome 19th c. buildings, the *Court House* and *Town Hall*. In Chapel Street, to the north-east, is the Municipal Library, which has a small collection of local antiquities. Farther east, in Seatown Place, can be seen an old windmill, a massive seven-storey structure. In Clanbrassil Street, which runs north from Market Square, stands St Nicholas's Church (RC: 18th c., with an older tower). St Patrick's Cathedral (1848) is modelled on King's College Chapel, Cambridge. It is not really a cathedral.

SURROUNDINGS. – 2 miles (3 km) north-east of the town a side road (R173) branches off the N1 and runs east into the *Cooley Peninsula*, a attractive hilly promontory between Dundalk Bay and Carlingford Lough, an arm of the sea to the north. A little way along the R173, at *Ballymascanlon* stands the *Proleek Dolmen (National Monument), with a 40 ton (40·6 tonne) capstone borne on only three uprights. Tradition has it that anyone who can throw a pebble on to the capstone so that it lies on the top will have a wish fulfilled.

On the north-east side of the peninsula lies the ancient little town of *Carlingford*, dominated by the massive King John's Castle (13th c.: National Monument) on a crag above the harbour. Near by can be seen the Tholsel, an old gate-tower in which the elders of the community used to meet. In a little street off the Square is the old Mint, a 15th c. fortified tower house with curious window carvings. Taaffe's Castle opposite the station has a large square keep (16th c.) with a fine spiral staircase.

2 miles (3 km) south-east, at *Greenore*, is an 18-hole golf-course.

Close to the Northern Ireland border, beautifully situated at the north end of Carlingford Lough, lies *Omeath*, from which there is a ferry service to Warrenpoint in Co. Down (Northern Ireland).

On the coast south of Dundalk is the little resort of *Blackrock* with a golf-course (18 holes), tennis courts and facilities for water-sports. Trout and salmon fishing in the River Fane.

3 miles (5 km) farther south, just off the N1, we come to *Dromiskin*. In the churchyard are a 56 ft (17 m) *round tower* and a high cross, both dating from the earliest days of a monastery established here in the 6th c. Adjoining is a 13th c. church. All of these are National Monuments. There are a number of well-preserved castles within a few miles' radius.

1¼ miles (2 km) south of Dromiskin, in *Castlebellingham*, stands Bellingham Castle, in a beautiful setting on the River Glyde, with handsome yew hedges. It has been renovated and is now a hotel.

From Dundalk the N52 runs south-west to Ardee (below). A more attractive route, however, is on the R171, which branches off the N52 and comes in 6 miles (10 km) to *Louth*, in earlier times a place of such importance that it gave its name to the county. St Mochta's House (National Monument) is a vaulted two-storey oratory (12th c.) with a stone roof. Near by are the ruins of a 14th c. church.

6 miles (10 km) farther south, on the River Dee, is the little town of *Ardee*, with a 9-hole golf-course and good fishing. It has two castles – Hatch's Castle and Ardee Castle, a square keep which now houses a small museum. St Mary's Church (Protestant), which incorporates parts of an older church, has a beautifully carved font.

3 miles (5 km) east of Ardee stand *Roadstown Castle*, a tall narrow keep with projecting towers at two opposite corners.

12 miles (19 km) west of Dundalk the R178 reaches *Carrickmacross* (Nuremore Hotel, A, 39 r.), with a convent which makes and sells high-quality lace. Around the town are several good fishing loughs. Golf-course, tennis courts.

7 miles (11 km) east of Carrickmacross the old schoolhouse of *Iniskeen* houses a local museum, with a section devoted to the old Great Northern Railway, which passed through the town. On the site of an old monastery is the 42 ft (13 m) high stump of a *round tower* (National Monument).

Just to the east of Dundalk on the R178 rises a 60 ft (18 m) high earthwork which is said to be the birthplace of the legendary hero CuChulainn. The site is now occupied by a building of 1780; fine views. A short distance away is *Castletown Castle* (15th c.), a four-storey structure with flanking towers.

4½ miles (7 km) north-west of Dundalk are the ruins of *Castleroche* (13th c.: National Monument), a triangular structure with bastions; it is particularly impressive when seen from the plain.

Dungarvan/Dún Garbhain

Map reference: D4.
Republic of Ireland.
Province: Munster. – County: Waterford.
Population: 6600.

ⓘ **Tourist Information office,**
St Mary Street,
Dungarvan;
tel. (058) 4 17 41.
Open July and August.

HOTELS. – *Lawlor's*, B*, 24 r.; *Devonshire Arms*, B, 20 r.; *Whitechurch House*, B, 16 r.; *Ormonde*, B, 13 r.

GUEST-HOUSE. – *Fountain*, Youghal Road, B, 11 r.

RESTAURANT. – *Seanachie*.

Dungarvan (Dún Garbhain, "Garvan's Fort") lies half-way along the Irish south coast in a sheltered bay at the mouth of the River Colligan, at the meeting-place of the N25 and N672. It is the administrative centre of Co. Waterford (apart from the city of Waterford itself), and is also a busy marketing centre, with leather-processing works. The town itself lies on both banks of the River Colligan, which is spanned by a bridge (1815) with a 74 ft (23 m) arch.

SIGHTS. – On the right bank of the river are the ruins of *Dungarvan Castle* (built 1185 and subsequently much altered), a massive circular keep surrounded by fortified walls. Near by are remains of the old town walls. ¼ mile (402 m) south, in the churchyard of the parish church can be seen the *Holed Gable*, a curious structure with a number of circular openings, the function of which is unknown.

In Abbeyside, on the left bank of the river, is a tower which belonged to a 13th c. Augustinian abbey and now serves as the belfry of the adjoining church. Near by stands a curious shell house.

SURROUNDINGS. – To the north of the town are the Comeragh and Monavullagh Mountains, rising to heights of up to 2500 ft (762 m).

To the east of Dungarvan, on the far side of the bay, lies *Clonea*, a popular little seaside resort with a good sandy beach, a 9-hole golf-course and two camp sites.

South of the town (ferry service) the *Cullingar Peninsula*, also has good beaches. There is a pleasant walk by way of *Ring*, with an Irish-language school, and the old-world little fishing village of *Ballynagaul* to *Helvick Head* (which can be reached also on the R674), wth fine views of Dungarvan Harbour and the hills to the north. The region south of Dungarvan Harbour, between the N25 and the sea, is the only area on the east coast where Irish is still the predominant language.

2½ miles (4 km) north-west of Dungarvan, on the N72, is a monument to the celebrated greyhound Master McGrath, that won the Waterloo Cup three times between 1868 and 1871 and was beaten only once in 37 races.

Dún Laoghaire

Map reference: C5.
Republic of Ireland.
Province: Leinster. – County: Dublin.
Population: 54,000.
ⓘ Tourist Information Office,
  St Michael's Wharf,
  Dún Laoghaire;
  tel. (01) 80 69 84–86, 80 57 60
  and 80 65 47.

HOTELS. – *Royal Marine*, A, 115 r.; *Victor*, Rochestown Avenue, B*, 60 r.; *Elphin*, Royal Marine Road, B, 20 r.

RESTAURANTS. – *Digby's Restaurant and Wine Bar*, 5 Windsor Terrace; *Creole*, 20A Adelaide Street; *Na Mara*, 1 Harbour Road.

Dún Laoghaire ("Leary's Fort": pronounced Dunleary) lies at the south end of the wide sweep of Dublin Bay, below the north-easterly foothills of the Wicklow Mountains. At the beginning of the 19th c. it was still a small fishing village: it is now an attractive suburb of Dublin, a seaside resort and residential town much favoured by retired people, and an important port, terminus of the mail-boat and car-ferry services from Holyhead (Anglesey). It is also Ireland's great yachting centre, with the headquarters of three major yacht clubs.

SIGHTS. – At the time of its construction (mainly 1817–21, by Rennie, though it took many more years to complete) the large *Harbour* was a masterpiece of contemporary civil engineering. Its east pier is a popular promenade, with concerts in summer.

In the town is the fine *National Maritime Museum*, housed in a former church (May–Sept. Tue.–Sun. 2.30–5.30 p.m.; admission charge), with some 500 exhibits. The emphasis is on Irish shipping, from the simple currachs of western Ireland to the most modern vessels of our own time.

A minor road leads from the harbour, skirting the bathing beach, to *Joyce's Tower*, situated on a rocky promontory with an extensive view over Dublin Bay. It was one of the Martello towers built during the Napoleonic Wars to watch for possible invasion attempts. In 1904 James Joyce lived for some time in the tower as guest of Oliver St John Gogarty, and he describes it in "Ulysses". It now houses a museum (Mon.–Sat. 10 a.m.–1 p.m. and 2–5.15 p.m., Sun. 2.30–6 p.m.; admission charge) containing original manuscripts and rare editions of Joyce's works as well as personal mementoes. The museum is open from May to September; at other times it can be seen on application to the Tourist Information Office.

SURROUNDINGS. – Along the coast to the north of the town, extending into the suburbs of Dublin, are the residential districts of Monkstown and Blackrock. *Monkstown* has a 19th c. church with towers like chess pawns. *Blackrock* has very popular seawater swimming-baths.

To the south, now joined on to Dún Laoghaire, is the ancient little town of *Dalkey* (Dalkey Island Hotel, B, 20 r.; Cliff Castle Hotel, C, 12 r.; Chez la Hiff Restaurant, 21 Railway Road; Baroque Restaurant, Main Street; Guinea Pig Restaurant, 17 Railway Road). In Main Street stand two relics of the town's medieval defences, Archbold's Castle (16th c.: National Monument) and another castle which is now the Town Hall.

Just off the coast lies a small islet, *Dalkey Island*, with an old church (National Monument) and a Martello tower. From Sorrento Terrace and Sorrento Park, on the town's south beach, there are magnificent views. The old granite quarries are a good practice ground for rock-climbers.

To the south of Sorrento Point stretches Killiney Bay, with the seaside resort of *Killiney* (Fitzpatrick's Killiney Castle Hotel, A, 48 r.; Court Hotel, A, 32 r.). The slopes of the hills are studded with villas of different periods set in gardens, while beyond the railway line, which here follows the coast, the beach is rocky. From Killiney Hill, topped by an obelisk of 1741, there are superb views of the hills and the sea.

To the west of Killiney, just off the R117, is the village of *Kilternan* (Dublin Sport Hotel, A, 52 r.). On a nearby hill can be seen the impressive *Kilternan Dolmen* (c. 2000 B.C.: National Monument), with a capstone 22 ft (7 m) long, 13¼ ft (4 m) across and 6 ft (2 m) thick borne on ten orthostats.

3 miles (5 km) west of Dún Laoghaire lies *Leopardstown Racecourse*.

Ennis/Inis

Map reference: D3.
Republic of Ireland.
Province: Munster. – County: Clare.
Population: 6200.

ⓘ **Tourist Information Office,**
Bank Place,
Ennis;
tel. (065) 2 83 66.

HOTELS. – *West County*, A, 110 r.; *Old Ground*, A, 60 r.; *Auburn Lodge*, B*, 20 r.; *Queen's*, B. 36 r.

RESTAURANTS. – *Golden Mountain*, 16 O'Connell Street; *Lady Gregory's*, Abbey Street.

EVENT. – *Fleadh Nua* (festival of music and dance, May).

Ennis (Inis, "River Meadow"), county town of Co. Clare and an important road and railway junction (N18, N68), lies on the River Suir in the west of Ireland. The River Fergus flows in broad curves through the town, which has preserved something of a medieval aspect with its narrow winding streets. Shannon International Airport is only 15 miles (25 km) from Ennis, which, with its extensive hinterland and its light industries, is a considerable market and commercial centre.

SIGHTS. – At the end of Abbey Street stands *Ennis Friary* (National Monu-ment), a Franciscan house founded in 1241 which in the mid 14th c. was a flourishing community with 375 friars and 600 students. The church dates from the original foundation but has been much altered. It has some very fine sculpture, including a figure of St Francis with the stigmata (on the south-west side of the tower), the MacMahon tomb of about 1475 (on the south wall), a royal tomb with scenes from the Passion and a small representation of the Scourging, with the "cock in the pot" (for an explanation of the legend, see Kilkenny, St Canice's Cathedral).

Near the abbey, in Harmony Row, is the *De Valera Museum and Library* (Mon.–Wed. and Fri. 11 a.m.–1 p.m., 2.15–5.30 p.m. and 7–9 p.m., Thu. 11 a.m.–1 p.m. and 2.15–5.30 p.m.), with material on Ennis and the surrounding area and the history of Ireland. Among the exhibits is the fountain pen with which Eamon de Valera and Neville Chamberlain signed the 1938 treaty on the handing over of the Irish naval bases occupied by Britain.

At the cattle market, near the station, a railway engine commemorates the old West Clare narrow-gauge railway.

SURROUNDINGS. – 6 miles (10 km) east of Ennis on the R469 is *Quin* (Ballykilty Manor Hotel and

Quin Abbey

Craggaunowen Project: a crannog

Restaurant, B*, 11 r.), with *Quin Abbey (1402: National Monument), the well-preserved ruins of a Franciscan friary built on the foundations of an earlier castle, the bastions of which can still be seen. The church has tombstones of the 15th to 19th c.; well-preserved cloister. On the other side of the little river stands St Finghin's Church (13th c.: National Monument); the tower is a later addition.

Farther south-east on the R469 we come to *Knappogue Castle*, a 16th c. tower house furnished in period style. In summer "medieval banquets" are held in a 19th c. annexe.

To the south is another restored castle, the 16th c. Craggaunowen Castle, which is part of a larger enterprise, the *Craggaunowen Project (Mar.–Oct. 9.30 a.m.–5.30 p.m.). The castle itself contains a small collection of medieval religious art from the Hunt Collection (see Limerick, National Institute for Higher Education), mostly from the Continent. In the grounds can be seen reconstructions of structures from the earliest periods of human settlement in Ireland, including a crannog (lake dwelling) in a small lough and a stone ring-fort, both with huts and implements of the period. In a glass shed is displayed the leather boat in which Tim Severin and his crew re-enacted the medieval voyages of St Brendan in 1976 and 1977. It is planned to build a megalithic chamber tomb and a small wooden church of the Early Christian period.

The R462 continues south to *Sixmilebridge*, a pretty little village with what has been called a "Georgian doll's house", Mount Ievers (1736). From here a minor road runs south-west to the village of *Bunratty* (Fitzpatrick's Shannon Shamrock Hotel and Restaurant, A, 100 r.; MacCloskey's Restaurant, Bunratty House Mews). Here, on the banks of a stream, stands *Bunratty Castle (15th c.: National Monument), which, after an eventful history of destruction and rebuilding, was acquired in 1954 by Lord Gort and

magnificently restored; it is now managed by the Shannon Free Airport Development Ltd. The great hall and banqueting hall, chapel and residential apartments are furnished with a splendid collection of period furniture (open daily 9.30 a.m.–5.30 p.m.; admission charge), and "medieval banquets" for visitors are held in the banqueting hall. In the basement is a shop.

Bunratty Castle

In the grounds of the castle is the *Bunratty Folk Park (daily 9.30 a.m.–5.30 p.m.; admission charge), an open-air museum in which typical farm-workers', fishermen's and craft-workers' cottages, domestic equipment and furnishings, have been re-erected.

Bunratty attracts large numbers of tourists, being only 7 miles (11 km) from *Shannon International Airport* (Tourist Information Office, tel. (061) 6 16 64 and 6 16 04; Shannon International Hotel, A, 118 r.). The airport, the most westerly in Europe, was opened in 1945, with the world's first duty-free shop. Since it lost its importance as a port of call for transatlantic flights a development company, Shannon Free Airport Development Ltd, has established a variety of industries here (precision tools, electronic apparatus, industrial diamonds, etc.). The town of *Shannon* has a population of 7000.

From Shannon Airport the N18 runs north to Ennis. On the left of the road can be seen the fine ruin of *Urlanmore Castle*. On the wall of an upper room in the keep are medieval outline drawings of animals.

Beyond this we come to *Newmarket on Fergus* (Dromoland Castle Hotel, A, 69 r.; Clare Inn, A, 121 r.). Dromoland Castle, now a hotel, is a mansion of 1830, with beautiful gardens, an old tower and a large stone fort within the grounds.

2 miles (3 km) south of Ennis on the N18 are the ruins of *Clare Abbey* (National Monument), founded in the 12th c. and extended at various times down to the 15th c. In the River Fergus is the ruined Clare Castle.

3 miles (5 km) south-west of Ennis on the N68, in a beautiful setting on a lough, are the remains of *Killone Abbey* (12th c.: National Monument), one of Ireland's few nunneries.

North-west of Ennis (the N85 to Fountain Cross, then 4 miles (6 km) to the left on the R476) lies the site of

Dysert O'Dea High Cross

*Dysert O'Dea (National Monument), with a church, a round tower and a high cross. The present church dates from the late 17th c., when it was reconstructed more or less in its original form (12th–13th c.) It has a fine Romanesque doorway carved with beautiful geometric designs, foliage and rather Mongoloid masks. At the north-west corner of the church stands the stump of a round tower, still 40 ft (12 m) high, and in a field to the east is a *high cross*, with an unusual figure of the Crucified Christ, fully clothed, on the east side; the other sides are divided into panels with a variety of geometric patterns, human figures and interlace designs with animals.

Enniscorthy/Inis Coirthe

Map reference: D5.
Republic of Ireland.
Province: Leinster. – County: Wexford.
Population: 5000

ⓘ Tourist Information Office,
Castle Hill,
Enniscorthy;
tel. (054) 23 41.
Open July and August.

HOTEL. – *Murphy-Floods*, Town Centre, B, 22 r.

RESTAURANT. – *Tavern*, 5 Templeshannon.

EVENT. – *Strawberry Fair* (July).

Enniscorthy (Inis Coirthe, "Rock Island") lies in the south-east corner of Ireland on the main road from Dublin to Wexford. The town is built on the west side of the River Slaney, both banks of which rise sharply above the river. The Slaney is navigable up to this point and carries a considerable traffic between Enniscorthy and Wexford, 15 miles (24 km) south.

SIGHTS. – The town developed as a market and distribution centre around *Enniscorthy Castle* (1586, restored: National Monument), a rectangular keep with corner towers which now houses an interesting museum (local archaeological finds and bygones from the Stone Age onwards, local crafts).

St Aidan's Cathedral, commandingly situated above the river, is a neo-Gothic church by Pugin (1840).

East of the town rises *Vinegar Hill*, with remains of a windmill (National Monument); fine views.

Killone Abbey

SURROUNDINGS. – 8 miles (13 km) north of Enniscorthy on the N11 we come to *Ferns*, still an episcopal see. The road crosses the site of an Augustinian abbey (National Monument), with the remains of three churches and other buildings. The present Protestant church incorporates some work from an earlier building; in the churchyard are three high crosses. Ferns Castle (National Monument) is a large rectangular keep with circular towers at three of the corners; in one of the towers is a beautifully vaulted 13th c. chapel.

Farther north-east on the N11 are *Gorey*, once an important cattle market, and (on the coast, reached on the R742) *Courtown* (Courtown Hotel, B*, 28 r.), a popular family seaside resort with beautiful sandy beaches and an 18-hole golf-course.

The *Blackstairs Mountains* to the west of Enniscorthy offer ample scope for hill walkers and climbers.

View of Enniscorthy

Enniscrone

See Inishcrone

Enniskerry/Ath na Scairbhe

Map reference: C5.
Republic of Ireland.
Province: Leinster. – County: Wicklow.
Population: 1200.

ⓘ Tourist Information Office,
Bray;
tel. (01) 86 71 28–29.
Open July and August.

HOTELS. – *Summerhill*, B, 10 r.; *Powerscourt Arms*,
C, 11 r.

RESTAURANTS. – *Enniskerry Lodge Inn*, Cloon;
Summerhill Hotel.

Enniskery (Ath na Scairbhe, "Rugged Ford"), one of the prettiest villages in Ireland, lies south-east of Dublin and west of Bray in a wooded hollow in the foothills of the Wicklow Mountains.

SIGHTS. – Enniskerry is a good base for walks in the hills and for a visit to Powerscourt House.

½ mile (800 m) south of the village is the entrance to the demesne of *Powerscourt, with gardens and a landscaped park which rank among the most beautiful in Ireland (open from mid March to the end of October, 10.30 a.m.–5.30 p.m.; admission charge). Tinnehinch Bridge, spanning the Dargle, is a celebrated beauty-spot. Powerscourt House itself, an imposing granite mansion (by Richard Cassels, 1731) approached by a mile-long avenue, was gutted by fire in 1974. From the house, which stands on high ground, the gardens extend down the slope, with terraces, statuary, tessellated pavements, ornamental lakes and wrought-iron gates. In the grounds are plantations of exotic trees, masses of rhododendrons and other flowering shrubs, Italian and Japanese gardens and a deer-park. From various viewpoints there are magnificent prospects of the surrounding hills – Great Sugar Loaf, 1630 ft (497 m); Kippure, 2430 ft (740 m).

It is an hour's walk to the celebrated *Powerscourt Waterfall*, the highest in Ireland, tumbling over a 400 ft (720 m) high cliff and at its most impressive after a rainy spell. The waterfall may be visited all year (10.30 a.m.–8 p.m.; admission charge).

Powerscourt: an ornamental gate . . .

. . . and the gardens

2 miles (3 km) upstream the Glencree River joins the Dargle, flowing down from Glendoo Mountain through a beautiful valley. An attractive road ascends the valley to *St Kevins*, one of series of barracks built by the British authorities along the Military Road after the 1798 Rising. Near by is a German military cemetery.

SURROUNDINGS. – 2 miles (3 km) north of Enniskerry the Dublin road goes through the *Scalp*, a rocky gorge littered with granite boulders which was hewn through the hills by glaciers in the last Glacial period.

Fanad Peninsula

Map reference: A4.
Republic of Ireland.
Province: Ulster. – County: Donegal.
(i) **Tourist Information Office,**
   Derry Road,
   Letterkenny;
   tel. (074) 2 11 60.

HOTELS and RESTAURANTS. – See Letterkenny.

The Fanad Peninsula on the north coast of Ireland, with spectacular cliff scenery, extends northward for some 12 miles (20 km) between the narrow inlet of Mulroy Bay to the west and Lough Swilly, the broad estuary of the River Swilly, to the east. At the tip of the peninsula is Fanad Head.

CIRCUIT OF THE PENINSULA. – From *Letterkenny* (see entry) the N56 runs north to *Milford*, a fishing centre at the head of Mulroy Bay. The village has a modern church. Near by is a waterfall known as the Grey Mare's Tail. There is good fishing in *Lough Fern* and other small loughs in the neighbourhood.

From Milford the R246 goes north along the east side of the fjord-like Mulroy Bay. Just before *Kerrykeel* (also spelt Carrow-keel) is a prehistoric chamber tomb with a massive capstone between 6 and 10 ft (2 and 10 m) in size. Kerrykeel lies at the foot of Knockalla Mountain, the "Devil's Backbone".

The R246 and its continuation lead to *Fanad Head*, at the northern tip of the peninsula (fine views). The return is down the west side of the peninsula, on the new

Knockalla road (8 miles (13 km)), with breath-taking scenery. Beyond *Portsalon*, which has a picturesque little harbour and an 18-hole golf-course, are the spectacular tunnels through the cliffs known as the Seven Arches, up to 300 ft (90 m) long, 20 ft (6 m) wide and 30 ft (9 m) high, and the Great Arch of Doagh Beg.

Knockalla Mountain, which can be seen ahead, falls steeply down to the lough. On the hill is a 19th c. gun position directed against a possible French invasion.

The R247 leads past Otway golf-course (9 holes) to *Rathmullan* (Rathmullan House Hotel, A, 21 r.; Fort Royal Hotel, B*, 22 r.; Pier Hotel, C, 16 r.), an attractive seaside resort with a sandy beach. At Rathmullan are the ruins of a Carmelite friary (15th c.: National Monument), with a church which a 17th c. bishop converted into his residence, and another gun position. From here in 1607 the Earls of Tyrone and Tyrconnell sailed away to France with their friends and supporters: the "Flight of the Earls" which was followed by the confiscation of great tracts of Irish land and the bringing in of large numbers of English and Scottish settlers.

There is a passenger ferry from Rathmullan across Lough Swilly to Fahan on the Inishowen Peninsula (see entry).

Fermoy/Mainistir Fhear Muighe

Map reference: D3.
Republic of Ireland.
Province: Munster. – County: Cork.
Population: 3100.
(i) **Tourist Information Office,**
   Fermoy;
   tel. (025) 3 11 10.

HOTEL. – *Grand*, B, 19 r.

The little market town of Fermoy (Mainistir Fhear Muighe, "Abbey of the Plainsmen") lies inland from the Irish south coast between the foothills of the Knockmealdown and Nagles Mountains. It has excellent salmon and trout fishing, and angling competitions are regularly held in the area. There is also good coarse

Fanad Head ▶

fishing; the Blackwater is the only river in Ireland in which roach are to be found. There are the remains of four castles on the banks of the river near the town.

SURROUNDINGS. – The north-south road (the N8) intersects with the N72, running east–west, in Fermoy. 10 miles (16 km) north of the town on the N8 is *Mitchelstown*, a little country town with a creamery producing butter and cheese. It was an 18th c. planned town which expanded in the 19th c. Kingstown College (1780) is an attractive group of 18th c. buildings.

7 miles (11 km) north-east, in Co. Tipperary, are the *Mitchelstown Caves*. The Old Caves, which are difficult of access, provided a refuge for a 16th c. Earl of Desmond with a large price on his head. The New Caves, discovered in 1833, have fine stalactitic formations; they can be seen on a guided tour (2 miles (3 km)).

In hilly country 6 miles (9·5 km) north-west of Mitchelstown, on the R655, we come to *Labba-molaga*, with the ruins of a modest Early Christian church (National Monument).

4½ miles (7 km) south-east of Fermoy is *Castlelyons*, with the remains of a 15th c. Carmelite friary (National Monument): a church, with a beautiful west doorway and tower, and other buildings. A few miles east, on a crag above the River Bride, stands a 14th c. tower house, *Conna Castle* (National Monument).

From Fermoy the N72 runs west, passing Ballyhooly Castle, to **Mallow** (Central Hotel, B*, 21 r.; Grill-n-Griddle Restaurant, 53–54 Main Street), an important sugar-manufacturing centre situated in the wooded valley of the Blackwater, a river well stocked with fish. In addition to good fishing the town has a golf-course (18 holes) and a racecourse, and there is also hunting in the area. In the 18th and 19th c. Mallow was a much-frequented spa, and still preserves something of the atmosphere of those days. It has a number of notable buildings – the Court House, the Market House, the picturesque half-timbered Clock House, some good 18th c. dwelling-houses and few relics of its heyday as a fashionable spa, the old Spa House, the racecourse and the three gushing Springs in Fermoy Road. At the south-east end of the town are the ruins of *Mallow Castle* (16th c.: National Monument), with a small museum. Near by are the remains of an earlier castle.

North of Mallow on the N20, close together, are *Ballybeg Abbey* (13th c.: National Monument), with a very fine dovecot, and the little town of *Buttevant*, with a ruined church which belonged to a Franciscan friary (13th c.: National Monument); fine choir and crypt (underbuilding on a steep river-bank).

A short distance to the north-east are the ruins of *Kilcolman Castle*, in which the poet Edmund Spenser (1552–99) lived for 13 years.

At *Killavullen*, to the east of Mallow, on a crag above the Blackwater, stands the ancestral home of the Hennessy family, producers of the world-famous Hennessy cognac.

The little market town of *Kanturk*, 12 miles (20 km) west of Mallow (Isle of the Syke Hotel, B, 16 r.), has a large early 17th c. fortified house of the MacCarthys; it now belongs to the Irish National Trust.

9 miles (15 km) north-east are the ruins of *Liscarroll Castle* (National Monument), a handsome tower house built in the 13th c. but much altered in later centuries; it is surrounded by a walled outer ward with defensive towers.

North of Kanturk on the R579, at *Tullylease*, are the ruins of a monastery of the 13th–15th c. (National Monument). It has a number of early gravestones built into the walls, including one on the east end of the church with fine ornament in the style of the 8th c. "Book of Lindisfarne" and a Latin inscription.

North-west of Fermoy on the R512 can be seen the *Labbacallee Cairn* (National Monument), an unusually large Neolithic wedge-shaped gallery grave with a rectangular main chamber and a smaller chamber to the rear. A short distance away is a roofless chamber tomb.

A short distance farther on we come to *Glanworth*, with an old 13-arched bridge over the River Funshion (view). In the surrounding area are a number of ruined castles on the banks of the river.

Galway/Gaillimh

Map reference: C2.
Republic of Ireland.
Province: Connacht. – County: Galway.
Population: 38,000.
ⓘ **Tourist Information Office**
(Aras Fáilte),
Eyre Square,
Galway;
tel. (091) 6 30 81.

HOTELS. – *Great Southern*, Eyre Square, A*, 120 r.; *Corrib Great Southern*, Dublin Road, A, 110 r.; *Galway Ryan*, Dublin Road, A, 96 r.; *Ardilaun House*, Taylor's Hill, A, 71 r.; *Flannery's Motor Inn*, Dublin Road, B*, 98 r.; *Skeffington Arms*, Eyre Square, B*, 21 r.; *Anno Santo*, Threadneedle Road, B*, 14 r.; *Imperial*, Eyre Square, B, 62 r.; *Atlanta*, Dominick Street, B, 20 r.; *Hilltop*, Dalysfort Road, C, 10 r.

GUEST-HOUSE. – *Adare House*, Father Griffin Place, B, 10 r.

RESTAURANTS. – *Eyre House*, 10 Eyre Square; *Lydon House*, 5 Shop Street; *Claddagh Rooms* (Great Southern Hotel), Eyre Square.

EVENT. – *Oyster Festival* (Sept.).

Galway (Gaillimh, "Gailleamh's Place") is picturesquely situated at the north-east end of Galway Bay, at the point where the short tidal River Corrib, coming from Lough Corrib, pours its abundant flow of water into the Atlantic.

Galway is the see of the diocese of Co. Galway, and has a university (part of the National University of Ireland), in which much of the teaching is in Irish (summer courses for visitors in July and August). Irish culture and language are also promoted by the Irish theatre, An Taiohbhearc. For centuries Galway had active trading relations with Spain, and it has preserved something of this Spanish influence. In the field of architecture, for instance, it is seen in the houses built round an open courtyard.

HISTORY. – There was a settlement on this site from the earliest times. After the building of a castle in 1124 and its capture by Richard de Burgo in 1232 Galway rapidly developed into a flourishing Anglo-Norman town. The "fourteen tribes of Galway" – aristocratic merchant families – made the town a kind of city state and held to the English connection in spite of all attacks by the Irish. The town was destroyed by a great fire in 1473 but was soon rebuilt. Trade with the countries of western Europe, particularly Spain, brought wealth and prosperity. During the 16th and 17th c. there was a celebrated grammar school here which is said at one time to have had 1200 pupils. In the 17th c. the town supported the Irish cause, and suffered extensive destruction at the hands of Cromwell's forces; and there was further damage when it was taken by William of Orange's troops in 1691.

SIGHTS. – The central area of Galway lies on the east bank of the River Corrib, but between Eyre Street, by the station, and the river few old buildings have survived, though a number of houses have stones with coats of arms – relics of Galway's heyday – built into their walls. *Eyre Square* (18th c.) is now landscaped as a memorial garden to US President J. F. Kennedy. On its north-west side stands *Browne's Gateway*, the doorway of an old patrician mansion which has been re-erected here. There is a striking monument in the square to the Irish-language poet Pádraic O'Conaire (1882–1923), who is represented sitting on a rock. From Eyre Square the town's main shopping street (William Street, Shop Street) runs down to O'Brien's Bridge.

*Lynch's Castle (16th c.: National Monument), a large grey building with coats of arms on the façade, now occupied by a bank, was the residence of the Lynches, an aristocratic family which provided several mayors of Galway. One of the Lynches, while in office as mayor, condemned his own son to death for the murder of a Spanish visitor and carried out the sentence with his own hands when no one else was willing to do it: hence the origin of the term "lynch law". A black marble tablet on the wall of the old prison in Market Street marks the spot where the execution is said to have taken place.

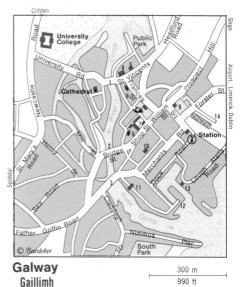

Galway
Gaillimh

300 m
990 ft

1 Salmon Weir Bridge
2 O'Brien's Bridge
3 Claddagh Bridge
4 Court House
5 Town Hall
6 Franciscan Friary
7 Lynch's Castle
8 St Nicholas's Church
9 J. F. Kennedy Memorial Garden
10 Taiohbhearc Theatre
11 Spanish Arch
12 Port
13 Aran Passenger Terminal
14 Bus Terminal

*St Nicholas's Church (National Monument), also in Market Street, was built in the 14th c. and, although much altered in later centuries, has preserved the aspect of a medieval parish church. Notable features are the triple gables of the west front, the gargoyles (rare in Ireland) and, in the interior, a number of tombs and a reader's desk.

The River Corrib is spanned by three bridges. The one farthest upstream, built in 1818, is the *Salmon Weir Bridge*, where hundreds of salmon can be seen in spring on their way up river to the huge expanse of Lough Corrib (see entry) – a journey of only 4 miles (6 km) from the sea.

There is a strong tidal movement on the river here, with a rapid ebb at low tide and an equally rapid flow upstream when the tide changes.

Near the bridge, on the east bank of the river, is the handsome classical *Court House* (1800). Close by, in Frances Street, can be seen an old *Franciscan Friary*, with a chapel containing a number of fine tombs.

The *Cathedral* (St Nicholas and the Assumption), on the right bank, was consecrated in 1965. One of the largest

The Spanish Arch and the River Corrib

churches in Ireland (330 ft (100 m) long by 155 ft (47 m) wide), it occupies the site of a prison in which many Irish patriots were confined; the cost of building it was met almost wholly by public subscription. Good mosaics in the side chapels.

The middle bridge, *O'Brien's Bridge*, is the oldest, its existence being first recorded in 1342. The Claddagh Bridge (a swing bridge) at the south end of the town takes its name from an old fishermen's quarter on the right bank of the Corrib which was occupied for centuries by a fishermen's guild but has now given place to modern buildings. The only relic of the old guild is the "Claddagh ring", a traditional form of wedding-ring with two hands clasping a heart which was worn as an amulet and handed down from mother to daughter. On the east side of the Corrib, below Claddagh Bridge, is the old town gate known as the *Spanish Arch*, leading to Spanish Parade, once the favourite promenade of Spanish merchants. The arch now houses the *Galway City Museum*, with material on the history of Galway and old weapons found in Galway Bay.

Near by is the busy *Harbour.* The boats to the *Aran Islands* (see entry) sail from the east side of the harbour, at the end of

Lough Atalia Road (for air services see below).

SURROUNDINGS. – North-east of Galway on the N17, *Claregalway* has the ruins of a Franciscan friary (National Monument) founded in 1290 and enlarged in the 15th c. On a tombstone in the church is a representation of a primitive plough.

6 miles (9 km) east of the town, at *Carnmore*, lies Galway's airfield, from which there are regular flights by Aer Arann to the Aran Islands and Dublin (see entries).

Continuing from Carnmore to Oranmore and going south from there on the N18, we come to *Clarinbridge*, a pretty little village where the excellent local oysters and shellfish can be sampled. An Oyster Festival is held here in September.

1¼ miles (2 km) beyond Clarinbridge, at Kilcolgan, the N67 branches off on the right. ¾ mile (1 km) west of the main road can be seen the ruined *Drumacoo Church* (National Monument), with finely carved windows and doorway. Here, too, is St Surney's Well, a notable holy well.

Immediately west of Galway and now joined on to it is *Salthill* (Tourist Information Office, tel. (091) 6 30 81, open June–Aug.; Warwick Hotel, B*, 49 r.; Salthill Hotel, Promenade, B*, 47 r.; Sacré Cœur Hotel, B*, 42 r.; Banba Hotel, B, 31 r.; Beach Hotel, B, 22 r.; Rockland Hotel, B, 19 r.; Galway Bay Hotel, C, 58 r.; Glendawn House Guest-house, B, 14 r.; Osterley Lodge Guest-house, B, 11 r.; Galleon Grill Restaurant), a leading seaside resort on the north side of Galway Bay. Its Irish name is Bothar na Tra ("Shore Road"). From the beautiful seafront promenade above a broad sandy beach there are extensive views of the hills of Clare, the Burren and the Aran Islands.

The R336 follows the coast to Barna and *Spiddal* (Bridge House Hotel, B*, 14 r.; Park Lodge Hotel, B, 25 r.), a pretty little resort with good fishing. This coastal area is a great favourite with artists and photographers.

From Spiddal a narrow but very beautiful road leads through the *Iar Connacht Hills* to Oughterard on Lough Corrib.

Glencolumbkille/ Gleann Cholaim Cille

Map reference: B3.
Republic of Ireland.
Province: Ulster. – County: Donegal.
Population: 250.

ⓘ Tourist Information Office,
Glencolumbkille;
tel. 17.
Open June to September.

HOTEL. – *Glencolumcille*, B, 19 r.

RESTAURANT. – *Glencolumcille Hotel.*

Glencolumbkille (Gleann Cholaim Cille, "St Columcille's Glen") is a picturesque holiday resort in the north of Ireland, at the most westerly point in Co. Donegal. It lies in a valley opening into Glen Bay, on the Atlantic, with a sandy bay and magnificent cliff scenery in the surrounding area. The area around Glencolumbkille is one of the Irish-speaking parts of Donegal. Here St Columcille (Columba) lived in solitude and meditated. Another tradition has it that Bonnie Prince Charlie spent some time here during his flight from Britain.

SIGHTS. – Glencolumbkille and the surrounding area are rich in remains of the past, including portal graves, cairns and souterrains. In the churchyard of the Protestant parish church is a souterrain roofed with huge stone slabs.

On 9 June (St Columcille's day) every year there is a *pilgrimage* here, when the pilgrims make a 3 mile (5 km) circuit of 15 stations, marked by a series of stone slabs and pillars inscribed with crosses and geometric designs on the slopes around the village; the largest of these stones is by the church (National Monument). Pilgrims must go round the circuit three or seven times, sometimes throwing a stone on the piles which have grown up around the stations. The pilgrimage must always be completed before sunrise.

On the west side of the village is the *Glencolumbkille Folk Museum*, an open-air museum consisting of four reed-thatched cottages representing different

The coast at Malinmore

periods in Irish life and containing furniture and utensils of the period. There is a shop in which local craft products can be bought. The whole project was the brainchild of Father James McDyer.

SURROUNDINGS. – South-west of Glencolumbkille lies *Malinmore*, a pretty little resort with a bay and picturesque cliffs. Near by, at Cloghanmore, is a court cairn (National Monument) some 3500 years old.

There is good fishing in the coastal waters extending south to the island of *Rathlin O'Birne*, which has a number of antiquities (6th c.) and a lighthouse.

Glendalough/ Gleann da Locha

Map reference: C/D5.
Republic of Ireland.
Province: Leinster. – County: Wicklow.

HOTEL. – *Royal*, B*, 13 r.

RESTAURANT. – *Royal Hotel.*

The celebrated monastic settlement of Glendalough (Gleann da Locha, "Glen of the Two Lakes") lies 25 miles (40 km) south of Dublin, some miles in from the Irish east coast.

From Laragh, on the road (R755) which runs south from Bray through the hills to Arklow, a side road leads up a wooded valley to the west and comes in rather more than a mile (2 km) to Glendalough, a site famed both for its monastic remains and for its scenic beauty.

Around the two lakes from which the place takes its name are the impressive, and for the most part well-preserved, remains (National Monument) of a religious centre which was once of great importance in Ireland. The valley of the River Glenealo, surrounded by hills

between 2130 and 2460 ft (650 and 750 m) and rapidly narrowing farther upstream, offers ample opportunities for walkers, climbers and rock-climbers.

HISTORY. – In the 6th c. St Kevin, seeking solitude, settled in this remote valley as a hermit. His piety and learning, however, soon attracted so many disciples that he founded a monastery. When he died in 618 at a great age Glendalough's great days were only beginning: after his time the Glendalough school is said to have had more than a thousand students. The annals tell of Viking raids and a number of fires in the 12th c. An Abbot of Glendalough, Laurence O'Toole, became Archbishop of Dublin in 1163. The Anglo-Normans made the monastery subject to the see of Dublin; then, after a fire in 1398, the monastery steadily declined. In 1875–80 the buildings were restored, and since then they have been well maintained.

THE **MONASTIC SETTLEMENT

The best starting-point for a tour of the site is the *Upper Lake*, where the first nucleus of the settlement was established. *Teampull na Skellig*, the little rectangular "Church of the Rock", stands on an artificially levelled platform on the lake and can be reached only by boat. 220 yd (200 m) farther east is a cavity in the cliff, probably a Bronze Age burial-place but now known as *St Kevin's Bed* or hermitage. Near a small bridge stands *Reefert Church* (11th c.), with a nave and chancel; the projecting stones at the corners supported the rafters.

Between the Upper and the *Lower Lake*, to the right of the car park, are an old stone fort and three stone crosses, and beside the Lower Lake another cross; all four are stations on the pilgrimage circuit.

The main group of monastic buildings, dating from the heyday of the monastery, lies downstream, near the hotel. The precinct was entered through the gateway,

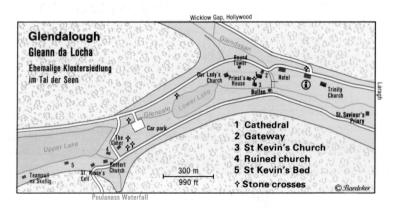

1 Cathedral
2 Gateway
3 St Kevin's Church
4 Ruined church
5 St Kevin's Bed
✣ Stone crosses

Glendalough Round Tower

St Kevin's Church

which has two round-headed granite arches. Near the gateway is the *round tower, 102 ft (31 m) high and 16 ft (5 m) in diameter at the base; it is still in its original condition apart from the roof which is reconstructed from the old stones.

To the west of the round tower stands the granite-built *Church of Our Lady* or St Mary's Church (10th c.), in which St Kevin's tomb was venerated until the 18th c. Beyond this is the *Priest's House*, a 12th c. building in Irish Romanesque style with an interesting carving of much earlier date on the lintel of the doorway. Just beyond it are a large granite cross (6th or 7th c.), the *"Cathedral"*, the largest church on the site, with a nave, chancel and sacristy (11th and 12th c.), and, finally, *St Kevin's Church, erroneously called St Kevin's Kitchen. This is a barrel-vaulted oratory of hard mica schist with a steeply pitched roof and a round-tower belfry (12th c.); it contains numerous gravestones, capitals and other architectural fragments found in the monastic precinct, including a 12th c high cross, with a Crucifixion, a figure of an abbot and interlace ornament, which may once have stood on the pilgrim road to Glendalough. St Kevin's Church outside the enclosure is of relatively little interest.

On the road to Laragh, to the right, stands *Trinity Church* (11th–12th c.), and a mile (1·5 km) east of the cathedral, beyond the river, is the latest complex of buildings, *St Saviour's Priory* (12th c.; reconstructed about 1875): a church with fine Romanesque carvings on the chancel arch and windows and some conventual buildings.

The whole site lies within *Glendalough Forest Park*, which extends north-west up the valley. Two small artificial lakes (reservoirs) and the Hill of Camaderry (2296 ft (700 m)) contribute to the beauty of the scenery.

Glengarriff/ Gleann Garbh

Map reference: E2
Republic of Ireland.
Province: Munster. – County: Cork.
Population: 150.

ⓘ Tourist Information Office,
Glengarriff;
tel. (027) 6 30 84.
Open July and August.

HOTELS. – *Casey's*, A, 20 r.; *Eccles*, Glengarriff Harbour, B, 35 r.; *Mountain View*, B, 20 r.; *Golf Links*, B, 16 r.

RESTAURANT. – *Mountain View Hotel*.

Glengarriff (Gleann Garbh, "Rugged Glen") lies in south-western Ireland at the mouth of a 6 mile (10 km) long valley where the River Glengarriff flows into Bantry Bay. It is wholly given up to the holiday and tourist trade, with accommodation for visitors in private houses as well as in the hotels.
In the favoured climate of this region, to which the Gulf Stream brings moist warmth, a mantle of vegetation of almost tropical luxuriance – fuchsias, yews, hollies and arbutus – covers the rocky slopes of the hills reaching down to the sea.

SURROUNDINGS. – Of the many little islands in the bay the one most worth visiting is *Garinish Island*, which lies offshore to the east of the R572. The gardens, with their magnolias, rhododendrons, camellias, etc., are particularly beautiful. The house in which George Bernard Shaw wrote much of "Saint Joan" in 1923 is open to the public (daily 10 a.m.–5.30 p.m.; admission charge).

The R572 winds its way between the Caha Mountains and the sea along the shores of Bantry Bay and around Adrigole Harbour to *Castletownbere* (Craigie's Cametingane House Hotel, B, 13 r.; Old Bank Restaurant, Bank Place; Wheel Inn Restaurant, Waterfall). Offshore can be seen the striking silhouette of *Bere Island*, on which there is a sailing school.

From *Dunboy Castle* (destroyed 1602) 2 miles (3 km) south-east there is a magnificent view.

Off the tip of the peninsula, separated from it by Dursey Sound, lies *Dursey Island*, which also affords splendid views.

North of Castletownbere the R571 crosses a saddle in the Slieve Miskish Mountains to *Eyeries*, a trim little village, in the neighbourhood of which is a huge ogham stone 17 ft (5·2 m) high (National Monument), looking like a work of modern sculpture.

The road runs north-east from Eyeries to *Lauragh* in Co. Kerry, with the beautiful gardens of Derreen House open to visitors in summer. From here it is possible to return to Glengarriff by way of the Healy Pass (1066 ft (325 m)) and Adrigole.

Gort/Gort lase Guaire

Map reference: C3.
Republic of Ireland.
Province: Connacht. – County: Galway.
Population: 1100.
(i) **Tourist Information Office**
(Aras Fáilte),
Eyre Square,
Galway;
tel. (091) 6 30 81.

HOTEL. – *Glynn's*, B, 14 r.

RESTAURANT. – *O'Grady's*, The Square.

The little market town of Gort (Gort lase Guaire, "Guaire's Field by the Shore") lies to the south of Galway

Gardens on Garinish Island

Bay in western Ireland, at the junction of the N18 and N66. It is laid out
around a large central square with
two early 19th c. churches.

SURROUNDINGS. – There are many features of
interest in the surrounding area. On the north side of
the town, to the west of the N18, lies *Coole Park*
(destroyed in 1941), once the home of Lady Gregory,
one of the founders of the famous Abbey Theatre in
Dublin. Many Irish writers and poets were guests here.
Nothing of this remains except a magnificent avenue
of cedars and a copper beech which bears the initials
of many writers (G. B. Shaw, Yeats, O'Casey and
others). The estate is now a national forest and deer-
park.

Monastic church, Kilmacduagh

South-west of Gort on the R460 are the ruins of the
monastic site of **Kilmacduagh**, with several churches
and a round tower. The *round tower*, 112 ft (34 m)
high, is excellently preserved, but leans about 2 ft
(60 cm) out of the perpendicular; the entrance is 25 ft
(7·8 m) above the ground. Beside it is the Cathedral
(12th/15th c.), with nave, chancel and transepts; in
the north transept are fine popular-style representations of the Crucifixion. To the right of the cathedral
stands St John's Church (12th c.), and adjoining it a
fortress-like 13th c. building, probably the abbot's
lodging. At the north-west corner of the precinct is
O'Heyne's Church (13th c.), with a fine chancel arch,
and close by are the remains of another small church.
On the other side of the road, opposite the cathedral, is
St Mary's Church (12th c.). The whole site, set in green
pastureland on the shores of a lough, with the Burren
Hills in the background, is exceedingly picturesque.

Yeats' Thoor Ballylee

4½ miles (7 km) north-east of Gort (just off the N66),
on the banks of a stream, stands *Thoor Ballylee*, a four-
storey 16th c. keep which was bought and restored by
W. B. Yeats, who lived in it from 1921 to 1929. His stay
is commemorated by a stone tablet with a few lines of
verse by him. The castle now contains a museum with
mementoes of the poet, including the first edition
of his works (open July and Aug. 9 a.m.–9 p.m.,
Mar.–June, Sept. and Oct. 10 a.m.–6 p.m.; admission
charge).

South-east of Gort lies *Lough Cutra*. The River Beagh
flows out of the lough but – like other rivers in this
limestone country – disappears into the ground. The
lough itself is highly picturesque, with a number of
small wooded islets on which are the ruins of churches
and a castle. Commandingly situated on the shores
of the lough is Lough Cutra Castle, and early 19th c.
house, complete with tower and battlements, designed by John Nash for the first Viscount Gort
(1810); it is not open to the public.

Grand Canal

Map reference: C3–4.
Republic of Ireland.
Length: 80 miles.

The Grand Canal links Dublin Bay
with the Shannon (see entry), following a fairly direct westerly
course from Dublin (see entry), by
way of Naas and Tullamore (see
entries) to Shannon Harbour. Differences of height are accommodated by a total of 52 locks.

HISTORY. – Construction of the canal began in 1756,
and soon afterwards the project was taken over by a

Dublin company and carried forward as far as the River Morrell by 1777, one of the purposes of this section being to improve the city's water-supply. Two years later the completed section of the canal was opened to navigation. In 1785 the Barrow Line, a branch canal from Robertstown to Athy, was brought into use. In 1804 the whole canal was completed, and the first boats began to ply between Dublin and Shannon Harbour. Thereafter, until the middle of the 19th c., various other branch canals to towns lying near the main canal were constructed. With the development of the railway system the economic importance of the canal declined, and this decline continued in the 20th c., until about 1960 commercial traffic on the branch canals came to an end.

BOATING ON THE GRAND CANAL. – The Grand Canal is now used mainly for pleasure-boating. Boats are restricted to the following maximum dimensions: length 60 ft (18·5 m), width 13 ft (3·9 m), draught 4 ft (1·2 m), freeboard 9 ft (2·75 m). Every boat must bear a name or a number. The maximum permitted speed is 3 miles (5 km) an hour. Boats keep to the right, with overtaking on the left. The locks may be used only in daylight. At certain points boats can be hired.

Further information about boating on the Grand Canal can be obtained from the Inland Waterways Association of Ireland, 3 Herbert Street, Dublin 2.

FISHING. – The canal system is well stocked with fish, particularly bream, rudd and perch, and offers excellent opportunities for fishermen.

Royal Canal: see entry.

Horn Head/Corran Binne

Map reference: A4.
Republic of Ireland.
Province: Ulster. – County: Donegal.
(i) Tourist Information Office,
    Dunfanaghy;
    tel. 63.
    Open June to August.

Horn Head (Corran Binne, "Hollow in the Hills"), on the north coast of Donegal, is the terminal point of a peninsula extending out into the Atlantic. It is reached by way of the N56.

SIGHTS. – The best starting-point for excursions to Horn Head and the surrounding area is Dunfanaghy (Arnold's

Hotel, B*, 40 r.; Carrig Rua Hotel, B*, 23 r.), which has an 18-hole golf-course and the little harbour of Port-na-Blagh (Port-na-Blagh Hotel, A, 58 r.). Just over a mile (2 km) east, in a sheltered bay, rises Marble Hill. All these places have beautiful sandy beaches.

From Dunfanaghy there is a delightful walk along the west coast of the peninsula to Horn Head. The headland rises straight out of the water to a height of about 600 ft (180 m), with views northward of the boundless Atlantic, broken only by numerous islands and promontories, and inland of magnificent ranges of hills, with Muckish Mountain and Mount Errigal as backdrops. Horn Head is the haunt of innumerable seabirds.

It is also possible to drive to the tip of the peninsula. The best view of the cliffs is to be had from Traghlisk Point on the east side.

South-east of Marble Hill on the Ards Peninsula, which projects into the bay of Sheep Haven, is a Capuchin friary. Visitors may be admitted to the grounds on application.

To the south of the friary, beautifully situated on a promontory, are the ruins of Doe Castle (16th c.: National Monument), a four-storey keep surrounded by defensive walls and towers. In the burial ground are interred the chiefs of many leading Donegal families.

6 miles (10 km) south of Dunfanaghy lies Creeslough, with a picturesque bridge on the Duntally River, a waterfall and St Michael's Church, a fine modern building (by Liam McCormick and Partners, 1971).

From here there are attractive trips to two beautiful loughs, Glen Lough and Lough Veagh, to the south. On the quiet shores of Lough Veagh, in an otherwise bare and rugged region, are the young plantations and park of Glenbeigh. Around this turreted neo-Gothic mansion are beautifully laid out gardens and terraces with a profusion of exotic plants, particularly rhododendrons.

Doe Castle

Inishcrone/Inis Eascrach Abhann

Map reference: A2.
Republic of Ireland.
Province: Connacht. – County: Sligo.
Population: 500.
ⓘ Tourist Information Office,
Main Street,
Inishcrone;
tel. (096) 3 62 02.
Open June to September.

HOTELS. – *Benbulben House*, B, 18 r.; *Castle Arms*, C, 17 r.; *Killala Bay*, C, 16 r.; *Alpine*, C, 15 r.; *Atlantic*, C, 12 r.

RESTAURANT. – *Clark's*.

Inishcrone or Enniscrone (Inis Eascrach Abhann, "Watershed Island") is a popular seaside resort in north-western Ireland, situated on the east side of Killala Bay, at the mouth of the broad estuary of the River Moy. Three are two well-equipped bath-houses with sulphur and other medicinal baths.

SURROUNDINGS. – 2½ miles (4 km) north of the village on the NR297 can be seen the ruins of *Castle Firbis*, seat of the MacFirbis family, which produced a number of noted poets and annalists. One of them, about 1416, wrote the famous "Great Book of Lecan", a genealogical work now in the library of the Royal Irish Academy in Dublin. Two other celebrated codices came from here.

The R297 leads north, at some distance from the sea, to *Easky*, a small holiday resort with good sailing, surfing and fishing. In the neighbourhood are numerous forts, a large dolmen (prehistoric chambered tomb) and the Split Rock, a travelled boulder with a deep fissure.

At *Dromore West*, where the R297 joins the N59, is a waterfall. 6 miles (10 km) north-east on a by-road we come to *Aughris Head*, a beautiful rocky headland.

From Dromore West a minor road runs south through the Ox Mountains, past lonely Lough Easky (good trout fishing), to join the R294. *Tubbercurry* 4 miles (6 km) east has good fishing; boats can be hired.

4 miles (6 km) south-west of Tubbercurry, picturesquely situated on the River Moy, are the ruins of *Banada Abbey*, an Augustinian house (15th c.).

On the way back to Inishcrone the R294 follows the north side of *Lough Talt* (good trout fishing), in a beautiful setting in the Ox Mountains.

Inishowen Peninsula/Inis Eoghain

Map reference: A4/5.
Republic of Ireland.
Province: Ulster. – County: Donegal.
Population (Buncrana): 3500.
ⓘ Tourist Information Office,
Buncrana;
tel. 158.
Open June to August.

HOTELS. – IN BUNCRANA: *Lough Swilly*, B, 18 r.; *White Strand Motor Inn*, B, 12 r.

The Inishowen Peninsula (Inis Eoghain, "Eoghan's Island") is the northernmost part of Ireland; its most northerly point is Malin Head. On the west side of the peninsula Lough Swilly, a broad arm of the sea, cuts deep into the land; on the east side is the great expanse of Lough Foyle, beyond which is Northern Ireland. At its north-western tip is Malin Head, overlooking the open sea. Inishowen is reached on the N13 from Letterkenny (see entry). The R238 encircles the peninsula.

CIRCUIT OF THE PENINSULA. – The chief place on the peninsula is *Buncrana*, a popular seaside resort on the east side of Lough Swilly, with a 3 mile (5 km) long beach, Lisfannon Strand (golf-courses). Beautifully situated on the lough is O'Doherty's Keep, a well-preserved but architecturally undistinguished stronghold (14th/17th c.: National Monument). Beyond the bridge stands *Buncrana Castle* (by Vaughan, 1716), a handsome mansion with a beautiful interior, unfortunately falling into a state of disrepair.

From Buncrana the best plan is to take the by-road which goes north-west to *Dunree Head* (beautiful view from lighthouse) and then over a breath-takingly steep pass (gradients of up to 30 per cent), the Gap of Mamore. The magnificent scenery is best seen when travelling from south to north (as described here). At the north end of the road *Dunaff Head* has magnificent cliffs (much frequented by rock-climbers) and beautiful views.

At Clonmany we rejoin the R238. 2 miles (3 km) east is *Ballyliffin* (Strand Hotel, B*, 10 r.; Ballyliffin Hotel, B*, 10 r.), near the 2 mile (3 km) long Pollan Strand. In the dunes of the *Doagh Peninsula* are prehistoric rubbish dumps, in which highly interesting discoveries have been made. Picturesquely situated at the northern tip of the peninsula are the ruins of Carrickabrahey Castle.

The R238 continues to *Carndonagh*, a little market town (hosiery manufacture, distillery), a few hundred yards (metres) west of which, by the roadside, are three Early Christian monuments (all scheduled National Monuments), including an 8th c.

*cross, one of the earliest in Ireland. The cross has rounded stubby arms with interlace ornament; in the lower half is the figure of a man with extended arms, flanked by smaller figures; and the back also has interlace and a human figure. On either side of the cross are smaller stones with reliefs of David with his harp, a bird, a man with two bells and other devices. Other monuments can be seen in the churchyard.

3 miles (5 km) north is Malin, from which the R242 leads past a handsome 18th c. mansion, Malin Hall (1758), to *Malin Head*, with magnificent cliff scenery. $\frac{3}{4}$ mile (1 km) west is *Hell's Hole*, a remarkable chasm into which the sea rushes with great force.

From Malin Head a long range of cliffs up to 790 ft (240 m) high extends south-east to *Glengad Head*. Farther south is *Culdaff*, a fishing centre (sea trout). Near here, at *Clonca*, are a ruined church, a fine but badly weathered high cross with a representation of the Miracle of the Loaves and Fishes, two male figures and geometric ornament, and a finely carved tombstone (National Monuments).

At *Carrowmore* is a group of high crosses (National Monuments).

The R238 continues south-east to *Moville*, a popular resort on Lough Foyle. From here there is a ferry service (only in summer; cars not carried) to Oban in Scotland. $2\frac{1}{2}$ miles (4 km) north-west lies *Greencastle*, with the ruins of a large castle (1305: National Monument). Near by is a Martello tower (hotel) of 1810.

From Moville the R241 goes north-east to *Inishowen Head*, from which another range of magnificent cliffs (with views of Northern Ireland on the far side of Lough Foyle) extends north-west. The cliff scenery and the beautiful valley of Glenagiveny attract many visitors.

The circuit of the peninsula can be completed by following the R238 along the shores of Lough Foyle to *Muff* (border crossing to Londonderry (see entry) in Northern Ireland) and continuing west on the R239 to rejoin the R238 south of Burnfoot.

At the intersection of the R238 with the N13, to the south of the R239, stands a

Grianán of Aileach

notable modern church dedicated to *St Aengus (by MacCormick and Madden), a circular structure with a ring of windows and a curving tent roof surmounted by a glass pyramid. Its form may have been influenced by the *Grianán of Aileach (National Monument), 2½ miles (4 km) away to the south. (Grianán means "Palace of the Sun".) This imposing circular stone fort is commandingly situated on a 790 ft (240 m) high hill, surrounded by three concentric earth ramparts. The windowless wall, constructed without mortar, is 17 ft (5 m) high and 13 ft (4 m) thick at the base, and encloses a grass-covered area 79 ft (24 m) across, entered through a low doorway. The wall is terraced on the inside, with steps leading up to the three terraces, and within the thickness of the wall are small chambers and passages. The period of construction of the fort, which was the seat of the kings of Ulster from the 5th to the 12th c., is unknown. It was extensively restored in 1870; a black line distinguishes the original work from the restored part above it. From the walls of the fort there are breath-taking views over the plain and the loughs.

3 miles (5 km) north-west lies *Fahan*, from which there is a ferry to Rathmullan (see Fanad Peninsula). In the old monastic churchyard adjoining a modern church is a very ancient cross-slab (8th c.), with two crudely carved figures flanking a cross of elaborate interlace work; on one of the edges is a Greek inscription (a rarity in Ireland).

Kells/Ceanannus Mor

Map reference: C5.
Republic of Ireland.
Province: Leinster. – County: Meath.
Population: 2600.

ⓘ Tourist Information Office,
Drogheda;
tel. (041) 3 70 70.
Open July and August.

HOTEL. – *Headfort Arms*, B, 22 r.

RESTAURANTS. – *Headfort Arms Hotel*; *Murphy Inn*, Market Street.

Kells (Ceanannus Mor, "Great Residence") lies in the wooded valley of the Blackwater 25 miles (40 km) inland from the Irish east coast, at the intersection of the N3 and N52.

HISTORY. – A monastic settlement was established here by St Columba in the 6th c., and in the 9th c. monks from Iona, driven out by Viking raids, sought refuge at Kells. In later centuries the settlement was several times plundered and subsequently restored.

The town was fortified by the Anglo-Normans and maintained its importance until the Dissolution of the Monasteries in 1551.

SIGHTS. – The name of Kells is primarily associated with the famous "Book of Kells", a splendidly illuminated Gospel book which is now in the library of Trinity College in Dublin (see entry). A facsimile can be seen in *St Columba's Church*, a modern building on high ground in the centre of the town, surrounded by a churchyard, on the site of the old monastery. By the church stands a 100 ft (30 m) high *round tower* (10th c.: National Monument) with five windows at the top; the original roof is missing. Adjoining is the *South Cross or Cross of SS Patrick and Columba (National Monument), probably erected in the 9th c. It has a wealth of sculptured ornament. On the base are a train of chariots, animals and interlace; on the south face the Fall, Cain and Abel, the Three Young Men in the Fiery Furnace, and above this Daniel in the Lions' Den, the Sacrifice of Isaac, to the right SS Paul and Antony in the wilderness, and above this again David with his harp and the Miracle of the Loaves and Fishes; and on the west face the Crucifixion and Christ as Judge. There are also a representation of David killing the lion and the bear and a number of panels with interlace ornament and fabulous beasts.

33 yd (30 m) away can be seen the stump of a very large cross (National Monument) with unusual representations on the east side of the Baptism of Christ (with two rivers flowing together), the Marriage in Cana (?), the Presentation in the Temple (?), David with his harp and the Entry into Jerusalem (?), and on the west side Adam and Eve, Noah's Ark, etc. An unfinished cross beside the church reveals the sculptor's method of work.

Also in the churchyard stands the tower of a medieval church, with various gravestones built into the walls, including a fine one with the effigies of a man and his wife.

To the north-west, beyond Church Lane, is *St Columba's House (National Monument), an oratory with a steeply pitched stone roof (probably 10th c.). The interior measures 24 by 21 ft (7·2 by 6·3 m), with walls more than 4 ft (1·2 m) thick which incline inwards until they meet in a ridge. The wall of an upper chamber under the roof (entered on a steep ladder) serves to support the roof. The entrance was originally 6½ ft (2 m) above the ground.

In Cross Street stands another high cross, the *Market Cross* (National Monument), carved with Biblical scenes similar to those on the South Cross.

South Cross

St Columba's House

SURROUNDINGS. – The estate of *Headfort*, on the north-east side of the town, has a handsome Georgian house (1770), now occupied by a school.

12½ (20 km) west of Kells on the R168 and R154, in the *Slieve na Calliagh* (Witch's Hill) range, is the **Loughcrew** group of burials. Here some 30 Neolithic chambered cairns are distributed over two neighbouring peaks. Few of them have preserved their chambers intact. Perhaps the most interesting is Cairn T in the eastern group, 120 ft (36 m) in diameter, which has a large main chamber with side chambers and many stones with scribed ornament. A walk in these hills, 985 ft (300 m) above the plain, affords superb views of the fertile countryside of Meath.

3 miles (5 km) north-west of the Loughcrew tombs lies the little town of *Oldcastle*, near which are two good fishing lakes, Lough Ramor (with the village of *Virginia*, p. 82, on its northern shore) and Lough Sheeling.

From Kells the N3 runs north-west towards Virginia. Just outside the town, on the left, can be seen a memorial tower of 1791 on the *Hill of Loyd* (views). 2½ miles (4 km) farther on are the ruins of *St Ciarán's Church*, on the banks of the Blackwater, with three simple high crosses (National Monuments), an Early Christian gravestone and a holy well.

Kenmare/An Neidin

Map reference: E2.
Republic of Ireland.
Province: Munster. – County: Kerry.
Population: 1100.
ⓘ **Tourist Information Office,**
Kenmare;
tel. (064) 4 12 33.
Open June to September.

HOTELS. – *Park*, A*, 48 r.; *Kenmare Bay*, A, 100 r.; *Lansdowne Arms*, B, 15 r.; *Wander Inn*, B, 14 r.

RESTAURANT. – *Purple Heather*, Henry Street.

EVENT. – *Fruits de Mer Festival* (Oct.).

Kenmare (An Neidin, "Little Nest"), a friendly little seaside resort at the south-western tip of Ireland, lies at the outflow of the River Roughty into the long inlet known as the Kenmare River. The town is noted for its high-quality lace, and also for its excellent woollen goods.

SIGHTS. – At the northern end of the New Bridge can be seen *Cromwell's Fort*, which was held by British troops during the Cromwellian Wars, though Cromwell himself was never in Kenmare.

An old footbridge spans the River Finnihy, a tributary of the Kenmare River. Near the

bridge is a circle of 15 standing stones, 50 ft (15 m) in diameter, with a dolmen in the centre.

SURROUNDINGS. – Kenmare lies at the intersection of two roads running through very beautiful scenery – the N71, leading north–south, and the R569/N70 going east–west. The N71 runs north to *Killarney* (see entry), the R569 east up the valley of the River Roughty (good fishing) to *Kilgarvan*. From Kilgarvan a charming but rather difficult road runs south through the hills to Bantry Bay (Co. Cork).

From Kenmare the N71 winds its way south, passing through three tunnels, up the valley of the River Sheen, another good fishing river. The watershed is passed in a tunnel (good views from both ends), and the road then continues down to *Glengarriff* (see entry) through a heather-clad valley flanked by red rocks, with magnificent views.

The R571 runs south-west from Kenmare along the south side of the Kenmare River to the *Cloonee Loughs*, from which a chain of smaller loughs ascends a valley into the hills. The road continues to Lauragh (see Glengarriff).

Kenmare is also a good starting-point for a drive round the Beara Peninsula on the beautiful scenic road known as the *Ring of Kerry* (see entry), taking the N70, which branches off the N71 just to the north-west of the town.

Kerry

See Ring of Kerry

Kildare/Cill Dara

Map reference: C5.
Republic of Ireland.
Province: Leinster. – County: Kildare.
Population: 4000.
ⓘ **Tourist Information Office,**
Naas;
tel. (045) 9 76 36.
Open July and August.

HOTEL. – *Derby House*, C, 13 r.

RESTAURANTS. – *Leinster Lodge*, Dublin Street; *Jockey Hall* (Curragh Racecourse).

EVENT. *Feast of St Brigid* (1 Feb.).

Kildare (Cill Dara, "Church of the Oak") lies in the east of Ireland on the Dublin–Limerick road (N7), on a site raised slightly above the surrounding plain. It is the centre of Ireland's horse-breeding and training industry.

St Brigid of Kildare (453–521), who ranks with St Patrick as Patron Saint of Ireland, founded a famous double monastery for monks and nuns here, headed jointly by a bishop as abbot and an abbess. The nuns tended a perpetual fire which was extinguished only at the dissolution of the monastery.

SIGHTS. – The town's glorious past is recalled by *St Brigid's Cathedral* (1223), which has been much restored, most recently in 1875–96. It contains a number of medieval tombs, notably the tomb of one of the Fitzgeralds of Lackach (d. 1575). In the churchyard stands a fine *round tower*, 105 ft (32 m) high, which was probably one of the last to be erected in Ireland; it can be climbed without difficulty. The roof is modern.

Off the east side of the Market Place is a 15th c. tower, all that remains of Kildare Castle.

SURROUNDINGS. – On the *Hill of Allen*, 5 miles (8 km) north of the town on the R415, there once stood a castle belonging to the kings of Leinster. The site is now occupied by a tower (1859) with Latin inscriptions; extensive views.

On the south-eastern outskirts of Kildare, at Tully, is the *Irish National Stud*, which has produced many famous racehorses. Here, too, is the *Irish Horse Museum*, covering the history of the horse from the Bronze Age to the present day. Among the exhibits can be seen the skeleton of the celebrated Irish racehorse Arkle.

Adjoining the grounds of the National Stud are the *Japanese Gardens*, laid out by Japanese gardeners, using imported plants, at the beginning of the 20th c. The gardens portray symbolically the stages of man's life.

The National Stud, the Horse Museum and the Japanese Gardens are open to the public from Easter to October (Mon.–Sat. 10.30 a.m.–12.30 p.m. and 2–5 p.m., Sun. 2–5 p.m.; admission charge).

To the east of the National Stud, in the Curragh Plain, lies the world-famous *Curragh Racecourse*, where the Irish Derby is run every year at the end of June or beginning of July.

At the eastern edge of the Curragh Plain, on the River Liffey (bridge of 1319), we come to the little town of *Kilcullen*, 2 miles (3 km) south of which is *Old Kilcullen*. Once a walled town with seven gates, Old Kilcullen preserves the remains of a monastery founded by St Patrick (National Monument), with a very interesting fragment of a 9th c. high cross which has representations of David with the lion (north side), Samson with the lion (west side), bishops, unidentified figures and interlace ornament. There is another badly weathered cross-shaft. Near by are the remains of a round tower and of a Romanesque church (12th c.).

Between Kilcullen and Old Kilcullen, on the west side of the N78, stands the hill-fort of *Dún Ailinne*, once a stronghold of the kings of Leinster. Its 15 ft (4·5 m) high walls enclose an area with a diameter of 150 yd

(135 m). The ditch, unusually, runs inside rather than outside the walls. The site was occupied from the Bronze Age until about 1800.

7 miles (11 km) west of Kildare lies the ancient little market town of *Monasterevan*, with handsome late 19th c. houses.

To the south of the village is *Moore Abbey*, an elegant 18th c. house built on the site of an old monastery. It is now a home for the mentally handicapped.

North of Monasterevan the *Grand Canal* (see entry) crosses the River Barrow in an aqueduct.

Kilkee/Cill Chaoidhe

Map reference: D2.
Republic of Ireland.
Province: Munster. – County: Clare.
Population: 1400.

ⓘ **Tourist Information Office,**
O'Connell Street,
Kilkee;
tel. 72.
Open June to August.

HOTELS. – *Thomond*, B*, 23 r.; *Victoria*, B, 20 r.; *Halpin's*, 2 Evin Street, B, 11 r.

The attractive family holiday resort of Kilkee (Cill Chaoidhe, "Church of St Caoidhe") lies in the west of Ireland on a semicircular bay sheltered from the Atlantic by the Duggerna Rocks.

SIGHTS. – From Kilkee a road to the west passes the Duggerna Rocks, with bench-like rock formations (open-air concerts) and comes to *Lookout Hill*, 200 ft (60 m) above the sea, from which in clear weather there are beautiful far-ranging views (care required on the edge of the cliffs).

SURROUNDINGS. – 6 miles (10 km) north-east of the town on the N67 is the village of *Doonbeg*, with beaches which are noted for their very beautiful shells.

South-east of Kilkee on the N67 lies the little market town and port of *Kilrush* (Inis Cathaigh Hotel, B, 16 r.; Orchard Hotel, B, 16 r.). The harbour at Cappagh Pier, 2 miles (3 km) south on the Shannon Estuary, has good berths and supply facilities for ships.

From here a boat can be hired to *Scattery Island*, on which are the ruins of a 6th c. monastery (National Monument) founded by St Senan. The **round tower**, one of the tallest in Ireland (115 ft (35 m)), can be seen from some way off; it is unusual in having the entrance at ground-level. To the east is the "Cathedral", to the north a 12th c. Romanesque church, to the south-east an early church with medieval additions. In the vicinity are other ecclesiastical buildings. The monastery was a place of great importance in the 14th and 15th c. but was destroyed in the reign of Elizabeth I.

Newly built boats, when first launched, used to sail round the island "with the sun", and pebbles from Scattery carried in a ship were believed to protect it from shipwreck.

The N67 comes to an end 5 miles (8 km) south-east of Kilrush at *Killimer*, from which there is a car ferry across the Shannon Estuary to Tarbert (see Ballybunion). If you are travelling south this saves a detour of some 55 miles (89 km) round the estuaries of the Fergus and Shannon. Hourly departures in both directions (at the half-hour from Killimer, on the hour from Tarbert).

There is also a very pleasant run from Kilkee on a minor road south-west along the coast to Fooagh, once a small spa (chalybeate spring), and *Fooagh Point*, with a holy well and magnificent rock scenery (tunnels, caves, cliffs), and then across the peninsula to *Carrigaholt*. Above the harbour are the fine ruins of a tall, narrow tower house (15th c.: National Monument), in a well-preserved outer ward; the turret facing towards the pier is modern. There is an Irish-language college in the village.

A beautiful road leads south-west from Carrigaholt to Kilbaha, from which it is 2½ miles (4 km) to *Loop Head* (lighthouse). Off the point is an isolated section of cliff known as Diarmaid and Grainne's Rock. Breathtaking views.

Kilkenny/Cill Chainnigh

Map reference: D4.
Republic of Ireland.
Province: Leinster. – County: Kilkenny.
Population 9500.

(i) **Tourist Information Office,**
Shee's Almshouse, Rose Inn Street;
tel. (056) 2 17 55.

HOTELS. – *Newpark*, A, 44 r.; *Springhill*, B*, 44 r.; *Club House*, B, 25 r.; *Carmel*, C, 14 r.

RESTAURANTS. – *Lack House*, Dublin Road; *Mulhall's*, 6 High Street; *Newpark Hotel*.

EVENT. – *Kilkenny Arts Week* (concerts, exhibitions, etc., Aug.).

Kilkenny (Cill Chainnigh, "Canice's Church"), in south-eastern Ireland on the banks of the River Nore, is perhaps second only to Dublin in its attraction for visitors. Its narrow winding streets lend it an old-world aspect; its terraces of handsome Georgian houses give it elegance; and with all this it is a busy modern town and market centre for a fertile agricultural area.

HISTORY. – A church was built here in the 6th c. by St Canice. In pre-Norman times it was the seat of the kings of Ossory, and later it passed into the hands of the Ormonds. During the 14th c. a number of parliaments met in Kilkenny, including the one in 1366 which passed the infamous Statute of Kilkenny. This made it high treason for an Anglo-Norman (i.e. an Englishman settled in Ireland) to marry an Irish-woman, adopt Irish customs, speak Irish or wear Irish dress, and prohibited Irishmen from living in a walled town. Although rigorously enforced, the statute failed in its object of preventing the assimilation of Anglo-Normans and Irish. From 1642 to 1648 the town was the seat of the Confederation of Kilkenny, an independent Irish parliament which brought together both the Old Irish and the Anglo-Irish Catholics; later, however, the Confederation split into two camps and the Anglo-Irish allied themselves with the English. In 1650 Cromwell took the town, and the Irish garrison was allowed to march out with full honours.

From time immemorial Kilkenny has been divided into three districts or wards – Irishtown, with the Cathedral as its central landmark; High Town to the south, dominated by Kilkenny Castle; and on the other bank of the River Nore the eastern district, with St John's Priory.

Irishtown

At the north end of the town, just off Vicar Street, stands *St Canice's Cathedral, one of Ireland's finest cathedrals (9 a.m.– 1 p.m. and 2–6 p.m.). Built on the site of an earlier church, it was begun about 1251 and completed in 1820. The massive squat tower (14th c.) and the walls of the aisles, transepts and clerestory are all topped by crenellations. In spite of much restoration (most recently in 1863–64) the interior has preserved its spacious character. It contains many fine monuments, including the tombs of the son of Henry de Ponto (1285: the oldest) and of Edmund Purcell (1549), both in the north aisle. The Purcell tomb has a carving of a theme frequently found in Irish sculpture – a cock crowing on the edge of a cooking-pot. This is a representation of the old Irish legend that after Christ's Resurrection a servant carried the news to the High Priest's kitchen. The cook scoffed at the story – as unlikely, he said, as that the cock cooking in the pot would come to life again: whereupon the cock jumped out of the pot and crowed.

In the choir can be seen the tombs of Bishop de Ledrede (d. 1360) and Bishop Rothe; in the south transept the tomb of the eighth Earl of Ormond and his wife (1539); and in the south aisle the tombs of Viscount Mountgarret, in armour, Bishop Walsh (1585) and a lady in old Irish dress.

In the north transept is St Ciarán's Chair, of black marble, and in the nave a 12th c. font.

St Canice's Cathedral

By the south transept stands a 100 ft (30 m) high *round tower* with numerous windows; the roof is not original. From the top (admission charge) there are fine views of the city and surrounding area.

From the Cathedral *St Canice's Steps* (1614) lead down to Dean Street.

High Town

Parliament Street, running south from the Cathedral, crosses the little River Bregagh, the boundary between Irishtown and High Town. On the right, in Abbey Street, are the *Black Freren Gate* (one of the old town gates) and beyond this *Black Abbey* (c. 1230), the church of an old Dominican friary. Of the original church there remain only the nave, south transept (14th c.) and tower (15th c.). Notable features of the interior are a medieval alabaster carving of the Trinity and a crudely carved oak figure of St Dominic.

Off Parliament Street on the left can be seen the ruins of *St Francis's Friary* (National Monument), a Franciscan house founded about 1232 and extended in 1321, when the beautiful seven-light east window was inserted. The slender tower has fine sculpture. The Abbey

Museum contains a variety of interesting antiquities.

Farther down Parliament Street stands *Rothe House, an Elizabethan merchant's house built round two courtyards

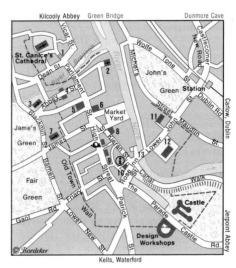

Kilkenny
Cill Chainnigh

	300 m
	990 ft

1 St Canice's Steps
2 St Francis's Friary
3 Black Abbey
4 Black Freren Gate
5 Rothe House
6 Court House
7 St Mary's Cathedral
8 Kyteler's Inn
9 Town Hall
10 She Almshouse
    (Tourist Office)
11 St John's Priory
12 Kilkenny College
13 John's Bridge

(1594; restored 1966). It is now the headquarters of the Kilkenny Archaeological Society, with their library and museum (open daily 3–5 p.m.; admission charge). On the opposite side of the street is the *Court House* (1794).

To the right, higher up, can be seen *St Mary's Cathedral* (1843), with a tower 200 ft (60 m) high.

To the left, in St Kieran's Street, is the oldest building in the town, *Kyteler's Inn*. Restored, with an old-style interior, it is still an inn.

In High Street, the continuation of Parliament Street, we come to the *Tholsel* (1761), now the Town Hall, in which the civic insignia and muniments (dating back to 1230) are preserved.

South-east of the Town Hall is *St Mary's Hall*, originally built as a parish church (13th c.?) and now a community house. It has a number of monuments from the old church, notably the tomb of Richard Rothe (d. 1637) and, in the churchyard, a monument with figures of Faith, Hope and Charity and the Twelve Apostles.

Adjoining St Mary's Hall is *Shee's Almshouse*, founded in 1582 by Sir Richard Shee, which remained in use as an almshouse until 1895.

In the Parade rises *Kilkenny Castle*, begun by William de Marshal in the 13th c. From 1391 to 1931 the castle – in the course of centuries much altered and enlarged, particularly in the 17th c. by the first Duke of Ormonde and in the 19th c. (picture-gallery wing) – was the principal seat of the Butler family, Earls and Dukes of Ormond, a final "e" being added to Ormond to denote a Duke. Finely situated on the high river-bank and surrounded by gardens, the castle is now open to the public (June–Sept., daily 10.30 a.m.–1 p.m. and 2–6.30 p.m.; 30 Sept.–31 May,

11 a.m.–1 p.m. and 2–5.30 p.m., except Mondays; conducted tours). Across the street are the old stables, now housing the *Kilkenny Design Workshops*, which have made a great contribution to the improvement of the design and packaging of Irish products.

Eastern District

The western and eastern districts of Kilkenny are linked by two bridges spanning the River Nore, John's Bridge and Green Bridge, rebuilt after a disastrous flood in 1763.

From the important street intersection at Shee's Almshouse John's Bridge leads into Lower John Street. In this street is *Kilkenny College*, a handsome Georgian building of 1782, successor to St John's College (founded 1666), which counted Jonathan Swift and George Berkeley among its pupils. Across the street is *St John's Priory* (13th c.: National Monument). Of the church there survives only the chancel, with beautiful windows and capitals; the Lady Chapel (rebuilt 1817) is still used for worship.

Along the banks of the river stand a number of mills, including corn-mills which are still in operation.

SURROUNDINGS. – North of the city on the N77 is **Dunmore Cave** (National Monument). Beyond a large entrance hall are three easily accessible chambers, in the last of which can be seen the Market Cross, a stalagmite over 20 ft (6 m) high; the chambers to the left of the entrance are more difficult of access. Conducted tours.

The road continues north past *Foulsrath Castle* (8 miles (13 km): now a youth hostel) to *Ballyragget* (10 miles (17 km)), with the ruins of a 15th–16th c. Ormond castle, a keep standing in a walled outer ward with four round towers. One Countess of Ormond was celebrated for leading her forces into battle.

7 miles (11 km) east by way of the R694, on the N78, we come to *Castlecomer*, a small planned town established in 1636. It has a 9-hole golf-course and good salmon fishing in the River Dinan.

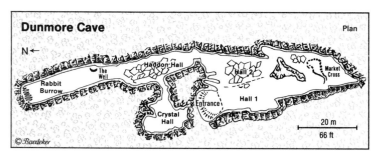

4½ miles (7 km) east of Kilkenny, reached on a minor road which branches left off the N10, stands *Clara Castle* (15th c.: National Monument), an unusually well-preserved six-storey tower house which still has the original oak beams, giving an excellent impression of the character of a fortified dwelling of the period. Among features of particular interest are the forecourt, a passage with a "murder hole" (a hole in the roof through which intruders could be pelted with missiles), a fine fireplace and a secret room.

Rather over a mile (2 km) farther on the R702 goes off on the right to *Gowran*, with a fine old parish church (*c.* 1275: National Monument) whose tower (14th or 15th c.), on the site of the original choir, has been incorporated in the present 19th c. church. The interior has fine pointed arches and columns of black marble; good sculpture and monuments (14th–17th c.). There are race-meetings on Gowran Park Racecourse throughout the year.

11 miles (18 km) south of Kilkenny, reached on the N9 from Gowran or the R700 direct from Kilkenny, lies *Thomastown*, with a ruined 13th c. church (National Monument) and, in the Roman Catholic parish church, a High Altar from Jerpoint Abbey (below).

North of Thomastown on the N9 it is well worth stopping in the village of *Kilfane* to see the over-life-size effigy of Sir Thomas de Cantwell on his tomb (13th c.: National Monument) in the church.

From Kilfane a minor road runs east to join the R703, which leads to *Graiguenamanagh*, on the River Barrow (fishing). In this little town is *Duiske Abbey* (National Monument), a Cistercian house. In the churchyard, on the south side of the chancel, are two small granite high crosses with carvings of Biblical scenes and abstract ornament.

5 miles (8 km) south-east of Thomastown on the wooded banks of the River More, here spanned by a graceful 18th c. bridge, lies *Inistioge*, with the remains of an Augustinian abbey founded in 1210. The nave, Lady Chapel and tower of the church still survive. The tower, of which the lower part is square and the upper part octagonal, is now a mausoleum.

From Inistioge *Brandon Hill* (1677 ft (511 m)) can be climbed. On the summit are a cairn and a stone circle; fine views of the Barrow and Nore valleys.

1½ miles (2·5 km) south-west of Thomastown stands *Jerpoint Abbey* (National Monument), one of Ireland's most beautiful monastic ruins (open from June to September; admission charge). The abbey, founded in 1158, was occupied by the Cistercians from 1180 until its forced dissolution in 1540.

The layout shows Cistercian influence. The church, with aisles, transepts and a projecting rectangular east end, is flanked on the south by the cloister (restored), round which are the conventual buildings. Of these only the sacristy, chapter-house and day-rooms on the east side have been preserved. Over the crossing, as the rule of the Order required, rises the handsome 15th c. tower (fine views from the top). The nave is divided into two parts, the monks' choir and the lay brothers' choir. The church has many fine monuments, including the tombs of Bishop O'Dulany of Ossory (d. 1202), Katerine Poher and Robert Walsh (d. 1501; by Rory O'Tunney) and two 13th c. knights. Note the rows of "weepers" on the tombs.

In the cloister are a fine series of carved figures, which have been called "a Late Gothic picture-book",

Jerpoint Abbey

Jerpoint Abbey is one of the most impressive monastic ruins in Ireland. It was founded in the 12th c., probably by Donal, Lord of Ossory.

Originally a Benedictine house, the abbey passed into the hands of the Cistercians in 1180. It was much influenced by the French Abbey of Clairvaux, the most famous monastic house in the West.

The most notable features of the architecture are the cloister and the tower (both 15th c.). There is an abundance, unusual in a Cistercian house, of fine sculpture.

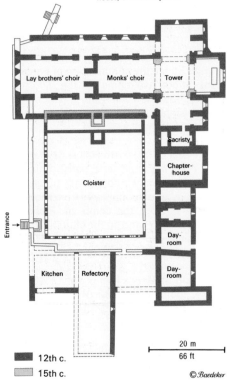

12th c.
15th c.

20 m
66 ft

© Baedeker

between the twin columns in the arcading. They were the work of Rory O'Tunney, of whom nothing is known except that he came from a great family of sculptors and is believed to have been active between 1501 and 1552.

Between the church and the cloister can be seen a fine figure of St Christopher.

A little farther west of Thomastown, on the Mount Juliet demesne, is the Kilkenny Hunt stud-farm.

6 miles (10 km) west of Thomastown, at *Kells* (not to be confused with the better-known Kells (see entry) in the north of the Republic), are the extensive remains of a fortified Augustinian priory (National Monument) founded in 1193. The surviving buildings date from the 14th and 15th c. The church, with nave, transepts, chancel and Lady Chapel, has a tower over the crossing and two other towers, one of which was probably the prior's lodging. On the south side of the church are remains of the conventual buildings, laid out around an inner court surrounded by a wall with two towers, to the south of which is a spacious outer court enclosed by a wall with five towers.

2 miles (3 km) south of Kells on a narrow by-road lies *Kilree*, with the remains of a monastery (National Monument): a roofless round tower 95 ft (29 m) high, a ruined church (good 17th c. monument in choir) and a badly weathered high cross (9th c.?) with representations of Biblical scenes and geometric ornament.

6 miles (10 km) south-west of Kilkenny on the N76 is *Callan*, a busy little market town which was strongly fortified in medieval times and has preserved a number of old buildings. Of the 15th c. Augustinian priory (National Monument) only the church, a long rectangular building with a central tower, survives; fine carved choir-stalls.

In the town centre are the ruins of St Mary's Church (16th c.: National Monument), with good details. The choir (restored), which is still used for worship, contains an old font. In the nave are a number of good monuments (16th and 17th c.), including that of John Tobyn, by Rory O'Tunney.

Outside the town is a large motte (13th c.: National Monument), 40 ft (12 m) high and 150 ft (46 m) long.

5 miles (8 km) south of Callan, on the borders of Co. Tipperary, we come to *Killamery*, with a 9th c. high cross (National Monument). The decoration, badly weathered, includes a chariot procession, a hunting scene, David with his harp and other Biblical themes, together with much geometric and animal ornament.

North-west of Kilkenny on the R693 is *Freshford*, with a church of 1730 (National Monument) which has a beautiful Romanesque doorway from an earlier church incorporated in its west front.

1 mile (1·5 km) south-west is *Ballylarkin*, with the ruins of a small 13th c. church (National Monument). This has a narrow doorway and a single window and, in the interior, fine consoles and good sedilia.

The R693 continues west from Freshford to *Urlingford*, in flat heath country. From a crossroads 2 miles (3 km) south-east can be seen a total of 12 castles.

4½ miles (7 km) north of Urlingford on the N8, beyond Johnstown, is *Fertagh*, with a 100 ft (30 m) high round tower (National Monument).

From Urlingford the R689 runs south to the ruins of *Kilcooly Abbey* (National Monument), in Co. Tipperary, a daughter house of Jerpoint (p. 148) founded in 1182. The entrance is on the west side of the property. The church, built in 1445–70 on the site of an earlier church, contains a wealth of sculpture. The screen between the south transept and the sacristy has a whole series of reliefs – the Crucifixion, St Christopher, a bishop, a mermaid with a mirror followed by two fish, coats of arms of the Butler family. Notable among the monuments in the choir is the tomb of Piers FitzJames Og Butler, with his reclining effigy as a knight and panels of saints and Fathers of the Church as weepers. Rory O'Tunney, who carved this tomb about 1526, was also responsible for the monument of William Cantwell and Margaret Butler and that of John Cantwell and Elicia Stouc. In front of that altar is the gravestone of Abbot Philip (d. 1463). An unusual feature is the pair of stone seats against the piers at the end of the nave.

Among the remains of the conventual buildings is a corbel-vaulted circular dovecot.

Killaloe/Cill Dalua

Map reference: D3.
Republic of Ireland.
Province: Munster. – County: Clare.
Population: 1000.

ⓘ **Tourist Information Office,**
Killaloe;
tel. (061) 7 61 55.
Open June to August.

HOTEL. – *Lakeside*, B, 14 r.

RESTAURANT. – *Gastronome's Good Eating House*, Main Street.

The little town of Killaloe (Cill Dalua, "Dalua's Church") lies inland in south-western Ireland, at the point where the Shannon emerges from Lough Derg and makes its way between the Arra Mountains and Slieve Bernagh into the Limerick Plain. Killaloe is a good centre for water-sports, including water-skiing and trips in cabin cruisers. A 13-arched bridge carries the R498 over the Shannon to Ballina (Co. Tipperary) and on to Limerick (see entries).

SIGHTS. – *St Flannan's Cathedral*, built in 1185, occupies the site of an earlier church and incorporates its Romanesque doorway. Beside it is an interesting stone, one of the few in Ireland to bear an inscription in Viking runes and one in ogham with the same meaning: "A blessing on Thorgrim, who made this stone." Also within the precincts of the Cathedral is *St Flannan's Oratory* (12th c.: National Monument), a small Romanesque church with a beautiful doorway and a well-preserved stone roof.

Near the Roman Catholic parish church is *St Molua's Oratory* (11th c.: National Monument), with a nave and a stone-roofed chancel. This little church was re-erected here in 1929 after being removed from an island in the Shannon which was due to be submerged under a hydro-electric scheme.

SURROUNDINGS. – To the north of the town extends *Lough Derg*, a long straggling lough with the boundary between Co. Clare and Co. Tipperary running along the middle. A beautiful road (R463) flanks the west side of the lough, passing the large fort of *Beal Boru*, from which King Brian Boru took his title, to *Tuamgraney*, which has an 11th–12th c. church; near by is a ruined castle.

1¼ miles (2 km) farther north, in a beautiful setting, is the fishing centre of *Scarriff* (Clare Lakelands Hotel, B,

Killaloe, on the Shannon

24 r.), near Scarriff Bay, into which flows the River Graney, coming from two good fishing loughs (brown trout, pike). 5 miles (8 km) north-east lies *Mountshannon*, another popular fishing centre.

Of the many islands in Scarriff Bay the most interesting is **Inishcealtra**, also known as *Holy Island*; it lies a mile (1·5 km) south-east of Mountshannon, where a boat can be hired. In the 7th c. St Caimin founded a monastery on the island, which was still being visited by pilgrims and penitents at the end of the 17th c. It is now a peaceful and charming little spot, with five churches, an 80 ft (24 m) high round tower, a hermit's cell and a churchyard with numerous crosses and inscribed stones (all National Monuments).

11 miles (18 km) west of Scarriff, on a hill near the R352, we come to the fishing centre of *Tulla*. In karstic terrain at nearby *Kiltanon* is an underground stream with interesting limestone caves called the Toumeens.

The R468 branches off the road to Tulla and runs north to *Feakle* (Smyth's Village Hotel, B, 12 r.), continuing into the beautiful valley of *Lough Graney*, which is famous for its pike.

Killarney/Cill Airne

Map reference: D2.
Republic of Ireland.
Province: Munster. – County: Kerry.
Population: 7700.

(i) **Tourist Information Office,**
Town Hall, Main Street,
Killarney;
tel. (064) 3 16 33.

HOTELS. – *Great Southern*, A*, 180 r.; *Europe*, Fossa, A*, 168 r.; *Dunloe Castle*, Beaufort, A, 140 r.; *Torc Great Southern*, A, 96 r.; *Three Lakes*, A, 70 r.; *Aghadoe Heights*, A, 55 r.; *Castlerosse*, A, 40 r.; *Cahernane*, A, 36 r.; *Killarney Ryan*, Cork Road, B*, 168 r.; *International*, B*, 88 r.; *Gleneagle*, B*, 74 r.; *Dromhall*, B*, 58 r.; *Lake*, Muckross Road, B*, 55 r.; *Arbutus*, B*, 35 r.; *East Avenue House*, B*, 16 r.; *Muckross*, B, 32 r.; *Whitegates Inn*, Muckross Road, B, 15 r.

GUEST-HOUSES. – *Gardens*, Countess Road, B, 19 r.; *Loch Fein Farm*, Fossa, B, 12 r.; *Linden House*, New Road, B, 11 r.; *Aisling House*, Countess Road, B, 10 r.; *Tuscar*, Fossa, B, 10 r.

RESTAURANTS. – *Deenach Grill*, College Street; *Gaby's Seafood Restaurant*, 17 High Street; *Linden House*, New Road.

EVENTS. – *Pan-Celtic Week* (May); *Bach Festival* (July).

Killarney (Cill Airne, "Church of the Sloe") lies near the coast in the south-west corner of Ireland. Near by are the beautiful Killarney lakes.

SIGHTS. – The beauty of the surrounding area and the wide range of recreation and leisure activities it offers make Killarney one of Ireland's most popular tourist centres. Once a typical little country town but now largely given over to the tourist trade, Killarney itself has little in the way of sights.

The Roman Catholic cathedral, St Mary's (by Pugin, 1855) and the Protestant parish church, also St Mary's, are both in Early English style.

Opposite the Franciscan church (1860), near the station, stands a monument to the "four poets of Kerry" – Pierce Ferriter (d. 1653), Geoffrey O'Donoghue (d. 1677), Aodhagan O'Rahilly (d. 1728) and Eoghan Ruadh O'Sullivan (d. 1784).

SURROUNDINGS. – Visitors who want to see the **Killarney lake district** have the choice between doing so on their own or taking advantage of the sightseeing trips organised by local agencies. Most people opt for a package covering travel in a jaunting-car (a light open horse-drawn car), on ponyback and by boat. One such trip – almost the standard tour – is the following: by jaunting-car from Killarney round the north side of the Lower Lake to *Kate Kearney's Cottage*; from there on a pony, in a jaunting-car or on foot over the *Gap of Dunloe* and down to the Upper Lake; then by boat from the south end of the lake by way of the Middle Lake to *Ross Castle*; and finally back to Killarney by jaunting-car.

The lakes around Killarney, of varying size, lie in a breath-taking beautiful landscape of mountains and hills formed by glacial action. The largest of the lakes is the *Lower Lake*, also known as *Lough Leane*, immediately south-east of Killarney. It is separated by a tongue of land from the smaller *Middle Lake* or *Muckross Lough*. A narrow channel links these two lakes with the *Upper Lake*, the smallest of the three. 4 miles (6 km) away to the east is *Lough Guitane*. To the south, where the hills rise to 2700 ft (820 m) are numbers of smaller lakes, mostly mere hill tarns. The shores of all these lakes have a dense covering of woodland – oak, arbutus, bamboos, giant ferns, etc. In early summer the roads are bordered by banks of tall foxgloves and the hillsides are covered with huge and brilliantly coloured rhododendron bushes.

Near the town is *Ross Castle*, a tower house surrounded by walls with round towers. There was an old prophecy that the castle would be taken only by an attack from the water. In 1652, taking advantage of this, Cromwell's General Ludlow had a large boat brought up and launched in the Lower Lake: whereupon the defenders, seeing this as the fulfilment of the prophecy, at once surrendered.

From the pier at Ross Castle visitors can be rowed out to the quiet little island of *Innisfallen*, with the remains of a monastery (National Monument). Here at the beginning of the 13th century were written the "Annals of Innisfallen", now in the Bodleian Library in Oxford. On the north-east side of the island is a small 12th c. church of red sandstone. Innisfallen still preserves the old native woodland of Ireland – rowan, ash, yew and holly.

The N71 goes round the east end of the Lower Lake to *Muckross Lough*, with an entrance (car park) to the *Bourne Vincent Memorial Park* (admission free: closed at dusk). This 10,870 acre (4400 ha) National Park, presented to the nation in 1932 by the Bourne family and Senator Vincent of California, takes in a large area of the lake district. ½ mile (800 m) from the entrance, in a lovely woodland setting, we come to

In the Killarney lake district

Rhododendrons in bloom

Jaunting-car in Muckross Park

*Muckross Friary (15th c.: National Monument), one of the best-preserved Franciscan abbeys in Ireland. The church, with a massive central tower, contains a number of tombs. The very beautiful cloister is surrounded by arcading in different architectural styles, and in the centre is a huge yew (a tree frequently found in monasteries, since it provided good wood for carving).

Farther down on the main road, in a park with magnificent plantations of rhododendrons, stands *Muckross House*, where a former house was occupied by Rudolph Erich Raspe (1737–94), author of "The Adventures of Baron Munchausen". It can be reached by car from another entrance on the N71 (car park at the house). In it are the *Kerry Folk Life Museum*, to which are attached a number of workshops (smithy, weaver's shop, pottery, saddlery) and a *Natural History Museum* (daily 10 a.m.–7 p.m., Oct.–Apr. 11 a.m.–5 p.m., closed Mondays in winter; admission charge).

Farther along the north side of Muckross Lough with its curiously shaped limestone rocks is Brickeen Bridge, leading to *Dinis Island*, where boats can be hired for trips on the three lakes.

The road continues along the lake to join the N71, which here traverses the park between the lakeside and Torc Mountain (1740 ft (530 m)). On the east side of the hill the River Torc flows down from a little mountain lake known as the *Devil's Punchbowl* and plunges over a 60 ft (18 m) high sandstone cliff to form the beautiful *Torc Cascade*. The path to the top of *Mangerton Mountain* (2756 ft (840 m)) passes the Devil's Punchbowl. From the top there are breathtaking views of hills near and far, lakes, valleys and arms of the sea – at their most impressive when passing clouds cast their shadows and showers of rain are gusting by.

The road continues south-west, flanked by rocky hillsides, to the Upper Lake, and comes to *Derry-*

cunnihy, a place of enchanting beauty where a waterfall dashes down over rocks in a setting of dense greenery. To the north-east the old road to Killarney goes through a wildly beautiful valley. Higher up, on the Kenmare road, is one of the finest viewpoints in the area, Ladies' View.

From the Upper Lake it is possible to return to Ross Castle by boat, sailing along narrow waterways with wooded shores, past the "Eagle's Nest" and Dinis Island.

The western part of the National Park extends from the Upper Lake to the south-west shore of the Lower Lake by way of Purple Mount (2698 ft (822 m)) and its foothills. This range of hills is separated from Macgillicuddy's Reeks (see entry) to the west by the rocky defile known as the *Gap of Dunloe*, best reached from the R562, which follows the north side of the Lower Lake. From the road to the Gap, which goes off on the left just after the golf-courses, can be seen Dunloe Castle, set amid trees, and a group of ogham stones (National Monument). It is customary to drive as far as Kate Kearney's Cottage, but from there the climb to the pass (some 2½ miles (4 km)) is usually continued in a jaunting-car, on a pony or on foot. It is possible to drive farther, but this could lead to a protracted dispute with the jarveys who drive the jaunting-cars. There are five little lakes, fed by a rapid mountain stream. The highest of these is Serpent Lake, into which St Patrick is said to have consigned all the snakes he expelled from Ireland. The mighty rocks bearing the marks of glacial action which flank the gorge give an excellent echo. From the top of the pass (784 ft (239 m)) there are superb views of hills, valleys and lakes in the varied shades of green, yellow and brown presented by the vegetation and the red sandstone rocks.

3 miles (5 km) from Killarney, on high ground to the right of the R562, stand the church and round tower of *Aghadoe* (National Monuments), formerly belonging to a monastery. Built into the south wall of the

church is an ogham stone. To the south-west of the church are the ruins of a circular keep (13th c.: National Monument), in a rectangular enclosure surrounded by walls and a moat. From the hill above there are panoramic views of the lakes and their islands, the twin hills to the south-east known as the Paps (2248 ft (685 m)), Mangerton Mountain and Carrantuohill (3360 ft (1024 m)) to the south-west.

Killybegs/Na Cealla Beaga

Map reference: B3.
Republic of Ireland.
Province: Ulster. – County: Donegal.
Population: 1600.
(i) **Tourist Information Office,**
Donegal;
tel. (073) 2 11 48.
Open June to August.

HOTELS. – *Killybegs*, A, 34 r.; *Bay View*, B, 19 r.

RESTAURANT. – *Cold End*, Main Street.

EVENT. – *Killybegs Sea Angling Club International Festival* (Aug.).

Killybegs (Na Cealla Beaga, "The Little Churches") is a fishing port in north-western Ireland, on the south coast of Donegal. It lies in an inlet off Donegal Bay which forms a natural harbour.

Killybegs is an important herring-fishing station, with fish-processing and sail-making as associated industries. The arrival of the fishing fleet and the unloading of the catch is a sight not to be missed. Killybegs also produces the famous Donegal hand-tufted carpets, which are to be found in Buckingham Palace and on Cunard liners. Visitors can be shown round the workshops.

There are also ample facilities for sport and recreation – tennis, sea angling and various water-sports (snorkelling and scuba-diving). An International Sea Angling Festival and a regatta are held in August every year.

Two local beauty-spots are *Carntullagh Head*, opposite the harbour, and *Drumanoo Head* to the south of the town.

SURROUNDINGS. – 5 miles (8 km) east of Killybegs lies *Dunkineely*, with good fishing. From here a road runs past a ruined castle and along a narrow tongue of land for 5 miles (8 km) to *St John's Point*, which has excellent fishing grounds and good beaches.

From *Crownarad Mountain* (1595 ft (486 m)), 3 miles (5 km) west of Killybegs, there are magnificent views. Beyond this, on the R263, is the picturesque village of *Kilcar*, a centre of the Donegal hand-woven tweed industry. South of the village, on *Muckross Head*, are cliffs and caves which can be reached on foot at low tide.

Killybegs harbour

The Slieve League cliffs

Kinsale harbour

2¼ miles (4 km) farther on, inland, we come to *Carrick*, situated on the River Glen some distance above its outflow into beautiful Teelin Bay.

Between Carrick and the little seaside resort of *Teelin* a side road goes off on the right to *Slieve League*, with the highest sea-cliffs in Europe (1936 ft (590 m)).

Beyond Teelin a footpath and a road lead to the remote Lough O'Mulligan and the cliffs on *Bunglass Point* (1008 ft (307 m); car park), from which there are superb views. Experienced hill-walkers can continue on "One Man's Pass", a 2 mile (3 km) path along a narrow ridge, with precipitous slopes on either side, to Slieve League. This walk requires a good head for heights and solid footwear.

Glencolumbkille: see entry.

Kinsale/Ceann Saile

Map reference: E3.
Republic of Ireland.
Province: Munster. – County: Cork.
Population: 1800.
(i) **Tourist Information Office,**
    Pier Road,
    Kinsale;
    tel. (021) 77 22 34.

HOTELS. – *Acton's*, A, 58 r.; *Blue Haven*, 3 Pearse Street, B*, 10 r.; *Perryville House*, B*, 10 r.; *Trident*, B, 40 r.

GUEST-HOUSE. – *Folk House*, B, 18 r.

RESTAURANTS. – *Blue Haven Hotel: Max's Wine Bar*, Main Street; *Vintage*, Main Street.

Kinsale (Ceann Saile, "Tide Head") lies on the Irish south coast, overlooking the broad estuary of the River Bandon. It became an English town in 1602, closed to Irish residents until the end of the 18th c., and still preserves something of the atmosphere of that period. Many of its older houses have been well restored, though a modern hotel introduces a jarring note.

This was once an important naval harbour. In 1601 a Spanish fleet landed a force of several thousand men to support the Irish against the English, but the Spaniards were forced to surrender to English forces. One consequence of this English victory was the "Flight of the Earls", after which Ireland's position as a dependency of England was confirmed.

William Penn, founder of the State of Pennsylvania, was a native of Kinsale.

Kinsale is now a popular holiday resort and excursion centre. The harbour is now a fishing port (mackerel) and a well-equipped fishing centre.

SIGHTS. – The town's most notable building is *St Multose's Church* (12th c.), now the parish church. On the north-west side of the church stands the tower, with a Romanesque doorway. Above the doorway can be seen a 15th c. figure of St Multose, who is credited with the foundation of a monastery which once stood here. The church has an interesting collection of tombstones (17th c.) and a fine font.

Near the church, higher up the hill, is an attractive group of almshouses of 1682.

In Carmel Avenue stands the "French Prison", a three-storey tower house (15th or 16th c.: National Monument) with charming ogee-arched windows. Other interesting buildings are the Court House of 1706, now occupied by the Kinsale Regional Museum (open on weekdays in summer 11 a.m.–1 p.m., and 3–5 p.m.; admission charge), and the ruined Carmelite Friary (14th c.).

The best view of the town is from Compass Hill.

SURROUNDINGS. – In Summer Cove, 2 miles (3 km) south of the town along the east side of the harbour inlet, can be found the well-preserved star-shaped Charles Fort (1677), the walls of which still stand 40 ft (12 m) high. At the south-west corner is a lighthouse, and within the fort are the ruins of 19th c. barracks. Conducted tours (caution required on the outer defences). On the opposite side of the inlet is a similar fortification, James Fort.

2 miles (3 km) east of Kinsale lies another inlet, Oyster Haven, with good bathing. On the shore are the imposing ruins of Mount Lang Castle (1631).

The R600 runs south-west from Kinsale to the village of Ballinspittle, above which is the Ballycateen Ringfort, with three deep ditches and a total diameter of 400 ft (120 m). 5 miles (8 km) south of Ballinspittle the Old Head of Kinsale reaches far out to sea, with a ruined castle and a lighthouse in magnificent cliff scenery. The "Lusitania" was torpedoed 12 miles (16 km) south of here in 1915.

To the west of the promontory lies Garrettstown (Coakley's Atlantic Hotel, B*, 22 r.), a quiet holiday resort with a sheltered bay.

From Garrettstown the road runs west, passing close to Coolmain Castle and Kilbrittain Castle (not open to the public), to Kilbrittain, from which the R603 leads north of Bandon (Munster Arms Hotel, B*, 30 r.), on the N71, which has a 9-hole golf-course and good trout fishing. The town was established in 1608 to house English settlers. Kilbrogan Church (1610), the parish church, was one of the first Protestant churches in Ireland. Along the banks of the River Bandon, a good fishing stream, are several ruined castles – on the Inishannon road Shippool Castle (1543) and Downdaniel Castle (1476).

Letterkenny/Leitir Ceanainn

Map reference: B4.
Republic of Ireland.
Province: Ulster. – County: Donegal.
Population: 6400.
(i) Tourist Information Office,
Derry Road,
Letterkenny;
tel. (074) 2 11 60.

HOTELS. – Mount Errigal, Ballyraine, B*, 55 r.; Gallagher's, B*, 26 r.

RESTAURANTS. – Christy's, 88A Lower Main Street; Golden Grill.

Letterkenny (Leitir Ceannain, "Hillside of the O'Cannons"), county town of Co. Donegal, lies on rising ground above the River Swilly in the far north of Ireland, overlooking the outflow of the river into Lough Swilly, a 25 mile (40 km) long inlet opening off the Atlantic.

SIGHTS. – The principal landmark of Letterkenny, a long straggling town on the slopes of the O'Cannon Hills, is the 215 ft (65 m) high spire of St Eunan's Cathedral (1901), finely decorated with Celtic motifs and stained glass by Harry Clarke and Michael Healy.

SURROUNDINGS. – From Letterkenny the R245 runs 8 miles (13 km) north to Rathmelton. 2½ miles (4 km) along this road a side road can be taken which passes the ruins of Killydonnell Abbey, with beautiful and varied views of Lough Swilly. Rathmelton is a friendly little fishing centre with a fine harbour and old warehouses along the front.

14 miles (22 km) south-east of Letterkenny on the N14, on the River Foyle (which marks the frontier with Northern Ireland), lies Lifford (Intercounty Hotel, B, 24 r.), facing Strabane on the other side of the frontier. It is, jointly with Letterkenny, the administrative centre of Co. Donegal, and has the only greyhound-racing track in the county.

From Lifford a minor road leads west to the hamlet of Beltany, 2 miles (3 km) south of Raphoe. Here, on a hill, can be seen a stone circle 153 yd (140 m) in diameter, with 64 standing stones, probably of Bronze Age date (access through the premises of a new factory); beautiful panoramic views.

Raphoe has an 18th c. neo-Gothic church with towers and transepts. From here the L80 runs south to Ballybofey (Jackson's Hotel, B*, 39 r.), in a beautiful moor and woodland setting (golf and tennis; trout fishing in the River Finn; shooting for small game).

7½ miles (12 km) north-west of Letterkenny (the R250/R251), on the River Glashagh, is a ruined church, Temple Douglas, in which St Columba is said to have been baptised. The R251 continues to the little village of *Church Hill*, near which are three small loughs (good fishing), on one of which, Gartan Lough, lies the village of *Gartan*, where Columba was born in 521. He is commemorated by a modern high cross. The inscription on St Columba's Stone refers to him as "son of Felim and Eithne, of the royal houses of Aeileach and Leinster".

North-east of Gartan Lough on the N56, reached on minor roads, we come to the fishing centre of *Kilmacrenan*, where Columba founded a monastery. Only the ruins of a 15th c. Franciscan abbey and an old parish church are to be seen today. 2 miles (3 km) west is the *Rock of Doon*, a large slab of stone with a flattened upper surface which was the place of coronation of the O'Donnell kings. It is well worth climbing the rock for the sake of the extensive views of the surrounding moorland from the top. At the foot of the rock is the *Holy Well*, visited by pilgrims for the sake of its healing powers.

The road north from Kilmacrenan crosses the *Barnesbeg Gap* to the coast (see Horn Head).

Rosguill Peninsula: see entry.

Limerick/ Luimneach

Map reference: D3.
Republic of Ireland.
Province: Munster. – County: Limerick.
Population: 61,000.
ⓘ **Tourist Information Office,**
The Granary, Michael Street,
Limerick;
tel. (061) 31 75 22.

HOTELS. – *Limerick Ryan*, Ennis Road, A, 168 r.; *Limerick Inn*, Ennis Road, A, 133 r.; *Two Mile Inn*, Ennis Road, A, 125 r.; *Jury's*, Ennis Road, A, 96 r.; *Cruise's Royal*, O'Connell Street, A, 73 r.; *Glentworth*, Glentworth Street, B*, 70 r.; *Royal George*, O'Connell Street, B*, 70 r.; *New Greenhills*, Ennis Road, B*, 55 r.; *Woodfield House*, Ennis Road, B*, 21 r.; *Railway*, Parnell Street, B, 10 r.

GUEST-HOUSES. – *Clifton House*, Ennis Road, B, 23 r.; *Alexandra House*, O'Connell Street, B, 11 r.; *Parkview*, Ennis Road, B, 5 r.

RESTAURANTS – *Copper Room* (Jury's Hotel); *Granary Tavern*, Charlotte Quay; *Olde Tom*, 19 Thomas Street.

Limerick (Luimneach, "Bare Spot"), the third city of the Republic of Ireland, lies on the River Shannon in the south-west of the island, at the point where the river begins to open out into its estuary. Here there was the most westerly ford on the river, round which, at the junction of busy traffic routes, a considerable town grew up. A number of main roads met here, and Shannon Airport is only 15 miles (24 km) away.

The curious verse form known as the limerick is often thought to be derived from the city of Limerick. One theory is that the form was first used orally in O'Twomy's pub in Mungret Street by a poet named Andrew McGrath in the late 18th c. and brought from there to London.

ECONOMY. – Limerick has a harbour which is not particularly large but is kept very busy. The city's main industries are flour-milling, tobacco, ready-made clothing, cement and steel cord. Limerick-cured hams and bacon enjoy a wide reputation.

HISTORY. – In the 9th c. the Danes established a base here from which they could plunder the interior of the country. They were driven out by the celebrated Irish King Brian Boru, after which possession of the town alternated between the Irish and the Anglo-Normans. In 1210 King John ordered a bridge and a castle to be built here. In later centuries the town grew in size and maintained its allegiance to the English Crown. During the 17th c. it was several times besieged and captured. The last occasion was in 1691, the year of the broken treaty, when, after a valiant defence, 10,000 Irish troops were granted the right, under a treaty signed by King William of Orange himself, to march out with full military honours; but the English Parliament, rejecting the religious freedom guaranteed in the treaty, refused to ratify it. The Irish troops thereupon went to France and took service in the army of Louis XIV; and in the course of the next 50 years hundreds of thousands of Irishmen followed their example and entered the service of France or Spain. During the 19th c. the town expanded south-westward along the banks of the Shannon.

SIGHTS. – Limerick is made up of the older district of *English Town* to the north, at the junction of the Shannon and the Abbey rivers, and two districts to the south of the Abbey River, *Irish Town* and *Newtown Pery*.

English Town

Crossing the Shannon on *Sarsfield Bridge* (1824–35) and turning right along Clancy's Strand, with a fine view of the city, we come to *Thomond Bridge*, on the site of the first Shannon bridge built by King John. At the end of the bridge is the Treaty Stone, on which the 1691 treaty is said to have been signed. To the right, rising imposingly above the Shannon, stands *King John's Castle*, a pentagonal fortress with a main block, three round corner towers, a bastion and a two-storey gatehouse. The interior was spoiled by the building of barracks in the 18th c. North-east of the castle, in Town Walls Playground, can be seen remains of the old town walls.

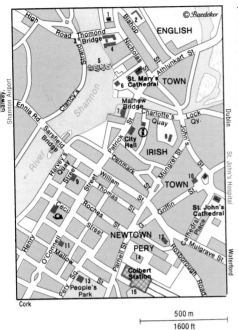

Turning right at the end of Castle Street into Nicholas Street, we come to *St Mary's Cathedral* (Church of Ireland), which preserves much 15th c. work (west doorway 12th c.). The oak *choir-stalls (a rare feature in Ireland), with misericords of fantastic animals, date from 1489. There are a number of notable monuments. From the tower (120 ft (36 m) high) fine views may be enjoyed.

In St Augustine's Place stands the handsome *City Court House* (1764).

Irish Town

To the south, beyond Mathew Bridge, is the *Custom House* (1769). From here, going along Charlotte's Quay and turning right, we come to St John's Hospital, in the grounds of which are remains of the old *town walls*, including two gates. There are also remains of walls, still standing to a considerable height, on the other side of the street. The Roman Catholic *St John's Cathedral* (1856–94) near by has the tallest tower in Ireland (280 ft (8 km)). Adjoining the Cathedral lies *St John's Square*, once a select 18th c. square, which is now protected as a National Monument and in course of rehabilitation. One of the restored buildings houses the *Limerick Museum* (open on weekdays 10 a.m.–1 p.m. and 2.15–5 p.m.)

Limerick
Luimneach

1 St Munchin's	9 Theatre
2 Town Wall	10 City Museum
3 Treaty Stone	11 Library
4 King John's Castle	12 Theatre
5 Curragour Fall	13 Library, Museum, Art Gallery
6 Court House	14 Bus Station
7 Custom House	15 Priory Park
8 Town Wall	

View over the Shannon towards Limerick

Georgian house doors

Newtown Pery

South-west of Irish Town extend the later additions to the city. The main street is *O'Connell Street*, almost a mile (1·5 km) long, which is now the heart of the city. At the end of the street stands the O'Connell Monument, honouring Daniel O'Connell, who won emancipation for Irish Catholics.

This part of the city is celebrated for its handsome Georgian houses with their brightly painted front doors. A particularly fine throughfare is Mallow Street, at the east end of which is the *People's Park.* In the park can be found the Public Library, Art Gallery (modern Irish painters) and Museum (antiquities, material on Irish history).

Plassey

3 miles (5 km) east of the city centre in Plassey (N7) we come to the *National Institute for Higher Education* (NIHE), which provides training designed to meet the needs of Ireland in a new Europe in the fields of administration, economics and technology. Associated with the Institute are an institute of physical education and a museum which houses part of the valuable *Hunt Collection (art from the Bronze Age to the 18th c.). The museum is open in summer (9.30 a.m.–5.30 p.m.; admission charge). The rest of the collection can be seen at the Craggaunowen Project (see Ennis).

SURROUNDINGS OF LIMERICK. – 8 miles (13 km) from Limerick, at the northernmost tip of Co. Limerick, is *Castleconnell*, a well-known fishing centre on the Shannon which in the 18th c. was a much-frequented spa. Below the town, at an old castle, is a long stretch of rapids on the river.

7½ miles (12 km) east of Limerick at Barringtonsbridge, on the R506, we come to *Clonkeen Church* (National Monument), a beautiful little Romanesque building. Farther east, under the Slievefelim Mountains, is *Glenstal Abbey*, now a Benedictine school, with a 19th c. circular "donjon", a modern church (1853) and an old terraced garden (restored).

12½ miles (20 km) south of Limerick, at Holycross on *Lough Gur*, lies a *prehistoric site (National Monument) of exceptional interest. During the 19th c. the lough was partly drained, when evidence of occupation going back to the Neolithic period was found. The following features are particularly notable: No. 4, a wedge-shaped passage grave (*c.* 2000 B.C.); No. 7, a stone fort (8th c.); No. 8, an oval stone fort (Early Christian period); No. 12, a Neolithic burial-place surrounded by a double earthwork, with a standing stone in the middle; No. 16, a burial mound with a circle of standing stones (*c.* 1500 B.C.); No. 17, a fine double stone circle with an earth rampart and a ditch (age uncertain); No. 22, a small stone circle of large slabs; No. 23, a crannog (originally an artificial islet, now linked with the shore); and No. 28, an imposing stone circle (*c.* 2000 B.C.), a cult site with an almost monumental entrance. There are also two medieval structures, Bourchier's Castle (16th c.) and Black Castle (14th c.), and the ruined 17th c. New Church.

On the way south from Lough Gur to Kilmallock a detour can be made, taking a road on the left at Bruff, to *Hospital*. The church (National Monument), originally belonging to an establishment of the Knights Hospitallers founded in 1215, contains three very interesting tombs with effigies.

Kilmallock, 21 miles (34 km) south of Limerick on the R512, is an ancient little country town. The Collegiate Church of SS Peter and Paul (15th c.: National Monument) incorporates 13th c. work (round tower) and has some fine monuments. King's Castle (14th c.: National Monument) and Blossom's Gate in Emmet Street bear witness to the importance of the town in medieval times.

To the north of the town can be found the ruins of a *Dominican abbey (13th–15th c.: National Monument), with a church which has some good carving, a fine five-light west window and notable monuments in the chancel. The 90 ft (27 m) high tower is borne on unusually narrow arches.

6 miles (10 km) south-east of Kilmallock lies the little market town of *Kilfinane*, at the foot of the Ballyhoura Mountains. Its most striking feature is an unusually large motte, 130 ft (39 m) high and 50 ft (15 m) in diameter at the base and 20 ft (6 m) at the top. From the summit there is a magnificent view of the great expanse of the "Golden Vale".

In *Glenosheen*, a beautiful side valley to the south-east of Kilmallock, stands *Castle Oliver*, a 19th c. structure complete with battlements, towers and bastions which is approached by two avenues with curious lodges at the gates. Near the castle is one of the "follies" built to provide employment during a famine. Castle Oliver is said to have been the birthplace of the famous Lola Montez, mistress of King Ludwig I of Bavaria.

From Kilmallock the R518 and R520 lead west to *Newcastle West* (River Room Hotel, B, 15 r.), 20 miles (32 km) south-west of Limerick, a busy market town with the ruins of a 12th c. Templar castle.

Farther north we come to *Ardagh*, where the famous Ardagh Chalice, now in the National Museum in Dublin, was found.

5 miles (8 km) south of Newcastle West is *Glenquin Castle* (15th c.: National Monument), a well-preserved six-storey tower house; the battlements are modern. To the west lies *Abbeyfeale* (Leen's Hotel, B, 15 r.), a good base for trout and salmon fishing in the River Feale.

From Limerick the N69 runs west to the ferry port of *Tarbert* (see Ballybunion). There are a number of places of interest on this important road.

2½ miles (4 km) from Limerick are the ruins of *Mungret Abbey* (National Monument), once an important monastic school, which preserves three of its original six churches.

4 miles (6 km) west stands *Carrigogunnell Castle* (National Monument), prominently situated on a volcanic crag. It is an imposing structure with two towers (15th and 16th c.), unfortunately in a poor state of preservation. From the castle there are fine views of the Shannon and the surrounding area.

In *Kildimo* can be seen the remains of a small Templar church (13th c.) and a parish church of 1705. Beyond this, on a hill, is little Killulta Church (12th c.: National Monument), with a triangular window, and, near by, *Dromore Castle*, a Victorian "fairy-tale castle" (1867–70), which has been derelict since 1950. 2½ miles (4 km) farther on, to the left of the road beyond Kilcornan, stands Killeen Cowpark Church (15th c.: National Monument).

In another 4 miles (6 km) the road comes to *Askeaton*, on the River Deel. On a rocky islet in the river, near the bridge, rise the ruins of *Desmond Castle* (15th c.: National Monument), a tower house with a banqueting hall measuring 30 ft by 90 ft (9 m by 27 m), with fine windows, blind arcading and vaulting. On the east side of the river are the well-preserved remains of a *Franciscan abbey (15th c.: National Monument): church with fine windows, beautiful cloister with two fine marble arches and a figure of St Francis, refectory and other conventual buildings.

7 miles (11 km) beyond this we come to *Foynes*, a small port picturesquely situated on the estuary of the Shannon. The harbour has excellent facilities for yachts. From Knockpatrick Hill (565 ft (172 m)), south of the town, there are extensive views over the Shannon Estuary. On the summit of the hill are a ruined church and a holy well.

8 miles (13 km) west, beautifully situated on the banks of the Shannon, here 1¼ miles (2 km) wide, lies *Glin*. Above the harbour rears Hamilton's Tower (19th c.). Outside the town stands Glin Castle, a ruined tower house, on the estate of the Fitzgeralds, Knights of Glin, who have been established here in uninterrupted succession for 700 years. The modern house (Georgian of 1780, altered in neo-Gothic style in 1820) has handsome rooms with good stucco ceilings (staircase, hall, library) and is furnished in period style (Irish, 18th c.) with family portraits of the 18th to 20th c. It can be seen by prior arrangement (groups only).

Lismore/Lios Mor Mochuda

Map reference: D4.
Republic of Ireland.
Province: Munster. – County: Waterford.
Population: 900.

ⓘ **Tourist Information Office,**
St Mary Street,
Dungarvan;
tel. (058) 4 17 41.
Open July and August.

HOTELS. – *Ballyrafter House, B*, 14 r.; *Lismore*, C, 15 r.

Lismore (Lios Mor Mochuda, "Mochuda's Great Enclosure") lies near the Irish south coast on the broad Blackwater, a good fishing river which is spanned by a handsome stone bridge of 1775. North of the town the Knockmealdown Mountains rise to heights of up to 2560 ft (780 m).

SIGHTS. – As early as the 7th c. there was a monastery here renowned for its learning, at which King Alfred of Wessex is said to have studied in the 9th c. *Lismore Castle*, magnificently situated on a high crag, probably occupies the site of the monastery. Built by King John in the 12th c., it survived the upheavals of later centuries and in 1602 came into the hands of Richard Boyle, first Earl of Cork, whose son Robert Boyle (1627–91) became the celebrated scientist who formulated Boyle's Law. The castle, which was much enlarged in the 19th c., now belongs to the Duke of Devonshire. The house is not accessible to the public, but the gardens are open from mid May to mid September (Tue. and Fri. 2–5 p.m.).

St Carthage's Cathedral (17th c.: National Monument) was built by Richard Boyle, incorporating parts of an earlier 13th c. church (chancel arch, windows in south transept). The elaborate MacGrath tomb (1557) has representations of the Crucifixion, an Ecce Homo and various saints and Apostles; built into the west wall of the nave are a number of early gravestones. The slender and graceful spire was the work of George Richard Pain (1827).

SURROUNDINGS. – 4½ miles (7 km) east of Lismore, where the Blackwater turns south, lies *Cappoquin*, a charmingly situated little town with good fishing in the Blackwater and its tributary streams. The river is tidal up to this point.

4½ miles (7 km) north of Cappoquin, in the hills, stands *Mount Melleray Abbey*, a Trappist house built in 1833. Visitors can be accommodated in the guesthouse.

A mile (2 km) south of Cappoquin, at the village of *Affane*, is Affane House, a large Georgian mansion. Here Sir Walter Raleigh – who is said to have introduced potatoes and tobacco to Ireland – planted the first cherry trees to grow in the British Isles.

At *Villierstown*, south of Affane, *Dromana Castle* has a curious gateway in the "Indian" style.

5 miles (8 km) west of Lismore is *Ballyduff*, with Ballyduff Castle, a fortified manor-house of 1628. Near here is the elaborate entrance, in neo-Early Gothic style, to Ballysaggartmore House, which was never built because of lack of funds.

Londonderry/ Derry/Doire

Map reference: A/B4.
Northern Ireland.
Province: Ulster. – District: Londonderry.
Population: 54,000.

ⓘ **Derry City Council,**
Guildhall,
Londonderry;
tel. (0540) 6 51 51.

HOTELS. – *White Horse Inn*, 68 Clooney Road, A, 44 r.; *Everglades*, Prehen Road, A, 38 r.; *Broomhill House*, Limavady Road, B, 21 r.

GUEST-HOUSE: *Eleonora Slevin*, 15 Northland Road, B, 7 r.

RESTAURANTS. – *Inn at the Cross*, 171 Glenshane Road; *New York*, 64 Strand Road; *Woodburn*, Blackburn Crescent.

EVENT. – *Relief of Derry Celebrations* (commemorating the siege of 1688–89, 12 August).

Londonderry or Derry (Doire, "Oak Wood"), the second city of Northern Ireland, lies on the River Foyle, just above its outflow into Lough Foyle, the largest inlet on the north coast of Ireland. It is an important port and industrial town (synthetic fibres, ceramics).

HISTORY. – A monastery was founded here by Columba in 546. Later the monastery and the settlement which had grown up around it were several times attacked and destroyed by the Vikings. In 1618 the town and the town walls were rebuilt. In recent years Londonderry has been one of the main centres of sectarian violence in the conflict between Catholics and Protestants in Northern Ireland.

SIGHTS. – The old town of Londonderry is surrounded by the best-preserved

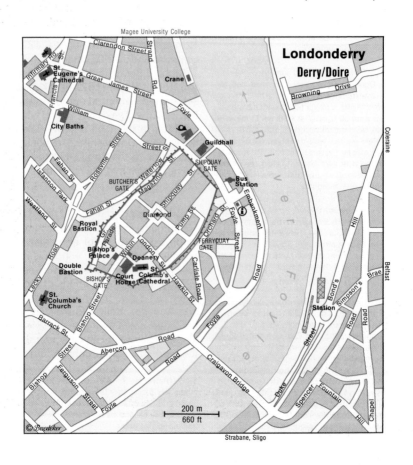

Strabane, Sligo

*town walls in the United Kingdom. Apart from the addition of three later gates they are preserved exactly as they were in 1618. There is a pleasant walk round the town on the walls; the best view of the town is from the Walker Monument on the Royal Bastion.

The four original gates which gave admittance to the old town are Butcher's Gate, Shipquay Gate, Ferryquay Gate and Bishop's Gate, the finest of the four.

The four principal streets, coming from the four old gates, meet – still following the medieval town plan – in the central square, which has been known since the 17th c. as the *Diamond*. The Town Hall formerly stood here, but after being destroyed during one of the many sieges of the town it was moved to another site. The square's feature is now a war memorial.

There are still numbers of Georgian houses in the old town, particularly in Shipquay Street, Magazine Street and Bishop Street. In Bishop Street are the Deanery (1833) and the classical-style Court House (19th c.).

Immediately east of the Court House stands *St Columb's Cathedral* (Protestant), built in the 17th c. and Gothicised in the 19th c. The roof is borne on brackets carved with the heads of 16 bishops of the town. Eight of the 13 bells in the bell-tower date from the 17th c. Incorporated in the bishop's throne is the throne of Bishop Bramhall, who consecrated the cathedral in 1633. The chapter-house contains documents on the history of the town and the locks and keys of the four old town gates.

To the south-west, outside the walls, we come to *St Columba's Church* (Church of Ireland), a 19th c. neo-Gothic building on the site of an earlier church. In the churchyard is St Colum's Stone, at which St Columba is believed to have prayed.

Outside the old town on the north is the neo-Gothic *Guildhall* (1912), which has a collection of relics and mementoes of Irish history.

From the Guildhall Strand Road runs north to *Magee University College* (1865), the grounds of which extend to the banks of the Foyle.

A handsome modern bridge, *Craigavon Bridge* (1933), 400 yd (365 m) long, crosses the Foyle to the east bank, where a new modern district of Londonderry is in course of development.

Craigavon Bridge, Londonderry

Giant's Causeway

SURROUNDINGS. – From the east bank of the Foyle the A2 runs by way of two charming villages, Eglinton and Ballykelly, to *Limavady*, an old town in the valley of the Roe. From here the A37 continues east to *Coleraine* (Lodge Hotel, B*, 15 r.; Bohill Auto Inn, B, 30 r.), one of the oldest English settlements in this area. This busy little town on the navigable River Bann is noted for its salmon, and as the site of the new University of Ulster.

From Coleraine the road leads north to the coast, coming in 6 miles (10 km) to *Portstewart* (Carrig-na-Cule Hotel, 2 The Promenade, B*. 33 r.; Edgewater Hotel, 88 Strand Road, B*, 30 r.; Strand Hotel, 90 Strand Road, B, 39 r.; Windsor Hotel, 8 The Promenade, B, 28 r.), with beautiful sandy beaches and a picturesque port. There is also good bathing at *Portrush* (Northern Counties Hotel, B*, 94 r.; Skerrybhan Hotel, 3–5 Lansdowne Crescent, B, 32 r.; Eglinton Hotel, 49 Eglinton Street, B, 32 r.), 4 miles (6·5 km) farther east. Offshore lie the *Skerries*.

The road continues east, passing *Dunluce Castle* (14th c.), on a rocky island linked with the mainland by a bridge, and *Bushmills*, with the world's oldest working whiskey distillery (*c.* 1600; conducted visits).

Beyond Bushmills, on the coast, we come to the ****Giant's Causeway**, one of Ireland's most extraordinary natural phenomena. It is a rock formation of polygonal (three- to nine-sided) basalt columns varying in size and height. Some of the groups of columns have fanciful names – the Lady's Fan, the Giant's Organ, the Horseshoe and so on. The most impressive, reached by way of the Shepherd's Path, is the Amphitheatre, with columns up to 80 ft (24·4 m) high and numerous lower blocks of basalt resembling giant seats.

The coast road continues to *Ballintoy* (13 miles (21 km)). To the east of the village is a gorge 60 ft (18 m) across, spanned from May to September (the fishing season) by the Carrick-a-Rede rope bridge, which enables the salmon fishers to reach the fishing grounds.

Beyond Ballintoy lies *Ballycastle* ('Oul' Lammas Fair, Aug.; Antrim Arms Hotel, Castle Street, C, 12 r.), a picturesque little port surrounded by woodland. Here a boat can be hired to go to *Rathlin Island*, 6 miles (10 km) offshore. In earlier times the island, which is still inhabited, was a Viking base. It is the setting of one of the familiar legends of Scottish history, the story of Robert the Bruce and the spider.

The road from Ballycastle to Cushendall (p. 65) is one of Ireland's most beautiful coast roads. It follows the Antrim coast past the famous ***Glens of Antrim**, nine in number – Glenarm, Glencoy, Glenariff, Glenballyemon, Glenaan, Glencorp, Glendun, Glenshesk and Glentaise. From Cushendall it is possible to continue on the coast road to Belfast (47 miles (76 km); see entry), or alternatively to take the beautiful road along *Glenariff* (A43) and return by way of Kilrea and Dungiven to Londonderry.

Longford/ Longphort

Map reference: C4.
Republic of Ireland.
Province: Leinster. – County: Longford.
Population: 4000.

ⓘ **Tourist Information Office.**
Main Street,
Longford;
tel. (043) 4 65 66.
Open June to August.

HOTELS. – *Longford Arms*, B*, 51 r.; *Annaly*, B, 49 r.

RESTAURANTS. – *Fountain Blue*, Dublin Road; *Old Spinning Wheel*, Ballymahon Street.

Longford (Longphort, "Fortress"), county town of Co. Longford, lies in the centre of Ireland, north-east of Lough Ree, at the junction of four roads – the N4, N5, N63 and T15.

SIGHTS. – A prominent landmark in the town is the dome of the neo-Renaissance *St Mel's Cathedral* (by Joseph Keane, 1840–93).

Longford takes its name from a fortress of the O'Farrels of which no trace remains.

The town offers a wide range of leisure activities – golf, tennis, fishing, shooting, horse-racing and greyhound-racing.

SURROUNDINGS. – 16 miles (26 km) north-east of Longford, on the R194, lies *Granard*, a fishing centre. Near the town stands a large motte (12th c.: National Monument), perhaps the largest of its kind in Ireland. On top of it is a statue of St Patrick, erected in 1932 to mark the 1500th anniversary of his coming to Ireland.

2½ miles (4 km) east, beginning at Lough Kinale and extending 6 miles (10 km) north-west to Lough Gowna, is a section of the "Black Pig's Dyke", a system of defensive earthworks, dated to between 300 B.C. and A.D. 300, which cuts obliquely across northern Ireland. Here the dyke is up to 20 ft (6 m) high and 30 ft (9 m) thick at the base, with a ditch on either side.

Lough Gowna is noted for its very fine trout.

8 miles (13 km) south-west of Granard (7½ miles (12 km) south-east of Longford) lies *Edgeworthstown*. Edgeworthstown House was the birthplace of the celebrated novelist Maria Edgeworth (1767–1849), whose works depict the social conditions of her time in both castle and cottage. Scott and Wordsworth were among the many distinguished writers who visited the house.

On the way from Edgeworthstown to Ballymahon (the N55, going south-west) a short detour can be made, on a side road on the main line, to *Ardagh*, with St Mel's Church (National Monument), said to have been founded by St Patrick.

Ballymahon is picturesquely situated on the River Inny; good fishing. 5 miles (8 km) east is *Pallas*, where Oliver Goldsmith was born.

From Ballymahon the R392 runs north-west to *Lanesborough*, on the Shannon, which here flows into *Lough Ree*. There is good trout fishing in both the river and the lough; in summer boats can be hired. Lanesborough is a popular stopping-place on cruises on the Shannon (see entry). Near the town, on the east bank of the river is a peat-fired power-station.

On the island of *Inchcleraun* in Lough Ree, 6 miles (10 km) south, are the ruins of an early monastery (National Monument), with remains of five churches and other buildings.

Lough Corrib

Map reference: C2.
Republic of Ireland.
Province: Connacht. – County: Galway.
(i) Tourist Information Office,
Eyre Square,
Galway;
tel. (091) 6 30 81.

Lough Corrib, north of Galway Bay in the west of Ireland, is nearly 30 miles (45 km) long but at some points no more than a few hundred yards (metres) wide. The lough is dotted with numerous islands – said to number 365 in all. They can be best seen from a viewpoint on high ground.

The *scenery of Lough Corrib is of striking beauty. Round the green shores of the lough, with their clumps of trees and expanses of pastureland, are countless little bays, promontories and peninsulas, reaching out to the tiny islets which form a kind of continuation of the land. To the east of Lough Corrib is low-lying country, to the west are hills, and on the horizon to the north are the mountains of Connemara. The lough is linked with Lough Mask, to the north, by underground streams; and from its southern end flows the River Corrib, reaching the sea after a course of only 4 miles (6·5 km).

Round Lough Corrib

It is possible to drive right round Lough Corrib, but with the exception of a short stretch at the north end of the lough the road runs at some distance from its shores, which can be reached on various side roads.

From *Galway* (see entry) the N59 goes north-west to *Moycullen* (8 miles (13 km)), a good fishing centre. A side road (5 miles (8 km) leads to *Knockferry*, where boats can be hired; there is also a ferry to the east side of the lough.

The road continues, passing *Ross Lake* (good rough fishing), to *Oughterard* (Connemara Gateway Hotel, A, 48 r.; Sweeney's Oughterard House Hotel, A, 20 r.; Corrib Hotel, B*, 22 r.; Egan's Lake Hotel, B*, 22 r.; Ross Lake House Hotel, B*, 12 r.; Currarevagh House Guest-House, A, 15 r.; 9-hole golf-course), the

Lough Corrib

"Gateway to Connemara". This little town, in a beautiful green setting on the River Owenriff, is a well-known fishing centre. 3 miles (5 km) south-east, on a rocky islet, stands *Aughnanure Castle* (1500: National Monument), a six-storey tower house in an inner and an outer ward with round towers. The castle has been restored and is open to the public in summer (11 a.m.–1 p.m. and 3–7 p.m.; admission charge).

From Oughterard a boat can be taken to the picturesque island of *Inchagoill*, with the remains of two churches (both National Monuments). The smaller of the two dates from the 5th c. the other (12th c.; restored) is a good example of Irish Romanesque architecture.

The narrow road which runs north along the shore of the lough is a dead end: to drive round the lake it is necessary to continue on the N59.

From the road intersection at *Maam Cross* (see Connemara) the R336 leads north to Maam Bridge, from which the L101 runs east to *Cornamona*, a fishing centre in a beautiful setting which is also a good base for walks and climbs in the hills to the west. Westward extend the mountains of Connemara, with Joyce's Country, and to the south, on either side of the long

Dooras Peninsula, are the waters of Lough Corrib with its countless islands.

South-west of Cornamona, occupying almost the whole of a little islet, rise the imposing ruins of *Castle Kirke*, also known as *Hen's Castle* (12th c.: National Monument), a large tower enclosed by curtain-walls.

The road continues for 5 miles (8 km), skirting the lough for much of the way, to *Clonbur*, on the isthmus between Loughs Mask and Corrib, with a fine view of Mount Gable to the west.

The route along the R346 and R334, passing through *Cong* (see entry) and coming in 14 miles to *Headford* (Angler's Rest Hotel, B, 15 r.), a little market town and fishing centre. There are a number of prehistoric ring-forts in the neighbourhood. 1½ miles (2 km) north-west stand the extensive and interesting ruins of *Ross Abbey, or Ross Errilly (National Monument), a Franciscan house founded about 1351 which was occupied until 1753. Most of the surviving remains, including the tower and the double south transept, date from the 16th c. The cloister has beautiful arcading. To the north of it is an inner court surrounded by conventual buildings, including a kitchen with a tank for fish, a bakery with its oven and the

Ross Abbey
Ross Errilly

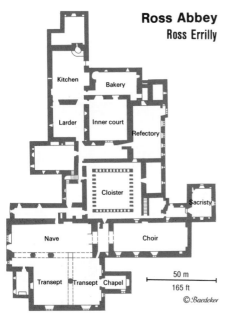

Lough Erne

Map reference: B4.
Northern Ireland.
Province: Ulster.

(i) **Fermanagh District Council**,
Town Hall,
Enniskillen;
tel. (0365) 2 50 50.

HOTELS. – IN ENNISKILLEN: *Killyhevlin*, B*, 23 r.; *Lakeland*, B*, 22 r.; *Railway*, 34 Forthill Street, B, 22 r.; *Fort Lodge*, B., 12 r.

RESTAURANTS. – IN ENNISKILLEN: *Railway Hotel*, 34 Forthill Street; *Crow's Nest*, 12 High Street; *Fort Lodge Hotel*.

Lough Erne, a long, straggling and much-indented lake system some 20 miles (32 km) from north to south and up to 6 miles (9·5 km) wide, lies in the north of Ireland, a little way east of Donegal Bay. It is *Ireland's most beautiful lake.

The ruins of Ross Abbey (Ross Errilly) lies only a mile or two from the eastern shores of beautiful Lough Corrib.

The abbey was founded about 1351, probably by Raymond de Burgo. Soon afterwards it was occupied by Franciscans, who remained here until 1753.

Over the centuries the abbey was much altered and rebuilt, particularly in the 15th c. The striking tower was built in 1498.

The cloister with its beautiful arcading is the architectural gem of this little abbey.

The northern part of the lough is called *Lower Lough Erne*, the southern part *Upper Lough Erne*. Upper Lough Erne is intricately patterned with bays and inlets and has numerous small islands in the southern half. The west end of Lower Lough Erne, with sluices to regulate the water-level, is almost on the border with the Republic.

refectory with a reader's desk. Altogether this is one of the best-preserved ruins of a Franciscan friary in Ireland.

5 miles (8 km) south of Headford a narrow road goes off on the right to *Annagh-down*, with the ruins of Annaghdown Abbey (National Monument). There are some remains of 12th c. work, but the principal church ("Cathedral") and the conventual buildings are 15th c.

Visitors returning to Galway by boat and passing through the channel which connects the south end of the lough with the River Corrib will see on the left the ivy-covered ruins of *Menlough Castle* and on the right the new buildings of University College Galway.

Lough Erne is a paradise for water-sports enthusiasts and fishermen. In summer motor launches ply on the lake, and house boats can be hired.

Enniskillen

The chief place in the Lough Erne area is the lively holiday resort of **Enniskillen** situated between the Lower and the Upper Lough, which are linked with one another by the River Erne.

On the highest point in the town stands the Protestant *St Macartan's Cathedral* (17th–18th c.), in which the colours of the Royal Inniskilling Dragoon Guards and the Royal Inniskilling Fusiliers are laid up.

Enniskillen Castle (National Monument) now houses a military museum (uniforms, arms, etc.). *Portora Royal School*, founded in the early 17th c., can claim Oscar Wilde and Samuel Beckett among its former pupils.

Lough Erne

The town owes its popularity mainly to the charm of the surrounding area, with its two loughs, its numerous rivers and streams and its beautiful parks. To the south of the town is *Castle Coole* (by Richard Johnston and James Wyatt, 1789–98), perhaps the finest classical mansion in Ireland.

Just north of Enniskillen, at the southern end of Lower Lough Erne, lies **Devenish Island**, with the remains of a monastery founded in the 6th c. by St Molaise. This has a 12th c. *round tower*, perfectly preserved, which is one of the finest in Ireland. It is 82 ft (25 m) high, tapering towards the top. There are also some remains of St Mary's Abbey and the Great Church (12th c.) and a fine cross 6 ft (2 m) high.

Tour of the Lake District

Lower Lough Erne extends north-west from Enniskillen. The A46 runs along the south side, the A47, A35 and A32 round the north and east sides.

We leave Enniskillen not on the A46, which keeps close to the lough, but on the B81, which goes north-west, at some distance from the lough, to *Monea*, with the ruins of an early 17th c. castle. The church has a mid 15th c. window from one of the churches on Devenish Island (above).

From Monea a minor road leads north to join the A46. In the lough can be seen the island of *Inishmacsaint*, which has the remains of a 12th c. church.

Farther on the road passes, on the left, the beautiful *Lough Navar Forest*, in which there are a number of small loughs. A side road leads to a viewpoint 985 ft (300 m) above Lough Erne.

The A46 continues to the little town of *Belleek*, on the border between Northern Ireland and the Republic. From here a road runs west to *Ballyshannon* (see Bundoran). To continue the tour of the lake district, however, we cross the River Erne, which flows out of Lough Erne into Donegal Bay, and follow the A47 along the north side of the lough. After passing the *Castle Caldwell Forest Reserve* (with the ruins of Castle Caldwell on a promontory in the lough), we come to a road fork. The left-hand road leads to *Pettigo*, in the Republic: we continue on the A47, which bears right and crosses a bridge on to long, straggling *Boa Island*. In *Caldragh* churchyard are two pagan figures of the 5th c. A.D.

At *Kesh* it is worth making a detour in a north-westerly direction to *Omagh* (Royal

Arms Hotel, 51 High Street, B*, 21 r.; Silverbird Hotel, 5 Gartin Road, B, 32 r.; McGirr's Restaurant, Mountjoy East; Top of the Town Restaurant, 13 John Street), at the junction of the rivers Drumragh and Camowen. This is a good base for salmon fishing and for walks in the Sperrin Mountains, north-east of the town.

Beyond Kesh, on the A35, is a road fork. The main road, bearing left away from the lough, makes for Irvinestown, but the more attractive alternative is the minor road (B82) which closely follows the shores of the lough. After passing a number of boating harbours it reaches *Castle Archdale Forest*, with the 18th c. mansion of that name. From here a boat can be taken to *White Island*, another charming little island with the remains of a Romanesque church.

Soon afterwards the B82 rejoins the main road (now the A32), which leads back to Enniskillen.

The route round **Upper Lough Erne**, with its intricate pattern of inlets and waterways, is on the A509, B127, A34, B514 and A4.

Leaving Enniskillen on the A4, we turn left a mile or so out of the town into the A509, which comes in 5 miles (8 km) to the popular holiday resort of *Bellanaleck* (boat hire). The route then continues to *Derrylin*, just beyond which the B127 goes off on the left and crosses the lough to the fishing centre of *Lisnaskea*, with the ruins of Castle Balfour. The A509 continues straight ahead to enter the Republic, joining the N3, the road to Cavan (see entry).
From the hill above Lisnaskea there are extensive views of the Upper Lough. From here, on the A34 and A4 or on the rather shorter B514 which runs close to the lough, we return by way of Castle Coole (see above, under Enniskillen) to our starting-point.

An interesting trip from Enniskillen is to the **Marble Arch Caves**, on the northern slopes of the Cullcagh Mountains, a system of underground caves with lakes, waterfalls, stalactites and stalagmites. To reach them, leave Enniskillen on the A4 and A32 and then take a side road on the right. The caves are open to visitors for a distance of 766 yd (700 m) – conducted tours daily from 11 a.m.

Lough Neagh

Map reference: B5.
Northern Ireland.
Province: Ulster.

Lough Neagh, a few miles west of Belfast, is the largest lake in the British Isles, with an area of 150 sq. miles (388 sq km). It is 18 miles (29 km) long by 11 miles (17·5 km) wide, with a greatest depth of 40 ft (12 m). It receives the water of 10 tributary streams and is drained by the River Bann, which flows out of the north end. Lough Neagh has an abundance of fish. There is no road or footpath running close to the shores of the lough, which are low and covered with vegetation.

SIGHTS. – From Belfast a road leads west to *Glenavy*, from which there is a good view of the lough. Boats can be hired here.

Offshore is beautiful *Ram's Island*.

Another route to Lough Neagh is to take the road north-west to **Antrim** (also reached from Glenavy on the A26), which has given its name to the magnificent stretch of coast to the north-west (see Londonderry). The town lies at the outflow of Six Mile Water into the lough. *Antrim Castle* (1622) was burned down and rebuilt more than once in the course of its history. The castle gardens were laid out by Le Nôtre, who designed the gardens of Versailles. 1 mile (1·2 km) north of the town, in the grounds of Steeple House, stands an excellently preserved *round tower* (89 ft (27 m) high).

Loughrea/Baile Locha Riach

Map reference: C3.
Republic of Ireland.
Province: Connacht. – County: Galway.
Population: 3400.
(i) **Tourist Information Office,**
    Eyre Square,
    Galway;
    tel. (091) 6 30 81.

HOTEL. – *O'Dea's*, Bride Street, B, 12 r.

RESTAURANTS. – *Fifth Avenue House*, Main Street; *Meadow Court*.

The thriving little town of Loughrea (Baile Locha Riach, "Town on the Grey Lough"), the see of the Bishop of Clonfert, lies in the west of Ireland a few miles inland from Galway Bay, at the junction of the N6 and N66.

SIGHTS. – *St Brendan's Cathedral, externally a modest and unassuming church, is notable for a magnificent series of *stained-glass windows* illustrating the development of Irish stained glass in the 20th c., with work by A. E. Childe, Michael Healy, Evie Hone and Sarah Purser among others. The church has other fine examples of modern art, including a series of Stations of the Cross.

Near by are the remains of a Carmelite friary (13th–15th c.; National Monument).

SURROUNDINGS. – 12 miles (20 km) north of the town on the R350, near *Bullaun*, stands the *Turoe Stone* (3rd c.: National Monument), an oval granite block 3 ft (90 cm) high with curvilinear relief ornament in a style characteristic of the La Tène period on the rounded upper half, which is separated from the undecorated lower part by a band of meander pattern. The stone formerly stood close to a nearby ring-fort, and no doubt served some ritual purpose.

Going south-east from Loughrea along the shores of Lough Rea and turning left at Carrowkeel, we pass through Duniry and come to *Pallas*, which has an imposing 16th c. castle (National Monument), a well-preserved tower house in an outer ward. The curtain-walls with their parapet walks and towers are largely undamaged.

20 miles (30 km) south-east of Loughrea at the north end of Lough Derg, where the Shannon flows into the lough, lies *Portumna* (Westpark Hotel, B*, 229 r.), with a 9-hole golf-course, good fishing and facilities for sailing and rowing (new marina). On the outskirts of the town, in the beautiful Portumna Forest Park, are Portumna Castle (1618: National Monument), a large fortified mansion with corner towers, and the ruins of a Dominican friary (National Monument): a church with a beautiful east window and various conventual buildings.

3 miles (5 km) north-east of Portumna stands *Derryhiveny Castle* (1653: National Monument), with fine fireplaces on the upper floors.

The R349 and R348 run north-west from Loughrea through an area which becomes steadily more stony and barren, coming in 12 miles (20 km) to **Athenry**, a little town which was a place of some consequence until the end of the 16th c. and has preserved many medieval buildings. Athenry Castle (1235–50: National Monument) is a ruined tower house with roof gables within the remains of curtain-walls with two corner towers. The Dominican Friary (National Monument), founded in 1241 and in subsequent centuries much altered and several times destroyed, is represented by a ruined church containing a number of funerary monuments. The Market Cross, of which only the base and the top part survive, has reliefs of the Crucifixion and the Virgin and Child (15th c.). The remains of the medieval town walls (probably early 14th c.) show the extent of the old town; the tower-like north gate is well preserved.

Around Athenry are several prehistoric and numerous medieval structures.

Louisburgh/Cluain Cearban

Map reference: C2.
Republic of Ireland.
Province: Connacht. – County: Mayo.
Population: 300.
ⓘ **Tourist Information Office,**
Louisburgh;
tel. 50.
Open July and August.

HOTELS: *Old Head*, B*, 10 r.; *Killadoon Beach*, B, 10 r.

Louisburgh (Cluain Cearban, "Kerwan's Meadow") is a fishing village and holiday resort on the south side of Clew Bay, in the west of Ireland. It is beautifully situated in a coastal plain with good fishing rivers bounded by Croagh Patrick on the east and the Mweelrea Mountains (2576 ft (785 m)) on the south and

Turoe Stone

St Brendan's Cathedral ▶

Old Head, Louisburgh

Off the coast to the north-west lies a quite holiday retreat, hilly **Clare Island**, which belonged in the 16th c. to the legendary Grace O'Malley. The castle (National Monument) by the small harbour is said to have been built by her; it is now a coastguard station and not open to the public. The island, which has a population of 160, can be reached by boat from Roonagh Quay, 4 miles (6 km) west of Louisburgh. Sailings are irregular.

Grace O'Malley (c. 1530–1600), the "Uncrowned Queen of the West", shared with the rest of her family a taste for piracy, operating from her base on Clare Island. The fame of this remarkable woman reached London, and Queen Elizabeth I expressed a desire to know her. It is said that Grace O'Malley went to Court, where she rejected all the favours shown her by the Queen, whom she treated as an equal. On her way home she called at Howth Castle in Dublin but was refused admittance, since the family were at dinner: whereupon Grace abducted the young son of the house and released him only on a promise that in future unexpected visitors would be bidden to a meal. For centuries thereafter an extra place was laid at the dinner-table in Howth Castle and the castle doors were left open.

Grace O'Malley also treated her husbands in a fashion very much her own. When she married her second husband she made it a condition that after one year of marriage each partner should have the right to dissolve the marriage by pronouncing the words "I dismiss you." During the year she insinuated her henchmen into the various family properties, and at the end of it, when her husband returned one day to their tower house at Carrigahooley she called to him from a window "I dismiss you" and refused to let him in.

$1\frac{1}{2}$ miles (2·5 km) south-west of the harbour stand the ruins of *St Bridget's Church* (c. 1500: National Monument). In the choir are medieval frescoes with an extraordinary mingling of human figures and animals, the meaning of which is unknown; the only scene which can be understood is a figure of the Archangel Michael weighing souls.

On the south side of the island, commandingly situated on the cliffs, is a promontory fort.

fringed on the seaward side by cliffs and sandy beaches. North-east of the village the promontory of *Old Head*, from which there are fine views, extends into the bay.

SURROUNDINGS. – To the east of Louisburgh *Croagh Patrick (2471 ft (753 m)), Ireland's holy mountain, rises abruptly out of the plain. It can be climbed either from *Lecanvey* Church or from *Murrisk*, farther to the east. Near Murrisk are the ruins of a small monastery (aisleless church, with tower; living-quarters). The final climb is up a steep slope covered with quartzite scree (strong footwear essential!). It is a strenuous ascent, rewarded by ever more extensive views. From the top the prospect extends northward over Clew Bay, studded with little islands, to the hills of the Curraun Peninsula, north-eastward to Mount Nephin – a view which is at its finest at sunset – southward over the Mweelrea Mountains to the Twelve Bens in Connemara, and westward to Clare Island at the mouth of Clew Bay.

There is a great pilgrimage to Croagh Patrick on the last Sunday in July, commemorating the 40 days of penance which St Patrick is said to have spent here in the year 441. In the chapel on the flat top of the hill a service is held for the pilgrims, many of whom leave their battered footwear at the final station of the pilgrimage.

South of Louisburgh the L100 climbs gradually to the *Doo Lough*, enclosed by steep rock faces. The lakes in the *Vale of Delphi* (see Connemara) offer good salmon and trout fishing. This is a good point from which to climb the *Mweelrea Mountains*, from the slopes of which there are magnificent views.

A minor road runs south-west from Louisburgh to the River Carrownisky (trout and salmon) and *Killeen*, an isolated little village with good beaches.

Macgillicuddy's Reeks/Na Cruacha Dubha

Map reference: D/E2.
Republic of Ireland.
Province: Munster. – County: Kerry.
ⓘ **Tourist Information Office,**
Town Hall, Main Street,
Killarney;
tel. (064) 3 16 33.

Macgillicuddy's Reeks (Na Cruacha Dubha, "The Black Mountains") lie on the Iveragh Peninsula in the south-west corner of Ireland. In this range of ancient red sandstone hills are Ireland's highest peaks,

Carrantuohill (3414 ft (1040 m)), Beenkeragh (3262 ft (994 m)) and Caher (3150 ft (960 m)). They offer good climbing, and from the two highest peaks there are far-ranging views over Dingle Bay to the north-west, the Killarney lakes and the south Kerry hills. No less fine are the nearer views of the gorges, the green valleys and the little lakes glittering far below.

A good base from which to explore Macgillicuddy's Reeks is *Glencar* (Hotel, B*, 29 r.), a fishing and climbing centre beautifully situated in the Caragh Valley, to the west of the Reeks. The ascent of Carrantuohill from here – or from the Black Valley farther east – involves no rock-climbing, but the boggy soil and vegeta-tion cover of low-growing scrub make this a fairly strenuous climb.

From the north side of the range rock-climbers can tackle the Devil's Ladder, a steep rock face 600 ft (183 m) high, which is approached by way of the Gaddagh Valley and Hag's Glen with its two little mountain lakes. The less experienced should engage a knowledgeable local guide (enquire at Tourist Information Office in Killarney). Climbers can get advice and simple accommodation in Walsh's Climbers' Inn in Glencar.

North of Glencar lies the long *Lough Caragh*, with a rich pattern of colour – lush greenery and rhododendrons along the shores of the lough, the red sandstone of the hills and the peat-brown water of the lough itself. At the north end, where the River Caragh flows out of the lough, is the village of *Caragh*. There is good salmon and trout fishing in the river and the lough.

4 miles (6 km) east of Glencar, below the west side of Carrantuohill, is *Lough Acoose*, nestling picturesquely in the foothills of the range.

Macroom/ Maghcromtha

Map reference: E3.
Republic of Ireland.
Province: Munster. – County: Cork.
Population: 2500.
(i) **Tourist Information Office,**
    Tourist House, Grand Parade,
    Cork;
    tel. (021) 27 32 51.

HOTELS. – *Castle*, B , 16 r.; *Victoria*, B, 22 r.

GUEST-HOUSE. – *Coolcower House*, C, 13 r.

RESTAURANT. – *Castle Hotel.*

Macroom (Maghcromtha, "Sloping Field") lies on the River Sullane, to the west of Cork in south-western Ireland. It is a busy little town, a marketing centre for the surround-ing area. The area to the west of the town is predominantly Irish-speaking (part of the Gaeltacht), and women of the older generation still wear the traditional hooded cloaks.

SIGHTS. – In the Square are a number of Georgian houses and the fine early 19th c. Market House. On the east bank of the river can be seen the ruins of *Macroom Castle* (gutted by fire in 1922), with a massive gatehouse. The church is 19th c. (by G. R. Pain).

SURROUNDINGS. – The roads east (to Cork) and west of Macroom are noted scenic routes.

The R618 follows a winding course by way of Carrigadrohid Castle, situated on an island, and *Dripsey* (noted woollen-mills), in the valley of the River Lee, which here sometimes widens into the aspect of a lake, to *Cork* (see entry).

The N22, the direct road to Cork, runs south-east along the west side of Carrigadrohid Reservoir. In 12 miles (20 km) a side road diverges on the right to *Kilcrea*, with the well-preserved remains of a Franciscan abbey (15th c.: National Monument) in a beautiful setting on the banks of the River Bridge. The remains include the church, with a fine sacristy and a bell-tower, and conventual buildings. There is also the keep of an old castle.

12 miles (20 km) south of Macroom, reached on the N22, then (to the right) the R584, traversing a hilly area, and (to the left) the R585, lies *Kinneigh*. Here, on the site of an early monastery, stands an unusual *round tower* (National Monument), 65 ft (20 m) high, with the lower 18 ft (5·5 m) hexagonal.

The R584 goes west from the N22 to *Inchigeelagh*, a little place very popular with fishermen and artists; it is picturesquely situated at the east end of *Lough Allua*, a long narrow lake well known for its white water-lilies.

Near the west end of the lough we come to the hamlet of *Ballingeary*, from which the road climbs to the celebrated *Pass of Keimaneigh*. Here it runs for more than a mile (2 km) between sheer rock faces, the austerity of which is relieved by the ferns and flowering plants which find a foothold in crevices in the cliffs. Just before the summit of the pass a narrow road branches off on the right to *Gougane Barra Forest Park* and Lough Gougane Barra (Gougane Barra Hotel, B*, 32 r.). From this dark and lonely lough, surrounded on three sides by high hills, flows the River Lee, falling in cascades down the rocky hillside and in times of heavy rain filling the whole valley with the sound of rushing water. In late autumn there is a pilgrimage to the site of a monastery founded by St Finbar in the 7th c. on a little island in the lough which is connected to the shore by a causeway. There are remains of old buildings and a modern neo-Romanesque church.

From these barren hills the R584 quickly descends to the pleasant valleys on Bantry Bay.

From Macroom the N22 leads north-west up the valley of the River Sullane, passing *Carrigaphooca Castle* (15th c.: National Monument), to the pilgrimage centre of *Ballyvourney*. Of the monastery founded by St Gobnat in the 7th c. there remain a circular building with an inner diameter of 20 ft (6 m) and walls 5 ft (1·5 m) thick, a well and the Saint's grave.

The N22 then continues through the Derrynasaggart Mountains to *Killarney* (see entry).

Monaghan/ Muineachain

Map reference: B5.
Republic of Ireland.
Province: Ulster. – County: Monaghan.
Population: 6200.
(i) **Tourist Information Office,**
Court House,
Monaghan;
tel. (047) 8 11 22.
Open June to August.

HOTELS. – *Hillgrove*, B*, 43 r.; *Four Seasons*, B*, 24 r.; *Westenra Arms*, B, 11 r.

RESTAURANT. – *Sartos Bistro and Wine Bar*, Glaslough Street.

Monaghan (Muineachain, "Little Hills"), county town and market centre of Co. Monaghan, lies in the north of the Republic, near the border with Northern Ireland, at the junction of the N2, N12 and N54.

There was a settlement here in the 9th c., but the present town dates from the 18th and 19th c.

SIGHTS. – The parish church (St Patrick's) is neo-Gothic. Near the church stands the fine *Court House* (1829), which now houses the County Museum. In Market Place is the small and elegant *Market House* (1792), in neo-classical style. In Old Cross Square is the Old Infirmary Building (1768), and near this is the Market Cross (1714).

On the south side of the town, on high ground, stands the neo-Gothic *St Macartan's Cathedral*; its slender spire is a local landmark.

SURROUNDINGS. – 7 miles (11 km) north of Monaghan on the R185 lies the picturesque little village of **Glaslough**, on the outskirts of which is the park of Leslie Castle (not open to the public). To the west of the town, around Lough Emy, can be seen large numbers of wild swans.

14 miles (22 km) south-east of Monaghan on the N2 we come to *Castleblayney*, near which is *Lough Muckno*, the largest and most beautiful of the Monaghan lakes. Like other loughs in the area, it offers good fishing. Outside the town stands Hope Castle, now a guest-house run by Franciscan nuns.

12 miles (20 km) farther south on the N2 is *Carrickmacross* (Nuremore Hotel, A, 39 r.), with a convent which makes high-quality lace. Around the town are several good fishing loughs. Golf-course, tennis courts.

7 miles (11 km) east of Carrickmacross in the old schoolhouse of Inniskeen is a local museum, with a section devoted to the old Great Northern Railway, which passed through the town. On the site of a monastery stands the 42 ft (13 m) high stump of a *round tower* (National Monument).

13 miles (21 km) south-west of Monaghan, on the frontier with Northern Ireland, lies *Clones*, the site of a monastery founded by St Tighearnach in the 6th c. Clones crochet lace, once widely exported, is still made here.

In the main square, the Diamond, can be seen a 15 ft (4·5 m) high cross (10th c., restored: National Monument) with representations of Adam and Eve, Cain and Abel, Daniel in the Lions' Den and the Arrest of Christ on the west side, and the Adoration of the Kings, the Twelve Apostles (?), the Last Supper and the Crucifixion on the east side.

In an ancient graveyard are a 75 ft (23 m) high *round tower* and a church-shaped tomb with finials. In another graveyard near by stands a ruined 12th c. church known as the Abbey (National Monument). In both graveyards are a number of unusual 17th and 18th c. tombstones.

Monasterboice/ Mainistir Buithe

Map reference: C5.
Republic of Ireland.
Province: Leinster. – County: Louth.
ⓘ **Tourist Information Office,**
Drogheda;
tel. (041) 3 70 70.
Open July and August.

Monasterboice (Mainistir Buithe, "St Buithe's Abbey"), an early monastic site celebrated for its crosses, lies near the Irish east coast, 6 miles (10 km) north-west of Drogheda on the R168.

HISTORY. – A little-known saint, St Buithe, founded a monastery here about the year 500. In 1097 the round tower was gutted by fire, destroying the monastic library. The monastery survived only until the beginning of the 12th c.

The Monastic Site

Within the old graveyard are preserved two churches, a round tower and three high crosses (all National Monuments), together with two early gravestones and a sundial.

The most impressive feature, near the entrance to the graveyard, is the *South Cross* or ****Muiredach's Cross**, one of the finest high crosses in Ireland. It takes its name from an inscription on the west side asking for "a prayer for Muiredach". Dated to the 10th c., it stands 16 ft 9 in (5·10 m) high and has reliefs on all four sides which are remarkable both for their form and their execution. A variety of scenes are represented in square panels on the shaft. On the east side are Adam and Eve, Cain and Abel, David and Goliath (?), Moses striking water from the rock (?), the Adoration of the Kings, Christ as Judge surrounded by good and bad souls, and Michael weighing souls; on the church-shaped summit of the cross is the meeting of SS Paul and Antony in the desert. On the west side can be seen the Arrest of Christ (?), Doubting Thomas (?), Christ with SS Peter and Paul (?), the Crucifixion and an unidentified scene. On the north side are SS Paul and Antony again, the Scourging, the Hand of God and interlace ornament and on the south side the Flight into Egypt, Pilate and more interlace ornament. On the base are hunting scenes, interlace ornament and meander patterns.

The *West Cross* or ***Tall Cross** is unusually high (21 ft (6·45 m)) and also richly decorated. Not all the 22 scenes represented can be identified. On the east side are David killing the lion, the Sacrifice of

Muiredach's Cross

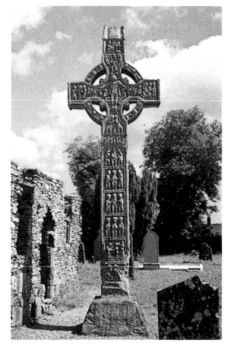

Tall Cross

Isaac, the Three Young Men in the Fiery Furnace, the Arrest of Christ, the Ascension and St Michael with the Devil. On the west side are the Watching of the Tomb, the Baptism, the Mocking of Christ, the Kiss of Judas and the Crucifixion. The base has ornamental patterns.

Of the *North Cross*, in the north-east corner of the graveyard, only the upper part and a section of the original shaft survive. The old sundial (pre-Gothic), enclosed within a railing, is a decorated granite block over a 6 ft (1·8 m) high; its age cannot be determined.

The ruins of the two churches are of no particular interest. The round tower, 50 ft (15 m) in diameter, stands 108 ft (33 m) high even though the top section is missing. The entrance, 6 ft (1·8 m) above the ground, is now reached by a modern flight of steps; the tower can be climbed.

Mullingar/ Muileann Cearr

Map reference: C4.
Republic of Ireland.
Province: Leinster. – County: Westmeath.
Population: 7900.
ⓘ **Tourist Information Office,**
Dublin Road,
Mullingar;
tel. (044) 4 86 50.

HOTELS: *Bloomfield House*, A, 33 r.; *Greville Arms*, B*, 24 r.

RESTAURANT: *Granby*, 9 Dominic Street.

Mullingar (Muileann Cearr, "Carr's Mill"), county town of Co. Westmeath and market centre of an agricultural area (mainly stock-farming), lies on the River Brosna in north-eastern central Ireland, at the junction of three railway lines and the intersection of two main roads, the N4 and N52. The town is almost encircled by the Royal Canal (see entry).

SIGHTS. – The town is dominated by the Roman Catholic *Cathedral of Christ the King* with its 140 ft (42 m) high twin towers. Attached to the church is an ecclesiastical museum.

The *Town Hall* and the *Court House* are handsome 18th c. buildings.

SURROUNDINGS – Mullingar lies between two large loughs, *Lough Owel* to the north and *Lough Ennell* to the south, where there are a championship golf-course, a pitch and putt course and a camp site. There is fishing for brown trout in both loughs and in the River Brosna.

North of Mullingar on the N4, between Lough Owel and Lough Derravaragh, lies *Multyfarnham*, with a modern Franciscan college built on the site of a 14th c. monastery, the church of which, with a fine tower, has been restored. In the grounds of the college are life-size Stations of the Cross.

The R394 runs north from Mullingar, passing several small loughs, to Castlepollard. On the way there, 7 miles (11 km) from Mullingar, we come to Crookedwood, to the right of which is *Taghmon*, with a ruined 15th c. church (National Monument) and a four-storey fortified tower house; both the church and the house have vaulted roofs.

At *Castlepollard* stands Tullynally Castle (formerly Pakenham Hall), an 18th c. mansion altered in the 19th c. It has associations with the 18th c. novelist Maria Edgeworth (see Longford) and the Duke of Wellington. The kitchen, main tower, museum and park are open to the public (Sun. 2.30–6 p.m.; admission charge).

2½ miles (4 km) east of Castlepollard, between two hills, lies *Fore*, a very ancient settlement where St Fechin founded a monastery in the 7th c. The monastic church (*c.* 900: National Monument) has been preserved, and in the churchyard are a high cross and a 15th c. tower house known as the Anchorite's Cell, with a 19th c. mausoleum built on to it. The original monastery was superseded in the 13th c. by a Benedictine priory; its fortress-like ruins (National Monument) are ¼ mile (400 m) away. They consist of a church, two tower houses, part of a cloister, domestic buildings and a dovecot. Not far distant, in the fields, are two gates (National Monuments), relics of the old town walls.

15 miles (24 km) south of Mullingar the N6 reaches *Tyrrelspass*, an 18th c. planned village of well-built houses laid out in a crescent round the village green. It won an award in the 1976 European Architectural Heritage Year. On the village green is an unusual memorial to those who died in the struggle for Irish independence – three children of different ages on their way to school.

Naas/Nas na Ri

Map reference: C5.
Republic of Ireland.
Province: Leinster. – County: Kildare.
Population: 8300.
ⓘ **Tourist Information Office,**
Naas;
tel. (045) 9 76 36.
Open July and August.

HOTELS. – *Curryhills House*, Prosperous, B*, 10 r.; *Town House*, B*, 10 r.

RESTAURANTS. – *Fair View House*, Fair Green Street; *Manor Inn*, Main Street.

Naas (Nas na Ri, "Assembly Place of the Kings"), county town of

The "Wonderful Barn", Leixlip

Castletown House: an interior

Co. Kildare, lies 21 miles (34 km) south-west of Dublin on the N7, on the edge of the Curragh Plain (see Kildare), celebrated as a horse-breeding area. 2½ miles (4 km) south on the R411 is Punchestown Race-course (see below), which is famous for its steeplechases.

HISTORY. – In early times Naas was the seat of the kings of Leinster, whose palace was on the North Mote, to the north of the town. The settlement was fortified by the Normans, and remains of one of their castles are incorporated in the Church of Ireland rectory. Naas was plundered in 1315 by Robert and Edward Bruce. It is now a thriving industrial town.

SURROUNDINGS. – 7 miles (11 km) north of Naas is *Clane*, with a Jesuit school, Clongowes Wood College, opened in 1814. The old chapel is a good example of neo-classical architecture; the new one has fine stained glass by Evie Hone and Michael Healy.

8 miles (13 km) north-east of Clane, on the Royal Canal (see entry), is *Maynooth*, a little town (15 miles (25 km) from Dublin on the N4) best known for its seminary, St Patrick's College, now part of the National University of Ireland. It was established by the British authorities in 1795, on the site of an earlier college founded in the 16th c. but soon suppressed by Henry VIII, to enable Roman Catholic priests to be trained in Ireland. It is now the largest seminary for priests in Ireland and in the British Isles, and in recent years has also admitted laymen and women. The handsome college buildings, grouped round two large courts with well-tended lawns, are mostly 19th c. They include a church and a small museum with antiquities and works of art illustrating the history of the Church in Ireland and its missionary activity. To the right of the college gates can be seen the remains of *Maynooth Castle* (13th–17th c.: National Monument) – a large keep, a gatehouse and part of the curtain-walls.

At the east end of the main street lies the large demesne of Carton House, a classical-style mansion (not open to the public) built by Richard Cassels in 1739.

4½ miles (7 km) east of Maynooth on the N4 is *Leixlip*. The remains of a 12th c. castle overlook the salmon-leap which gave the place its name (Danish *lax-hlaup*), where there is now a hydroelectric dam with a salmon-ladder.

A mile (1·5 km) south-west of the town (on private property) stands the *"Wonderful Barn"*, a conical structure of brick and stone built in 1743 for Lady Connolly of Castletown House. Each storey has a vaulted ceiling and a circular hole in the floor through which goods stored in the barn were hauled up. A spiral stone staircase winds up on the outside of the building.

South-east of Leixlip, on the Liffey, we come to *Celbridge*, 2½ miles (4 km) upstream from which is *Castletown House*, a splendid Palladian mansion built by the Italian architect Alessandro Galilei in 1722 for William Conolly, Speaker of the Irish House of Commons. A broad flight of steps leads up to the entrance in the centre of the three-storey main block, which is linked by curving colonnades with the two end wings. The interior (open Apr.–Sept., Mon. and Wed.–Sat. 11 a.m.–6 p.m., Sun. 2–5 p.m.; admission charge) has superb stucco decoration; the staircase and the Pompeian Gallery are particularly fine. The house was formerly the headquarters of the Irish Georgian Society, who furnished it with Irish period furniture.

© Baedeker

Castletown House

Pompeian Gallery

Dining-room   Hall   Staircase Hall

1 Brown Study
2 Red Drawing-room
3 Green Drawing-room

4 Print Room
5 Volunteer Room
6 Pastel Room
7 Cartoon Room

2 miles (3 km) north-west of the house stands *Conolly's Folly*, a large obelisk-crowned triumphal arch (perhaps designed by Richard Cassels) erected by William Conolly's widow to provide employment during the difficult year 1740.

2½ miles (4 km) south of Castletown House, on the Grand Canal (see entry), is *Lyons House*, an 18th–19th c. mansion with a beautiful interior, now occupied by an agricultural college.

From Maynooth the N4 and T41 run west to *Johnstown*, with a large 19th c. mansion, and *Carbury*, with the extensive remains, commandingly situated on a hill, of Carbury Castle (14th–16th c.), an imposing pile with its pointed gables, chimneys and towers. ¾ mile (1 km) north, also on a hill, can be seen the remains of Carrick Castle (14th c.) and a 13th c. church.

North-east of Naas is *Kilteel*, with the ruins of a fine Romanesque church and a castle (National Monument). The church (12th c.) has a richly decorated chancel arch, with figures of Adam and Eve, David and Goliath, Samson with the lion, an acrobat, a man with a drinking-horn and an abbot with his crosier.

3 miles (5 km) south-east of Naas we come to *Punchestown*. Near the racecourse, on the Woolpack Road (the medieval road from Dublin to Kilkenny), stands the *Long Stone of Punchestown* (National Monument), a huge tapering granite monolith 23 ft (7 m) high. When it was re-erected after collapsing in 1931 a Bronze Age burial was found at the foot of the stone.

9 miles (14 km) south of Naas is Russborough House (see Wicklow Mountains).

A mile (2 km) south-west of Naas on the N7 are the massive remains of *Jigginstown House* (National Monument), begun by the Earl of Strafford in 1633 as a country residence for himself and for the entertainment of Charles I, but left unfinished after Strafford's execution in 1641. It was one of the first houses to be built entirely in brick, and, with a frontage of 374 ft (114 m), it would have been one of the largest mansions in Ireland. In its present state the most notable features are the groin-vaulted basement and a series of handsome rooms on the ground floor.

7 miles (11 km) south-west of Naas on the N7 lies *Droichead Nua* or Newbridge, a former garrison town which now has some thriving industries and the research centre of Bord na Móna, a Government body responsible for the development of the country's extensive reserves of peat. Golf-course; greyhound-racing. On the banks of the Liffey is a motte 40 ft (12 m) high and 180 yd (16·5 m) across.

9 miles (15 km) north-west of Naas the R409 reaches *Robertstown*. Here, at the highest point on the Grand

Canal (see entry), is the old Canal Hotel, built in 1801 for passengers on the canal. From April to October candlelight banquets in 18th c. style are held in the hotel, preceded by a visit to the *Falconry of Ireland* and a trip on the canal in a horse-drawn boat (Mon.–Sat., beginning 7.30 p.m.; banquet at 9.30 p.m.). The canal frontages of the village and the hotel have been restored to their early 19th c. appearance, and the old boats have also been rehabilitated (excursions by arrangement). At the Falconry a wide variety of trained hunting-birds can be seen in action.

3 miles (5 km) west, in an extensive area of bogland, the *Bog of Allen*, are Allenwood power-station (peat-fired) and a factory making peat briquettes.

Navan/An Uaimh

Map reference: C5.
Republic of Ireland.
Province: Leinster. – County: Meath.
Population: 4100.

ⓘ **Tourist Information Office,**
Drogheda;
tel. (041) 3 70 70.
Open July and August.

HOTELS. – *Ardboyne*, Dublin Road, A, 26 r.; *Beachmount House*, B, 16 r.

RESTAURANT. – *Dunderry Lodge* (outside the town).

Navan (An Uaimh, "The Cave") lies in undulating country north-west of Dublin, at the junction of the River Boyne and the Blackwater. The largest town in Co. Meath, it is a busy market centre and an important road junction (the N3, N51, R162 and R161).

SIGHTS. – The Roman Catholic church (1836) has a fine figure of Christ Crucified (1792) by Edward Smythe. West of the town is a large motte which is a favourite viewpoint.

SURROUNDINGS. – A mile (2 km) north-east of the town on the N51, at *Donaghmore, is the site of an early monastery, with a well-preserved round tower and a church (National Monuments). St Patrick is said to have founded his first monastery in Ireland here. The tower (10th c.?) has a round-headed doorway 12 ft (3·6 m) above the ground with a relief of the

Crucifixion above it and a human mask on either side of the architrave. The church is 15th c. There are early gravestones in the churchyard.

On a hill to the east stands *Dunmoe Castle* (National Monument): two sides of an original rectangular structure (16th c.) with round towers at the corners.

6 miles (10 km) south of Navan, beyond the village of Bective (on the R161, to the left), are the ruins of *Bective Abbey (12th c.: National Monument), a Cistercian house founded from Mellifont (see Drogheda). Of the original buildings there remain only the chapter-house and some parts of the church. In the 15th c. the monastery was fortified, and from this period date the beautiful cloister and the tower and great hall (the refectory?) of the post-Dissolution mansion built on the site.

Near by are the ruins of Assey Castle and Ballinter House, an 18th c. mansion by Cassels.

7½ miles (12 km) west of Navan on the N51 *Rathmore* has a ruined 15th c. church (National Monument). The nave and chancel are flanked by towers, and the outside of the fine east window has figural decoration. The interior has fine carving in the apse, on a number of tombs and on a font. On the north side of the church is a cross (1519) with reliefs of St Lawrence, St Patrick and an abbess.

Farther along the N51, just before Athboy, the *Hill of Ward* (384 ft (117 m); National Monument), an ancient cult site and meeting-place, can be seen on the left.

Tara: see entry.

New Ross/Ros Mhic Treoin

Map reference: D5
Republic of Ireland.
Province: Leinster. – County: Wexford.
Population: 5400.
ⓘ **Tourist Information Office,**
The Quay,
New Ross;
tel. (051) 2 18 57.
Open July and August.

HOTEL. – *New Five Counties*, A, 35 r.

RESTAURANT. – *Galley Cruising Restaurant* (tea and dinner cruises).

New Ross (Ros Mhic Treoin, "Wood of the Son of Treann") lies in the south-east corner of Ireland on the steep east bank of the River Barrow. It is one of the oldest towns in Co. Wexford, and its narrow winding streets – sometimes stepped lanes suitable only for pedestrians – still preserve something of the atmosphere of the Middle Ages. New Ross is an important inland port, and the broad river is busy with small boats. It is the market centre for the fertile surrounding area. A long bridge connects the town with its suburb in Co. Kilkenny, Rosbercon.

SIGHTS. – *St Mary's Church* (early 12th c.: National Monument) was a large parish church of which only the chancel and transepts remain; the nave was pulled down in the 19th c. to make way for a new church. Notable features are the three fine Gothic windows in the choir and a number of medieval tombs.

The *Tholsel* (Town Hall), built between 1749 and 1804, is a handsome neo-classical building with a cupola'ed bell-tower.

SURROUNDINGS. – 4 miles (6 km) south of New Ross, in the angle between the R733 and R734, lies the 400 acre (164 ha) *John F. Kennedy Memorial Forest Park*, opened in 1968, with finance provided by Americans of Irish descent. President Kennedy's great-grandfather came from the village of Dunganstown, to the west. The park is open to the public. From a hill in the park, Slieve Coilte (accessible by car), there are fine panoramic views.

4½ miles (7 km) farther south on the R733 we come to the imposing remains of *Dunbrody Abbey (National Monument), a 12th c. Cistercian house. The church, in austere Cistercian style, has a chancel, transepts, nave and crossing tower (15th c.). The surviving conventual buildings include the library and chapter-house on the east side and the refectory and kitchen on the south side.

Beyond this, at Arthurstown, stands *Ballyhack Castle* (15th c.: National Monument), a five-storey stronghold with vaulted rooms, situated at some distance from the road on the banks of the Barrow. From Ballyhack there is a passenger ferry over the broad estuary of the Barrow to Passage East (Co. Waterford).

From Ballyhack a road continues down the coast to the little fishing village of *Duncannon*, with a good sandy beach and an old fort on a rocky promontory guarding the entrance to the estuary. The road continues to *Hook Head*, at the tip of a long narrow peninsula.

On the east side of the peninsula is *Slade Castle* (15th–17th c.: National Monument), picturesquely situated beside a small fishing harbour. The 56 ft (17 m) high tower is battlemented, as are the lower parts of the castle. The lighthouse on Hook Head rests on a 700-year-old circular keep.

2 miles (3 km) north-east of Slade there is a road fork at which the right-hand road leads to *Fethard-on-Sea* (Naomh Seosamh Hotel, B, 23 r.; Innyard House Restaurant), which has good sandy beaches. A short distance away is Baginbun Head, where the first Normans landed in Ireland in 1169. 4½ miles (7 km) north of Fethard the R733 crosses the R734. 2½ miles (4 km) east of the intersection can be seen the ruins of *Tintern Abbey* (11th and 15th c.: National Monument), a Cistercian house. The tower and chancel of the church were converted into a dwelling-house in the 16th c.

Portlaoise/Port Laoise

Map reference: C4.
Republic of Ireland.
Province: Leinster. – County: Laois.
Population: 4000.

ⓘ **Tourist Information Office,**
James Fintan Lalor Avenue,
Portlaoise;
tel. (0502) 2 11 78.
Open June to August.

HOTELS. – *Killeshin*, B*, 44 r.; *Montague*, Emo, B, 16 r.

RESTAURANT. – *Egan's Hostelry*, 24–25 Main Street.

EVENT. – *Stradbally Steam Rally* (Aug.).

Portlaoise (Port Laoise, "Fort of Laois"; pronounced Portleesh) lies in south-eastern central Ireland on the railway line from Dublin to Cork. It is an important road junction (the N7, N8, N80).

SIGHTS. – The town was destroyed in the 17th c. and no buildings of that period survive. The Court House and the town gate are early 19th c.

Just outside the town, at Ivyleigh, is the *Irish Veteran Car Museum* (seen by appointment). Most of the vehicles on display are pre-1914.

SURROUNDINGS. – 11 miles (18 km) north-east of Portlaoise on the R419 is *Portarlington*, an old Huguenot settlement, with a fine Market House (1800) and a number of handsome Georgian buildings. North of the town rises the prominent cooling tower of Ireland's first peat-fired power-station.

2¼ miles (4 km) east of Portarlington are the imposing ruins of *Lea Castle* (13th c.), a square keep with round corner towers.

From Portlaoise the N80 runs east to Stradbally (7 miles (11 km)), passing on the way the *Rock of Dunamase*, an imposing 200 ft (60 km) high crag with the ruins of a large and forbidding castle (10th–17th c.): a rectangular keep, bastioned and turreted walls, a gatehouse, curtain-walls and a moat. Fine panoramic views.

Stradbally has a *Steam Museum* (seen by appointment) with historic steam-engines.

7½ miles (12 km) south-east of Portlaoise lies *Timahoe*, with a well-preserved **round tower** (12th c.: National Monument) nearly 100 ft (29 m) high and 56 ft (17 m) diameter at the foot. Visitors can see the interior of the tower.

8 miles (13 km) south-west of Timahoe on minor roads is *Abbeyleix*, an attractive little planned town laid out by an 18th c. Viscount de Vesci on the site of an old monastery. The de Vesci mansion, Abbeyleix House (1773), stands in a beautiful park (open Easter to end September 2.30–6.30 p.m.; admission charge).

6 miles (10 km) south of Abbeyleix the N8 comes to *Durrow* (Castle Arms Hotel, B, 15 r.). 7½ miles (12 km) north-west of this on the R434 are the *Aghaboe* churches (National Monument), parts of which date from the 13th and 15th c.

To the west of Portlaoise the *Slieve Bloom Mountains* rise to 1700 ft (520 m), with beautiful valleys which are best reached, on attractive minor roads, from *Mountrath*. The rivers offer both game and coarse fishing.

7 miles (11 km) north-west of Portlaoise is *Mountmellick*, almost completely encircled by the River Owenass (trout fishing). Here the Quakers opened their first school in Ireland in 1677; and at Rosenallis, 4½ miles (7 km) north-west at the foot of the Slieve Bloom Mountains, they established their first large cemetery. At Mountmellick, and also to the north of Portlaoise, are swarms of drumlins (whale-backed mounds of boulder clay, of glacial origin).

Ring of Kerry

Map reference: D/E1/2.
Republic of Ireland.
Province: Munster. – County: Kerry.

ⓘ **Tourist Information Office,**
Cahirciveen;
tel. (0667) 21 41.
Open July and August.

ⓘ **Tourist Information Office,**
Waterville;
tel. 60.
Open June to September.

The largest of the peninsula which project into the Atlantic in Kerry, in the south-west of Ireland, is the Iveragh Peninsula, bounded on the south by the estuary of the Kenmare River, on the west by the Atlantic and on the north by Dingle Bay. At the east end of the peninsula *Macgillicuddy's Reeks* (see entry) tower up above the Killarney lakes.

A scenic road, the famous ****Ring of Kerry**, runs round the peninsula, keeping close to the coastline for most of the way. Starting from *Kenmare* at the south-east corner of the peninsula, the route (here on the N70) runs west to *Waterville* and then north and north-east to *Killorglin*; from there the R562 goes inland to *Killarney*, from which the N71 leads south to Kenmare.

The total length of the circuit is 100 miles (158 km); a detour to Valentia Island at the north-east corner of the peninsula will add at least another 25 miles (40 km). In suitable weather the Ring of Kerry is a road of extraordinary scenic beauty; it is not really possible, therefore, to do it

Staigue Fort

justice in a day trip. It should be remembered also that at the height of the season there is very heavy traffic on the roads.

**Round the Ring of Kerry

The trip can be made either in a clockwise or an anti-clockwise direction: there is nothing to choose between the two. It is described here clockwise from Kenmare.

From *Kenmare* (see entry) the N70 runs west along the north side of the inlet known as the Kenmare River. On the right can be seen the foothills of Macgillicuddy's Reeks, on the left, over the water, the Caha Mountains.

At *Templenoe* is a church of 1816. Beyond this, at the ruins of Dromore Castle, is a viewpoint and car park. In 7½ miles (12 km) the valley of the Blackwater (salmon and trout fishing) opens up on the right. The river plunges down to the sea in a deep gorge; from the road a footpath leads down through dense, almost tropical vegetation to the shore. A charming little road ascends the valley and over an 850 ft (250 m) pass to Glencar and Lough Caragh (see Macgillicuddy's Reeks).

4 miles (6 km) farther on is *Tahilla* (freshwater and sea fishing), and beyond

this *Parknasilla* (Great Southern Hotel, A*, 60 r.), a beautifully situated holiday resort with a mild climate all year round in which palms, pines, bamboos and jasmine flourish.

The road now turns inland, coming in 2 miles (3 km) to *Sneem*, a fishing centre in a narrow inlet. The Protestant church (16th c., much altered) has an unusual weathervane in the form of a salmon. There is good walking and climbing in the hills to the north and west, which rise to 2166 ft (660 m).

At *Castlecove*, 8 miles (13 km) west of Sneem, a very narrow road leaves the N70 on the right and comes in just over a mile (2 km) to a large stone fort on a hill between two valleys. This is *Staigue Fort* (National Monument), a circular structure of drystone walling, 90 ft (27 m) in diameter and over 16 ft (5 m) high, surrounded by a ditch. The walls are 13 ft (4 m) thick, with staircases on the inside and small chambers in the thickness of the wall. The date of the fort is uncertain.

The N70 then continues for some distance along the sea with its many small islands and then turns inland to *Caherdaniel* (Derrynane Hotel, B*, 51 r.; Dominique's Restaurant; trout fishing; swimming, surfing), near which is a small stone fort similar to Staigue. In Derrynane Bay

Coastal scenery, Derrynane

stands Derrynane Abbey, the ancestral home of Daniel O'Connell (1775–1847). The house now contains a museum with mementoes of the "Great Liberator" (Apr.–Oct., Mon.–Sat. 9 a.m.–6 p.m., Sun. 11 a.m.–7 p.m.; Nov.–Mar., Mon.–Sat. 1–5 p.m., Sun. 1–6 p.m.). Here, too, is the beautiful Derrynane National Park (open all year). At Derrynane Pier a boat can be hired to cross to the famous rocky islet of *Skellig Michael* (see Skellig Islands).

The N70 now climbs to the Coomakista Gap (690 ft (210 m)), from which there are magnificent views, and runs down to Ballinskelligs Bay. To the right, in a beautiful setting, lies Lough Currane. On *Church Island* in this freshwater lough are a destroyed 12th c. church (National Monument) with a Romanesque doorway, remains of monks' dwellings and a number of gravestones with Christian symbols.

From a narrow road which follows the south side of Lough Currane can be seen the ruins of a castle which has been engulfed by the lough. On the west side of the lough are the horseshoe-shaped stone fort of Beenbane and the ruins of a thick-walled beehive hut (both National Monuments).

Waterville (An Coirean, "The Little Whirlpool"; Tourist Information Office, see

above; Waterville Lake Hotel, A, 50 r.; Butler Arms Hotel, A, 37 r.; Waterville Beach Hotel, B*, 40 r.; Waterville Hotel, The Jolly Swagman, B, 20 r.; Bay View Hotel, B, 24 r.; Huntsman Restaurant; Sheilin Seafood Restaurant) lies some 40 miles (60 km) west of Kenmare on the narrow strip of land between Lough Currane and Ballinskelligs Bay. The abundance of fish in the local rivers and loughs and in the sea makes this a popular centre for both freshwater and sea fishing.

From Waterville two lonely and beautiful minor roads, which join after 10 miles (16 km) or so, traverse the middle of the Iveragh Peninsula and then descend to *Killorglin* (p. 178). The more southerly of the two passes a number of loughs well stocked with fish.

To the west of Waterville there are good beaches in Ballinskelligs Bay. Across the bay is the village of *Ballinskelligs*. From both Waterville and Ballinskelligs there are boats to the *Skellig Islands* (see entry).

The N70 continues north from Waterville. In some 7 or 8 miles (12 or 13 km) a road branches off on the left to *Portmagee*. From here a very beautiful but narrow road leads south to the *Coomanaspig Gap* (1080 ft (330 m)), from which there are splendid views of the bays and rocky islands in the Atlantic.

From Portmagee a bridge (1970) crosses a narrow strait to **Valentia Island** (Valentia Heights Guest-House, B, 8 r.; Ring Lyne Guest-House and Restaurant). This bare rocky island offers excellent opportunities for sea fishing. From *Bray Head* (788 ft (240 m)) at its western end there are magnificent views of the Atlantic cliffs. At its eastern end is *Knights Town*, from which there is a ferry to the mainland. The road from the ferry joins the N70 a few miles beyond the side road to Portmagee.

Farther on is *Cahirciveen* (Tourist Information Office, see above; Ringside Rest Hotel, B, 24 r.; Bentee Hotel, C, 14 r.; Teach Chullain Restaurant, Main Street), at the foot of Bentee Mountain (1227 ft (374 m)). From here boats sail (in good weather) to the celebrated *Skellig Islands* (see entry), which rear out of the water, 9 miles (14 km) out to sea, like the peaks of sunken mountains.

Facing Cahirciveen across the broad Valentia River can be seen the ruins of Ballycarbery Castle. To the north-east of the castle, reached on a side road which leaves the N70 on the left, are two good stone ring-forts – *Cahergall* (National Monument), 105 ft (32 m) in diameter, with two stone structures within the walls; and, commandingly situated on a hill, *Leacanabuaile* (9th c.: National Monument), with staircases, chambers in the thickness of the walls and underground rooms.

The N70 continues north-east up the wide valley of Kells. On the left rises Knockadober (2230 ft (680 m)), on the right a range of peaks of much the same height. Between them are fine views of the sea and the hills. The road then keeps close to the foot of Drung Hill, running high above the sea at some points, passes an old coaching inn, with magnificent views of Dingle Bay and the hills of the Dingle Peninsula, and descends to Glenbeigh.

The beautifully situated little holiday resort of *Glenbeigh* (Towers Hotel, A, 22 r.; Glenbeigh Hotel, B*, 18 r.) has good fishing. A mile (2 km) west is a beautiful sandy beach, Rossbeigh Strand.

From Glenbeigh it is 9 miles (15 km) through an undulating morainic landscape to the little town of *Killorglin*

(Bianconi Inn Guest-House, B, 19 r.), where the famous Puck Fair is held every year on 10–12 August.

After crossing the River Laune (salmon fishing) the road forks. The N70 continues straight ahead to Milltown, west of which are the ruins of *Kilcolman Abbey* (13th c.: National Monument), and *Tralee* (see entry), while the R562 turns east and, following the river, continues on the Ring of Kerry. 4 miles (6 km) from the road fork, $\frac{1}{2}$ mile (800 m) away on the banks of the river, stands *Ballymalis Castle* (16th c.: National Monument), the picturesque ruin of a four-storey tower. Extensive views of Macgillicuddy's Reeks.

The road now traverses the *Killarney lake district* (see entry) and climbs, with fine views to the rear, to *Moll's Gap*, and then descends through beautiful scenery, with many bends, to Kenmare, the starting-point of the drive. (Killarney to Kenmare, 21 miles (34 km)).

Roscommon/Ros Comain

Map reference: C3.
Republic of Ireland.
Province: Connacht. – County: Roscommon.
Population: 1700.
(i) **Tourist Information Office,**
    Roscommon;
    tel. (0903) 63 56.

HOTEL. – *Abbey*, B*, 25 r.

Roscommon (Ros Comain, "Coman's Wood"), county town of Co. Roscommon, lies on the southern slopes of a gentle hill 20 miles (32 km) north of Athlone in central Ireland, at the junction of three main roads – the N60, N61 and N63. It takes its name from St Coman, who founded a monastery here in the 6th c.

SIGHTS. – Of the original monastery nothing survives, but there still exists the ruins of a *Dominican abbey* founded by Felim O'Conor, King of Connacht, in 1253. In a canopied niche on the north wall of the church (National Monument) is the founder's tomb (*c.* 1290), with the figures of eight armed retainers.

***Roscommon Castle** (National Monument), built in the 13th c. but much altered subsequently. It is an imposing square structure with round bastion towers at the corners and a twin-towered gatehouse.

SURROUNDINGS. – 11 miles (18 km) north of Roscommon, at *Tulsk*, where the N5 crosses the N61, are the remains of a castle and a Dominican friary. 3 miles (5 km) north-west of this, at *Rathcroghan*, stretches an area of high ground some 2 sq. miles (5 sq. km) in extent with a number of earthworks. The site (National Monument) is believed to have been the place of coronation of the kings of Connacht. The earliest feature is a low mound, probably a passage grave. There are also various square, round, oval or irregularly shaped areas enclosed by earth walls. A standing stone within a stone ring-fort is said to mark the grave of Dathi, the last pagan King of Ireland. In the immediate vicinity are other ring-forts and megalithic tombs.

12 miles (19 km) north-west of Roscommon the R367 branches off the N60 on the right and reaches *Ballintober*, with the ruins of a castle built about 1300 – a square structure with polygonal towers at the corners of its massive walls, two projecting gate-towers on the east side and a moat.

5 miles (8 km) farther north-west on the R60 is *Castlerea*, a little town offering a variety of leisure activities (golf, tennis, fishing). Near the town is a 19th c. mansion, Clonalis House, with period furniture and a fascinating collection of Irish manuscripts, documents and books (open May, June and September, Sat.–Mon. 2–6 p.m.; July and August, Wed.–Mon. 2–6 p.m.; admission charge).

Roscrea/Ros Cre

Map reference: D4.
Republic of Ireland.
Province: Munster. – County: Tipperary.
Population: 4200.
(i) Tourist Information Office,
   Kichham Street,
   Nenagh;
   tel. (067) 3 16 10.

HOTELS. – *Racket Hall*, B*, 10 r.; *Pathe*, B, 22 r.

GUEST-HOUSE. – *Tower*, Church Street, B, 11 r.

RESTAURANT. – *Tower Guest-House.*

Roscrea (Ros Cre, "Crea's Wood"), a small country town with some industry, lies in southern central Ireland at the junction of the N7, N62 and R421. It is a good base for walking and climbing in the Slieve Bloom Mountains.

SIGHTS. – The town grew up around a monastery founded by St Cronan in the 7th c. Of the Romanesque *St Cronan's Church* (12th c.: National Monument) built on the old monastic site there survives only the west front with the doorway and blind arcading on either side; the rest was pulled down in 1812 to make way for the new parish church. To the north of the church is a high cross (12th c.) with representations of Christ, a bishop and two other figures (the Virgin and St John?). The modern road bisects the monastic site, so that the 10th c. round tower (National Monument) is cut off from the church; originally 80 ft (24 m) high, it survives to a height of 60 ft (18 m).

Near by, in Castle Street, are the ruins of *Roscrea Castle* (13th c.: National Monument), with massive curtain-walls, several towers and an elaborate system of staircases and passages leading to the various defensive stations. The holes in the walls for the chains of the drawbridge can be seen from the street.

In Abbey Street are remains of a 15th c. Franciscan friary – a gateway, the walls of the choir and the bell-tower, the buttresses of which form the entrance to the modern Roman Catholic parish church.

SURROUNDINGS. – 2 miles (3 km) east of the town, near the golf-course, stands the ruined church (12th–13th c.: National Monument), with a finely decorated west doorway and chancel arch, of *Mona Incha Abbey*, founded in the 7th c. on an island in an area of bogland.

4 miles (6 km) south-east of Roscrea in the Timoney Hills are a stone circle and over 200 standing stones scattered over a wide area.

20 miles (32 km) south-west of Roscrea on the N7, in a fertile plain, lies the town of **Nenagh** (Tourist Information Office, see above; Nenagh Motor Inn, B, 20 r.; Ormond Hotel, B, 17 r.; Brocagh-on-the-Water Restaurant, Kilgarvan Quay). Its main feature of interest is the massive keep of *Nenagh Castle* (early 13th c.: National Monument), a five-storey round tower 100 ft (30 m) high with walls up to 20 ft (6 m) thick; the upper part is 19th c. Of the other towers of this pentagonal Norman stronghold of the Butlers there remains only one of the towers of the gatehouse.

A few hundred yards (metres) away are the ruins of a Franciscan friary destroyed in 1650.

6 miles (10 km) north-west of Nenagh, on Lough Derg, is the little holiday resort of *Dromineer* (fishing, water-sports).

17 miles (27 km) north of Nenagh, at *Lorrha*, are three churches (all National Monuments) – a ruined Dominican church with interesting details (13th c., with later alterations); the remains of an Augustinian church (15th c.); and, to the south, another church, still in use, with sculptured decoration on the doorway, including a pelican (symbol of self-sacrificing love).

Rosguill Peninsula

Map reference: A4.
Republic of Ireland.
Province: Ulster. – County: Donegal.
ⓘ **Tourist Information Office**,
Derry Road,
Letterkenny;
tel. (074) 2 11 60.

The Rosguill Peninsula is one of the little peninsulas on the indented coastline of Co. Donegal, in the extreme north of Ireland, bounded on the east by Mulroy Bay and on the west by Sheep Haven. The beauty of its scenery attracts many visitors. Like much of Donegal, this is still a predominantly Irish-speaking area. The hand-woven tweed for which Donegal is famous is made here.

Atlantic Drive

The **Atlantic Drive**, encircling the greater part of the peninsula, is one of Ireland's finest scenic roads. The starting-point of the circuit (of about 12 miles (20 km)) is *Carrigart* (Carrigart Hotel, A, 56 r.), a pleasant holiday resort (golf, tennis, swimming, riding, sea fishing) which can be reached either from the south-east on the N56 (from Letterkenny, see entry), with a beautiful stretch of road around Mulroy Bay, or from the south-west.

From Carrigart a narrow road goes north, keeping along the west side of Mulroy Bay, and in 4 miles (6 km) bears west across the peninsula to beautiful *Tranarossan Bay* (dunes with interesting flora in spring). The road follows the Atlantic coast and then winds its way southward, with views of Sheep Haven, to *Downings* (Beach Hotel, B, 22 r.), a holiday resort with a good sandy beach. Visitors can inspect a tweed factory where Donegal tweed can be bought.

Less than a mile (1 km) south lies the resort of *Rosapenna* (Rosapenna Golf Hotel, A, 40 r.), with its beautifully situated championship golf-course. Both Downings and Rosapenna are sea-fishing centres.

The Rosses/Na Rosa

Map reference: A/B3.
Republic of Ireland.
Province: Ulster. – County: Donegal.
ⓘ **Tourist Information Office**,
Dungloe;
tel. (075) 2 12 97.
Open June to August.

Tranarossan Bay, on Ireland's Atlantic coast

HOTELS. – IN DUNGLOE: *Oston na Rosann*, B, 48 r.; *Sweeny's*, B, 13 r.

The much-indented coastal area known as the Rosses (Na Rosa, "The Headlands") in north-western Donegal extends from Gweebarra Bay in the south to Inishfree Bay in the north – a tract of generally flat country of grey rocks, little loughs and tiny fields enclosed by drystone walls. It is a predominantly Irish-speaking area.

Circuit of the Rosses

The only place of any size in this still largely unspoilt region is *Dungloe* on the N56. From here the N56 and another beautiful road to the east run north-east to *Gweedore* (see Bloody Foreland). To the right of the N56 lies *Lough Anure*, which is of geological interest for its evidence of glacial action.

South-west of Dungloe we come to another interesting geological feature, the *Talamh Briste* – a narrow chasm about $\frac{1}{4}$ mile (400 m) long but only a few yards (metres) wide. Not far from this fissure is *Crohy Head*, with fine cliffs and interesting caves.

From Dungloe the R259 runs north-west following the Atlantic coast, with beautiful and constantly changing views. Just outside the town, at a fork, the left-hand road keeps close to the coast, with views of the numerous offshore islands, and runs along a narrow strip of land between Lough Meela and the sea. On the left can be seen Rutland Island, with the sand-covered remains of a harbour constructed in 1796. In 5 miles (8 km) the road comes to *Burtonport*, an important fishing port, where it is claimed that more salmon and lobsters are landed than at any other port in Ireland or in the British Isles.

To the west, beyond a number of smaller islands, lies *Aranmore Island* (or Aran Island: not to be confused with the Aran Islands; see entry), to which there is a boat service from Burtonport (Mon.–Sat. 10.30 a.m.). At Leabgarrow landing-stage is a youth hostel. The island's wild heather-covered plateau ends on its west coast in cliffs and sea-caves which provide nesting-places for countless seabirds. A small lough in the centre of the island, Lough Shure, has rainbow trout.

The R259 pursues a winding course between the sea and various inland loughs, going north, east and finally south to Gweedore, where it joins the N56. Near here, on the River Gweedore, can be seen a beautiful little waterfall.

From Dungloe there is also a lonely road traversing the Rosses from the N56 to the R259.

Royal Canal

Map reference: C4/5.
Republic of Ireland.
Length: 90 miles.
ⓘ **Inland Waterways Association of Ireland,**
3 Herbert Street,
Dublin 2.

Like the Grand Canal (see entry), the Royal Canal starts from Dublin and links Dublin Bay with the Shannon (see entry). Its course is farther north than that of the Grand Canal, joining the Shannon above Lough Ree. Differences in height are accommodated by 47 locks.

HISTORY. – The construction of the Royal Canal was begun in 1792, after more than 30 years' planning and preparatory work. Each section was brought into use as it was completed, and the link with the Shannon was established in 1817, leading to a considerable increase in freight and passenger traffic. Branch canals were constructed to link up with towns near the main canal. But, as with the Grand Canal, increasing competition from the railways brought economic difficulties. Finally the canal was bought by a railway company and a railway line was built alongside it (1845). During the second half of the 19th c. traffic on the canal continued to decline, and some of the branch canals and canal harbours were filled in. By the middle of the 20th c. freight transport had stopped completely, and in 1961 the canal was officially closed to commercial traffic. The Royal Canal Amenity Group now works for the preservation of the canal as a historical monument and a recreational facility.

The Royal Canal offers excellent facilities for pleasure-boating and cruising. The maximum size of boat permitted is determined by the dimensions of the smallest lock, which is 75 ft (22·9 m) long and 13 ft (4 m) wide, with a draught of $4\frac{1}{2}$ ft (1·4 m). The lowest bridges over the canal have a clearance of 10 ft (3·05 m).

For fishing enthusiasts there are bream, roach, rudd, tench, pike and the occasional trout.

On the banks of the Shannon at Killaloe

River Shannon

Map reference: B–D3/4.
Republic of Ireland.
Length: 230 miles (370 km).

The Shannon, Ireland's longest river, rises in Co. Cavan, flows through the limestone plains of central Ireland and reaches the Atlantic just beyond Limerick. With its loughs, tributary streams and canals it forms a widely ramified system of waterways traversing a fifth of the area of Ireland. The banks of the Shannon, apart from the few places of some size through which it flows, are thinly populated and for much of their length bordered by pasture-land. Since there is no industry along the river the light over the water is of unusual clarity. Apart from a short non-navigable stretch in its upper course the gradient down to Killaloe is so gentle that only six locks are required over this considerable distance.

In recent years there has been an active development of facilities for recreation and the tourist trade on the Shannon between Battlebridge (at its outflow from Lough Allen) and Killaloe. There are marinas for cabin cruisers of all types and sizes at Carrick-on-Shannon, Athlone and Killaloe (see entries).

A leisurely cruise along these peaceful waters is one of the great holiday pleasures that Ireland can offer. Care is, however, required on the two largest lakes in the Shannon area, Lough Ree at Athlone and Lough Derg at Killaloe, since a sudden wind can whip up heavy waves. Lough Ree in particular, with its low-lying shores and great expanse of open water, should be crossed only in good weather conditions.

For information about the hire and operation of cabin cruisers, see p. 215.

*Cruising on the Shannon

Boats starting from *Carrick-on-Shannon* (see entry) will no doubt first explore the upper course of the Shannon, the River Boyle and its loughs, and above all beautiful *Lough Key* (near the town of Boyle; see entry), with its wooded islands and its Forest Park (forest trails, bog garden, restaurant, shop).

Sailing downstream from Carrick-on-Shannon, we pass through the *Jamestown Canal* (possible visits to Drumsna and Jamestown) into beautiful *Lough*

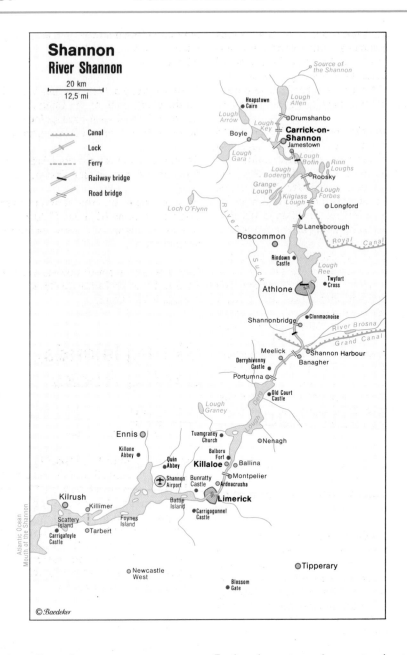

Shannon
River Shannon

20 km
12,5 mi

Canal
Lock
Ferry
Railway bridge
Road bridge

Source of
the Shannon

Lough
Allen

Heapstown
Cairn

Lough
Arrow

Lough
Key

Drumshanbo

**Carrick-on-
Shannon**

Boyle

Jamestown

Lough
Gara

Lough
Bofin

Rinn
Loughs

Lough
Bodergh

Roosky

Grange
Lough

Lough
Forbes

Loch O'Flynn

Kilglass
Lough

Longford

River

Lanesborough

Roscommon

Royal   Canal

Rindown
Castle

Lough
Ree

Twyfort
Cross

Suck

Athlone

Shannonbridge

Clonmacnoise

River Brosna

Grand Canal

Meelick

Shannon Harbour

Derryhivenny
Castle

Banagher

Portumna

Old Court
Castle

Lough
Graney

Ennis

Tuamgraney
Church

Nenagh

Killone
Abbey

Balboru
Fort

Quin
Abbey

Killaloe

Ballina

Shannon
Airport

Bunratty
Castle

Montpelier

Ardnacrusha

Kilrush

Battle
Island

Limerick

Killimer

Carrigogunnel
Castle

Scattery
Island

Foynes
Island

Tarbert

Carrigafoyle
Castle

Atlantic Ocean
Mouth of the Shannon

Newcastle
West

Tipperary

Blossom
Gate

© Baedeker

Boderg. From here a narrow passage through the reed-beds gives access to the lonely Corronadoe loughs, a paradise for bird-watchers and anglers. At Dromod on *Lough Bofin* is a beautiful little harbour (which can accommodate only a small number of boats). Farther south lies Rooskey with its quay. Beyond this extends a narrower tree-lined stretch of the Shannon, leading into *Lough Forbes* and, beyond the junction with the Royal Canal (see entry), to Termonbarry with its large lock. From Termonbarry, or from Cloondara on the other side of the river, *Strokestown* and *Longford* (see entry) can be visited.

Farther downstream is an extensive tract of bogland which is worked by the Irish peat development board, Bord na Móna. At *Lanesborough* (see Longford) the Shannon is spanned by a bridge of nine arches. The river then opens out into the great expanse of **Lough Ree** (the "Lake of Kings"). On several islands in the lough, including Inchbofin (National Monument), Inishturk and Inchmore, are remains of early monastic settlements. On Inchclearaun (also known as Quaker Island after a 19th c. inhabitant) Clothra, sister of Queen Maeve, is said to have been killed by a slingstone hurled from the shores of the lough.

South of *Athlone* (see entry) and its lock the river pursues a quiet winding course through flat country until the towers of **Clonmacnoise** (see entry) appear on the horizon. This is surely the finest approach to the old monastic city (landing-stage).

At *Shannonbridge* an old bridge of 16 arches spans the Shannon. Here can be seen remains of fortifications of the Napoleonic period. From *Shannon Harbour* boats once sailed to Dublin on the Grand Canal (see entry). The ruins of buildings dating from that period still convey some feeling of Regency elegance.

Below Shannon Harbour the river becomes wider, passing the old towns of Banagher (see Birr) and Portumna (see Loughrea), and then flows into **Lough Derg** (see Killaloe), the largest of the many Shannon lakes, studded with islands. The landscape now changes: the shores become more fertile, farms and villages appear more frequently and there is an air of greater prosperity. The south end of Lough Derg is surrounded by hills, and ranges of ancient red sandstone mountains mark out the horizon on both sides.

The town of *Killaloe* (see entry) is noted not only for its remains of the past but also for its large marina and its water-skiing facilities.

For visitors who have hired a boat the trip ends at Killaloe. Boat-owners can go farther, though sailing lower down the Shannon is considered difficult and hazardous. For the next 18 miles (29 km) the river, which hitherto has been fairly sluggish, falls rapidly. At *Ardnacrusha* (Hill of the Cross) is a huge hydroelectric power-station built in 1925–29, with a dam at Parteen, a head-race $8\frac{1}{2}$ miles (14 km) long bringing the water to the power-station, four turbines and two locks. This first and largest of Ireland's power-stations produces some 350,000,000 kWh of electricity annually. It is an impressive experience to visit the power-station (Mon.–Fri. 10 a.m.–noon and 2.30–4 p.m.); the approach by road from Limerick or Killaloe is along the north bank of the Shannon. In the huge locks boats are raised and lowered more than 100 ft (30 m). There is also a fish-lift in which fish – mainly salmon – are raised in 3 hours to the upper canal (the head-race). From the power-station the water is

led in a tail-race a mile (1·6 km) long to rejoin the river above Limerick, at a point where it is already tidal.

Most of the city of *Limerick* (see entry) lies on the south bank of the Shannon, with docks and moorings for sea-going vessels of up to 10,000 tons (10,161 tonnes).

Beyond Limerick, on the right, is *Shannon International Airport* (see Ennis).

Between here and the Atlantic, over a distance of some 60 miles (100 km) the Shannon opens out into its funnel-shaped estuary.

Near Kilkee (see entry) there is a car ferry (return) between Tarbert in Co. Kerry and Killimer in Co. Clare.

Skellig Islands/ Skellig Rocks

Map reference: E1.
Republic of Ireland.
Province: Munster. – County: Kerry.

The Skellig Islands or Skellig Rocks, a group of small rocky islets, lie off the south-west coast of Ireland some 9 miles (14 km) west of the Iveragh Peninsula. Skellig Michael in particular is notable for its remains of an early monastic settlement, which give a vivid impression of the rigours of the ascetic life on these remote and barren rocks.

Visiting the Islands

The ****islands** can be reached – when the sea is calm – by boat from Waterville, Ballinskelligs or Cahirciveen (see Ring of Kerry).

The boat first passes **Little Skellig**, an island inhabited by tens of thousands of seabirds of many species, particularly gannets. The dense swarms of birds taking off from their nesting-places, soaring up, swooping down again and all the time uttering their harsh cries form a sight – and a sound – not to be forgotten. Binoculars should be taken.

On **Skellig Michael**, the largest of the islands, a lighthouse, standing 164 ft

View of Little Skellig

Monastic settlement, Skellig Michael

(50 m) above the sea, is reached on a safe path from the landing-stage. (Before leaving the boat, check the time of departure: it is strictly forbidden to spend the night on the island.)

From here 670 steps hewn from the rock a thousand years ago lead up to the saddle between the island's two rocky peaks; then visitors must turn right to reach the narrow artificial terraces with the well-preserved remains (National Monument) of the monastic settlement founded by St Finan in the 9th c. – six beehive huts with a circular exterior and a rectangular interior; two boat-shaped stone oratories; lower down, remains of a church, probably of the 12th c.; small gardens, a well, gravestones and remains of a sundial; and finally enclosure walls on the edge of a dizzy precipice.

The higher of the two peaks, to the left of the saddle, is to be recommended only to those with a good head for heights.

After the monks left the island in the 13th c. many pilgrims continued to come, climbing to the highest point to kiss the ancient stone standing upright in the rock.

Skibbereen/ Sciobairin

Map reference: E2.
Republic of Ireland.
Province: Munster. – County: Cork.
Population: 2100.

ⓘ **Tourist Information Office,**
    14–15 Main Street,
    Skibbereen;
    tel. (028) 2 17 66.

HOTELS. – *Liss Ard House*, A, 10 r.; *West Cork*, B*, 42 r.; *Eldon*, B, 26 r.

RESTAURANTS. – *Ivanhoe*, 67 North Street; *Sean Og's*, Market Street.

Skibbereen (Sciobairin, ''Little Boat Harbour''), one of the chief places in Co. Cork, lies near the southern tip of Ireland, beautifully situated on the River Ilen, which a mile (2 km) below the town opens out into a winding estuary with numerous islands. It is a fishing port and market town, and a good centre from which to explore the surrounding area. It has a neo-classical parish church of 1820.

SURROUNDINGS. – From Skibbereen the R596 leads south-east to *Castletownshend*, a favourite haunt of artists. In the middle of the steep and picturesque village street is a clump of trees. On its south-western outskirts stands Drishane House, home of Edith Somerville (1858–1949), co-author with Violet Martin, whose pseudonym was Martin Ross, of "Some Experiences of an Irish R.M." and other works depicting life in the Anglo-Irish houses of their time.

North-west of the village rises the massive *Knockdrum Fort* (National Monument), a ring-fort 95 ft (29 m) in diameter with 10 ft (3 m) thick stone walls, a narrow entrance protected by a guard-chamber and underground rooms.

At the south end of the R595, 7 miles (11 km) south-west of Skibbereen, we come to the pleasant holiday resort of *Baltimore*, a well-known fishing centre which also has a sailing school. Offshore, like a breakwater protecting the town's sheltered harbour, lies *Sherkin Island*, with the ruins of a castle and a monastery; there is a ferry service from Baltimore.

Farther out, also with a boat service from Baltimore, is *Clear Island*, whose inhabitants, living off the tourist track as they do, have preserved something of their older way of life and still speak Irish. There are two Irish-language colleges on the island. The ruins of a church (12th c.: National Monument) and a cross-slab bear witness to an Early Christian settlement here. Magnificent cliff scenery at *Fastnet Rock*, Ireland's most southerly point.

On the way back to Skibbereen a side road can be taken which bears east past *Lough Ine*, a clear sea lough where the rich fauna is kept under observation by a Cork University marine biological station.

10 miles (16 km) west of Skibbereen, at Ballydehob, the R593 turns south-west and comes to *Schull*, round which are a number of old copper-mines. From Mount Gabriel (1312 ft (400 m)) there are good panoramic views. From here there is an attractive run to *Crookhaven*, which has a safe harbour. A narrow road runs out to *Mizen Head*, from the highest point of which (765 ft (230 m)) there is a magnificent view of the Atlantic coast.

Sligo/Sligeach

Map reference: B3.
Republic of Ireland.
Province: Connacht. – County: Sligo.
Population: 17,200.

(i) **Tourist Information Office,**
Aras Reddan, Temple Street,
Sligo;
tel. (071) 6 12 01.

HOTELS. – *Sligo Park*, A, 60 r.; *Southern*, Lord Edward Street, B, 52 r.; *Silver Swan*, B*, 24 r.; *Clarence*, Wine Street, B, 15 r.

RESTAURANTS. – *Kate's Kitchen*, 24 Market Street; *Bonne Chère*, 45 High Street.

Sligo (Sligeach, "Shelly River"), county town of Co. Sligo, lies in the north-west of Ireland, on a well-wooded plain encircled by hills. Most of the town is on the south side of the broad River Garavogue, which flows from Lough Gill, to

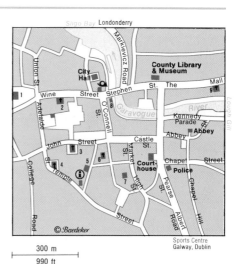

Sligo
Sligeach

1 Railway Station and Bus Terminus
2 Methodist Church
3 St John's Cathedral (C of I)
4 Cathedral of the Immaculate
Conception (St John; RC)
5 Theatre
6 Presbyterian Church
7 Dominican Friary
8 Yeats Building
9 Church of Ireland

the east, into Sligo Bay. Sligo is the most considerable town in north-western Ireland, the see of both a Catholic and a Protestant diocese and an important road junction, at the meeting-place of the N14, N15 and N16. It is also the terminus of a railway line from Dublin, with the Republic's most northerly railway station.

The poet W. B. Yeats lived for some time in Sligo. Courses for foreign students are run in the Yeats English Language School in July and August every year.

HISTORY. – Sligo appears in the records for the first time in 537. In 807 it was plundered by Norse pirates. It became the residence of Maurice Fitzgerald, Earl of Kildare, in 1245. Later rival clans contended for possession of the town. It was destroyed by Cromwell's troops in 1641 and again in 1645.

SIGHTS. – In Stephen Street, on the north side of the River Garavogue, is the *County Library*, housed in an old church (open June–Sept., Thu. and Fri. 10.30 a.m.– 12.30 p.m. and 2.30–4.30 p.m.; Nov.– Mar., Tue. and Fri. 2.30–4.30 p.m.; May and October, Tue.–Fri. 2.30–4.30 p.m.). Attached to the Library are the Sligo County Museum and Art Gallery. The County Museum, in the old rectory, contains material on the history of the region and mementoes of W. B. Yeats, including first editions of his works, letters and family photographs. The Art Gallery (on the upper floor of the Library) has pictures by a variety of artists; of particular interest are the works by Jack Butler Yeats, the poet's brother.

From the County Library a bridge leads over to the south bank of the river. To the left are the oldest buildings in Sligo – the church, cloister and conventual buildings of *Sligo Abbey (National Monument), a Dominican friary founded by Maurice Fitzgerald in 1253 and rebuilt in 1416 after a fire. The church has a double-aisled nave and transepts; the choir dates from the original foundation, the transepts from the 16th c. Notable features are the canopied tomb of Cormack O'Crean (1506), on the north side of the nave, with a Crucifixion and other figures in low relief, and the O'Conor Sligo monument (1624) on the south side. Three sides of the beautiful 15th c. cloister have survived, with the sacristy and chapterhouse (13th c.).

550 yd (500 m) west are the town's two principal churches, St John's Church (Church of Ireland) in John Street, a neo-Gothic building of 1812, and the Roman Catholic St John's Cathedral (neo-Romanesque, 1869–74) in Temple Street.

SURROUNDINGS. – To the east of the town lies Lough Gill, 5 miles (8 km) long and well stocked with salmon, trout and pike, which rivals Killarney for sheer natural beauty. A drive round the lough 23 miles (37 km) is an experience not to be missed. On a peninsula between its north-western end and the River Garavogue stands Hazelwood House, a beautiful little Palladian mansion by Richard Cassels (1731). To the north is picturesque Lough Colgagh, above which are the large Deerpark court grave and other prehistoric structures. From the top of the hill there is a fine view of the lough.

The road passes Newtown Castle (16th c.) and comes to the east side of the lough and Dooney Rock, a popular viewpoint, celebrated by Yeats in his poem "The Fiddler of Dooney". Not far away, off the southern shore of the lough, can be seen Inishfree Island, Yeat's "lake isle of Inisfree".

From here the route continues on the R287 to Dromahair, and 4 miles (6 km) beyond this takes a right turn and runs down through a valley to the south side of the lough. From here can be seen Church Island, with a ruined church (National Monument), and the smaller Cottage Island. To the north is Cairns Hill, on which there are various prehistoric remains. Then back to Sligo on the N4.

17 miles (28 km) south-east of Sligo on the N4 we come to Lough Arrow. At the near end of the lough, opposite Castle Baldwin, a road on the left leads to the Heapstown Cairn (National Monument), probably a passage grave, and continues east to Lough Nasuil. In 1933 this remarkable little lough, some 330 yd (300 m) in diameter and normally containing some 1,308,000 cu. yd (1,000,000 cu. m) of water, suddenly emptied, remained dry for three days and as suddenly filled up again.

To the south, beautifully situated on the shores of the lough, is Ballindoon Friary (16th c.).

6 miles (10 km) farther on we return to the N4 at Ballinafad, which has a 6th c. castle (National Monument) with massive corner towers. 3 miles (5 km) north, on a lonely hill in the Bricklieve Mountains, can be found the prehistoric site of Carrowkeel (National Monument), with 14 burial mounds, all circular except one which is oval, containing different types of tomb chamber. They are dated to 2500–2000 B.C. Below the burial site are the remains of 50 round stone huts, perhaps occupied by the men who constructed the graves. From the top of the hill there is a beautiful view of Lough Arrow.

A few miles (kilometres) west rises Keshcorran Hill (near Kesh, just off the R295), in which are a number of caves. 6 miles (9 km) north is Ballymote, with the massive ivy-covered ruins of a castle with six round towers, which gives a powerful impression of a medieval stronghold. Built about 1300, the castle was the subject of frequent attack until it was finally slighted about 1700.

The R293 continues north and joins the N17. To the west of the junction, on the banks of the River Owenmore (salmon fishing), extends the beautiful demesne of Anaghmore, with exotic trees and rare shrubs. 2½ miles (4 km) north-east on the N17 is Collooney, also on the Owenmore, near which stands a fine 18th c. house, Makree Castle.

1½ miles (2 km) north, at Ballysodare, is a picturesque series of rapids on the River Owenmore, with a salmon-ladder bypass for the fish. On the left bank can be seen the ivy-clad ruins of a 7th c. monastery.

10 miles (16 km) west of Ballysodare near Screen, at the foot of 1970 ft (600 m) high hills, lies Lough Achree, Ireland's "youngest lough", which came into being in 1490 as the result of an earthquake.

At the west end of Sligo Bay are two charming little places, both 5 miles (8 km) from Sligo and with regular bus services in summer – Strandhill to the south-west and Rosses Point to the north-west.

Strandhill has a golf-course (18 holes) and good sheltered sandy beaches which also offer excellent surfing. To the south is an easily climbed hill, Knocknarea (1096 ft (334 m)), on the summit of which is a huge cairn (National Monument) 36 ft (11 m) high and 197 ft (60 m) in diameter, popularly supposed to be the grave of Queen Maeve; from the top there are magnificent views. On the south-west side of the hill is a deep chasm between sheer limestone cliffs.

On the east side of the hill lies the Carrowmore Bronze Age cemetery, which has the largest concentration of megaliths in Ireland. The site has unfortunately been damaged by gravel-working. Most of the tombs are passage graves. There are also a number of stone forts and standing stones.

Across the water from Strandhill can be seen Rosses Point (Ballincar House Hotel, A, 20 r.; Yeats Country Ryan Hotel, B, 79 r.; Moorings Restaurant), with a famous championship golf-course, good sheltered sandy beaches and a sailing school.

Chambered tomb, Carrowmore

Boating harbour, Rosses Point

Tara/Teamhair na Riogh

Map reference: C5.
Republic of Ireland.
Province: Leinster. – County: Meath.

24 miles (38 km) north-west of Dublin, at the village of Tara (Teamhair na Riogh, "Tara of the Kings") a narrow side road leaves the N3 on the left and ascends the famous Hill of Tara, a low grassy hill from which there are extensive views to the north and west.

HISTORY. – From the 3rd c. onwards this was the seat of kings – at first petty priest-kings and later the high kings of Ireland. Every three years popular assemblies were held here at which laws were promulgated and disputes between the clans were settled. With the spread of Christianity Tara lost its importance as a cult site but remained the seat of the high kings until its abandonment in 1022.

Centuries later, in 1843, Tara was again the scene of a great assembly – a mass meeting at which Daniel O'Connell made a speech calling for Catholic Emancipation.

Hill of Tara

The *Hill of Tara (National Monument) has a whole series of grass-covered earthworks. Nothing remains of the timber or wattle-and-daub buildings of the Celtic period, the finest of which were said to have doors set with precious stones and furnishings of gold and bronze.

The central area of the complex, the *Rath of the Kings*, is surrounded by a great rampart. In the middle of the enclosure are two small circular earthworks, *Cormac's House* and the *Royal Seat*. To the north, still within the enclosure, is the *Mound of the Hostages*, a passage grave of about 1800 B.C., which was supposed to be the site of the royal coronation stone, Lia Fáil. Beside Cormac's House stands a pillar-stone commemorating Irish rebels killed in the 1798 Rising, now erroneously given the name of Lia Fáil. Here, too, can be seen a modern statue of St Patrick, who is said to have converted High King Laoghaire.

South of the Rath of the Kings we come to another earthwork, the Rath of King Laoghaire, and abutting it on the north is the *Rath of the Synods* (2nd–4th c.), once surrounded by a ring-wall, which was badly mutilated at the beginning of this century by British Israelites seeking the Ark of the Covenant; systematic excavations have been carried out here since 1952. Close by is a graveyard with many old gravestones.

Farther north two parallel earthworks 600 ft (180 m) long and 100 ft (30 m) apart have a depression between them, traditionally identified as the *Banqueting Hall*. An old print shows a banquet in progress, with the high king's guests seated in order of rank and dignity. Archaeologists believe, however, that this feature may have been the ceremonial approach to a cult site.

To the west of the Banqueting Hall lie other earthworks known as the Rath of Gráinne and the Sloping Trenches, probably cult sites.

On another hill ½ mile (800 m) south of the Hill of Tara is the fort known as *Rath Maeve*, (National Monument), 240 yd (220 m) in diameter, surrounded by a rampart and a ditch.

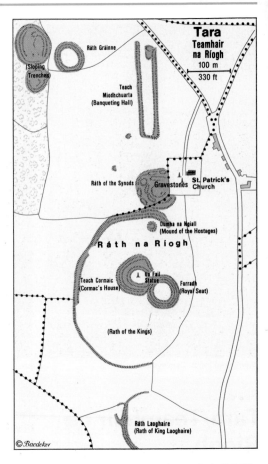

Thurles/Durlus Eile

Map reference: D4.
Republic of Ireland.
Province: Munster. – County: Tipperary.
Population: 7400.
(i) **Tourist Information Office,**
Holycross (Tipperary);
tel. 41.
Open May to September.

HOTELS. – *Hayes*, Liberty Square, B*, 37 r.; *Anner*, B*, 14 r.

RESTAURANT. – *Hayes Hotel*.

The little market town of Thurles (Durles Eile, "Strong Fort of Ely") lies in the fertile plain of the River Suir in the south of Ireland. It is an important road junction (N62, N75, R498) and is on the Dublin–Cork railway line. It is the cathedral town of the archdiocese of Cashel and Emly.

SIGHTS. – At the bridge over the Suir stands the keep of *Bridge Castle* (12th c.), and near the Square the smaller *Black Castle* (15th c.). The Cathedral (1865–72), in Lombard Romanesque style, has a Baroque High Altar by Andrea Pozzo (17th c.) which came from the Gesù Church in Rome. In a mortuary chapel the tomb of Archbishop Croke (1824–1902), who took an active part in the struggle for Irish independence and was the first patron of the Gaelic Athletic Association, founded in 1884, now one of Europe's largest amateur sports federations.

SURROUNDINGS. – 2 miles (3 km) north of the town, to the right of the N62, can be seen *Brittas Castle*, an unfinished 19th c. building with an imposing battlemented tower.

4 miles (6 km) south of Thurles, on the right bank of the Suir, is *Holy Cross Abbey (13th–15th c.: National Monument), a Cistercian house founded in the 12th c. The abbey possessed a fragment of the True Cross which made it a great place of pilgrimage. The church, re-roofed and restored in 1975 as part of European Architectural Heritage Year, is aisled, with transepts and a massive tower over the crossing. The chancel, transepts and crossing are beautifully vaulted. The choir (15th c.) with its east window and stone sedilia bearing coats of arms is particularly fine. In the north transept, partly preserved, is a wall-painting (a feature rare in Ireland) depicting a stag-hunting scene in shades of brown, red and green. Between two chapel recesses in the south transept is a columned

Holy Cross Abbey, on the banks of the Suir

and arched structure, probably the shrine in which the relic of the True Cross was exhibited. From here a staircase leads to the upper floor with the monastic living-quarters. On the east side of the beautiful and well-preserved cloister lies the chapter-house (not open to the public); the refectory on the south side has been destroyed.

3 miles (5 km) north-west of Holy Cross Abbey *Ballynahow Castle* (16th c.: National Monument) has one of the few round keeps in Ireland. Two vaulted roofs of the original five has been preserved.

Tipperary/Tiobrad Arann

Map reference: D3.
Republic of Ireland.
Province: Munster. – County: Tipperary.
Population: 5000.
ⓘ Tourist Information Office,
Main Street,
Tipperary;
tel. (062) 5 14 57.

HOTELS. – *Glen*, B*, 24 r.; *Royal*, Bridge Street, B, 18 r.; *Ballyglass House*, B, 11 r.

GUEST-HOUSE. – *Ach na Sheen House*, A, 10 r.

RESTAURANT. – *Royal Hotel*.

Tipperary (Tiobrad Arann, "Well of Arann") is a market and industrial town (dairy products, linoleum, etc.) in the south of Ireland, situated in the fertile Golden Vale which extends from Cashel in the east into Co. Limerick to the west. South of the town extends the long ridge of the Slievenamuck Hills. Its name became widely known in the popular song "It's a long way to Tipperary" sung by British troops before and during the First World War.

SIGHTS. – Little is left of the old town. The most notable remains of the past are the chancel arch of a monastic church (13th c.) and the ruins of a 17th c. grammar school.

SURROUNDINGS. – 6 miles (9 km) east of Tipperary on the N74 (the road to Cashel; see entry), in the Golden Vale, are the ruins of *Thomastown Castle*, built in the 17th c. and enlarged in neo-Gothic style about 1812. This was the birthplace in 1790 of Father Theobald Matthew, the "Apostle of Temperance" (see Cork). The castle fell into disrepair from the end of the 18th c., and the park, which once had a large French-style garden, now forms part of an afforestation scheme.

2 miles (3 km) farther east the road crosses the Suir at the village of *Golden*. Picturesquely situated on a rocky islet in the river stands a ruined castle. Beyond the bridge a road on the right leads to the ruins of Ireland's largest medieval monastery, *Athassel Priory (13th–15th c.: National Monument), an Augustinian house founded by William de Burgh and dissolved in the mid 16th c. The remains cover an area of 4 acres (1·6 ha). The church, 213 ft (65 m) long, has an aisled nave, a choir and transepts, with a handsome tower over the crossing. In the choir is the tomb of a

Norman knight (13th c.). Practically nothing is left of the cloister, around which are the extensive conventual buildings, surrounded by a high wall. In front of the gatehouse was a bridge giving access to the priory. Until the mid 14th c. there was a little town here of which no trace remains.

9 miles (15 km) west of Tipperary lies *Emly*, which until the Reformation was the see of an archibishop. The cathedral town of the present archdiocese of Cashel and Emly is Thurles (see entry).

Tralee/Traigh Li

Map reference: D2.
Republic of Ireland.
Province: Munster. – County: Kerry.
Population: 16,500.
(i) **Tourist Information Office,**
32 The Mall,
Tralee;
tel. (066) 2 12 88.

HOTELS. – *Brandon*, A, 154 r.; *Early of Desmond*, A, 50 r.; *Ballygarry House*, B*, 16 r.; *Brenner's*, B, 43 r.; *Imperial*, B, 36 r.; *Ballyroe Country Club*, B, 16 r.; *Horan's*, B, 12 r.; *Meadowlands*, C, 24 r.

RESTAURANTS. – *Cordon Bleu*, The Square; *Stella*, 7 Lower Castle Street.

EVENT. – *Rose of Tralee International Festival* (Aug.).

Tralee (Traigh Li, "Beach of the River Lee"), the lively county town of Co. Kerry, lies in the south-west of Ireland, 2 miles (3 km) above the outflow of the River Lee into Tralee Bay. Tralee once had a harbour, linked with the sea by a canal. It is now mainly a market town and tourist centre, and also the gateway to the Dingle Peninsula (see entry) with its many remains of the past. The famous Ring of Kerry (see entry) is within easy reach.

SIGHTS. – Since Tralee was set on fire by its garrison in 1643 and again in 1691 before its surrender to the enemy, no older buildings have survived.

The 19th c. Dominican *Church of the Holy Cross* (by Pugin) has fine stained glass by Michael Healy in the sacristy. Other features of interest are a number of Georgian houses in the centre of the town, a memorial commemorating the 1798 Rising in Denny Street, the early 19th c. *Court House*, now roofless, with an Ionic portico, and the municipal park, with the Ashe Memorial Hall.

SURROUNDINGS. – 8 miles (13 km) west of Tralee, in a sheltered situation on Tralee Bay, is the little port of *Fenit*, a good centre for sea fishermen and underwater divers. St Brendan the Navigator (483–578) was born in the neighbourhood. 2 miles (3 km) from the village stands Fenit Castle.

5 miles (8 km) north-west of Tralee on the R551 lies **Ardfert**, around which are important medieval remains. St Brendan founded a monastery here, to which a group of churches (National Monuments) in the churchyard belonged – the fortress-like St Brendan's Cathedral, with a beautiful 12th c. west doorway and blind arcading and a 13th c. nave and choir (fine lancet windows); to the north-west the little Romanesque Church of Temple na Hoe, which has quoin-shafts with carved capitals; and the 15th c. Church of Temple na Griffin.

A few hundred yards (metres) east are the ruins of a *Franciscan friary* (13th–15th c.: National Monument). The church has cylindrical columns and a beautiful south window. Two sides of the 15th c. cloister, originally roofed with stone slabs, have survived.

Near Ardfert is Banna Strand, where Roger Casement was landed from a German submarine in 1916 to take part in the Easter Rising. He was quickly captured near by and after being tried and found guilty of treason was executed later that year.

Farther north on the R551 lies *Ballyheige*, a quiet seaside resort with a good sandy beach. On beautiful Kerry head, to the west of the village, the hexagonal quartz crystals known as "Kerry diamonds" can be found.

Trim/Baile Atha Truim

Map reference: C5.
Republic of Ireland.
Province: Leinster. – County: Meath.
Population: 2100.
(i) **Community Tourist Information Office,**
Castle Street,
Trim.

HOTEL. – *Wellington Court*, B*, 20 r.

RESTAURANT. – *Tonga*, Market Square.

The little market town of Trim (Baile Atha Truim, "Town of the Elder-Tree Fort") lies on the River Boyne in a fertile plain north-west of Dublin. Here within a small space are gathered remains of a great past both religious and military.

HISTORY. – In 1172 Hugh de Lacy, a vassal of Henry II, built a castle on a site close to the spot where St Patrick had founded a monastery in the 5th c. The castle changed hands several times, being successively fought over, destroyed, rebuilt and enlarged. Richard II held the future Henry V and the Duke of Gloucester prisoner here. In the 14th c. the town which had grown up around the castle was walled. The Irish Parliament met here several times during the 15th c. In 1649 the town fell into Cromwellian hands.

SIGHTS. – Trim's most prominent landmark is the *Yellow Steeple* (National Monument), the last relic of an Augustinian abbey built in the 14th c. on a bare hill above the river. This finely proportioned tower, which still exceeds a height of 126 ft (38 m), formerly stood on the north side of the church.

Near by is *Talbot's Castle*, built in 1415 but later modernised and converted into a school. Among its pupils was Arthur Wellesley, the future Duke of Wellington. He later lived in Patrick Street, where there is a monument to him.

A little way south of the Yellow Steeple are the two-storeyed ruins of *Sheep Gate*, the only surviving town gate.

On the south side of the Boyne rises a magnificent stronghold, **Trim Castle** (National Monument), the largest Anglo-Norman castle in Ireland, covering an area of 3 acres (1·2 ha). In the centre of the area, on its highest point, is the square keep, with turrets at the four corners and projecting towers (only three out of the original four survive) in the middle of each of the 11 ft (3·3 m) thick walls, giving the massive structure a cruciform plan. There was a drawbridge operated from the tower on the south side. The outer ward is surrounded by a curtain-wall with semicircular towers (five of which remain) and a moat. The parapet walks originally linked up with the town walls.

Other features of interest in the town are a number of Georgian houses and the façade of the prison (1827).

A museum in the Education Centre puts on special exhibitions of material from the country's larger museums.

SURROUNDINGS. – About ½ mile (1 km) east of the town, at an old bridge over the Boyne, we come to *Newtown Trim*, with the ruins of the Abbey of SS Peter and Paul (National Monument). Of the very large Cathedral (13th c.; transitional Romanesque/Gothic) built for the see of Meath there remain only the choir, the crossing and a small section of the nave. On the south side of the church are some remains of conventual buildings. To the east is a smaller church (13th c.), with a fine double tomb of the late 16th c.

In the *Boyne Valley* between Trim and Navan are a number of typical Norman castles – massive rectangular structures flanked diagonally by two round towers.

Tuam/Tuaim

Map reference: C3.
Republic of Ireland.
Province: Connacht. – County: Galway.
Population: 4400.

ⓘ **Tourist Information Office,**
    Town Hall,
    Tuam;
    tel. (093) 2 44 63.
    Open July and August.

HOTEL. – *Imperial*, B, 26 r.

RESTAURANT. – *Cre na Cille*, High Street.

Tuam (Tuaim, "Burial-Place") lies to the east of Lough Corrib on the N17, in the west of Ireland. It is a thriving little market town with some industry, including a sugar factory, and is a good centre for fishing.

Tuam was a place of great ecclesiastical importance from an early period. The town's first and second Protestant archbishops were associated with the production of the first Irish translation of the New Testament in 1602. It is now the see of a Roman Catholic archbishop and a bishop of the Church of Ireland.

SIGHTS. – The 19th c. ***St Mary's Cathedral** (Church of Ireland) in Galway Road incorporates the barrel-vaulted chancel, with a beautifully carved chancel arch and a fine east window, of the original church (12th and 14th c.). In the south aisle is the shaft of a 12th c. high cross with interlace and other ornament. The choir-stalls are Italian Baroque (*c.* 1740).

In the Market Square stands another *high cross* (12th c.: National Monument) assembled from various fragments, with a number of figures and interlace ornament.

Near by, in Shop Street, is the *Mill Museum*, with an operational corn-mill and milling equipment.

SURROUNDINGS. – 8 miles (13 km) north-east of Tuam on the N83 lies *Dunmore*, an old place with the ruins of a castle and an abbey (both National Monuments). The castle (14th c.) consists of a sturdy four-storeyed rectangular tower with gables. The abbey was an Augustinian friary founded in 1425 by a member of the Bermingham family; all that survives is the church, with a massive central tower borne on arches.

2 miles (3 km) east of Tuam stands *Bermingham House* (1730), with good plasterwork and fine furniture (open on weekday afternoons).

7 miles (11 km) south-east of Tuam on the R347 and N63 (the Roscommon road), picturesquely situated on a small lough, are the ruins of *Knockmoy Abbey* (National Monument), a Cistercian house founded in 1190. The nave is undecorated but the choir has some fine carving. On the north wall is one of Ireland's few examples of medieval wall-painting, dating from about 1400. Only the outlines, drawn in black, have survived. The scenes depicted are Christ in the attitude of blessing, the Martyrdom of St Sebastian and the legend of the three dead and the three living kings. Under the three dead kings was the inscription: "That which you are, we were; that which we are, you will be." The east wing of the conventual buildings is well preserved, but the cloister no longer exists.

2½ miles (4 km) north-west of Tuam, at *Kilbennan*, are a partly collapsed round tower and the ruins of a small church (both National Monuments), on the site of an old Franciscan friary.

Tullamore/Tulach Mhor

Map reference: C4.
Republic of Ireland.
Province: Leinster. – County: Offaly.
Population: 7900.
ⓘ **Tourist Information Office,**
　Emmet Square,
　Birr;
　tel. (0509) 2 02 06.
　Open May to September.

GUEST-HOUSE: *Oakfield*, B, 10 r.

RESTAURANT: *Bridge House.*

Tullamore (Tulach Mhor, "Great Assembly Hill"), county town of Co. Offaly, lies almost exactly in the centre of Ireland at the junction of the N52 and N80 and on the Dublin–Galway railway line. Until 1804 Tullamore was the terminus of the Grand Canal (see entry) from Dublin. It is now a considerable market and industrial town, with maltings and a distillery (Irish Mist). Tullamore Dew is nowadays produced elsewhere.

SIGHTS. – Tullamore has no old buildings, since in 1785, when it was a smaller place than it is now, most of the town was destroyed by the explosion of a large balloon which crashed here. Notable later buildings are St Catherine's Church (1818), the 19th c. Market House and Court House, and buildings erected during the early period of the Grand Canal.

SURROUNDINGS. – 4½ miles (7 km) north of Tullamore is *Durrow*, where St Columcille founded a monastery in the 6th c. Here in the 7th c. was written

and illuminated the famous "Book of Durrow", now in Trinity College in Dublin. Almost the only relic of the monastery is a *high cross (10th c.: National Monument) with fine figural reliefs. On the east side are the Sacrific of Isaac and Christ in Glory, flanked by David with his harp on the left and David killing the lion on the right; on the west side the Watching of the Tomb, the Scourging, the Arrest of Christ and the Crucifixion; on the south side Adam and Eve, Cain and Abel, a warrior and a horseman; and on the north side two groups of figures. The cross is in the grounds of Durrow Abbey (private property): visitors should, therefore, behave with circumspection.

22 miles (35 km) north-east of Tullamore, on the eastern boundary of Co. Offaly, lies the pretty little market town of *Edenderry*, which has a number of attractive early 19th c. buildings. On a hill south of the town are the ruins of Blundell's Castle. To the west can be seen a number of castles, including Srah Castle (16th c.) and Ballycowen Castle (17th c.), typical fortified mansions of their periods.

6 miles (9 km) west of the town, reached on minor roads, is *Rahan*, on the Grand Canal, where there was a monastery from the 8th to the 18th c. Two churches belonging to the monastery (both National Monuments) can still be seen. The larger of the two (Romanesque) has a beautiful doorway and good carving on the chancel arch and two windows; the nave is 18th c., on earlier foundations. The smaller church dates from the Early Christian period but has been much altered.

Farther west, visible from a considerable distance over the plain, are the tall cooling towers of *Ferbane* power-station, which is fuelled by peat.

14 miles (22 km) north-west of Tullamore, near the R436, stands the parish church (Roman Catholic) or *Boher*, which preserves the 12th c. *Shrine of St Manchán*. The yew-wood casket containing the Saint's remains is contained within a portable metal reliquary decorated with animal symbols and bronze figures (later additions).

Waterford/Port Láirge

Map reference: D4.
Republic of Ireland.
Province: Munster. – County: Waterford.
Population: 40,000.
ⓘ **Tourist Information Office,**
　41 The Quay,
　Waterford;
　tel. (051) 7 57 88.

HOTELS. – *Ardree*, A, 100 r.; *Tower*, The Mall, A, 81 r.; *Granville*, Meagher Quay, A, 50 r.; *Bridge*, The Quay, B*, 40 r.; *Dooley's*, The Quay, B*, 36 r.

GUEST-HOUSE. – *Portree*, Mary Street, B, 13 r.

RESTAURANTS. – *Stonecourt*, 16–17 O'Connell Street; *Teaser's*, 124 The Quay; *Tower Hotel.*

EVENT. – *Waterford International Festival of Light Opera* (Sept.).

Waterford on the River Suir

Waterford (Port Láirge, "Láirge's Landing-Place"), county town of Co. Waterford, lies near the south-eastern tip of Ireland on the River Suir, some 20 miles (30 km) above its mouth. The river at this point is broad and deep, and has thus enabled the town to develop into a seaport of considerable importance. It has a variety of industries, but is particularly known for its glass. Waterford glass was famous in the early 19th c., and since its revival in 1947 again enjoys international reputation.

HISTORY. – In 853 the Danes established a settlement here which they called Vadrefjord. In 1170 Strongbow took the town, and it became second in importance only to Dublin among Anglo-Norman strongholds. In 1487, when the pretender Perkin Warbeck was crowned in Dublin, Waterford remained loyal to England, and in recognition of this Henry VII granted it the motto *Urbs intacta manet Waterfordia*, which still appears on the city arms. In 1649 Cromwell was forced to abandon the siege of Waterford, but it was taken by his forces in the following year. Forty years later, after at first supporting James II, it surrendered to William III.

SIGHTS. – From the bridge over the Suir the street know as the Quay – successively called Merchants' Quay, Meagher's Quay and Parade Quay – runs along the south bank of the river for ¾ mile (1·2 km). Most of the principal sights of Waterford can be seen by going down various streets and lanes opening off the Quay.

Parallel to Merchants' Quay is O'Connell Street. At the corner of this street and Bridge Street can be seen a church tower, all that remains of an old Dominican house, *Blackfriars Priory* (1226–1541). A short distance along O'Connell Street the Public Library houses the *Waterford City Art Gallery* (open Mon., Wed. and Fri. 2–5.30 p.m. and 7–9 p.m., Thu. and Sun. 11 a.m.–1 p.m. and 2–5.30 p.m.), with

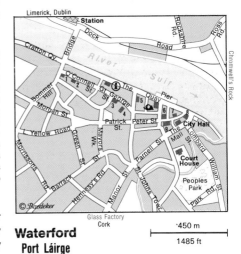

**Waterford
Port Láirge**

·450 m
1485 ft

1 Blackfriars Priory
2 Library, City Art Gallery
3 Chamber of Commerce
4 St Patrick's Church
5 Holy Trinity Cathedral

6 St Olaf's Church
7 French Church
8 Reginald's Tower
   (City Museum)
9 Christ Church Cathedral

works by modern Irish painters (Jack B. Yeats, Paul Henry, Mainie Jellett, Evie Hone, Bea Orpen and Sean O'Sullivan) and sculpture by Eddie Delaney and Oisín Kelly.

O'Connell Street leads into Great George Street, on the right-hand side of which is the *Chamber of Commerce*, a handsome building by John Roberts (1794). Near by, in a lane off Broad Street, we reach *St Patrick's Church* (mid 18th c.), with a charming gallery.

Across from St Patrick's, between Parade Quay and High Street, stands *Holy Trinity Cathedral*, also by Roberts (1793), with a late 19th c. façade. Going down Parade Quay, we pass on the right the *French Church* (National Monument), with a 15th c. nave, chancel and tower, all that is left of a monastery founded in 1240. From the 17th to the 19th c. the nave was used as a hospice for paupers, while the choir became a place of worship for Huguenot refugees and the Lady Chapel a place of burial for the leading families of the town.

At the far end of the Quay The Mall, an attractive street with a number of Georgian houses, branches off on the right at a sharp angle. On the corner is an imposing round tower known as *Reginald's Tower*, with walls 10 ft (3 m) thick, which was once part of the Danish defences; it now houses the City Museum. Beyond the tower are the *City Hall* (by Roberts, 1782), which has been preserved in its original state, and the Theatre Royal, also by Roberts (1788). Beyond these again stands the city's principal Protestant church, *Christ Church Cathedral* (by Roberts, 1779), with a spacious interior and two fine tombs, the Rice monument (1469) and the Fitzgerald monument, of Carrara marble. On the south side of the Cathedral is the Bishop's Palace (18th c., restored 1975).

A short distance away, off The Mall to the left, we come to the dignified *Court House* of 1849, in grounds which are linked with the People's Park to the south by a footbridge over the little John's River.

Opposite the People's Park on the north side of the Suir, in the Ferrybank district, can be seen *Cromwell's Rock*, from which Cromwell is said to have watched the siege of the town (fine view).

1½ miles (2·5 km) from the city centre on the Cork road (N25), the continuation of The Mall, is the *Waterford Glass Factory*, famous for its hand-cut crystal. Visitors may see a film of the glass-making process.

SURROUNDINGS. – 6 miles (10 km) east of Waterford on the R683 lies *Passage East*, where the River Suir flows into the inlet called Waterford Harbour, after joining the River Barrow at Cheekpoint. This was once a fortified town, where Strongbow landed in 1170 with 1200 men, going on to take Waterford. There is a passenger ferry to Ballyhack, on the other side of Waterford Harbour.

On the west side of the mouth of Waterford Harbour, south-east of the city, is *Dunmore East* (Haven Hotel, B*, 17 r.; Candlelight Inn, B*, 11 r.; Ocean Hotel, B, 14 r.), a seaside resort prettily situated on the slopes running down to the sea, with a boating harbour and a good beach (underwater diving).

From Waterford the R675 runs south to Tramore Bay. A minor road on the right leads in 2½ miles (4 km) to the fine *Knockeen Dolmen* (National Monument), believed to be 4000 years old, with a rectangular chamber roofed by two overlapping capstones.

The main road comes in 8 miles (13 km) to the popular family resort of *Tramore* (Grand Hotel, B*, 50 r.; Shalloe's Cliff Hotel, Strand Street, B*, 17 r.; Seaview Hotel, B, 11 r.; O'Shea's Hotel, C, 19 r.; Crobally House Guest-House, B, 15 r.), with a beautiful sandy beach 3 miles (5 km) long and recreation facilities for every taste (fishing, horse-racing, golf, amusement park).

Leaving Waterford on the N25, which runs west up the Suir Valley, and turning right into the R680, we come in 9 miles (15 km) to *Portlaw*, an old Quaker settlement, with tanneries which contribute a large proportion of Ireland's leather production. On the west side of the town is *Curraghmore*, one of the most beautiful demesnes in the country, with an interesting shell house (open to the public only on Thursday and bank holiday afternoons). An avenue over a mile (2 km) long leads to the house (by John Roberts, 1745), seat of the Marquess of Waterford, with good interior decoration and some fine paintings (not open to the public).

A few miles (kilometres) north-west of Waterford (the N9, then the N24), in Co. Kilkenny, stand the imposing ruins of *Granagh Castle* (National Monument) high above the north bank of the Suir, with a 13th c. keep and curtain-walls reinforced by towers and a 16th c. great hall.

Westport/Cathair na Mart

Map reference: C2.
Republic of Ireland.
Province: Connacht. – County: Mayo.
Population: 3400.
ⓘ Tourist Information Office,
The Mall,
Westport;
tel. (098) 2 57 11.

HOTELS. – *Westport Ryan*, A, 56 r.; *Westport*, B*, 49 r.; *Castle Court*, B*, 40 r.; *Clew Bay*, B*, 32 r.; *Railway*, B*, 19 r.; *Grand Central*, B, 20 r.

RESTAURANTS. – *Ardmore House*, The Quay; *Asgard Tavern and Restaurant*, The Quay.

EVENTS. – *International Sea Angling Festival; Westport Horse Show* (June).

Westport (Cathair na Mart, "Stone Fort of the Cattle") lies in the north-west of Ireland on Clew Bay, at the south-east corner of which (Westport Bay) the River Carrowbeg flows into the sea. Before the coming of the railway the town – a planned settlement established by the Earl of Altamont in 1780, probably to the design of a French architect – was a considerable port; it is now an angling centre, with good fishing in Clew Bay.

The little River Carrowbeg flows down the centre of The Mall, the town's main street, with lime trees on both sides of the river, which is spanned by attractive old bridges.
The Protestant church (1880) has Art Nouveau carving.
At the south end of The Mall is a pleasant square, the Octagon, with an unusual clock-tower on the site of a monument destroyed in 1922.

Continuing south from The Mall and bearing right, we come to the entrance to *Westport House, seat of the Marquess of Sligo (open Apr.–Oct. 2–6 p.m., mid May–mid Sept. 10.30 a.m.–6.30 p.m.; admission charge). The house, built by Richard Cassels in 1730–34 and enlarged by James Wyatt, is one of the finest mansions in Ireland, with good plasterwork, English and Irish pictures and much else besides. In the basement is a shopping arcade.

In the beautiful grounds are fountains, operated by tidal power, and a zoo.

SURROUNDINGS. – 7 miles (11 km) north of Westport on the N59, which leads into northern Mayo, is *Newport* (Newport House Hotel, A, 20 r.; Black Oak Inn, B, 5 r.), a fishing centre (sea fishing in Clew Bay, trout in the neighbouring loughs) dominated by an old railway viaduct. In the church (1914) can be seen a beautiful stained-glass window (Last Judgment) by Clarke (1930). In the surrounding countryside are numerous drumlins (mounds of boulder clay left by glaciers), and many of the islets in Clew Bay are drumlins which have been engulfed by the sea.

From Newport the R317 runs north-east along the beautiful valley of the Newport River. To the right of the road lies *Lough Beltra*, with the Castlebar radio transmitter.

The N59 continues west from Newport, passing on the right *Lough Furnace* and *Lough Feeagh*, in a beautiful side valley. To the left, in a quiet bay, are the ruins of *Burrishoole Abbey* (15th c.: National

Westport House

Grace O'Malley's Tower

Monument), a Dominican house. Of the church there remain the nave, choir and south transept (windows) and the squat central tower. There is also a fragment of the cloister.

A few miles (kilometres) farther west, in another inlet on the left of the road, stands *Carrigahooley Castle* (15th c.: National Monument), formerly called Rockfleet Castle, a four-storey tower with corner turrets which once belonged to the formidable Grace O'Malley (see Louisburgh).

7 miles (12 km) beyond this we reach *Mulrany* (Great Western Hotel, B, 55 r.), a little place with a mild climate in which fuchsias, rhododendrons and Mediterranean heaths flourish. Golf and tennis; sea fishing.

From Mulrany the R319 crosses the large *Curraun Peninsula* to Achill Island (see entry). An attractive little road encircles the whole of the peninsula, with constantly changing scenery and views to the south of Clew Bay and Clare Island. In the centre of the peninsula rises the hill from which it takes its name, Curraun (1815 ft (553 m)).

4 miles (6 km) souh-east of Westport, on a side road off the R330, in the village of *Aghagower*, can be found the ruins of a round tower and a church (National Monuments) – relics of a monastery founded by St Senach, who was consecrated as a bishop by St Patrick. The round tower, the top of which is missing, stands 60 ft (18 m) high; the entrance is modern. The church is 15th c.

Wexford/Loch Garman

Map reference: D5.
Republic of Ireland.
Province: Leinster. – County: Wexford.
Population: 11,500.
(i) **Tourist Information Office,**
Crescent Quay,
Wexford;
tel. (053) 2 31 11.

HOTELS. – *Talbot*, A, 104 r.; *White's*, Abbey street, A, 55 r.; *Ferrycarrig*, Ferrycarrig Bridge, B*, 40 r.; *Kincone Lodge*, B*, 14 r.; *County*, C, 13 r.

GUEST-HOUSE. – *Whitford House*, New Line Road, B, 20 r.

RESTAURANTS. – *Captain White's*, North Main Street; *Farmers' Kitchen*, Rosslare Road; *Selskar Restaurant* (White's Hotel), Abbey Street.

EVENT. – *Wexford Festival of Opera* (Oct.).

Wexford (Loch Garman, "Garman's Loch"), county town of Co. Wexford, lies at the south-eastern tip of Ireland in Wexford Harbour, a sheltered inlet opening off St George's Channel. The picturesque old town with its narrow winding streets is a typical example of an Anglo-Norman settlement. The modern town is noted for the manufacture of agricultural machinery.

SIGHTS. – Wexford's winding Main Street runs roughly parallel to the long waterfront on Wexford Harbour. Almost everything of interest in the town can be seen by going down the side streets to right and left.

At the north-west end of the town are *Westgate*, the only surviving town gate out of the original five, and remains of the town walls. Near by can be seen the ruins of *St Selskar Abbey* (15th c.: National Monument).

At the interesection of Main Street and Quay Street is a little square called the Bull Ring, recalling the Norman pastime of bull-baiting, and a bronze memorial to the 1798 Rising.

Between Rowe Street and Allen Street (on the right of Main Street), in High Street, stands the 18th c. *Theatre Royal*, where the Wexford Opera Festival is held annually at the end of October.

To the left, along Henrietta Street, is Crescent Quay, on which is a statue of Commodore John Barry (1745–1803), erected by the United States Government in honour of the father of the American Navy.

An old lightship moored at the quay now houses a *Maritime Museum* (open May–Sept. and during the Festival, 10 a.m.–8 p.m.; admission charge).

To the right of Main Street, near St Peter's Square, are the ruins of *St Patrick's Church* with interesting old gravestones in the churchyard.

The neo-Gothic Church of the Assumption in Bride Street and Church of the Immaculate Conception in Rowe Street, both with spires 233 ft (71 m) high, are known as the *Twin Churches*, having been built at the same time (1851–58) by the same architect, Robert Pierce.

SURROUNDINGS. – To the east of the town extends the great expanse of *Wexford Harbour*. On the north side is a wildfowl reserve, notable particularly for the great numbers of lesser white-fronted geese which winter there every year; there are also many swans. For the benefit of visitors there are a car park, a screened approach, an observation tower and a collection displaying the species which frequent the reserve.

Ferry at Rosslare Harbour

The N25 leads south-east from Wexford to Rosslare Harbour. A detour can be made on the R739 (on the left) to *Rathmacknee Castle* (15th c.: National Monument), which is excellently preserved and gives a good impression of what a 15th or 16th c. Irish castle was like. Within the outer ward stands the five-storey keep, with the battlements characteristic of the period. The walls of the outer ward are over 23 ft (7 m) high and 4 ft (1·2 m) thick, with a massive round tower at the north-east corner and a smaller square tower at the north-west corner.

From the castle a minor road returns to the N25 at Killinick Station, and just beyond the village a road branches off on the left to the little town of *Rosslare* (Kelly's Hotel, A, 97 r.; Casey's Cedars Hotel, A, 34 r.; Golf Hotel, B, 25 r.; Jimmy's Steak and Seafood Restaurant, Strand Road), which claims to be one of the sunniest and driest places in Ireland. Its wide bay has a 6 mile (10 km) long beach of safe sand and shingle, and other holiday attractions include golf, tennis and sea fishing.

3 miles (5 km) away at the south end of the bay lies *Rosslare Harbour* (Tourist Information Office, tel. (053) 3 32 32; Great Southern Hotel, A, 100 r.; Rosslare Hotel and Restaurant, A, 25 r.; Tuskar House Restaurant), terminus of car ferries from Fishguard in Wales and Le Havre in France, with a long pier. To the east, 6 miles (10 km) out to sea, can be seen the *Tuskar Rock* (lighthouse, 1815), around which there is good fishing for bass.

6 miles (10 km) south of Rosslare Harbour is *Carnsore Point*, at the extreme south-eastern tip of Ireland. On the point are a ring-fort and a holy well. To the west, separated from the sea only by a thin strip of land, lies *Lady's Island Lake*. On an island in the lake, now connected with the shore by a causeway, are the ruins of an Augustinian house and a Norman castle with a leaning tower (12th c.).

Just over a mile (2 km) farther west, at *Tacumshane*, can be seen one of the only two intact windmills in Ireland (built 1846, restored 1952), with part of the original wooden equipment.

The area around *Tomhaggard*, 4 miles (6 km) west, was settled by the first Anglo-Normans to reach Ireland, and over the centuries was so strongly held and defended that the settlers did not mix with the Irish population. As a result the distinctive dialect of the original settlers, who mostly came from Wales, was preserved into the 19th c.

From Tomhaggard the R739 continues to Kilmore and *Kilmore Quay*, a remote and picturesque fishing centre on Forlorn Point. From here a boat can be taken to the rocky **Saltee Islands** (Little Saltee and Great Saltee). These uninhabited islands are Ireland's largest bird reserve, the nesting-place of some 30 species, including cormorants, puffins, razorbills and fulmars. (Before visiting the islands, consult the Tourist Information Office in Wexford.)

$7\frac{1}{2}$ miles (12 km) west of Kilmore stands *Coolhill Castle*, a well-preserved 16th c. stronghold on an elongated plan.

3 miles (5 km) north-west of Wexford (N11), at Ferrycarrig, the *Slaney River*, hitherto a wide and sluggish stream, is caught between steep wooded banks and becomes a rushing torrent. On a crag high above the river are the massive ruins of a 15th c. castle. On the opposite bank a tower commemorates Irish soldiers who fell in the Crimean War.

Wicklow/Cill Mhantain

Map reference: D5.
Republic of Ireland.
Province: Leinster. – County: Wicklow.
Population: 5200.
ⓘ **Community Tourist Information Office,**
Wicklow;
tel. (0404) 29 04.

HOTELS. – *Grand*, B, 16 r.; *Strabreaga*, C, 12 r.

RESTAURANTS. – *Knockrobin House*; *Old Rectory*.

Wicklow (Cill Mhantain, "St Mantan's Church"), county town of Co. Wicklow, lies 32 miles (51 km) south of Dublin at the southern end of a wide curving bay on the Irish Sea. Here the River Vartry reaches the sea, after opening out into an inland lagoon 2 miles (3 km) long, separated from the sea by a grassy spit of land (now a promenade and recreational area). The Vikings took advantage of this safe harbour, establishing themselves in the old monastic settlement founded by St Mantan in the 5th c. and renaming it Wykinglo.

SIGHTS. – The old town of narrow streets grew up in the shelter of *Black Castle* (12th c.), a Norman stronghold on a rocky promontory east of the town, which until the 17th c. was subject to repeated attacks as rival clans contended for its possession.

There are some remains of a Franciscan friary (13th c.) in the garden of the parish priest's house. Built into the 18th c. parish church is a beautiful Romanesque doorway.

SURROUNDINGS. – From *Wicklow Head*, 2 miles (3 km) south-east of the town, there are fine views. Unusually, there are three lighthouses on the point. Farther south the sandy beaches of the "Silver Strand", now spoiled by excessive numbers of caravans, extend down to *Brittas Bay* and *Mizen Head*.

The R750 and N11 run north-west from Wicklow to Rathnew and *Ashford* (Cullenmore Hotel, B, 10 r.; Bel Air Hotel, C, 12 r.; restaurants in both hotels), beautifully situated on the River Vartry.
Close to the village, along the banks of the river, are the very beautiful *Mount Usher Gardens*, with many varieties of trees, plants and shrubs, including subtropical species. The gardens, then covering little more than an acre (0·4 ha), were originally laid out by Edmund Walpole in 1860; they now extend to some 20 acres (8 ha). The gardens, with shops, a tea-room and a collection of carriages, traps and snares, etc.,

are open to the public throughout the year (Mon.–Sat. 10 a.m.–5.30 p.m., May–mid Sept. also Sun. 2–5.30 p.m.; admission charge).

Higher up the Vartry Valley we reach the *Devil's Glen*. This well-known beauty-spot is a deep chasm the craggy sides of which are covered with trees and shrubs. On entering the glen the river falls nearly 100 ft (30 m) into the Devil's Punchbowl. There are fine views of the waterfall from paths constructed in the glen.

Wicklow Mountains

Map reference: C/D3.
Republic of Ireland.
Province: Leinster. – County: Wicklow.
ⓘ **Community Tourist Information Office,**
Grand Parade,
Arklow;
tel. (0402) 3 24 84.
Open June to September.
Community Tourist Information Office,
Wicklow;
tel. (0404) 29 04
Tourist Information Office,
Bray;
tel. (01) 86 71 28–29.
Open July and August.

The Wicklow Mountains, a range of granite hills, extend for some 40 miles (60 km) from just south of Dublin, continuing southward through Co. Wicklow. Their eastern slopes run down towards the Irish Sea, while their western slopes border the plain of the River Barrow.

Only two passes, the Sally Gap and the Wicklow Gap, offer a route through the hills from east to west. This is a solitary region of hills flecked brown and purple, dark lakes and conical peaks, often enough shrouded in mist. Until the 18th c. the inaccessible high valleys in the hills offered a relatively safe retreat for refugees, outlaws and criminals. After the 1798 Rising British forces built a strategic highway, the Military Road, to permit better control of the area.

The **Military Road** begins at Rathfarnham, now a suburb of Dublin, and runs 15 miles (25 km) south, as the R115, to the *Sally Gap*. From there it continues as an unclassified road, at first through the hills and then down *Glenmacnass* to *Laragh* (12½ miles (20 km)). From Laragh it follows the R755 south for rather more than a mile (2 km) and then bears right and winds its way, again as an unclassified road, through the hills to *Aghavannagh* in the valley of the Ow, where it comes to an end (about 9 miles (15 km)). The guard-posts to be seen at various points on the route are a reminder of the original purpose of the road.

Through the Wicklow Mountains

From *Rathfarnham*, just outside Dublin, the road leads south, climbing steadily. Ahead, to the right, can be seen Kippure 2517 ft (767 m) with its television tower; to the rear there is a fine view of Dublin. Soon afterwards the road to Enniskerry diverges to the left. The R115 then continues south, past two small lakes and over a boggy plateau, the source of Dublin's River Liffey and of the Dargle, which flows east and lower down the valley forms the spectacular **Powerscourt Waterfall**.

At the *Sally Gap* (1657 ft (505 m)), the watershed, the R115 joins the R759, which runs south-east, high above the forest-covered shores of *Lough Tay*, to its junction with the R755. From here it is a short distance to *Roundwood*, an attractive village in the wooded valley of the Vartry and a good fishing centre. To the east is a large artificial lake, the Vartry Reservoir, to the west *Lough Dan*, a long narrow lough in a beautiful setting below the granite foothills of the Wicklow Mountains. 2½ miles (4 km) south of Roundwood lies the pretty village of *Annamoe*.

From the Sally Gap the R759 continues north-west down the Liffey Valley, below the massive bulk of Kippure to the right, and after passing through *Kilbride* joins the N81.

The Military Road winds its way southward from the Sally Gap over bare moorland, crossing a number of streams flowing down from the hills on the right of the road, Gravate (2396 ft (730 m)), Duff Hill (2406 ft (733 m)) and Mullaghcleevaun (2839 ft (865 m)). It then descends the rugged valley of *Glenmacnass*, passing a waterfall (best seen from the other side of the valley), to *Laragh*, at the meeting-place of a number of valleys (and the roads and rivers which follow them). From here the R755, coming from the north-east, continues south-east,

following the River Avenmore, down the beautiful *Vale of Clara* to *Rathdrum*.

From Laragh the R756 climbs westward, passing in a side valley on the left the famous monastic site of **Glendalough** (see entry), to the *Wicklow Gap* (1595 ft (486 m)), between Tonelagee (2734 ft (833 m)) to the north and Camaderry (2337 ft (712 m)) to the south. Camaderry lies within the *Glendalough Forest Park* (nature reserve), the boundary of which is skirted by the road. 2½ miles (4 km) beyond the pass a narrow road on the right leads to Glenbridge Youth Hostel, in a lonely valley bottom. In another 4 miles (6 km) another road goes off on the right and runs north to the Lacken Reservoir or *Poulaphuca Lake*, with an area of 8 sq. miles (2000 ha) which contributes to Dublin's water-supply and is also harnessed to produce electric power.

The R756 now runs down to Hollywood. Rather more than a mile (2 km) south of the village, at *Athgreany*, is a large stone circle of uncertain age (National Monument) known as the "*Piper's Stones*", with an isolated stone, the "Piper", outside the circle.

4 miles (6 km) north of Hollywood on the N81, past the reservoir, stands *Russborough House, a Palladian mansion by Richard Cassels and Francis Bindon (1740–50), now occupied by the Beit family. The main house, with a flight of steps up to the entrance, is linked by colonnades to two substantial wings. The house has fine plasterwork by Francini and contains Sir Alfred Beit's valuable art collection, including works by Goya, Rubens, Velázquez and Vermeer and a display of Irish silver (open Easter to end of October on Sundays and bank holidays, June to September also Wednesdays, July and August also Saturdays, 2.30–6.30 p.m.; admission charge).

2½ miles (4 km) farther north lies *Blessington* (Downshire House Hotel, A, 25 r.), with a church of 1669. Fishing permits for the reservoir (brown trout) can be obtained here.

Rather more than a mile (2 km) south of Laragh the Military Road bears right into the hills, climbs to 1267 ft (386 m) and then descends into Glenmalure. At a crossroads in the hamlet of Drumgoff a

narrow road branches off on the right, climbs into wild and lonely country and then degenerates into a footpath. This area at the foot of *Lugnaquilla Mountain*, Ireland's second highest peak (3095 ft (943 m)), was frequently a retreat for political refugees. From here the valley of the Avonbeg, to the south-east, falls to the *Avondale Forest Park* on the R752.

From Drumgoff the Military Road climbs again to 1510 ft (460 m) and ends in 5 miles (8 km) at *Aghavannagh*, in a remote valley basin enclosed by hills. There is a youth hostel here in one of the old British guard-posts.

From the watershed at Aghavannagh a road goes south-east down the valley of the River Ow (trout) to Aughrim. Another road leads west over a plateau at the foot of the Wicklow Mountains and down to *Baltinglass*, on the River Slaney (9-hole golf-course; trout fishing). In the village can be seen the remains of the Cistercian *Abbey of Vale Salutis* (12th c.: National Monument), with ornamental carving in the nave and choir which shows a mingling of Irish Romanesque and Cistercian forms. Part of the cloister has been restored; the tower and east window are 19th c.

North-east of the village rises Baltinglass Hill (1237 ft (377 m)), on the summit of which is a large Neolithic chambered cairn (National Monument). This is now enclosed within a later ring-fort (500 B.C.– A.D. 500?), the stone walls of which can still be seen. Fine views from the top of the hill.

5 miles (8 km) north of Baltinglass at *Castleruddery*, on the east side on the N81, are a large stone circle 100 ft (30 m) in diameter and a motte (both National Monuments). There is a transport museum at Castleruddery.

The Wicklow Way

The long-distance trail known as the **Wicklow Way**, opened in 1983, runs for 80 miles (126 km) from *Marley Park*, Co. Dublin (car park; bus service from Dublin), to *Clonegal* in Co. Carlow. Within easy reach of the Way, which is marked by signposts, are convenient parking-places, so that it is possible to walk sections of the route. The course of the Way takes it past a variety of hills, valleys, parks and other beauty-spots, including the Powerscourt Waterfall (pp. 127, 203).

The first section of the Way follows the eastern slopes of the hills, ending near Lough Tay at *Luggala*, on the R759, between the Sally Gap and Roundwood.

The second section makes for *Laragh*, passing the end of Glenmacnass, and then turns south-west by way of *Drumgoff* and *Aghavannagh* to *Moyne*. The final section runs south, past the Ballycumber Hills and other ranges of hills, by way of *Tinahely* and *Shillelagh* to *Clonegal*.

From Clonegal it is possible to continue – outside the Wicklow Mountains area – on the *South Leinster Way* to *Graiguena-managh*, Co. Kilkenny (25 miles (40 km)).

Walkers on the Wicklow and South Leinster Ways will encounter a great variety of wildlife on the hillsides and forest paths – red deer, hares, foxes, grouse and (more rarely) badgers. An information leaflet, "The Wicklow and South Leinster Way", can be obtained from the Irish Tourist Board.

Youghal/Eochail

Map reference: E4.
Republic of Ireland.
Province: Munster. – County: Cork.
Population: 5900.
ⓘ Tourist Information Office,
Youghal;
tel. (024) 9 23 90.
Open July and August.

HOTELS. – *Hilltop*, B*, 50 r.; *Monatrea House*, B, 14 r.

GUEST-HOUSE. – *Devonshire Arms*, B, 10 r.

RESTAURANTS. – *Aherne's Pub and Seafood Bar*, 163 North Main Street; *Clancy's Bar and Bistro*, Front Strand.

Youghal (Eochail, "Yew Wood"; pronounced Yawl) lies on Youghal Bay on the Irish south coast. Here the Blackwater River opens out into a sea lough which forms a safe harbour for shipping. This old-world little market town and fishing port is also a popular seaside resort, with good sandy beaches. Youghal is famous for its point lace, which is distinguished by its vivid patterns.

HISTORY. – From the 13th c. until its destruction by the rebel Earl of Desmond in 1579 Youghal was a flourishing place. Sir Walter Raleigh had close associations with the town, and later it passed into the hands of Richard Boyle, Earl of Cork. In 1649 it surrendered to Cromwell, who made Youghal the base for his campaigns in Ireland.

SIGHTS. – The N25, the Waterford–Cork road, traverses the town parallel to the Blackwater, dividing into two one-way streets in the old town centre. Approaching the town from the north, the road passes, in a churchyard (right) the ruins of *North Abbey* (National Monument), a Dominican house founded in 1268.

Just after the beginning of the one-way system William Street branches off North

River landscape, Youghal

Main Street on the right to *St Mary's Church*, a collegiate church founded in the early 13th c. and subsequently much rebuilt (most recently the choir in 1854). The church (aisled) has a separate tower. Notable features of the interior are the oak carving in the nave, the font and a number of tombs, in particular the elaborately sculptured monument of Richard Boyle (1619) in the south transept, where he lies buried with his two wives and nine of his sixteen children. In the churchyard are remains of the old fortifications (15th–16th c.), with walls and towers extending south-east along the west side of the town for a distance of some 656 yd (600 m).

North-east of the parish church stands *Myrtle Grove*, a stately Elizabethan mansion which belonged to Sir Walter Raleigh (not open to the public).

In Main Street are a number of old buildings. On the left are the remains of Tynte's Castle (15th c.), on the right the Red House, a brick building of 1706 in Dutch style, almshouses (1634) and St John's House, a hospital founded in 1360. At the end of the street rises the five-storey *Clockgate Tower, erected in 1771 in place of an old town gate; until 1837 the town prison, it now houses a small museum.

The Clockgate Tower is the starting-point of a signposted Tourist Trail which takes in the main features of interest in the town.

SURROUNDINGS. – North of Youghal on the N25 a side road goes off on the left up the west bank of the Blackwater, passing the ruins of Rinncru Abbey and Templemichael Castle, to the remains of *Molana Abbey*, beautifully situated on the river, with the church and the conventual buildings (chapter-house, refectory, kitchen) laid out round a cloister.

South-west of Youghal, the R633 leads to *Ballymacoda*, where Irish is still spoken, and the R629 to the fishing village of *Ballycotton*, situated on high ground above the sea, with good beaches and beautiful cliff scenery.

5 miles (8 km) north-west of Ballycotton is *Cloyne*, which was the see of a bishop in the 12th c. The Cathedral dates from 1250 but has been much altered and modernised; it contains a number of fine monuments and (by the north door) curious carvings with pagan symbols. On the opposite side of the street stands a round tower 100 ft (30 m) high, the original roof of which has been replaced by a battlemented top.

Near the town are large limestone caves. In the Castlemary demesne can be seen a prehistoric chambered tomb.

7½ miles (12 km) west of Youghal on the N25 lies *Killeagh*. North of the village, extending for some miles up the valley of the River Dissour, is *Glenbower State Forest*, which has preserved the character of the old natural forests of Ireland. South-east of Killeagh stands the round keep of *Inchiquin Castle* (13th c.).

4 miles (6 km) south-west of Killeagh we come to *Castlemartyr*. In the grounds of a Carmelite priory are the remains of the Seneschal's Castle – a 15th c. outer ward with angle towers, a keep of the same period and 17th c. domestic quarters. There are other castles in the neighbourhood.

6 miles (10 km) farther west is *Midleton*, a busy little market and industrial town with a handsome 18th c. Market House and a church designed by the Pain brothers (19th c.). Nearly all of the Republic's distilling is done here.

Practical Information

When to go

The best time to go to Ireland is between the end of March and the end of October. July and August, the warmest months, are best for seaside holidays. In spring – April or May – the countryside is at its greenest. Autumn can also be very pleasant, since the weather in September tends to be mild and dry.

Although, thanks to the oceanic climate, it is never particularly cold in Ireland, there is a good deal of rain. As a rule, however, it takes the form of showers and does not last long.

See also Introduction to Ireland, Climate (p. 11).

Getting to Ireland

By air

The Republic of Ireland has four international airports (Dublin, Cork, Shannon and Connacht Regional, Knock, Co. Mayo); Northern Ireland has one (Belfast Aldergrove). The Republic's national airline is Aer Lingus, which flies both international and domestic services.

There are regular services from many airports in Britain to the Irish international airports and (less frequently) to certain regional airports; from the United States and Canada to Belfast via London Heathrow and Gatwick and to Shannon and Dublin in the Republic; and from many European cities to Dublin and Belfast. Many visitors from Europe, America and other parts of the world will, of course, fly to a British airport and get a connecting service from there.

The flight from British airports takes an hour or less.

Services from British airports. – There are services to **Dublin** from London Heathrow (Aer Lingus, British Airways). London Gatwick (Aer Lingus, Dan Air), Birmingham (Aer Lingus, British Airways), Blackpool (Manx Airlines), Edinburgh and Glasgow (Aer Lingus), the Isle of Man (Manx Airlines), Leeds/Bradford and Liverpool (Aer Lingus), Manchester (Aer Lingus, British Airways) and Newcastle (Dan Air), Bristol (Aer Lingus), Luton (Ryan Air), and summer-only services from Bristol, Cardiff, East Midlands and Jersey; to **Cork** from London Heathrow (Aer Lingus, British Airways), London Gatwick (Dan Air), Birmingham (British Airways), Manchester (Aer Lingus) and Plymouth (Brymon Airways), and summer-only services from Bristol, Cardiff, Isle of Man and Jersey; to **Shannon** from London Heathrow (Aer Lingus, British Airways); to **Waterford** from London Gatwick (Ryan Air), and to Connacht Regional (Knock) from Luton (Ryan Air).

There are services to **Belfast** from London Heathrow (British Airways, British Midland), London Gatwick (Dan Air), Aberdeen (Air Ecosse), Birmingham (British Airways), Bristol and Cardiff (Dan Air), East Midlands (British Midland), Glasgow (British Airways), Leeds/Bradford (Air UK), Manchester (British Airways) and Newcastle (Dan Air), and summer-only services from Jersey; to **Belfast Harbour** from Blackpool (Jersey European), Edinburgh (Loganair), Exeter (Jersey European), Glasgow (Loganair), Isle of Man (Jersey European, Manx Airlines), Liverpool (Manx Airlines), Manchester (Loganair) and Teesside (Jersey European), and summer-only services from Blackpool; and to **London-derry** from Glasgow (Loganair).

By sea

There are many passenger and car ferry services between British and Irish ports:

From English and Welsh ports to the Republic: Fishguard/Rosslare (Sealink), Holyhead/Dun Laoghaire (Sealink), Holyhead/Dublin (B+I), Liverpool/Dublin (B+I), Pembroke/Rosslare (B+I). The crossing from Fishguard to Holyhead takes about $3\frac{1}{2}$ hours, from Liverpool about $7\frac{1}{2}$ hours.

Liverpool and Holyhead can be reached by direct rail services from London Euston Station, Fishguard and Pembroke from London Paddington Station.

From the Isle of Man to Dublin and Belfast (Isle of Man Steam Packet Company).

From Scottish ports to Northern Ireland: Stranraer/Larne (Sealink Scotland), Cairnryan/Larne (Townsend Thoresen). The crossing takes about $2\frac{1}{2}$ hours.

From Liverpool to Belfast (Belfast Car Ferries).

There are also a number of services from French ports: Le Havre/Rosslare (5 sailings weekly), Le Havre/Cork (weekly), Cherbourg/Rosslare (twice weekly), Roscoff/Cork (weekly).

Passport and Customs Regulations

British citizens do not, of course, require a passport to go to Northern Ireland and do not need one to enter the Republic if they are travelling direct from Britain. Nationals of other countries require a passport, or in some cases a national identity card.

If you are driving your own car you should carry your national driving licence and car registration document, as well as a "green card" (international insurance certificate).

Since both the United Kingdom and the Republic of Ireland are members of the EEC the customs regulations are similar. Personal effects, sports equipment, etc., can be taken in without payment of duty, and there are the usual duty-free allowances of alcohol, tobacco, perfume, etc. For goods obtained duty-free in the EEC or on a ship or aircraft, or bought outside the EEC, the allowances are 200 cigarettes or 100 cigarillos or 50 cigars or 250 grams of tobacco (or double these amounts for residents outside Europe); 1 litre of alcoholic drinks over 22 per cent volume (33·8° proof), or 2 litres of alcoholic drinks not over 22 per cent volume or fortified or sparkling wine, plus 2 litres of still table wine; 50 grams of perfume; 250 cc of toilet water; and other goods to the value of £28 sterling. For goods obtained duty-paid in the EEC the allowances are 300 cigarettes or 150 cigarillos or 75 cigars or 400 grams of tobacco; $1\frac{1}{2}$ litres of alcoholic drinks over 22 per cent volume or 3 litres of alcoholic drinks not over 22 per cent volume or fortified or sparkling wine, plus 4 litres of still table wine; 75 grams of perfume; 375 cc of toilet water; and other goods to the value of £120.

There are of course no customs barriers between Northern Ireland and the rest of the United Kingdom.

Time

The whole of Ireland observes Greenwich Mean Time which is 5 hours ahead of New York time. Summer Time is 1 hour in advance of Greenwich Mean Time and is in force from March to October.

Currency

Republic of Ireland

The unit of currency is the Irish pound or *punt* (IR£) of 100 pence (p). There are banknotes for £1, £5, £10, £20, £50 and £100 and coins in denominations $\frac{1}{2}$p, 1p, 2p, 5p, 10p, 20p and 50p.

The value of the Irish pound is at present somewhat less than that of the pound sterling.

There are no restrictions on the import of currency. Irish currency may be exported up to a limit of IR£100, foreign currency up to the equivalent of IR£500 or to a higher amount if declared on entry.

Northern Ireland

The unit of currency is the pound sterling (£) of 100 pence (p). There are banknotes for £5, £10, £20 and higher amounts, and coins in denominations of 1p, 2p, 5p, 10p, 20p, 50p and £1.

There are no restrictions on either the import or the export of currency.

In both parts of Ireland traveller's cheques, Eurocheques and the principal credit cards are widely accepted.

Language

English is spoken throughout Ireland. Although the old Celtic language of Ireland, known as Irish, Erse or Gaelic (see Introduction to Ireland, The Irish Language), is an official language of the Republic of Ireland jointly with English, it is the everyday language only in certain of the remoter parts of the country.

The Irish alphabet has fewer letters than the Latin alphabet – no j, k, v, V, w, x, y or

z. An acute accent over a vowel means that it is long. The traditional Irish uncial script will frequently be seen in road signs, etc.

The following list of Anglicised forms of Irish words may help in interpreting place-names, etc.:

abha	river
ard	hill
ath	ford
ball	town, settlement
beal	estuary
ben	hill
bord	office, board
bun	end
burren	stone
cahir	stone fort
cashel	stone fort
cavan	cave
cill	church
clochan	beehive-shaped stone hut
cnoc	hill
croagh	conical hill
derry	oak
drum	chain of hills
dun	hill fort
eireann	Irish
ennis (innis)	island, meadow
gal	river
grianan	palace
lis	stone fort
lough	lake, arm of the sea
mac	son
monaster	monastery
rath	ring-fort
skerry	small rocky islet
slieve	hill, mountain
tholsel	town hall

A useful English-Irish and Irish-English dictionary, with an outline of Irish grammar, is published by the Talbot Press in the Republic of Ireland (latest edition 1984).

For a fuller account of the Irish language, see "Teach Yourself Irish", published by the English Universities Press, London, 1961 (with later reprints).

Getting About in Ireland

By air

In addition to the four international airports in the Republic and Belfast International Airport in Northern Ireland there are a number of regional airports, including in particular Galway (Carnmore), Killarney (Farranfore), Waterford and Sligo in the Republic and Londonderry in Northern Ireland. Regular services between these places are flown by Aer Lingus and a number of domestic airlines, including Aer Arann, which has twice-daily flights between Dublin and Londonderry and daily flights from Galway to the Aran Islands (Mon.–Sat.: outward flight 9.30 a.m., return 5 p.m.).

Information:
Aer Lingus, 40 Upper O'Connell Street and 42 Grafton Street, Dublin, and 12 Upper Georges Street, Dun Laoghaire, tel. (01) 37 77 77; 38 Patrick Street, Cork, tel. (021) 2 43 31; 136 O'Connell Street, Limerick, tel. (061) 4 55 56.

Aer Arann, Carnmore Airport, Co. Galway, tel. (091) 9 43 48.

By rail or bus

In the Republic of Ireland the public transport authority responsible for running rail and bus services is the *Córas Iompair Eireann* (CIE). Modern trains run between Dublin and the larger towns, and there are bus services linking the smaller as well as the larger places. The principal routes are shown on the map on p. 213. Visitors can buy a "rambler ticket" covering both rail and bus travel (but not in the central areas of Dublin, Cork, Limerick and Galway). Information about these tickets can be obtained from all CIE offices and the larger railway stations.
Northern Ireland also has an extensive network of rail and bus services, with particularly good bus links between towns not served by the railway system. There are express buses from Belfast to numerous towns in the province, including the coastal resorts. "Runabout tickets" can be bought, covering a week's travel on either the rail or the bus network. The rail journey between Dublin and Belfast takes about $2\frac{1}{2}$ hours.

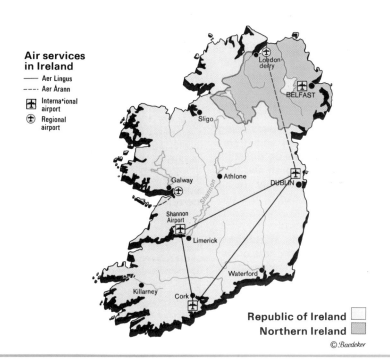

Air services in Ireland

— Aer Lingus
---- Aer Árann
⊞ International airport
⊕ Regional airport

Londonderry
BELFAST
Sligo
Galway
Athlone
DUBLIN
Shannon Airport
Limerick
Waterford
Killarney
Cork

Republic of Ireland ▢
Northern Ireland ▨

© Baedeker

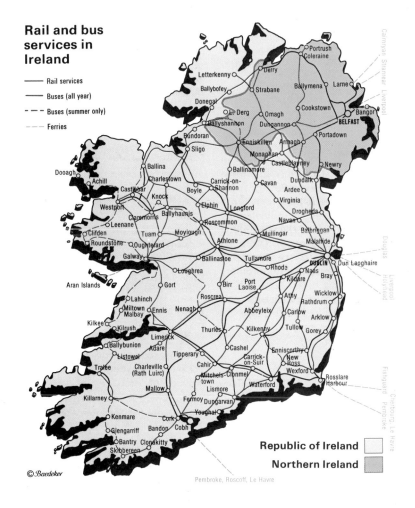

Rail and bus services in Ireland

— Rail services
— Buses (all year)
- - - Buses (summer only)
---- Ferries

Portrush
Coleraine
Letterkenny
Derry
Ballybofey
Strabane
Ballymena
Larne
Donegal
Cookstown
Bangor
L. Derg
Omagh
Ballyshannon
Dungannon
BELFAST
Bundoran
Portadown
Enniskillen
Armagh
Sligo
Monaghan
Newry
Ballina
Castleblayney
Dooagh
Ballinamore
Achill
Charlestown
Carrick-on-Shannon
Cavan
Dundalk
Castlebar
Boyle
Ardee
Knock
Virginia
Westport
Elphin
Longford
Drogheda
Claremorris
Ballyhaunis
Navan
Leenane
Tuam
Moylough
Roscommon
Balbriggan
Clifden
Oughterard
Athlone
Mullingar
Malahide
Roundstone
Ballinasloe
Tullamore
DUBLIN
Dun Laoghaire
Galway
Loughrea
Rhode
Bray
Aran Islands
Gort
Birr
Port Laoise
Kildare
Naas
Wicklow
Lahinch
Roscrea
Athy
Rathdrum
Miltown Malbay
Ennis
Nenagh
Abbeyleix
Carlow
Arklow
Kilkee
Kilrush
Thurles
Kilkenny
Tullow
Gorey
Ballybunion
Limerick
Adare
Listowel
Tipperary
Cashel
Enniscorthy
Tralee
Charleville (Rath Luirc)
Cahir
Carrick-on-Suir
New Ross
Wexford
Mitchels-town
Clonmel
Rosslare Harbour
Mallow
Lismore
Waterford
Killarney
Fermoy
Dungarvan
Kenmare
Cork
Youghal
Glengarriff
Bandon
Cobh
Bantry
Clonakitty
Skibbereen

Carinryan Stranraer Liverpool
Douglas
Liverpool Holyhead
Fishguard Pembroke
Cherbourg Le Havre Pembroke

Pembroke, Roscoff, Le Havre

Republic of Ireland ▢
Northern Ireland ▨

© Baedeker

By car

The roads in Ireland are generally good, though in country areas minor roads may be narrow and winding.

In the Republic the road numbering system is in process of change, the former T (trunk) roads and L (link) roads being renumbered as N (national) and R (regional) roads. Place-names on direction signs are given in both English and Irish forms, and distances are now being shown in kilometres instead of the traditional miles.

The classification of roads in Northern Ireland is the same as in the rest of the United Kingdom, with A (trunk) roads, B (secondary) roads and M for motorways.

Throughout Ireland traffic travels on the left, with passing on the right. At a junction of two roads of equal importance, unless otherwise indicated, traffic coming from the right has priority. Other driving regulations and road signs are in line with European standards.

Seat-belts must be worn by drivers and front-seat passengers. Motor-cyclists and moped-riders must wear helmets.

Drunk driving laws are strict. The blood alcohol limit is 0·8 per cent.

Speed limits. – In the Republic of Ireland the maximum permitted speed in built-up areas is 30 m.p.h. (48 kph), on most country roads 55 m.p.h. (88 kph); on some stretches of road there may be a 40 m.p.h. (64 kph) limit, indicated by signs. In Northern Ireland the speed limit in built-up areas is 30 m.p.h. (48 kph) unless a higher limit (40 or 50 m.p.h. (64 or 80 kph)) is indicated, on ordinary country roads 60 m.p.h. (97 kph) and on dual-carriageway roads and motorways 70 m.p.h. (112 kph).

Car rental

Irish and international car rental firms have offices throughout Ireland, particularly at international airports and ports and in the larger towns. There are many package holidays offering car rentals as part of the package.

If you propose to take a rental car over the border between the Republic and Northern Ireland this must be arranged with the car rental firm beforehand.

Car rental firms in the Republic of Ireland:

Avis
5 Mile Bridge, Ballinhassig, Cork,
tel. (021) 88 82 42.
Cork Airport, tel. (021) 96 50 45.
1 Hanover Street East, Dublin, tel. (01) 7 76 91–96.
Dublin Airport, tel. (01) 37 23 69.
Aras Fáilte, Eyre Square, Galway, tel. (091) 6 89 01.
Shannon Airport, tel. (061) 6 16 43.

Europcar
Cork Airport, tel. (021) 96 67 36.
Baggot Street Bridge, Dublin, tel. (01) 68 17 77.
Dublin Airport, tel. (01) 37 81 79.
Headford Road, Galway, tel. (091) 6 22 22.
Tourist Office, Rosslare, tel. (053) 3 21 81.
Shannon Airport, tel. (061) 6 16 18.
Meyler's Garage, Redmond Place, Wexford,
tel. (053) 2 21 22.

Hertz
Cork Airport, tel. (021) 96 13 55.
Leeson Street Bridge, Dublin, tel. (01) 60 22 55.
Dublin Airport, tel. (01) 37 16 93.
Dun Laoghaire, tel. (01) 80 16 18.
Sean Ashe Motors, Headford Road, Galway,
tel. (091) 6 52 96.
Punches Cross, Limerick, tel. (061) 4 55 66.
Shannon Airport, tel. (061) 6 16 39.

InterRent
14 Bridge Street, Cork, tel. (021) 50 87 66.
38 Pearse Street, Dublin, tel. (01) 77 07 04.
Dublin Airport, tel. (01) 37 99 00.
Waterford Road, New Ross, tel. (051) 2 14 03.
Shannon Airport, tel. (061) 6 18 77.
Newrath, Waterford, tel. (051) 7 65 58.
Ferrybanks, Wexford, tel. (053) 3 32 88.

Car rental firms in Northern Ireland:

Avis
Airport Road, Aldergrove Airport,
tel. (08494) 5 23 33.
69 Great Victoria Street, Belfast,
tel. (0232) 24 04 04.
Harbour Airport, Belfast, tel. (0232) 24 04 04.
Dunmore Street, Coleraine, tel. (0265) 36 54.

Hertz
Airport Road, Aldergrove Airport,
tel. (08494) 5 25 33.
Terminal Building, Harbour Airport, Belfast,
tel. (0232) 5 25 33.
173 Strand Road, Londonderry,
tel. (0504) 26 04 20.

Europcar
GMG Garages, 176 Shore Road, Belfast,
tel. (0232) 77 35 55.
Terminal Building, Belfast International Airport,
tel. (08494) 5 34 44.
Airport Road, Belfast Harbour Airport,
tel. (0232) 5 09 04.
96 Glenarm Road, Larne, tel. (0574) 7 93 60.

Distances by Road in Ireland

The distances between the larger towns in Ireland range, in general, between 50 and 200 miles (80 and 322 km). Thus from Cork to Limerick it is 65 miles (105 km), with an average journey time of 2 hours, while from Dublin to Killarney is 192 miles (309 km) – average time $5\frac{1}{2}$ hours. The greatest distances are, naturally, between the south-west (Killarney) and north-east (Londonderry) of the island.

The table shows the distances, miles and kilometres, between the principal towns in the Republic and Northern Ireland.

Distances in kilometres and in miles	Athlone	Belfast	Cork	Donegal	Dublin	Dundalk	Galway	Kilkenny	Killarney	Limerick	Londonderry	Portlaoise	Roscommon	Sligo	Waterford	Wexford
Athlone	●	227	219	183	126	145	93	126	232	121	209	74	32	117	174	188
Belfast	141	●	424	180	167	84	306	284	436	323	117	253	224	206	333	309
Cork	136	264	●	402	257	325	209	148	87	105	428	174	251	336	126	187
Donegal	114	112	250	●	222	158	204	309	407	296	69	257	151	66	357	372
Dublin	78	104	160	138	●	85	219	117	309	198	237	84	146	217	158	142
Dundalk	90	52	202	98	53	●	238	198	352	241	156	151	151	167	243	227
Galway	58	190	130	127	136	148	●	172	193	105	272	150	82	138	220	253
Kilkenny	78	177	92	192	73	123	107	●	198	113	335	51	158	245	48	80
Killarney	144	271	54	253	192	219	120	123	●	111	441	225	264	343	193	254
Limerick	75	201	65	184	123	150	65	70	69	●	328	114	151	232	129	190
Londonderry	130	73	266	43	147	97	169	208	274	204	●	282	211	135	383	378
Portlaoise	46	157	108	160	52	94	93	32	140	71	175	●	106	191	100	114
Roscommon	20	139	156	94	91	94	51	98	164	94	131	66	●	85	208	222
Sligo	73	128	209	41	135	104	86	152	213	144	84	119	53	●	293	307
Waterford	108	207	78	222	98	151	137	30	120	80	238	62	129	182	●	63
Wexford	117	192	116	231	88	141	157	50	158	118	235	71	138	191	39	●

Maps of Ireland

Visitors who propose to drive off the main roads in Ireland should supplement the general map in this Guide with more detailed maps of the areas they want to explore. The following is a selection of suitable maps:

Map of Ireland (12 miles (20 km) to the inch (25 mm)), published by the Ordnance Survey, Dublin: a map designed for the visitor, with through routes shown for main cities and towns.

Holiday Maps of Ireland (1:250,000), published by the Ordnance Survey, Dublin: four sheets (North, East, South, West) showing every motorable road, with places of interest marked; additional holiday information on reverse side.

Holiday Map of Ireland North, published by the Ordnance Survey of Northern Ireland.

Quarter-inch (7 mm) maps of Ireland, published by Bartholomew, Edinburgh: five sheets (Antrim–Donegal, Dublin–

Roscommon, Wexford–Tipperary, Cork–Killarney, Galway–Mayo), showing relief and much detail.

Quarter-inch (7 mm) map of Ulster, published by Bartholomew.

Map of Ireland (1:570,000), map of Ireland (motorways and main roads, 1:570,000) and map of Northern Ireland (1:290,000), published by Geographia, London.

Accommodation

Hotels and guest-houses

Ireland can offer visitors a wide range of hotels, from country-house hotels and other luxury establishments down to modest places which still offer good comfortable accommodation. There are also numerous guest-houses, which are smaller than the hotels but can offer more personal service.

The Irish Tourist Board publishes a list of hotels and guest-houses (price IR£1). The Northern Ireland Tourist Board's booklet, "All the Places to Stay" (95p), includes holiday homes (see below) as well as hotels and guest-houses.

Hotels are officially classified, in both the Republic and Northern Ireland, in five categories:

A*: hotels which are particularly well equipped and furnished and offer a very high standard of comfort and service; most bedrooms have private bathrooms.

A: hotels which provide a high standard of comfort and service; a large proportion of bedrooms have private bathrooms.

B*: hotels which offer very comfortable accommodation and good service; bedrooms with private bathrooms available.

B: hotels which are well kept and offer comfortable accommodation with good bathroom and toilet facilities.

C: hotels which are clean and comfortable with satisfactory service; hot and cold water and heating in bedrooms and adequate bath and toilet facilities.

Guest-houses are classified in four categories (A, B*, B and C) in the Republic and in two categories (A and B) in Northern Ireland.

Hotel tariffs in Dublin, Belfast and the well-known holiday centres are substantially higher than elsewhere. All prices include VAT (value-added tax).

Country houses

Many old country houses and mansions in the Republic have been converted into hotels and restaurants. Establishments of this kind belong to the Irish Country Houses and Restaurants Association, which issues a brochure listing them. Some of these houses serve meals only to residents; others cater also for non-residents; and others again are restaurants but have no accommodation for residents.

Such country houses are included in the lists of hotels and restaurants in the A to Z section of this Guide.

Holiday homes

Self-catering accommodation is available all over Ireland in cottages, bungalows, chalets, apartments and country houses. The Irish Tourist Board publishes a list of such holiday homes ("Self Catering", price IR£1·50), and they are listed in the Northern Ireland Tourist Board's booklet "All the Places to Stay".

Bed and breakfast

For those who want to be free in their choice of route and overnight accommodation the solution is "bed and breakfast" – comfortable rooms in private houses or farmhouses at reasonable prices with a substantial Irish breakfast. Some package tours also include vouchers for bed and breakfast accommodation.

Some houses of this kind also offer weekly stays.

The Irish Tourist Board publishes two lists, "Town and Country Homes" and "Farm Holidays in Ireland" (each 80p), and the Northern Ireland Tourist Board has a booklet "Farm and Country Holidays" (50p); but visitors will have no difficulty in finding plenty of other places with a "bed and breakfast" sign.

Youth hostels

Youth hostels offer overnight accommodation for young people at reasonable prices. An international youth hostel card must be produced; advance booking is advisable.

For information and lists of hostels, apply to the Irish and Northern Ireland Youth Hostel associations:

Irish Youth Hostel Association,
39 Mountjoy Square,
Dublin 1;
tel. (01) 74 57 34.

Youth Hostel Association of Northern Ireland,
56 Bradbury Place,
Belfast BT7 1RU;
tel. (0232) 22 47 33.

Camping and caravanning

There are numerous camp and caravan (trailer) sites throughout Ireland. Lists of approved sites, with details of facilities and prices, are published by the Irish Tourist Board ("Caravan and Camping Guide", IR£1) and the Northern Ireland Tourist Board ("Camping and Caravan Parks", 20p).
Before camping on private land permission should be sought from the owner or tenant.

For the rental of camping equipment:

O'Meara Camping (Ireland) Ltd,
160A Crumlin Road,
Dublin 12;
tel. (01) 75 23 14.

Irish drinks and Irish butter

Food and drink

The principal meals of the day in Ireland are breakfast, lunch, tea and dinner. Formerly the traditional Irish evening meal was "high tea", between tea and dinner, but this is now rarely served.

The Irish breakfast is a substantial meal, consisting of corn flakes or porridge, ham and eggs and sausages, toast, brown bread, butter and marmalade, accompanied by coffee, tea, milk or fruit juice.

Lunch is usually a modest meal, often consisting only of sandwiches and tea. Hotels and restaurants, however, offer a full menu; many have a reasonably priced tourist menu.

Tea, in the afternoon, may be accompanied by cakes, buns or biscuits.

Dinner in a restaurant always consists of several courses, with a choice of dishes for each course. Sherry, whiskey or gin may be taken as an aperitif.

The first course may be smoked Irish salmon, seafood cocktail or egg mayonnaise. This may be followed by leg of lamb with mint sauce, roast rib of beef, gammon steak, grilled sirloin steak, fried fillet of plaice with tartare sauce, or poached or grilled salmon, accompanied perhaps by Brussels sprouts, creamed mushrooms, celery au gratin, carrots Vichy, creamed potatoes or baked potatoes. Among popular desserts are lemon meringue pie, hot apple pie with ice cream and fruit salad with fresh cream.

One celebrated Irish speciality is Irish stew, consisting of mutton, potatoes, onions and seasoning, stewed for several hours.

Favourite Irish drinks are beer and whiskey. There is a wide range of beers, from light English ales to the dark Guinness stout with its foaming head, brewed in the celebrated Guinness Brewery in Dublin. A light lager is now also popular.

Irish whiskey is quite different from Scotch whisky, in spelling as well as in taste. It is drunk neat or with water. Whiskey is also drunk in the form of "Irish coffee" or "Gaelic coffee". To make this warm and comforting drink you first heat a glass by washing it out with hot water; then pour in a measure of Irish whiskey with a little sugar, fill up with hot black coffee, stir well and, after the mixture has settled, top it up with a good spoonful of fresh or whipped cream.

Irish whiskey is the basis of a liqueur, "Irish Mist", which is said to have originated in the town of Tullamore, in a process involving the addition of heather honey.

Among tourist attractions which have recently become popular in Ireland are the **"medieval banquets"** held in old castles such as Bunratty, Knappogue (near Quin, Co. Clare) and Dunguaire (Kinvara, Co. Galway). At these events substantial medieval-style meals, with wine, are served by young men and women in medieval costume to the accompaniment of old ballads and music.

Restaurants

The Irish Tourist Board publishes a list of restaurants, "Dining in Ireland Guide"

(IR£1), and the Northern Ireland Tourist Board also produces a useful booklet, "Let's Eat Out" (£1).

Some restaurants offer a tourist menu as well as à la carte meals. Some have a full licence entitling them to serve any alcoholic drinks; some have only a wine licence.

Pubs

The Irish pub is a national institution. Its main function is to provide liquid refreshment rather than food, but some pubs now also offer a "pub lunch" of sandwiches or a hot dish of some kind. They offer visitors an easy way of making friendly contact with local people.

Most pubs are open on weekdays from 10.30 in the morning to 11.30 at night in summer and 11 p.m. in winter. On Sundays they are open from 12.30 to 2 p.m. and from 4 to 10 p.m. In Dublin they close from 2.30 to 3.30 p.m. Closing times are strictly observed. In Northern Ireland pubs are closed on Sunday.

The following is a selection of typical pubs in the Republic of Ireland.

Co. Dublin
Conway's, 70 Parnell Street, Dublin 1
Sackville Lounge, Sackville Place, Dublin 1
Madigan's, 25 North Earl Street, Dublin 1
Mooney's, 1 Lower Abbey Street, Dublin 1
Bartley Dunne's, 32 Lower Stephen Street, Dublin 2
Cassidy's, 42 Lower Camden Street, Dublin 2
Davy Byrne's, 21 Duke Street, Dublin 2
Doheny and Nesbitt, 5 Lower Baggot Street, Dublin 2
Kehoe's, 9 South Anne Street, Dublin 2
McDaid's, 3 Harry Street, Dublin 2
Mulligan's, 8 Poolbeg Street, Dublin 2
Murphy's, "Scruffy's", 1 Powers Court, Dublin 2
Neary's, 1 Chatham Street, Dublin 2
O'Connell's, 29 South Richmond Street, Dublin 2
O'Donoghue's, 15 Merrion Row, Dublin 2
Palace Bar, 21 Fleet Street, Dublin 2
Stag's Head, Dame Court, Dublin 2
Essex Gate Bar, 34–37 East Essex Street, Dublin 2
Long Hall, 51 South Great Georges Street, Dublin 2
Toner's, 139 Lower Baggot Street, Dublin 2
O'Brien's, Sussex Terrace, Dublin 4
Ryan's, 51 Haddington Road, Dublin 4
Searson's, 42 Upper Baggot Street, Dublin 4
Humphrey's, 79 Ranelagh Road, Dublin 6
Slattery's, 217 Lower Rathmines Road, Dublin 6
Brazen Head, 20 Lower Bridge Street, Dublin 8
Lord Edward, 23 Christchurch Place, Dublin 8
Ryan's, Parkgate Street, Dublin 8
Kavanagh's, 1 Prospect Square, Dublin 9
Abbey Tavern, Howth
Joe May, Harbour, Skeries

Co. Cavan
Derragarra Inn, Butlersbridge

Co. Clare
Bofey Quin's, Corofin
Durty Nelly's, Bunratty
O'Connor's, Doolin

Co. Cork
Dan Lowrey's, 13 MacCurtain Street, Cork
Lyster's, Baltimore
Skibbereen Eagle, Tragumna (near Skibbereen)
Blue Haven, Kinsale
Overdraught, Minane Bridge
Spaniard, Kinsale

Co. Galway
Moran's, Kilcolgan
O'Connor's, Salthill
Paddy Burke's, Clarinbridge
Silver Teal, Moycullen

Co. Kerry
Lynch's, The Spa, Tralee
Purple Heather, Kenmare

Co. Louth
Monasterboice Inn, Monasterboice (near Drogheda)

Co. Mayo
Asgard, The Quay, Westport
Val's, Ballyhaunis

Co. Sligo
Hargadon's, O'Connell Street, Sligo
Redmond Bruen's (Austie Gillen's), Rosses Point

Co. Waterford
Katie Reilly's Kitchen, Tramore Road, Waterford
Seanachie, Dungarvan

Co. Westmeath
Annie Murphy's, Glassan

Co. Wicklow
Laragh Inn, Laragh

In many of the old pubs traditional ballads are still sung. There are also so-called "singing pubs" in which singers and instrumentalists come together to make music in a convivial atmosphere and the other customers can join in the singing.

Musical Events

The Irish have always been fond of singing and making music, many of their songs and ballads which are sung in Gaelic date from the 16th c. Songs with English words are found only from the mid 19th c. onwards.

There are numerous events in Ireland designed to preserve and promote traditional folk music. Thus the **All-Ireland Fleadh** (pronounced Flah) is an annual festival of folk music, held each year in a different town; but no less interesting than the official programme of competitions is the impromptu music-making that goes on in the crowded pubs and hotels and in the street.

The **Fleadh Nua**, held every year in Ennis, Co. Clare, at the end of May, provides a platform for both established and new groups and soloists; at this festival there is less spontaneous music-making. Similar festivals, on a smaller scale, are held in many other towns.

Tralee, Co. Kerry, is the home of **Siamsa** (pronounced She-amsa), the Folk Theatre of Ireland, which combines folk singing and dancing with dramatic performances. It puts on at least three shows a week during the summer, and also goes on tour. Galway's Gaelic theatre, An Taibhdhearc, also presents performances of traditional music.

For summer visitors there are ample opportunities to hear Irish folk music. In some 40 towns throughout the country there are folk evenings or *seisiun* ("sessions") at which people of all ages come together to sing, make music, dance and tell tales, when members of the audience are invited to join in. The large hotels and some restaurants also organise evening entertainments for visitors.

Singing pubs: see Pubs

Electricity

In the Republic 220 volts (50 cycles); in Northern Ireland 240 volts (50 cycles). Power sockets are of the British type; visitors from countries with a different type should take an adaptor.

Weights and Measures

Both in the Republic and in Northern Ireland the traditional British (non-decimal) weights and measures are still in use. A gradual process of change-over to the metric system is, however, under way.

Souvenirs

Among the most sought-after souvenirs of a visit to Ireland are hand-woven tweed, fine lace, hand-knitted jerseys, pipes, china, pottery, silver and hand-cut crystal. Smoked salmon is also a popular buy.

Articles which attract a high rate of VAT (value-added tax), such as crystal, can be despatched by the shop to your home address, so that you pay only the postage and save the tax.

Fine antiques can be found in antique shops, at auctions and in flea markets (Dublin, Cork, Limerick).

Many visitors like to take home examples of the traditional Irish crafts (pottery, hand-woven articles, basketwork, glass-blowing, etc.) which are still practised in many parts of Ireland. In some places there are holiday courses in these crafts.

For information on Irish crafts apply to the Crafts Council of Ireland, Thomas Prior Bridge, Ballsbridge, Dublin 4, tel. (01) 68 07 64.

Tipping

In most hotels and restaurants a service charge of 10, 12 or 15 per cent is automatically added to the bill. Otherwise a tip of between 5 and 15 per cent can be given.

Sports

In Ireland sport is an important element in everyday life. The desire to establish Irish independence of Britain in sport led to the establishment in 1884 of the **Gaelic Athletic Association**. *Gaelic football*, which combines features of association football and rugby was also actively promoted.

There is also a special Irish form of *bowling*, fought out with a heavy steel ball on quiet country roads in the south of Ireland between two towns or villages.

The great Irish game, however, is *hurling*, played by 15-men teams with hurling-sticks, which are rather like hockey-sticks with broader blades. The all-Ireland senior finals at Croke Park in Dublin are watched by over 80,000 fanatical spectators.

See also Golf, Fishing, Shooting, Riding and Water-sports, below

Greyhound-racing: see Calendar of events

Sport for the disabled. – The Irish Tourist Board produces a guide for the disabled, with the addresses of organisations and clubs (including the Irish Wheelchair Association and the National League of the Blind) which will advise disabled people interested in sport.

Climbing and Hill-walking

Ireland's inland hills and its coastal cliffs offer ample space for hill-walking, climbing and rock-climbing. Good walking country is to be found particularly in the hills of Wicklow, Kerry and Connemara. Guides and maps are readily available, and some long-distance trails such as the Wicklow and South Leinster Way and the Kerry Way are waymarked. Before setting out on a long walk climbers should consult the weather forecast. Further information can be obtained from the Federation of Mountaineering Clubs of Ireland, of which some 40 climbing clubs are members.

Address:
Federation of Mountaineering Clubs of Ireland,
20 Leopardstown Gardens,
Blackrock, Co. Dublin.

Golf

Golf is a popular sport in Ireland, and on summer evenings and at week-ends large numbers of people can be seen playing golf, often without any elaborate equipment. There are some 200 golf clubs, and numerous courses, about half of them 18-hole courses. There are golf-courses near most holiday hotels. Clubs can often be rented by visitors.

Golf-courses in the Republic of Ireland (map opposite)

1 Dublin area
Balbriggan Golf Club (9)
Ballinascorney Golf Club (9)
Carrickmines Golf Club (9)
Castle Golf Club (18)
Clontarf Golf Club (18)
Deerpark Golf Club (18)
Donabate Golf Club (18)

Golf-courses in the Republic of Ireland

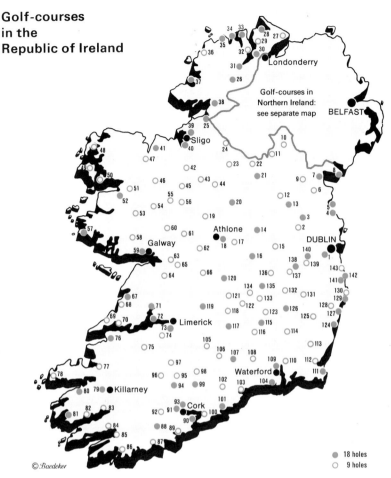

Golf-courses in Northern Ireland: see separate map

● 18 holes
○ 9 holes

© Baedeker

Dublin and County Golf Club (18)
Dublin Sport Golf Club (18)
Dun Laoghaire Golf Club (18)
Edmonstown Golf Club (18)
Elm Park Sports and Golf Club (18)
Forrest Little Golf Club (18)
Foxrock Golf Club (18)
Grange Golf Club (18)
Hermitage Golf Club (18)
Howth Golf Club (18)
Killiney Golf Club (9)
Lucan Golf Club (9)
Malahide Golf Club (9)
Milltown Golf Club (18)
Newlands Golf Club (18)
Portmarnock Golf Club (18 and 9)
Rathfarnham Golf Club (9)
Royal Dublin Golf Club (18)
Rush Golf Club (9)
Skerries Golf Club (18)
Slade Valley Golf Club (18)
Stackstown Golf Club (18)
St Anne's Golf Club (9)
Stepaside Golf Club (9)
Sutton Golf Club (9)
Woodbrook Golf Club (18)
  2 Trim Golf Club (9)
  3 Royal Tara Golf Club (18)
  4 Laytown and Bettystown Golf Club (18)
  5 County Louth Golf Club (18)
  6 Ardee Golf Club (9)
  7 Dundalk Golf Club (18)
  8 Greenore Golf Club (18)

  9 Nuremore Golf Club (9)
 10 Rossmore Golf Club (9)
 11 Clones Golf Club (9)
 12 Virginia Golf Club (9)
 13 Headfort Golf Club (18)
 14 Mullingar Golf Club (18)
 15 Edenderry Golf Club (9)
 16 Tullamore Golf Club (18)
 17 Moate Golf Club (9)
 18 Athlone Golf Club (18)
 19 Roscommon Golf Club (9)
 20 County Longford Golf Club (18)
 21 County Cavan Golf Club (18)
 22 Belturbet Golf Club (9)
 23 Ballinamore Golf Club (9)
 24 Blacklion Golf Club (9)
 25 Bundoran Golf Club (18)
 26 Ballybofey and Stranorlar Golf Club (18)
 27 Greencastle Golf Club (9)
 28 Ballyliffen Golf Club (18)
 29 Buncrana Municipal Golf Club (9)
 30 North West Golf Club (18)
 31 Letterkenny Golf Club (18)
 32 Otway Golf Club (9)
 33 Portsalon Golf Club (18)
 34 Rosapenna Golf Club (18)
 35 Dunfanaghy Golf Club (18)
 36 Gweedore Golf Club (9)
 37 Narin and Portnoo Golf Club (18)
 38 Donegal Town Golf Club (18)
 39 County Sligo Golf Club (18)
 40 Strandhill Golf Club (18)
 41 Enniscrone Golf Club (18)

42 Ballymote Golf Club (9)	**93** Mahon Municipal Golf Course (9)
43 Boyle Golf Club (9)	Douglas Golf Club (18)
44 Carrick-on-Shannon Golf Club (9)	Cork Golf Club (18)
45 Ballaghaderreen Golf Club (9)	**94** Mallow Golf Club (18)
46 Swinford Golf Club (9)	**95** Doneraile Golf Club (9)
47 Ballina Golf Club (9)	**96** Kanturk Golf Club (9)
48 Belmullet Golf Club (9)	**97** Charleville Golf Club (9)
49 Achill Golf Club (9)	**98** Mitchelstown Golf Club (9)
50 Mulrany Golf Club (9)	**99** Fermoy Golf Club (18)
51 Castlebar Golf Club (9)	**100** East Cork Golf Club (9)
52 Westport Golf Club (18)	**101** Youghal Gold Club (18)
53 Ballinrobe Golf Club (9)	**102** Lismore Golf Club (9)
54 Claremorris Golf Club (9)	**103** Dungarvan Golf Club (9)
55 Ballyhaunis Golf Club (9)	**104** Tramore Golf Club (18)
56 Castlerea Golf Club (9)	**105** Tipperary Golf Club (18)
57 Connemara Golf Club (18)	**106** Cahir Golf Club (9)
58 Willis Park Golf Club (9)	**107** Clonmel Golf Club (18)
59 Galway Golf Club (18)	**108** Carrick-on-Suir Golf Club (9)
60 Tuam Golf Club (9)	**109** Waterford Golf Club (18)
61 Mountbellew Golf Club (9)	**110** New Ross Golf Club (9)
62 Ballinasloe Golf Club (9)	**111** Rosslare Golf Club (18)
63 Athenry Golf Club (9)	**112** Wexford Golf Club (9)
64 Gort Golf Club (9)	**113** Enniscorthy Golf Club (9)
65 Loughrea Golf Club (9)	**114** Borris Golf Club (9)
66 Portumna Golf Club (18)	**115** Kilkenny Golf Club (18)
67 Lahinch Golf Club (18)	**116** Callan Golf Club (9)
68 Spanish Point Golf Club (9)	**117** Thurles Golf Club (18)
69 Kilkee Golf Club (9)	**118** Templemore Golf Club (9)
70 Kilrush Golf Club (9)	**119** Nenagh Golf Club (18)
71 Ennis Golf Club (18)	**120** Birr Golf Club (18)
72 Shannon Golf Club (18)	**121** Roscrea Golf Club (9)
73 Limerick Golf Club (18)	**122** Rathdowney Golf Club (9)
Castleroy Golf Club (18)	**123** Castlecomer Golf Club (9)
74 Adare Manor Golf Club (9)	**124** Courtown Golf Club (18)
75 Newcastle West Golf Club (9)	**125** Coollattin Golf Club (9)
76 Ballybunion Golf Club (18)	**126** Carlow Golf Club (18)
77 Tralee Golf Club (9)	**127** Arklow Golf Club (18)
78 Ceann Sibeal Golf Club (9)	**128** Woodenbridge Golf Club (9)
79 Killarney Golf and Fishing Club	**129** Blainroe Golf Club (18)
Killeen Course (18)	**130** Wicklow Golf Club (9)
Mahony's Point Course (18)	**131** Baltinglass Golf Club (9)
80 Dooks Golf Club (18)	**132** Athy Golf Club (9)
81 Waterville Golf Club (18)	**133** Abbeyleix Golf Club (9)
82 Parknasilla Golf Club (9)	**134** Mountrath Golf Club (9)
83 Kenmare Golf Club (9)	**135** Heath Golf Club (18)
84 Glengarriff Golf Club (9)	**136** Portarlington Golf Club (9)
85 Bantry Golf Club (9)	**137** Cill Dara Golf Club (9)
86 Skibbereen Golf Club (9)	**138** Curragh Golf Club (18)
87 Dunmore Golf Club (9)	**139** Naas Golf Club (9)
88 Bandon Golf Club (18)	**140** Bodenstown Golf Club (18)
89 Kinsale Golf Club (9)	**141** Delgany Golf Club (18)
90 Monkstown Golf Club (18)	**142** Greystones Golf Club (18)
91 Muskerry Golf Club (18)	**143** Bray Golf Club (9)
92 Macroom Golf Club (9)	

**Golf-courses in
Northern Ireland**

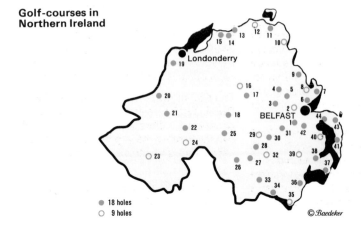

● 18 holes
○ 9 holes

© Baedeker

Golf-courses in Northern Ireland

1 Belfast area
Balmoral Golf Club (18)
Belvoir Golf Club (18)
Cliftonville Golf Club (9)
Dunmurry Golf Club (18)
Fortwilliam Golf Club (18)
Gilnahirk Golf Club (9)
Holywood Golf Club (18)
Knock Golf Club (18)
Knockbracken Golf Club (18)
Malone Golf Club (18 and 9)
Ormeau Golf Club (9)
Shandon Park Golf Club (18)
Royal Belfast Golf Club (18)
2 Greenisland Golf Club (9)
3 Massereene Golf Club (18)
4 Ballymena Golf Club (18)
5 Ballyclare Golf Club (18)
6 Carrickfergus Golf Club (18)
7 Whitehead Golf Club (18)
    Bentra Golf Club (9)
8 Larne Golf Club (9)
9 Cairndhu Golf Club (18)
10 Cushendall Golf Club (9)
11 Ballycastle Golf Club (18)
12 Bushfoot Golf Club (9)
13 Royal Portrush Golf Club (18, 18 and 9)
14 Portstewart Golf Club (18 and 18)
15 Castlerock Golf Club (18)
16 Kilrea Golf Club (9)

17 Moyola Park Golf Club (18)
18 Killymoon Golf Club (18)
19 City of Derry Golf Club (18 and 9)
20 Strabane Golf Club (18)
21 Newtownstewart Golf Club (18)
22 Omagh Golf Club (18)
23 Enniskillen Golf Club (9)
24 Fintona Golf Club (9)
25 Dungannon Golf Club (18)
26 County Armagh Golf Club (18)
27 Tandagree Golf Club (18)
28 Portadown Golf Club (18)
29 Craigavon Golf (and Ski) Centre (9)
30 Lurgan Golf Club (18)
31 Lisburn Golf Club (18)
32 Banbridge Golf Club (12)
33 Newry Golf Club (18)
34 Warrenpoint Golf Club (18)
35 Kilkeel Golf Club (9)
36 Royal County Down Golf Club (18 and 18)
37 Ardglass Golf Club (18)
38 Downpatrick Golf Club (18)
    Bright Castle Golf Club (18)
39 Spa Golf Club (9)
40 Mahee Island Golf Club (9)
41 Kirkistown Castle Golf Club (18)
42 Scrabo Golf Club (18)
43 Donaghadee Golf Club (18)
44 Bangor Golf Club (18)
    Carnalea Golf Club (18)
    Clandeboye Golf Club (18 and 18)
    Helen's Bay Golf Club (9)

Hunting

Fox-hunting is a popular Irish sport for good horsemen, not only for the "gentry" but for any small farmer who possesses a horse. The hunt can also be followed on foot. There are still some 50 hunts in Ireland with the season lasting from the beginning of November to the end of March.
It can sometimes be included in a package holiday.

Riding

Ireland is an ideal place for a riding holiday, whether you are a beginner or an experienced rider. Package riding holidays are offered by some travel firms.
Riding-schools organise courses for beginners, with experienced instructors. The horses are accustomed to strange riders and are generally well behaved. There are also courses in jumping and dressage (usually lasting a fortnight) for more experienced riders.
Another possibility is a pony-trekking holiday, usually lasting a week, with perhaps 4 hours in the saddle each day. In the Republic the most interesting treks are in Connemara, on the Dingle Peninsula and in Co. Sligo. In Northern Ireland there

are pony-trekking centres in Belfast and in Cos Antrim, Down, Londonderry and Tyrone.

Addresses and information about riding holidays in the Republic can be obtained from the brochure entitled "Horse Riding Holidays" published by the Irish Horse Board:

Irish Horse Board,
Naas Road, Dublin 12;
tel. (01) 50 11 60.

The Northern Ireland Tourist Board issues a free leaflet on pony-trekking and riding holidays.

Ireland is a great horse-breeding country, and **horse-racing** is a very popular spectator sport. There are more than 250 race-meetings every year on the country's 30 or so racecourses. The sport is promoted by the Racing Board and supervised by the Turf Club, a body with a long tradition behind it. Ireland's best-known racecourse is the Curragh in Co. Kildare.

The *Dublin Horse Show*, run by the Royal Dublin Society every year at the beginning of August, offers a full programme of events. It is also the largest market for Irish bloodstock and attracts numerous foreign buyers.

Horse-drawn caravans: see Getting about in Ireland, p. 212.

Fishing

Thanks to its numerous loughs (lakes) and rivers and its extensive coastal waters Ireland is one of the great fishing countries, offering a great variety of angling opportunities – game fishing (salmon and trout), coarse fishing and deep-sea fishing.

Since Irish fishermen are mainly interested in trout and salmon, no licence is required for **coarse fishing**, either in the Republic or in Northern Ireland. The principal species of coarse fish are pike, bream, tench, rudd, roach, perch, carp and eel.

For **game fishing** a licence is required;

it can be obtained from the office of the fishery board or district concerned and from certain tackle-dealers, shops and hotels. Most game-fishing waters are privately owned (enquire locally). The commonest species of trout is the brown trout. The best-stocked waters are in the west of Ireland (Lough Corrib, etc.).

There are excellent deep-sea fishing grounds off the west and south coasts of Ireland, in the warmer water brought by the Gulf Stream. The fish which can be caught in these waters include shark, ray, cod species, pollack, hake, bass, grey mullet and sea-bream. Tackle can be hired locally. The season is from spring to autumn.

Common Irish freshwater fishes

Rudd
Scardinius erythrophthalmus

Perch
Perca fluviatilis

Brown trout
Salmo trutta

Bream
Abramis brama

Pike
Esox lucius

Salmon
Salmo salar

Shooting

There is good shooting in Ireland for pheasant, grouse, partridge, snipe and various species of wild duck. A gun licence is required.

Deer-stalking is not available for visitors.

The shooting season is fixed each year by the Department of Agriculture; it is usually from the beginning of September to the end of January.

For the addresses of shooting clubs and organisers of shoots apply to the Tourist Board.

Water-sports

Sailing

The Atlantic Ocean and the Irish Sea offer excellent sailing waters. Around the Irish coast are numerous sailing centres and sailing schools for both beginners and the more experienced.

Boats can be rented at the following sailing centres:

Fingall Sailing School,
Malahide, Co. **Dublin**

Galway Sailing Centre,
Galway, Co. **Galway**

Riversdale Sailing Centre,
Ballinamore, Co. **Leitrim**

Skillet Sailing School,
Kinsale, Co. **Cork**

Valentia Marina Sailing Centre,
Valentia, Co. **Kerry**

Information about sailing courses (on both coastal and inland waters) can be obtained from:

Irish Yachting Association,
87 Upper Georges Street,
Dun Laoghaire;
tel. (01) 80 02 39

Irish Association for Sail Training,
c/o Irish Federation of Marine Industries,
Confederation House, Kildare Street,
Dublin 2;
tel. (01) 77 98 01

Northern Ireland Council of Royal Yachting Association,
49 Malone Road,
Belfast BT9 6RZ

Water-Skiing

There are opportunities for water-skiing on loughs (lakes) and rivers and especially off flat coastal areas. The necessary equipment and boats can be hired at many places.

Information: **Water Ski Association,**
20 Upper Merrion Street,
Dublin 2

Surfing

Surfing can be practised in Ireland anywhere where there is water: the necessary breeze can usually be relied on. Surfboards can be rented at many places.

Information: **Irish Board Sailing Association,**
79 Mount Anville,
Dublin;
tel. (01) 72 62 04

Scuba Diving

Irish coastal waters offer ideal conditions for scuba diving. The warm Gulf Stream keeps up the temperature of the water so that it is relatively pleasant even at some depth. At some points the coast falls steeply down, offering a variety of submarine fauna and flora. Some diving centres have equipment for hire.

Information: **Irish Underwater Council,**
60 Lower Baggot Street,
Dublin 2;
tel. (01) 78 58 44

Rowing

Ireland's numerous rivers and loughs (lakes) offer ample scope for rowing.

Information: **Irish Amateur Rowing Union,**
40 Crannagh Road,
Dublin 14;
tel. (01) 90 60 01

Canoeing

The Irish loughs (lakes) and rivers offer opportunities both for canoe touring and white-water canoeing. The best rivers are the Liffey, Barrow, Nore, Boyne, Slaney, Lee, Shannon, Suir and Munster Blackwater. Canoes can be rented.

Information: **Irish Canoe Union Training Unit,**
415 Eustace Street,
Dublin 2;
tel. (01) 71 96 90

See also Getting about in Ireland, by boat
(p. 215)

Assistance for the Disabled

The Irish Tourist Board publishes a free booklet, "Accommodation for the Disabled", which lists hotels and guesthouses with facilities for the disabled and wheelchair-users. The Northern Ireland Tourist Board's booklet "The Disabled Tourist in Northern Ireland" (50p) lists places to stay and things to see.

Public Holidays

Republic of Ireland

1 January
17 March (St Patrick's Day)
Good Friday
Easter Monday
First Monday in June (Whitsun Holiday)
Last Monday in August (August Weekend)
Last Monday in October (Autumn Bank Holiday)
25 and 26 December (Christmas)

Northern Ireland

1 January
17 March (St Patrick's Day)
Good Friday
Easter Monday
First Monday in May (May Day Bank Holiday)
A Monday in the second half of May (Spring Bank Holiday)
12 July (Orange Day, commemorating the Battle of the Boyne, 1690)
A Monday in the second half of August (Summer Bank Holiday)
25 and 26 December (Christmas)

Opening Times

Opening times of post offices: see Postal and Telephone Services

Republic of Ireland

Shops: Opening times vary, but are usually from 9 or 9.30 a.m. to 5.30 or 6 p.m. There is an early closing day on Wednesday, Thursday or Saturday, varying from place to place. Shopping centres stay open until 9 p.m. on Thursday and/or Friday. In some places shops remain open until 8 or 9 p.m. on Saturdays.

Banks are open Monday to Friday from 10 a.m. to 12.30 p.m. and 1.30 to 3 p.m., in Dublin to 5 p.m. on Thursday. They are closed on Saturdays, Sundays and public holidays except at Dublin and Shannon airports.

Opening times at **international airports:**
Dublin: daily 7 a.m.–11.30 p.m. April to September, daily 7.30 a.m.–9.30 p.m. October to March.
Shannon: daily 6.30 a.m.–5.30 p.m.
Cork: Monday 10 a.m.–2 p.m., Tuesday to Friday 10 a.m.–3 p.m.

Petrol (gas) stations are usually open from 9 a.m. to 6 p.m. On Sundays they have restricted opening times. In Dublin and Cork some petrol (gas) stations are open 24 hours a day.

Northern Ireland

Shops in Belfast are open on weekdays from 9 a.m. to 5.30 p.m. Outside Belfast they have one early closing day, varying from place to place. Most of the smaller shops close at lunchtime.

Banks are open Monday to Friday from 10 a.m. to 12.30 p.m. and 1.30 to 3.30 p.m. In small places the bank may be open on only two or three days in the week.

Postal and Telephone Services

Opening times
Post offices are usually open from 9 a.m. to 6 p.m.
Small country post offices close at lunchtime.

Postage rates
Letters from the Republic of Ireland to Britain and other EEC countries cost 28p, postcards 23p.
Letters to the United States and Canada cost 46p.

Letters and postcards from Northern Ireland cost 13p (second class) or 18p (first class) to Britain, 18p to EEC countries and 29p (air mail) to the United States and Canada.

Telephone
Local and long-distance calls can be made from coin-operated public call-boxes; international calls are best made from a post office or hotel. As a rule international calls can be dialled direct, but in smaller places they must go through the exchange.

International telephone codes: see p. 231.

Calender of Events

Events which take place in particular locations will be found in the A–Z section of this guide. In addition the following events take place at various places in the Republic and in Northern Ireland:

January
Many places — Hunting

February
1st
Kildare — Feast of St Brigid (tel. Kildare 523)

March
throughout Ireland — St Patrick's Week (middle of March), with parades in the larger towns
Many places — Opening racing season

April
Dublin — Grand Opera Season

May
Belfast — Lord Mayor's Show (parade with decorated floats and bands)
Cork — International Band Competition
Dublin — Spring Show and Industrial Fair Feis Ceoil (folk music)
Ennis — Fleadh Nua (festival of music and dance)
Killarney — Pan-Celtic Week

June
Dublin — Festival of Music in Great Irish Houses
Letterkenny — Donegal International Car Rally
Listowel — Writers' Week
Westport — International Sea Angling Festival
Westport Horse Show

July
Athlone — Athlone International Freshwater Gala Angling Festival
Shannon Boat Rally
Cobh — Cobh International Folk Dance Festival
Dublin — Dublin International Folk Festival
Enniscorthy — Strawberry Fair
Glenariff — Glens of Antrim Feis (Irish dancing and music)
Killarney — Bach Festival

August
Ballycastle — Oul' Lammas Fair
Birr — Birr Vintage Week (vintage cars, etc.)
Clifden — Connemara Pony Show
Dublin — Antiques Fair
Dublin Horse Show
Killorglin — Puck Fair
Killybegs — Killybegs Sea Angling Club International Festival
Kilkenny — Kilkenny Arts Week (concerts, exhibitions, etc.)
Letterkenny — Letterkenny International Folk Festival
Londonderry — Relief of Derry celebrations (12 August: commemorating the siege of 1688–89)
Stradbally (Co. Laois) — Stradbally Steam Rally (for rail enthusiasts)
Tralee — Rose of Tralee International Festival

September
Dublin — All Ireland Hurling Finals

Galway	Galway Oyster Festival	Wexford	Wexford Festival of Opera
Waterford	Waterford International Festival of Light Opera		
		November	
		Belfast	Belfast Festival of Queen's (drama and music at Queen's University)
October			
Ballinasloe	Horse Fair		
Castlebar	Castlebar International Song Contest		
Dublin	Dublin City Marathon	**December**	
Kenmare	Fruits de Mer Festival	Dublin	Dublin Grand Opera Society Winter Season

Greyhound-racing: This is a popular spectator sport in Ireland, accompanied by heavy betting. There are greyhound-racing meetings at many places throughout the year.

Pilgrimages: see Introduction to Ireland, Religion

Information

Republic of Ireland

Irish Tourist Board/ Bord Fáilte Éireann,
Head office:
Baggot Street Bridge,
Dublin;
tel. (01) 76 58 71

Great Britain
150 New Bond Street,
London W1Y 0AQ;
tel. (01) 493 3201

6–8 Temple Row,
Birmingham B2 5HG;
tel. (021) 236 9724

19 Dixon Street,
Glasgow G1 4AJ;
tel. (041) 221 2311

28 Cross Street,
Manchester M2 3NH;
tel. (061) 832 5981

Northern Ireland:
53 Castle Street,
Belfast BT1 1GH
tel. (084) 22 78 88

Foyle Street,
Londonderry;
tel. (0540) 26 95 01

United States of America:
757 Third Avenue,
New York NY 10017;
tel. (212) 418 0800

230 North Michigan Avenue,
Chicago IL 60601;
tel. (312) 726 9356

625 Market Street, Suite 502,
San Francisco CA 94105;
tel. (415) 957 0985

Canada
10 King Street East,
Toronto M5C 1C3;
tel. (416) 364 1301

Australia
MLC Centre, 37th Level,
Martin PLace,
Sydney 2000;
tel. (02) 232 7177

New Zealand
Dingwall Building, 2nd Floor,
87 Queen Street,
PO Box 279, **Auckland** 1;
tel. (09) 79 37 08

Northern Ireland

Northern Ireland Tourist Board
Head office:
River House, 48 High Street,
Belfast BT1 2DS;
tel: (0232) 24 66 09

Great Britain
11 Berkeley Street,
London W1X 6BU;
tel. (01) 493 0601

Olympic House, 142 Queen Street,
Glasgow G1 3BU;
tel. (041) 221 5115

38 High Street,
Sutton Coldfield B72 1UP
tel. (021) 354 1431

The Republic of Ireland
Tourist Information Desk, Clery's,
O'Connell Street,
Dublin 1;
tel. (01) 78 60 55

United States of America:
40 West 57th Street, 3rd Floor,
New York NY 10019;
tel: (212) 765 5144

Information in Ireland

In the Republic of Ireland information can be obtained locally from *tourist information offices* or, in one or two places, *community tourist information offices*. Information offices are usually open Monday to Friday from 9 a.m. to 4 p.m., Saturday from 9 a.m. to 1 p.m.; many of them are closed during the winter.
In Northern Ireland information can be obtained from *local councils*.
Some small places have no telepone dialling code, and calls must be obtained through the exchange.

Diplomatic and Consular Offices

In the Republic of Ireland

United Kingdom
Embassy,
31 Merrion Road,
Dublin 4;
tel. (01) 69 52 11

United States of America
Embassy,
42 Elgin Road,
Ballsbridge, **Dublin**;
tel. (01) 68 87 77

Canada
Embassy,
65 St Stephen's Green,
Dublin 2;
tel. (01) 78 19 88

Australia
Embassy,
Fitzwilton House,
Wilton Terrace,
Dublin 2;
tel. (01) 76 15 17

In Northern Ireland

United States of America
Consulate General,
Queen's House, 14 Queen Street,
Belfast BT1 6EQ;
tel. (0232) 22 82 39

International Telephone Codes

From Britain to the Republic of Ireland:
Dublin: 0001
Elsewhere: 010 353

From the Republic of Ireland to Britain: 03

From the United States or Canada to the Republic: 353
From the Republic to the United States or Canada: 16 1

From the United States or Canada to Northern Ireland: 44
From Northern Ireland to the United States or Canada: 010 1

From Australia to the Republic: 353
From the Republic to Australia: 16 61

From Australia to Northern Ireland: 44
From Northern Ireland to Australia: 101 61

From New Zealand to the Republic: 00 353
From the Republic to New Zealand: 16 64

From New Zealand to Northern Ireland: 00 44
From Northern Ireland to New Zealand: 010 64

When an international call is dialled any zero at the beginning of the local dialling code should be omitted.

Emergency Calls

Police, fire, ambulance
(throughout Ireland): dial **999**
(free call)

Breakdown assistance
(Automobile Association):

Republic of Ireland: **(01) 77 94 81**
Northern Ireland: **(0232) 4 45 38**